Mormon History

MORMON HISTORY

Ronald W. Walker,
David J. Whittaker,
and James B. Allen

with a contribution
by Armand L. Mauss

University of Illinois Press
URBANA AND CHICAGO

© 2001 by the Board of Trustees of
the University of Illinois
All rights reserved
Manufactured in the United States of America
c 5 4 3 2 1

⊚ This book is printed on acid-free paper.

Library of Congress Cataloging-in-Publication Data
Walker, Ronald W. (Ronald Warren), 1939–
Mormon history / Ronald W. Walker, David J. Whittaker, and
James B. Allen ; with a contribution by Armand L. Mauss.
p.   cm.
Includes bibliographical references and index.
ISBN 0-252-02619-5 (alk. paper)
1. Mormon Church—Historiography. 2. Church of Jesus Christ
of Latter-Day Saints—Historiography. I. Whittaker, David J.
II. Allen, James B., 1927– . III. Title.
BX8611.W34   2001
289.3'09—dc21   00-009378

*To those who labor to enlarge
the memory of the Mormon people*

Contents

Preface

WHEN WE BEGAN OUR Mormon bibliographic labor fifteen years ago, we agreed that a primary rule would govern our work: it should be as useful as possible. The first product of our work was our two-part *Studies in Mormon History, 1830–1997,* published by the University of Illinois Press in the year 2000. Reflecting our idea of utility, the work not only listed the authors and titles to more than 16,000 works of Mormon history but also indexed this material by topic. If a thesis, dissertation, article, or book treated a topic in a substantial manner, we wanted our readers to be able to find it by this topic.

This book is meant as a companion to *Studies in Mormon History.* Again, our desire is to be useful. Having spent so many years compiling and creating an indexed bibliography, we believed that our readers would want us to describe and interpret our work. We therefore hope that this volume will aid readers in several ways: by describing what has gone on in the past, including the various methods, themes, and interpretations that historians have used; by sketching the background and work of leading LDS writers; and by suggesting the pitfalls and strengths of previous writing, with an eye toward improving our professional craft. Our hope is to provide a handbook for those starting a study in Mormon history, although we suspect even the most seasoned historical veteran will find value in the chapters that follow. While much of our information may be found in specialized works on Mormon history writing, we bring this material together for the first time as a synthesis of modern scholarship dealing with the writing of Mormon history.

Mormon History is divided into two parts: interpretive chapters and two appendixes containing descriptive essays.

* * *

The first three interpretive chapters trace the history of Mormon historical writing. The first deals with the nineteenth century, the formative years of Mormon historiography. Although this period was filled with partisan controversy and therefore partisan and often ephemeral history, many items produced during this era remain worth reading, both because of their substance and because many of these works can now be used as primary sources. For instance, nineteenth-century histories may help us understand the Mormon nineteenth-century image, early Mormon and non-Mormon attitudes, and Mormon thought itself as the church was getting underway.

The second chapter deals with historical writing in the first half of the twentieth century, which can be characterized as a period of transition. During these years, historians began to edge away from past polemics to a more balanced and professional approach. It was also a time when leading scholars studied Mormon rural sociology, which made faith claims less relevant. Mormonism was increasingly studied for its own sake—how the Church of Jesus Christ of Latter-day Saints (LDS) helped settle the American West—rather than as a matter of religious truth.

Chapter 3 traces the rise of the "new Mormon history" following World War II. This was a period of rapid development, multidiscipline approaches, and unparalleled fecundity. It was also a time when academic, "detached" writing dominated, and as a result, tensions rose between Mormon scholars and Mormon church leaders, who preferred a more faith-oriented history. Because of the quality and quantity of Mormon history writing during this period, Mormon studies began to lay claim to being a subset in the broader historical discipline of western history.

From the beginning of the Mormon church, its members have been drawn to biography. Latter-day Saints have written diaries, produced autobiographies, and have written and read life stories. Because of this interest (well established by Mormonism's early Puritan forebears) and because of the establishment of biography as a new, twentieth-century literary genre, we devote chapter 4 to LDS biography. This chapter examines the Mormon fascination with biography, surveys important books in the field, and suggests ways that the biographical craft can be strengthened. Some readers may think that our advise is gratuitous. We admit our intrusion but are hopeful that it may bring improvement to a body of work that too often has lacked dimension and characterization—or even a theoretical method.

Chapter 5, entitled "Flowers, Weeds, and Thistles: The State of Social Science Literature on the Mormons," continues our collaboration with Armand L. Mauss, who, along with Dynette Ivie Reynolds, provided an important addendum to our *Studies in Mormon History.* In that work, Mauss and Reynolds permitted us to publish their social science bibliography of LDS literature, a literary cousin to historical writing. In the present volume, Mauss interprets the social science literature. He describes the progress of scholars in this field, and in the process, he provides a window to this growing and important body of work. We were especially anxious to include Mauss's essay, not simply because its content is important but also because it suggests the increasing interdisciplinary nature of Mormon scholarship.

Finally, the two appendixes are designed to help scholars with historical sources. These essays are therefore more descriptive than interpretive. Appendix A reviews the development of LDS print literature, emphasizing the first seventy-five years of Mormon publishing. This essay traces the history of Mormon imprints, suggests major strains of Mormon thought and practice as revealed by this printed word, and recommends directions for future research. The second appendix reviews the history of Mormon bibliographies and reference works. Although the contents of many of these past bibliographies are encompassed in our own work, we offer this essay because it points scholars to specialized fields of research. We also believe that a listing of bibliographies and source guides can be grist for future LDS cultural and intellectual histories.

This work goes to press not long after the death of Leonard J. Arrington, the dean of Mormon historians, and at the beginning of a new century. These events suggest a passing of an era and create in us a reflective mood that readers will find in our essays. However, if our reveries are not explicit on two points, we wish to be clear here: we leave our bibliographic work with a deep appreciation for those who have gone before us. We also share an optimism that predicts an even greater achievement for the future.

Mormon History

1. Beginnings: Nineteenth-Century Historical Writing

THE FIRST PHASE of Mormon historiography began shortly after the Church of Jesus Christ of Latter-day Saints was founded in 1830 and continued throughout the rest of the nineteenth century. During this first phase, important primary and secondary sources came into existence, major and long-lasting historical issues were raised and debated, and several seminal studies were completed. Nonetheless, most early works were not "history," at least in the modern sense of the term. Too often they lacked balance and failed to consider the full range of existing sources. Many were an antiquarian's delight of loosely organized and ill-fitting material. They were, however, the first steps toward a rich heritage of Mormon historical writing.

The virtues and defects of early Mormon history may be traced to the fact that it was highly partisan. Mormons believed that their church was the "only true and living church upon the face of the whole earth," and they wrote with the settled conviction that this belief generated. Theirs were providential or "faithful" histories in the tradition of the historical books of the Old Testament or such seventeenth-century Puritan religious works as William Bradford's *Of Plymouth Plantation* or Cotton Mather's *Magnalia Christi Americana.*[1] Mormon history, as written by the Mormons themselves, told of a new branch of God's chosen people who, like their New England forebears, dwelt in a "city upon a hill." They were part of a modern dispensation in which heavenly intentions were being made known in preparation for Jesus Christ's Second Coming.

Not surprisingly, non-Mormon writers disagreed. Often they were rival Christian ministers, apostate Mormons, or local journalists who had opposed the Mormons when they lived or preached in nearby communities. Reflecting their own partisanship, non-LDS chroniclers found little to praise in Mormonism and much to condemn. For many of them, the new religion was a fanatical sect that unprincipled church leaders used to plunder an unsuspecting flock.

These two groups of historians—the LDS writers of providential history and their non-Mormon antagonists—dominated nineteenth-century Mormon history and filled it with strong words and emotions. The two groups often could not even agree on what sources to use, much less arrive at similar conclusions. During its first phase, the writing of Mormon history was a battleground. Mormons wrote primarily to defend the faith, while their foes wrote with the hope of destroying the foundations of the Mormon "kingdom." There was little room for neutrality and no interest in asking the kinds of questions that, a century later, produced many outstanding, well-balanced works enjoyed by Mormon and non-Mormon alike.

Early Anti-Mormon Historical Writing

The first book about the Mormons, Eber D. Howe's *Mormonism Unvailed; or, A Faithful Account of that Singular Imposition and Delusion,* came from an opponent in 1834.[2] Howe was the editor of the *Painesville Telegraph,* published a few miles from Kirtland, Ohio, the first Mormon gathering point outside New York State. One of Howe's friends recalled that the newspaperman seemed to have little outward animosity for the Mormons, although his sister and perhaps his wife joined them.[3] Howe described his own religious beliefs as pliant—by his own admission he intended to "slide along" with prevailing opinion. Later in his life, he accepted spiritualism.[4]

Whatever the reason, shortly after the Mormons began to arrive in northern Ohio in the early 1830s, Howe started a spirited newspaper campaign against them. In 1834, he followed with the publication of *Mormonism Unvailed,* which was filled with passionate condemnations. One passage described Joseph Smith, the church's founding prophet, as one of the "vilest wretch[es] on earth." Similarly, Howe dismissed Smith's new book of scripture, the Book of Mormon, as a "fabrication" gauged to the "lowest of our passions."[5]

Mormonism Unvailed included nine anti-Mormon "letters" written by the Mormon dissident Ezra Booth, which the *Ohio Star* (Ravenna, Ohio) had earlier printed. More important, the book used the research of another former Mormon, Doctor Philastus Hurlbut ("Doctor" was his given name). The Mormons had earlier expelled Hurlbut for sexual misconduct and in the process gained his enmity. Hurlbut was so open with his threats against Joseph Smith and the Mormons that an Ohio court placed him under a $200 bond and required him to pay $300 in court costs.[6]

Some Mormons believed that it was Hurlbut, not Howe, who was the actual author of *Mormonism Unvailed.* If so, Hurlbut was a curious irony. His unusual first given name came from the folk traditions of the time: a seventh son was believed to have special spiritual or doctoring power.[7] Hurlbut attempted to use this same folk culture to discredit Smith. Traveling to New York State, Hurlbut gathered affidavits from those who claimed to have once known the Smith family. These affidavits described how Joseph Smith and other members of his family had participated in the popular, early nineteenth-century search for buried treasure. Howe and Hurlbut saw this activity as a proof of serious character flaws: the Smiths were "lazy" and "superstitious" and believed in "ghosts and witches."[8] Even before the publication of *Mormonism Unvailed,* two articles issued by mainline Christian magazines had made similar charges about the Smiths' money-digging and their supposedly unsavory character.[9]

But how had the uneducated Smith produced the difficult-to-explain Book of Mormon? To answer this question, which became a major theme in Mormon historiography, Howe and Hurlbut suggested the existence of a hidden conspiracy. They advanced the theory that a "talented knave" stood behind the public career of Joseph Smith and was actually responsible for producing the Book of Mormon. This conspirator was identified or "unvailed" (thus the book's title) as Sidney Rigdon, a "Campbellite" minister who later became a prominent Mormon. According to this theory, Rigdon had secured an unpublished romance novel, "Manuscript Found," written by the Reverend Solomon Spaulding, which allegedly had some of the names, archaic language, and story line of the Book of Mormon. After altering and embellishing Spaulding's original draft, Rigdon supposedly gave the book to Smith, who brought the "new scripture" to light in a supernatural-appearing way.[10]

The Hurlbut-Howe arguments had at least two problems. First, because the Palmyra affidavits that Hurlbut gathered contained stock phrases organized in a recurring pattern, Mormons charged that Hurlbut either had approached the Smith's neighbors with a prepared agenda in mind or had edited their responses to secure the result he desired. At the very least, it was clear that the indicting affidavits failed to convey a rounded portrait of the Smiths and their early New York experiences. Second, the Spaulding explanation for the Book of Mormon had little evidence to support it—as Howe himself was forced to admit. Howe acknowledged (but minimized) that Hurlbut had secured from Spaulding's widow the draft copy of "Manuscript Found," which, when examined, bore little similarity to the Book of Mormon. Faced with this difficulty, Howe offered the hypothesis that Spaulding must have written another draft of "Manuscript Found," yet to be discovered.

Howe was right about one thing. Writing his autobiography at the end of his career, he claimed that *Mormonism Unvailed* was the "basis of all the [non-LDS] histories" of Mormonism.[11] It was hardly an exaggeration. When discussing the origin of Mormonism, most nineteenth-century non-LDS articles and books were variations on the main themes of *Mormonism Unvailed:* Joseph Smith and his family were treasure hunters, the LDS Church began as a speculation, and the Book of Mormon could be explained by an elusive Spaulding manuscript. The last charge became an anti-Mormon theme as a small cottage industry tried to promote the conspiracy theory.[12] However, when the Spaulding manuscript was discovered among Howe's papers in Hawaii in 1884 and when no "second" manuscript came to light, the theory began to give way.[13]

Within eight years of the publication of *Mormonism Unvailed,* six other books appeared, each with a similar tone and content. The Reverend Daniel Kidder's *Mormonism and the Mormons: A Historical View of the Rise and Progress of the Sect Self-Styled Latter-day Saints* and the Mormon dissenter John C. Bennett's *History of the Saints; or, An Exposé of Joe Smith and Mormonism* not only borrowed many of Howe's ideas but also used large blocks of his text.[14] Dr. John A. Clark's memoir, *Gleanings by the Way,* devoted twelve of its thirty-three chapters to Mormon topics.[15] Clark, who had served as the Episcopal minister of Palmyra, New York, when the Book of Mormon was published, provided an account of an important interview he had had with Martin Harris, Smith's closest early Palmyra coworker. But for the most part, Clark followed Howe's general outline. If Rigdon had not been the conduit for getting the Spaulding manuscript to Smith, Clark reasoned, Smith must have gotten it in some other way. The Book of Mormon was surely beyond Smith's power and intelligence.[16]

The Presbyterian minister J. B. Turner's *Mormonism in All Ages; or, The Rise, Progress and Causes of Mormonism* had a slightly different view. In Turner's mind, the Book of Mormon, while still beyond Smith's ability, was too absurd for a man of Rigdon's learning. Turner therefore proposed an alternative thesis: young Smith himself had secured the Spaulding manuscript. Perhaps Smith had gotten the manuscript on an undocumented trip to northeastern Pennsylvania or eastern Ohio, the two areas where Spaulding lived after 1809.[17]

Neither of the two books written by the Episcopal minister Henry Caswall, *The City of the Mormons; or, Three Days at Nauvoo* and *The Prophet of the Nineteenth Century; or, The Rise, Progress, and Present State of the Mormons,* cited Howe as a source, but each seemed influenced by the Ohio journalist. According to Caswall, Smith was a "low juggler" without character or education. Caswall also charged the Smith family with trying to use Mormonism to make money. To these familiar arguments, the Episcopal minister added one of his own. He condemned Smith and his new religion as the unfortunate fruits of American religious democracy. In contrast to the stability of a church-state episcopacy, such as the Anglican establishment in Great Britain, Smith was guilty of "claiming immediate inspiration, interpreting the Scriptures according to his own fancies, and, in short, leading his followers into the lowest abyss of mental degradation."[18]

The themes of these early anti-Mormon books were restated some twenty-five years later in Pomeroy Tucker's *Origin, Rise, and Progress of Mormonism: Biography of Its Founders and History of Its Church.* Tucker was a longtime Palmyra resident who knew Joseph Smith and such early Mormon leaders as Oliver Cowdery and Martin Harris. Tucker had actually read the proof sheets for the first printing of the Book of Mormon. None of these experiences, however, left him with a favorable impression of Mormonism. Tucker charged that young Joseph was given to tall tales and "vagabondish" ways and that the Smith family was illiterate and whiskey-drinking. Tucker explained the new church's success in terms of the kind of members that it recruited: Mormonites were "fanatic masses" enrolled in a cause.[19]

Early Mormon Historical Writing

Mormons responded to the growing consensus of their detractors only occasionally. Five years before his death, Joseph Smith spoke of digging for Spanish treasure at the behest of a prosperous farmer on the "Big Bend" of the Susquehanna River, but the narrowly worded passage did not acknowledge the activity to be "money-digging."[20] In another refutation of the growing anti-Mormon chorus, several LDS pamphleteers challenged the Spaulding thesis by reminding their readers of Hurlbut's character shortcomings and by denying Rigdon's role in the alleged conspiracy.[21]

Generally, however, the Mormons simply ignored their opponents' charges and concentrated on telling their providential history, as required by Smith's formal revelations. "Behold, there shall be a record kept," said one that was received the day the church was organized.[22] Such counsel led to the establishment of the office of church historian and recorder, one of the first administrative positions of the new church and one usually occupied in the nineteenth century by a leading elder.[23] These early church historians and secretaries produced several unpublished manuscripts, including John

Whitmer's brief narrative of the church's first years, which was finally published in the twentieth century.[24]

The first major LDS historical material to be printed appeared in the 1834 and 1835 issues of the *Latter Day Saints' Messenger and Advocate,* the Mormon newspaper published at Kirtland, Ohio. The author of this material was "Second Elder" Oliver Cowdery, Joseph Smith's chief assistant, who used the literary device of eight serial letters to describe the origins of Mormonism. Cowdery reported that Smith's religious quest had begun when the teenager attended a neighborhood preaching revival. Later, his prayers brought the visit of an angel, who told him about ancient plates that were buried in a nearby hill. These "golden plates" contained the record of the Book of Mormon, which Smith later translated. As for the character of the Smith family, Cowdery had nothing but praise. Joseph's parents were "industrious, honest, virtuous and liberal to all," while Smith himself was an "upright, virtuous, and faithfully industrious young man."[25] Cowdery's letters were digressive, incomplete, and favorable to Smith and his family, but they were also an important source for early Mormon history and were reprinted at least seven times before the end of the century by the various branches of Mormonism.

Early Mormon pamphlets also played a role in defining the providential history of the church. Of these, Apostle Orson Pratt's *Interesting Account of Several Remarkable Visions, And of the Late Discovery of Ancient American Records,* published in 1840, was the most important.[26] To Cowdery's material on the coming forth of the Book of Mormon, Pratt added "Joseph Smith's history," which included such incidents as the emigration of the family to New York State when the boy was ten years old; Smith's "First Vision" theophany—the first time that this pivotal story appeared in print (even though Smith wrote an early unpublished version in 1832); the discovery, translation, and publication of the golden plates; and the formal organizing of the church. Pratt also added a list of short belief statements of the new movement. As Mormonism's first narrative history, *An Interesting Account of Several Remarkable Visions* broadly influenced all later Mormon-authored history and served as the framework for several important nineteenth-century works of history and doctrine. For instance, its sentences and paragraphs lay at the root of Joseph Smith's *Correspondence between Joseph Smith, the Prophet, and Col. John Wentworth;* numerous missionary brochures; and the church's later canonized thirteen statements of belief, the "Articles of Faith."[27]

The church's expulsion from western Missouri during the fall and winter of 1837–38 further encouraged church members to write history. Hoping to provide a record of their persecution and perhaps gain public assistance to ease their suffering, many Mormon expatriates wrote personal statements about their ordeal in Missouri.[28] In addition, several church members wrote historically minded pamphlets about the Missouri experience.[29] In turn, Missourians responded with their own version of events. According to one of these rejoinders, the Mormons were "fanatics" drawn from "the very dregs of eastern cities." This view carried the implication that the Saints' enthusiasm had earned them their reward.[30]

For Joseph Smith and several other church leaders, the Missouri "persecution" brought more than exile; they were incarcerated at Liberty, Missouri. The long months in the dreary jail gave the Mormon prophet a chance to reflect on his ministry, including the need to "keep a record." Shortly after gaining his freedom, Smith appointed a traveling committee to gather not only materials relating to the church's expulsion from Missouri but also "other historical matter connected with said Church."[31] About this time, Smith also resumed a chronicle of his doings. The Mormon leader, when later describing this journal, showed how defensive he had become after the tumultuous events of the Missouri period: "For the last three years I have a record of all my acts and proceedings, for I have kept several good, faithful, and efficient clerks in constant employ: they have accompanied me everywhere, and carefully kept my history, and they have written down what I have done, where I have been, and what I have said; therefore my enemies cannot charge me with any day, time, or place [of offense], but what I have written testimony to prove my actions; and my enemies cannot prove anything against me."[32] This sense of embattlement overtook much of Mormon writing during the nineteenth century.

These post-Missouri acts on the part of Smith led to the single most important historical project undertaken by Mormons during the first several decades of the church's history—a work that was for the Mormons as important and seminal as *Mormonism Unvailed* had been for their antagonists. In May 1838, Smith and his clerk, James Mulholland, began the "History of Joseph Smith." The project was not meant to be Smith's personal journal; rather, it was to be a church annal, a kind of documentary scrapbook covering the life and presidency of Mormonism's founding prophet.

One of the many scribes who worked on the project described its method: "The Prophet was to furnish all the materials; and our business, was not only to combine, and arrange in c[h]ronological order, but to spread out or amplify not a little, in as good historical style as may be."[33] In this case, "good historical style" meant reworking all the sources, whether written by Smith or by others, into a first-person narrative. Thus, while the document used many sources, it read like a personal journal, filled with "I's" and "we's."

When Smith died in 1844, the Smith annals were completed to the date of 5 August 1838.

For the next sixteen years after Smith's death, church clerks continued in a similar manner. They gathered materials wherever they could be found but continued to use Smith's voice throughout. Long excerpts, for instance, were taken from the diary of Heber C. Kimball, an early apostle who had often traveled with Smith. These were then woven into a seamless narrative as though Smith himself were speaking. Although the church historians Willard Richards and George A. Smith tried to make the record accurate in terms of dates and events and often consulted Smith's personal papers, the entire Nauvoo, Illinois, period of "Joseph Smith's History," 1838–44, was written in its final form by writers other than Joseph Smith. Often it included source material that Smith probably had never seen.[34]

"Joseph Smith's History" was first published in installments in early Mormon newspapers, even as it was still in the process of being written. The *Times and Seasons* of Nauvoo, Illinois, began to print the chronological history in March 1842 and continued until its suspension four years later. In the 1850s, Salt Lake City's *Deseret News* renewed the serialization, while the *Latter-day Saints' Millennial Star* in England produced parallel copies through both publishing spans.

By the end of the nineteenth century, "Joseph Smith's History" was still not available in book form, and church leaders authorized George Q. Cannon, a member of the First Presidency, to prepare a multivolume work. Cannon died shortly thereafter, leaving only the first ninety-six pages in galleys, and B. H. Roberts took over the project. From 1902 to 1912, Roberts produced what he inaccurately entitled the *History of the Church of Jesus Christ of Latter-day Saints: Period I, History of Joseph Smith, the Prophet, by Himself.* Even worse than causing confusion over Smith's lack of authorship, Roberts made corrections, deletions, and emendations to the six-volume work without explaining his reasons for doing so.[35]

The *History of the Church,* or, as it was also called, the *Documentary History of the Church,* had other imperfections. Relying on materials readily at hand, it failed to cover, in depth or at all, several important episodes. Moreover, at times it violated its usual chronological organization by allowing material to appear out of sequence. No doubt these flaws stemmed partly from the many different clerks who worked on the project. (During Joseph Smith's time alone, twenty-four scribes helped compile the *History of the Church,* thirteen of whom left the undertaking because they died or because they abandoned the church). The pressures of the Mormon trek west also prevented a complete or comprehensive work. But the most overwhelming fault of the *History of the Church* lay with its structure. Its first-person point of view made it impossible for readers to determine who was describing an event and why.

Nevertheless, the *History of the Church* was a remarkable achievement. When placed beside such warmly received nineteenth-century compilations as John Marshall's biography of George Washington or Jared Sparks's twelve-volume edition of the Washington papers, the Mormon multivolume project did not fare badly. In an era of cavalier editing, the work was almost always faithful to the materials it quoted; it did not "touch up" or delete details for effect. Because it reproduced sources abundantly, its breadth was unsurpassed as a nineteenth-century LDS work, and even to the present, it contains historical facts not easily found elsewhere. Despite its passion and point of view, the *History of the Church* remains a basic research tool for beginning students of the early Mormon experience.

"Middle Way" Historical Writing

Two books issued at midcentury tried to navigate between the competing extremes of *Mormonism Unvailed* and the *History of the Church*. The first was by the British literary figure Charles Mackay. Mackay had already written thirteen books before the *London Morning Chronicle* assigned him to report on conditions in Liverpool as part of its campaign to examine the "underside" of Victorian life. Mackay's investigation led him to the Latter-day Saints, who were active in the city, and the correspondent filed three long "letters" about their history and activity. These proved so popular that they were reissued in an expanded volume, *The Mormons; or, Latter-Day Saints, with Memoirs of the Life and Death of Joseph Smith, the "American Mahomet."*[36]

During the next decade, this influential book saw five London editions, a half-dozen more in the United States, and still others in revised and abridged printings in France, Germany, and even Sweden.[37] For the first time, Mormonism became a topic of international conversation among the educated classes. Nor did the influence of *The Mormons* quickly pass. Many later Mormon-related European and American books of adventure, poetry, and humor, as well as histories and novels, owed their material to Mackay's report. Even some of the illustrations of the book were long-lasting. At least six of *The Mormons*'s forty engravings were done by the Mormon Frederick Piercy, and these were used and reused in Mormon and Utah books into the twentieth century.

Several factors helped make Mackay's work a success. First, it was a convenient and accessible collection of Mormon and non-Mormon sources. Not so much a narrative synthesis as a compilation of materials tied together by a thin thread of commentary, the book quoted from the works of Orson Pratt, LDS mission tracts, the circular letters of the Mormon First Presidency, and the pro-Mormon lecture of Thomas L. Kane, which had been published as a small book under the same title in Philadelphia in 1850. To these, Mackay offered the counterweight of passages from *Mormonism Unvailed* and the exposé of the Nauvoo dissenter John C. Bennett.

Perhaps the book's popularity also stemmed from its exaggerated estimate of Mormon membership, wealth, and influence, which must have greatly alarmed Victorian readers. Mackay reported that the movement, only two decades old, had 300,000 members and was supported by perhaps as much as three-and-a-half tons of California gold. "Whatever the world may say of the Mormons," Mackay wrote, "they have succeeded in establishing the third political system that has grown out of Christianity. The Pope, the Queen of England, and Brigham Young, are alike heads of States and of Churches: and, what is perhaps as remarkable a fact, the only State Church in America is that which has been founded by Joseph Smith. . . . Their past history has been a singular one. Their future history promises to be even more remarkable."[38]

The second midcentury book that aimed at impartiality was John W. Gunnison's *Mormons; or, Latter-day Saints in the Valley of the Great Salt Lake*.[39] Gunnison was a West Point graduate who had been dispatched to Utah in 1849 to complete a U.S. Army–sponsored topographical survey.[40] When he was snowbound in the winter of 1849–50, the scholarly Gunnison began a study of his friendly but sometimes socially distant Latter-day Saint neighbors.[41] While Gunnison disliked the "theo-democracy" of the Mormon leaders, he found the rank-and-file Saints "strange and interesting." This distinction led him to ignore the popular prejudice of the time and aim at even-handedness. Let "reason regain its sway over erratic feeling," he wrote. He wanted his book to avoid both non-Mormon animosity and Mormon fanaticism.[42]

The first half of Gunnison's work described Mormon society in Utah, while the second was more historical. In detailing the Saints' history, Gunnison accepted the claims of the Hurlbut-Howe Palmyra affidavits and the Spaulding explanation of the Book of Mormon. But he also spoke of Joseph Smith's religious dreams and his natural "genius" for remolding Spaulding's secular tale into a dynamic religious tract. The Book of Mormon, he concluded, had an "ingenious" plot, which was "skilfully arranged" in the remarkable likeness of scripture.[43] Not content with just examining the origins of Mormonism, Gunnison produced a half-dozen well-written chapters that chronicled the Mormons' more recent history and in the process created the first narrative synthesis of the LDS past.

The Mormons could not have been pleased with Gunnison's dismissal of their providential claims. Shortly after the book's publication, one Mormon orator spoke of the author's "distant, learned[,] very polite, and unsolicited chronicles."[44] Nonetheless, the Saints were not entirely displeased with the book. Gunnison repeatedly praised the Utahns for their industry and "brotherly unity" and spoke admiringly of Brigham Young's "great shrewdness" and extraordinary "grasp of thought."[45] In short, the book offered Mormons the virtue of seeking to understand them, while it provided non-Mormons with a sensible passageway through the welter of contradictory sources. For these reasons and because of its craftsmanship, Gunnison's history passed through almost a dozen nineteenth-century editions.

Writings of First-Person Observers

The Gunnison book represented a literary type. During the nineteenth century, more than four hundred journalists, literary figures, ministers, military men, politicians, territorial appointees, and ordinary tourists visited the Mormons and recorded their impressions in articles, chapters in books, memoirs, and travel guides. This travel genre—the most prolific of all nineteenth-century literary forms dealing with the Mormon people—owed its popularity to the exotic image of the remote and polygamous Mormons during the era. The Saints were convenient grist for the mills of those writing for profit and interest.

These visitors' accounts started early in LDS experience with Nancy Towle's 1832 sketch of church proceedings at Kirtland, Ohio, in *Vicissitudes Illustrated, in the Experience of Nancy Towle* and continued with such works as Henry Caswall's *City of the Mormons* and Josiah Quincy's *Figures of the Past from the Leaves of Old Journals,* which offered a Boston blueblood's impressions of Joseph Smith and his Nauvoo, Illinois, headquarters.[46] However, most travel accounts about the Mormons had Utah as their setting, particularly in the last third of the century when the transcontinental railroad made the Great Basin settlements accessible. The Utah travelers included some of the most interesting men and women on the American and European scene: Henry Ward Beecher, Charles Farrar Browne (Artemus Ward), Samuel Clemens (Mark Twain), William "Buffalo Bill" Cody, John C. Frémont, Horace Greeley, and Rudyard Kipling—to name some of the more famous travelers.[47]

At their best, the travel accounts surveyed Utah's social and cultural scene and gave details that sometimes escaped the eye of the contemporary Saint. Examples of this literature included Richard F. Burton's *City of the Saints, and across the Rocky Mountains to California;* Fitz Hugh Ludlow's *Heart of the*

Continent: A Record of Travel across the Plains and in Oregon; and Jules Remy and Julius Brenchley's *Journey to Great-Salt Lake City.*[48] Other perceptive reports included Solomon Nunes Carvalho's *Incidents of Travel and Adventure in the Far West;* William Chandless's *Visit to Salt Lake;* John Codman's *Mormon Country: A Summer with the "Latter-day Saints";* William Hepworth Dixon's *New America;* Elizabeth Kane's *Twelve Mormon Homes Visited in Succession on a Journey though Utah to Arizona* and her posthumously published *A Gentile Account of Life in Utah's Dixie, 1872–73;* and Phil Robinson's *Sinners and Saints: A Tour across the States, and Round Them with Three Months among the Mormons.*[49]

Of course, other visitors were less discerning. Their accounts usually focused on Utah's peculiar institution of plural marriage and, in the process, often revealed more about the Victorian era's repressed sexuality than about any practice existing in the kingdom of the Saints. For example, Benjamin G. Ferris's popular *Utah and the Mormons: The History, Government, Doctrines, Customs and Prospects of the Latter-Day Saints* charged that Utah territory was filled with "gross sensuality" and that one Mormon leader furnished "separate stalls" for his wives, "as a farmer would his favorite cows."[50] Ferris, whose service as Governor Brigham Young's Washington-appointed territorial secretary apparently had been amicable, seemed transformed once he had left the territory and begun to write for the non-Mormon audience.

From today's perspective, it appears that Ferris and many other visitors to Utah consciously or unconsciously took advantage of the Saints' negative image—the rampant anti-Mormonism of the time created a promising publishing niche.[51] They were not the only writers to do so. Dissident Mormons also sought fame and fortune—and to expose supposed Mormon folly—by writing books. Hurlbut began the process, and it continued with more than a dozen exposés written during the remainder of the century. One of the most influential was the *History of the Saints,* authored by the Nauvoo dissident John C. Bennett. Bennett's book was a collection of anti-Mormon, fact-as-well-as-fiction documents, spliced together with occasional prose. To this day, it retains value for details normally excluded from more pietistic accounts of the Mormon "Kingdom on the Mississippi," although its lack of balance and clear animosity requires that it be read with caution.[52]

The public's interest in Mormonism's supposed "sins and sex" was so strong that the century saw the publication of a string of authoritative-sounding, first-person accounts that had their origins not so much in Nauvoo or the Great Basin but in the pulp publishing houses of eastern United States and London. These fanciful accounts were sometimes loosely based on actual people and events; sometimes their "facts" came only from the imagination of highly creative writers who knew little about Mormonism. But almost always they were lurid. Included in this group were Orvilla S. Belisle's *Mormonism Unveiled; or, A History of Mormonism;* Maria N. Ward's *Female Life among the Mormons* and its counterpart, Austin N. Ward's *Husband in Utah; or, Sights and Scenes among the Mormons;* and Catherine Waite's *Mormon Prophet and His Harem; or, An Authentic History of Brigham Young.*[53] Whatever their shortcomings, each of these works was popular enough to warrant repeated new editions. Some are still cited as legitimate sources by unsuspecting scholars.[54]

Other books were more firmly rooted in personal experience, although they still used the exaggerated and formulaic techniques of the exposé. *Mormonism: Its Leaders and Designs* was written by John Hyde, a former Mormon elder who eventually became a Swedenborgian minister.[55] Hyde joined the anti-Mormon tide by ascribing the church's growth to imposture, fanaticism, and delusion. While offering a chronological history of Mormonism, most of Hyde's pages were devoted to "documenting" the church's alleged excesses. Fanny Stenhouse's memoir followed a similar pattern. Its first edition seemed a promising start, but when it was published in its expanded and more famous 1874 version, *"Tell It All": The Story of a Life Experience in Mormonism,* its passages of invention and overwriting prevented what might have been a poignant account of the talented Stenhouse's estrangement from Mormonism.[56] Still less charity can be given to Ann Eliza Webb Young, who wrote *Wife Number 19; or, The Story of a Life in Bondage* in 1875.[57] Webb was Brigham Young's estranged plural wife, and she distorted Utah conditions and misrepresented her former husband in what seemed a clear quest for publicity and salved pique—not to mention the profits that might accrue from one of her national speaking tours.

William Hickman's *Brigham's Destroying Angel, Being the Life, Confession, and Startling Disclosures of the Notorious Bill Hickman* was marketed in 1873 as the memoir of Mormonism's chief "Danite" avenger.[58] Filled with frontier braggadocio and an occasional scene drawn from whole cloth, Hickman's book was edited by John Hanson Beadle, whose own exposé, *The History of Mormonism; Its Rise, Progress, Present Condition and Mysteries,* followed a year later.[59] Although some have suggested that *Brigham's Destroying Angel* was written by Beadle, not Hickman, Hickman's most recent biographer concluded otherwise.[60] Hickman apparently was one of several rough Utah frontiersmen who may have dispensed occasional summary justice to Utah's criminal element.

John D. Lee's *Mormonism Unveiled; or, The Life and Confessions of the Late Bishop, John D. Lee* was a more substantial memoir.[61] Lee had a contentious personality, but until he played a leading role in the Mountain Meadows massacre—the infamous Indian-Mormon killing of over a hundred California-bound emigrants in 1857—he was an energetic and dutiful southern Utah pioneer. His memoir, written shortly before his execution, was self-serving and minimized his role in the crime, but it contained valuable detail and was genuine in many of its emotions. Despite the hopeful expectation of some in the anti-Mormon community, Lee's book failed to implicate Brigham Young in the massacre.

Mormon Antiquarianism

Balancing the negative images of the travel account literature and the LDS exposés were the generally favorable, Mormon-authored biographies of the men and women of Mormonism's first generation. Examined more fully elsewhere in this volume, the most important of these were Edward W. Tullidge's three books, *Life of Brigham Young; or, Utah and Her Founders, Women of Mormondom,* and *Life of Joseph the Prophet;* Orson F. Whitney's *Life of Heber C. Kimball, an Apostle: The Father and Founder of the British Mission;* George Q. Cannon's *Life of Joseph Smith, the Prophet;* and B. H. Roberts's *Life of John Taylor, Third President of the Church of Jesus Christ of Latter-day Saints.*[62] In addition to these book-length works, there were several compilations of biographical sketches: the biographical appendix to Edward W. Tullidge's *History of Salt Lake City;* Andrew Jenson's *Biographical Encyclopedia;* Emmeline B. Wells's *Charities and Philanthropies . . . Woman's Work in Utah,* which treated Utah's first women doctors; and the *Juvenile Instructor* series "Heroines of Mormondom."[63] This tradition of biographical vignette continued into the twentieth century with Orson F. Whitney's *History of Utah* and Frank Esshom's *Pioneers and Prominent Men of Utah: Comprising Photographs, Genealogies, Biographies.*[64]

Generally, these nineteenth-century biographies tended to memorialize their subjects, neglect women, emphasize administrative considerations to the exclusion of the fuller dimension of human life, and stress career over character. Stylistically, they seldom moved beyond a chronological summary, which substituted quotation for a smoothly told narrative.

These fawning and disjointed qualities did not just beset early Mormon writing. They were also part of an age that celebrated the past and found little pejorative meaning in the word *antiquarian.* It was a time of "documania," when even newspapers printed historical documents for a fascinated reading public. "Every man was his own historian," wrote George Callcott of this nineteenth-century compulsion, "searching for himself in the old manuscripts and colonial records, enjoying the mysterious lure of the unknown, standing at the frontier of knowledge."[65] To further this quest, historical societies and historical journals were established, both of which gave "documents" center stage. It was a time when the compiler of records and the historian were one and the same.

As the century progressed, this "antiquarian" tendency increasingly manifested itself in Mormon writing. For instance, continuing the tradition of "Joseph Smith's History," Utah historians compiled documents pertaining to the Brigham Young presidency. These were chronologically organized as "Brigham Young Manuscript History" (sometimes called the "Documentary History of the Church"), now available at the LDS archives in Salt Lake City. The preliminary portion of this work formed the basis of volume seven of B. H. Roberts's *History of the Church* and was later published in a less abbreviated form as the *Manuscript History of Brigham Young, 1846–1847*, edited by Elden J. Watson.[66] Another example of this midcentury compiling was the 314-page "Histories of the Twelve," which contained important material on several Mormon leaders. Never completed and today seldom used, this collection was printed in successive runs of the *Deseret News* and the *Millennial Star.*[67]

Still another manifestation of the "antiquarian" impulse was the historical handbook. Organized as catechisms and compendia, these brief summaries offered quick and easily digestible information, especially for the rising generation. Following this pattern, the church historian George A. Smith published *Historical Address Delivered by President Geo. A. Smith* and *The Rise, Progress, and Travels of the Church of Jesus Christ of Latter-day Saints,* which surveyed such topics as the origin of plural marriage among the Mormons and the beginning of Utah's pioneer settlement.[68] Similarly, the Mormon-owned newspaper, the *Deseret News,* produced several commemorative booklets containing pioneer lore, including the *New Year's Issue* in 1893.[69] The *Salt Lake Tribune* followed suit with *Fifty Years Ago Today* in 1897, a booklet that honored the 1847 Mormon settlement of Utah.[70] In a similar vein, during the 1890s the *Deseret News,* the *Tribune,* and the *Salt Lake Herald* often issued important historical data in their special New Year's editions. Finally, Franklin D. Richards's *Compendium of the Faith and Doctrines of the Church of Jesus Christ of Latter-day Saints;* John Jaques's *Church of Jesus Christ of Latter-day Saints: Its Priesthood, Organization, Doctrines, Ordinances and History;* and Abraham H. Cannon's *Hand-book of Reference to the History, Chronology, Religion and Country of the Latter-day Saints* all contained brief summaries of material that was more pedagogical than historical.[71]

The historian who personified the LDS documentary method was Andrew

Jenson, a Danish convert who was an indefatigable gatherer of historical material.[72] Early in his career, Jenson issued an annual "chronology" of the church's immediate past events. He also produced the first volume of the already mentioned *Biographical Encyclopedia* and began the publication of the *Historical Record,* a history magazine of miscellany. After his appointment as an assistant church historian in 1891, Jenson began to compile historical material for most of the ecclesiastical units of the church. Some of these data were later printed in his *Encyclopedic History of the Church of Jesus Christ of Latter-day Saints;* most, however, remained in manuscript form at the LDS archives.[73]

Jenson's most ambitious project was the "Journal History," a chronologically arranged scrapbook of church history. This work eventually grew to more than eight hundred legal-size volumes, each three to five inches thick. Originally the "Journal History" contained a wide range of documentary material, including diary excerpts, speeches, letters, newspaper accounts, and the minutes of confidential church meetings. Unfortunately, Jenson's successors were less energetic, and by the middle of the twentieth century, the "Journal History" had become a much less rich resource. Whatever its most recent failings, however, the microfilmed and roughly indexed "Journal History" remains an important primary source for Mormon history. The original is located in the LDS Church library in Salt Lake City, and microfilm copies can be found at most large research libraries in Utah.

Another important collector of Mormon documents was the essayist, playwright, and historian Edward W. Tullidge. When writing his biographies of Joseph Smith and Brigham Young or penning his sketches of prominent Mormon women, Tullidge collected and published large masses of documents. He continued the procedure with his most important work, *The History of Salt Lake City.* That book, which included a much broader coverage of Mormon history than its title implies, offered perhaps the largest array of LDS source documents ever assembled in a single nineteenth-century book. Using pioneer journals, government documents, newspapers, and even pioneer hymns, *The History of Salt Lake City* also published the early city charter, territorial laws, and large blocks of correspondence between Mormon leaders and federal officials. Unfortunately, since Tullidge's book lacked scholarly citations and an index, its rich sources were difficult to access.[74]

Tullidge did more than provide documents. The *History of Salt Lake City* contained almost five dozen biographical sketches, many with accompanying steel engravings. Tullidge also recognized a fuller range of historical topics than did many of his contemporaries. As a result, he treated such topics as Utah's early theocratic conditions, commerce and mining, Salt Lake journalism, the Mormon theater, and the Godbeite movement to "reform" Mormonism, with which Tullidge himself had once been associated.

After contributing Mormon-related material to several national journals, including *Harper's* and the *Phrenological Journal,* Tullidge edited several Utah-based, history-oriented journals, including *Tullidge's Quarterly Magazine.* He closed out his career with the ponderously titled *Tullidge's Histories, Volume II: Containing the History of All the Northern, Eastern, and Western Counties of Utah; Also the Counties of Southern Idaho,* which aimed to do for the northern Mormon periphery what his Salt Lake history had done for the heartland.[75]

George Q. Cannon, a member of the LDS First Presidency, also gathered and printed several nineteenth-century antiquarian works. Given the assignment to oversee the education of the church's youth and the Mormon Sunday School movement, Cannon established a publishing press, George Q. Cannon and Sons, and issued numerous didactic, noninterpretive studies of the LDS past. One of Cannon's most important projects was the *Juvenile Instructor* (1866–1929), a magazine that offered LDS youth a variety of instruction, including articles dealing with history and biography. Cannon also published the "Faith-Promoting" series of popular biography, missionary journals, and vignette history—again largely directed at juvenile readers. The church leader even published his own biography of Mormonism's founder, *The Life of Joseph Smith, the Prophet* in 1888.[76] No doubt, Cannon's labors to promote education and refinement greatly strengthened the church's youth during a period when Mormonism was widely misunderstood. However, he was also responsible for a less helpful legacy. By stressing only the positive and faith-promoting aspects of Mormonism, he left the LDS youth who went on to attend eastern colleges and universities at a disadvantage. Unacquainted with the complexity and tensions of their faith, they were often unprepared to defend their religion to others—or, for that matter, to themselves.

The antiquarian spirit in the United States influenced Mormon historiography in yet another way—the writing of local history. During the last decades of the century, many cities, counties, geographical regions, and states printed commemorative histories of their past, and these, if the Mormon hegira had crossed into their boundaries, often included information about the Saints. Because these non-LDS works celebrated the new nation at a time when the Mormons were considered outside the American mainstream, their treatment of Mormonism was usually disparaging. If this approach sometimes provided misleading and even false information, on other occasions the local histories balanced the overly positive views of Mormon accounts and provided details that Mormon authors overlooked.

Several local histories deserve special mention. Helpful in assessing the attitudes of non-Mormons in Pennsylvania and New York where the church first originated were such books as Emily C. Blackman's *History of Susquehanna County, Pennsylvania;* Henry P. Smith's edited *History of Broome County [New York];* James H. Smith's *History of Chenango and Madison Counties, New York;* and Orasmus Turner's *History of the Pioneer Settlement of Phelps and Gorham's Purchase.*[77] Of the more than half-dozen local histories that had information about Mormonism's Missouri travail, *The History of Jackson County, Missouri* offered a chapter on the "Mormon War," while the *History of Caldwell and Livingston Counties, Missouri* devoted sixty pages to various church-related events.[78]

Thomas Ford's *History of Illinois: From Its Commencement as a State in 1818 to 1847* combined local history with personal memoir. Ford was governor of Illinois during the Mormons' last years in Nauvoo, and his policies contributed to the deaths of Joseph Smith and Hyrum Smith and to the expulsion of the Saints from Illinois. Not surprisingly, his account included a measure of self-justification. Ford condemned Joseph Smith for being a cunning tyrant with a propensity for "invention." He likewise charged the ordinary Saint with having a fierce "enterprising enthusiasm."[79] It was the Saints' peccadilloes, not the actions of their Illinois neighbors, that led to their persecutions, Ford seemed to say.

Emerging Synthesis History

Most of the information provided by the Utah travel accounts, the exposés written by LDS dissidents, and the nationally published local histories was narrowly focused and often prejudicial. Fortunately, however, during the last decades of the nineteenth century, there were signs that writing about the LDS past was beginning to mature and offer new perspectives. While still adversarial in tone, these later writers were no longer content merely to assemble large blocks of quoted material; they increasingly tried to mold or synthesize their sources into a more readable narrative. Moreover, some of these new "synthesis" historians sought a more satisfactory explanation of the Mormon past by promoting fresh interpretations.[80]

One indication of this new approach was the historical article. During the century, the eastern press published more than 125 articles on the Mormons, some of which made a lasting contribution. For instance, one of the earliest and most detailed accounts of the U.S. government's decision to dispatch troops to Utah in 1857—the so-called "Utah War"—was Albert B. Browne's series of articles, "The Utah Expedition: Its Causes and Consequences," which appeared in the *Atlantic Monthly* in 1859. Later, the U.S. Army gave its version of these events in W. R. Hamilton's "History of the Mormon Rebellion of 1856–57," which was serially published in 1890 and 1891 in the periodical *United Service.*

John Hay, a native of southwestern Illinois who eventually became U.S. secretary of state, wrote a literate account of the events that led to the killing of Joseph Smith. He argued that Smith's death was the result of the Mormon destruction of an opposition newspaper in Nauvoo, the LDS semisecret practice of plural marriage, and the church's alleged willingness to protect criminals operating along the Mississippi River.[81] Like Governor Thomas Ford's memoir, Hay's thesis led to the comfortable conclusion (for the Illinois citizenry at least) that the Saints' troubles were of their own making.

The most meaningful work of the rising generation of historians was published in books. Thomas Gregg, yet another anti-Mormon journalist, had opposed the Mormons when they had lived in Nauvoo, a few miles from his home in southwest Illinois. Although written almost half a century after this first encounter, *The Prophet of Palmyra* maintained Gregg's earlier point of view. Gregg argued that Joseph Smith lacked mental ability and proper character and asserted that the Book of Mormon contained little of religious worth. Yet, despite such views, Gregg was left wondering about the enigma of Joseph Smith and Mormonism: "That such a career as was his, with such remarkable results following, could be run in the enlightened Nineteenth Century, and in a land where Christianity and Civilization have shed their benign rays, is a mystery which the writer prefers to leave his readers to solve."[82]

Gregg's riddle repeatedly surfaced in the confrontational literature of the time. After emphasizing Smith's shortcomings and minimizing his talent, writers were then pressed to explain his success. William A. Linn's *Story of the Mormons: From the Date of Their Origin to the Year 1901,* the last of the century's non-Mormon histories, did no better at solving the puzzle. Linn used a variety of Mormon and non-Mormon sources, and his narrative was the most sophisticated of the anti-LDS writers. Yet his conclusions remained harsh. Linn made the usual charges about the Mormon leaders' motives and their "dictatorial power." In addition, he introduced themes that reflected the muckraking age in which he wrote, noting the incidence of foreign-born among the Mormons and charging the LDS Church with the conspiracy of trying to control the economic and political affairs of the Intermountain West. To Linn, Mormonism was an "American threatening" institution.[83]

If Linn's book summarized the anti-Mormon historical writing of the nineteenth century, it also impacted the future: such rising LDS writers as B. H.

Roberts felt compelled to respond to Linn's charges in books published in the new century. In addition, as the nineteenth century closed, some traditional non-LDS interpretations of Mormonism began to soften or give way. To maintain the Spaulding theory after the Spaulding manuscript had been discovered, both Gregg and Linn resorted to the idea of a second "Manuscript Found"—Sidney Rigdon must have found a second Spaulding draft. Moreover, as the Saints prospered in the arid Intermountain West, they could not be easily dismissed as dupes; their settlements showed industry and a striving for education and culture. The LDS economic and political power that Linn found alarming refuted the charge of Mormon incompetence and folly.

As old interpretations begin to fray, new approaches began to take their place. When T. B. H. Stenhouse started to research *Rocky Mountain Saints*, he was a Mormon stalwart who planned to write a Mormon defense. Church leaders allowed him to use the LDS archives. However, in the early 1870s, Stenhouse and his wife, Fanny, left the LDS Church to join William S. Godbe's "New Movement," which proclaimed itself as a reform of Mormonism. When Stenhouse's book finally appeared in 1873, it was both a Godbeite tract and an exorcism of his former beliefs. Like most non-Mormon books of the time, it contained charges of Danite "blood atonement," Mormon materialism, and Mormon theocratic power.[84]

Nevertheless, it did offer new insights. For the first time, a major narrative history suggested that Joseph Smith was sincere and had ability. Stenhouse saw the Mormon founder as "one of the earth's most remarkable men," but in line with the Godbeites' unusual program (Godbe accepted spiritualism as well as modernism), Smith was described as an unlearned spiritualistic medium who often misread the message of the otherworld.[85] More lasting were other Stenhouse interpretations. By juxtaposing the Mormon theocracy and the national government, sectarianism and pluralism, provincialism and contemporary culture, Stenhouse helped create several of the twentieth century's interpretive models of Mormonism. Stenhouse also argued that the Missouri confrontation during the late 1830s was two-sided, since both Missourians and Mormons shared the blame. He also believed that the Mormon difficulties in Illinois were based on political rivalry as well as religious prejudice. By employing such arguments, Stenhouse began the process of narrowing the extremes of nineteenth-century LDS historiography. The book was reprinted five times by 1905 and was one of the most influential of Mormonism's founding era.

As important was Hubert Howe Bancroft's *History of Utah: 1540–1886*, which, instead of focusing entirely on Utah as its title implied, devoted more than a quarter of its pages to detailing the story of early Mormonism.[86] Much about the book was fresh. Bancroft used the church's historical records as well as several hundred historical sketches written by a cross section of Utahns. To these local records, he added government and nationally published sources. This material was then assembled in Bancroft's unabashed, mass-production style, with Alfred Bates, one of the Bancroft's History Company's employees, writing much of the first draft.[87]

Bancroft's historical philosophy worked in the Saints' favor. Narrative history, Bancroft believed, should provide "a clear and concise statement of facts . . . , leaving the reader to make his own deductions and form his own opinions."[88] While the formula freed Bancroft's work from the polemics that typically filled many Mormon studies of the time, it also produced ambivalence: his matter-of-fact narrative favored the Utahns, but the non-Mormon point of view was retained in many footnotes and even in some narrative passages. This precarious balance was more than a reflection of personal philosophy or the interpretative extremes of Mormon studies. To secure access to church documents and assistance, Bancroft had agreed to let church leaders examine the work before it went to press. A favorable statement of the Mormon position was thus a sine qua non from the start.

Bancroft's *History of Utah* had a Mormon partner. Poet-historian-thespian Orson F. Whitney's four-volume *History of Utah* at last provided the Mormons with a major narrative history of their own.[89] Whitney, a first-generation Utahn who was immersed in the territory's lore and documents, wrote "old style" history, eloquently (sometimes grandiloquently) and without the detailed footnotes and bibliographic references that modern history was coming to demand. Whitney devoted a third of his first volume to Mormonism's pre-Utah years and later gave Mormon topics generous attention. His fourth volume was the best collection of biographical sketches, Mormon and Utahn, found in print. The magisterial series was later condensed into Whitney's *Popular History of Utah*.[90]

First-Century Trends

Mormon history, like Mormonism itself, traveled a great distance during the nineteenth century. Begun in the hothouse of millennial excitement and given to polemical views, writing history had matured both in terms of source availability and narrative style by the turn of the century. But, after seventy years, historians typically remained in two opposing camps, each more prone to argue the merits of Mormonism than to seek an understanding of the men and women who had enrolled in its cause. If several issues that had embroiled Mormon literature, such as the Spaulding theory, were becoming less compelling, other old interpretive questions continued to claim an interest: Joseph Smith's Palmyra origins, Mormon theocracy, and the church's supposed "anti-American" threat to national institutions. In all this, the amateur historian—sometimes the journalist, the traveler, the minister, or the Mormon apologist or dissident—dominated. Mormon historiography was still in the process of becoming.

Notes

1. The proclamation of Latter-day Saint religious exclusivity is taken from Mormon scripture: Doctrine and Covenants (present edition) 1:30. One cannot read of the Puritan historians without seeing many parallels with early Mormon writing. See Peter Gay, *A Loss of Mastery: Puritan Historians in Colonial America* (New York: Vintage Books, 1968); Richard S. Dunn, "Seventeenth-Century English Historians of America," in *Seventeenth-Century America: Essays in Colonial History,* ed. James Morton Smith (Chapel Hill: University of North Carolina Press, 1959), 195–225; and Kenneth Murdock, "Clio in the Wilderness: History and Biography in Puritan New England," *Church History* 24 (September 1955): 221–38.

2. Eber D. Howe, *Mormonism Unvailed; or, A Faithful Account of that Singular Imposition and Delusion* (Painesville, Ohio: By the author, 1834).

3. Arthur B. Deming, *Startling Revelations! Naked Truths about Mormonism* (Oakland, Calif.: n.p., 1888), 2.

4. Eber D. Howe, *Autobiography and Recollections of a Pioneer Printer* (Painesville, Ohio: Telegraph Steam Printing House, 1878), 64.

5. Howe, *Mormonism Unvailed,* 74.

6. Dean C. Jessee, ed. and comp., *The Personal Writings of Joseph Smith* (Salt Lake City: Deseret Book, 1984), 11 and 28 January and 1 and 7 April 1834, 26–27, 32.

7. For Hurlbut's name, see Sermon of George A. Smith, 10 January 1858, *Journal of Discourses,* 26 vols. (Liverpool, England: F. D. and S. W. Richards, 1854–86), 7:113. For folk tradition, see Aaron C. Willey, "Observations on Magical Practices," *Medical Repository* 3 (1812): 380; Andrew Jackson Davis, *Answers to Ever-Recurring Questions from the People* (Boston: William White, 1873), 99–100; and Earl W. Hayter, *The Troubled Farmer, 1850–1900: Rural Adjustment to Industrialism* (De Kalb, Ill.: Northern Illinois University Press, 1968), 41.

8. Howe, *Mormonism Unvailed,* 11.

9. A. W. B[enton], "Mormonites," *Evangelical Magazine and Gospel Advocate,* n.s., 2 (9 April 1831): 120; David S. Burnet, "Some Thing New—The Golden Bible," *Evangelical Inquirer* 1 (7 March 1831): 217–40. Later in the century, other articles appeared with similar content: Fayette Lapham, "The Mormons," *Historical Magazine,* n.s., 7 (May 1870): 305–7; Frederick G. Mather, "The Early Days of Mormonism," *Lippincott's Magazine* 26 (August 1880): 198–211; and Emily M. Austin, *Mormonism; or, Life among the Mormons* (Madison, Wis.: M. J. Cantwell, 1882), 31–33. Various late nineteenth-century local and state histories, cited later, carried on the theme.

10. Howe, *Mormonism Unvailed,* 100, 278–90.

11. Howe, *Autobiography and Recollections,* 45.

12. A sampling of the more important literature included Matilda Spaulding Davison, "The Mormon Bible," *Millennial Harbinger,* n.s., 3 (1839): 265–68; Edward Duffield Neill, "The Book of Mormon," *Historical Magazine,* 2d ser., 6 (August 1869): 68–69; Ellen E. Dickinson, "The Book of Mormon," *Scribner's Monthly* 20 (August 1880): 613–16; Robert Patterson, *Who Wrote the Book of Mormon?* (Philadelphia: L. H. Everts, 1882); and Ellen E. Dickinson, *New Light on Mormonism* (New York: Funk and Wagnalls, 1885). During the century, there were at least two dozen additional articles, many reprints or derivative re-statements, of the above pieces of literature.

13. James H. Fairchild, "Manuscript of Solomon Spaulding and the Book of Mormon" (paper read before the Northern Ohio and Western Reserve Historical Society, 23 March 1886, published as *Tract No. 77, Western Reserve Historical Society* [Cleveland, Ohio, 1886]), 187–200; James H. Fairchild, "Solomon Spaulding and the Book of Mormon," *Bibliotheca Sacra* 42 (January 1885): 173–74.

14. Daniel Kidder, *Mormonism and the Mormons: A Historical View of the Rise and Progress of the Sect Self-Styled Latter-day Saints* (New York: G. Lane and P. P. Sandford, 1842); John C. Bennett, *History of the Saints; or, An Exposé of Joe Smith and Mormonism* (Boston: Leland and Whiting, 1842).

15. John A. Clark, *Gleanings by the Way* (Philadelphia: W. J. and J. K. Simon, 1842).

16. Ibid., 225–26, 266–67. Clark's summary suggested the tone of his work: "You might as well go down into the Crater of Vesuvius and attempt to build an ice house amid its molten and boiling lava, as to convince any inhabitant in either of these towns [Palmyra and Manchester, New York], that Jo Smith's pretensions are not the most gross and egregious falsehood" (346).

17. J. B. Turner, *Mormonism in All Ages; or, The Rise, Progress and Causes of Mormonism* (New York: Platt and Peters, 1842), 213.

18. Henry Caswall, *The City of the Mormons; or, Three Days at Nauvoo* (London: J. G. F. and J. Rivington, 1842); Henry Caswall, *The Prophet of the Nineteenth Century; or, The Rise, Progress, and Present State of the Mormons* (London: J. G. F. and J. Rivington, 1843), vi (first quote), 8 (second quote). For a biographical sketch of Caswall, see Craig L. Foster, "Henry Caswall: Anti-Mormon Extraordinaire," *BYU Studies* 35, no. 4 (1995–96): 144–59.

19. Pomeroy Tucker, *Origin, Rise and Progress of Mormonism: Biography of Its Founders and History of Its Church* (New York: D. Appleton, 1867), 16 (first quote), 278–79 (second quote).

20. Joseph Smith, "History, 1839," in *Autobiographical and Historical Writings,* vol. 1 of *The Papers of Joseph Smith,* ed. and comp. Dean C. Jessee (Salt Lake City: Deseret Book, 1989), 282. See also Oliver Cowdery, "Letter VIII," *Latter Day Saints' Messenger and Advocate* 2 (October 1835): 201.

21. Parley P. Pratt, *Mormonism Unveiled* (New York: By the author, 1838); Benjamin Winchester, *The Origin of the Spaulding Story* (Philadelphia: Brown, Bicking and Guilbert, 1840); John E. Page, *The Spaulding Story concerning the Origin of the Book of Mormon* (Pittsburgh: n.p., 1843).

22. Doctrine and Covenants 21:1. For similar-minded instruction, see ibid., 47:1–4; 69:2–3, 8; and 85:1–2.

23. The history of the official church historian is beyond the scope of this essay, but the following literature provides an introduction to its establishment and functioning: Dean

C. Jessee, "Joseph Smith and the Beginning of Mormon Record Keeping," in *The Prophet Joseph: Essays on the Life and Mission of Joseph Smith,* ed. Larry C. Porter and Susan Easton Black (Salt Lake City: Deseret Book, 1988), 138–60; Charles P. Adams and Gustive O. Larson, "A Study of the LDS Church Historian's Office, 1830–1900," *Utah Historical Quarterly* 40 (Fall 1972): 370–89; A. William Lund, "The Church Historian's Office," *Improvement Era* 38 (April 1935): 220, 252; A. William Lund, "The Church Historian's Office," *Improvement Era* 59 (November 1956): 795, 853–54; Ronald K. Esplin and Max J. Evans, "Preserving Mormon Manuscripts: Historical Activities of the LDS Church," *Manuscripts* 27 (Summer 1975): 166–67; T. Edgar Lyon, "Church Historians I Have Known," *Dialogue: A Journal of Mormon Thought* 11 (Winter 1978): 14–22; and Howard C. Searle, "Early Mormon Historiography: Writing the History of the Mormons, 1830–1858" (Ph.D. diss., University of California at Los Angeles, 1979), 69–143.

24. This history was published in serial form (minus the last chapters) in the Reorganized Church of Jesus Christ of Latter Day Saints' John Whitmer, "Church History," ed. Heman C. Smith, *Journal of History* 1 (January–July, 1908); and more recently in F. Mark McKiernan and Roger D. Launius, eds., *An Early Latter Day Saint History: The Book of John Whitmer Kept by Commandment* (Independence, Mo.: Herald Publishing House, 1980). The original manuscript is in the RLDS Library and Archives, Independence, Missouri. Other unpublished works of the period included a six-page narrative written by Smith himself containing an account of his "First Vision"; a twenty-page genealogical memorandum of the Smith family; and a twenty-nine-page statement of early church events prepared in 1835–36 by Frederick G. Williams, Oliver Cowdery, and Warren Parrish, all at the LDS Historical Department, Salt Lake City.

25. Cowdery, "Letter VIII," 200–201.

26. Orson Pratt, *An Interesting Account of Several Remarkable Visions, and of the Late Discovery of Ancient American Records* (Edinburgh, Scotland: Ballantyne and Hughes, 1840).

27. Joseph Smith, *Correspondence between Joseph Smith, the Prophet, and Col. John Wentworth* (New York: John E. Page and L. R. Foster, 1844).

28. The instruction for this record-keeping is found in Doctrine and Covenants 123:1–6ff. See also Clark V. Johnson, "The Missouri Redress Petitions: A Reappraisal of Mormon Persecution in Missouri," *BYU Studies* 26 (Spring 1986): 31–44; and Clark V. Johnson, ed., *Mormon Redress Petitions: Documents of the 1833–1838 Missouri Conflict* (Provo, Utah: Religious Studies Center, Brigham Young University, 1992).

29. See, for example, Francis G. Bishop, *Brief History of the Church of Jesus Christ of Latter Day Saints* (Salem, [Mass.]: Blum and Son, 1839); John P. Greene, *Facts Relative to the Expulsion of the Mormons, or Latter-day Saints from the State of Missouri* (Cincinnati: R. P. Brooks, 1839); Parley P. Pratt, *History of the Late Persecution Inflicted by the State of Missouri upon the Mormons* (Detroit: Dawson and Bates, 1839); Sidney Rigdon, *An Appeal to the American People: Being an Account of the Persecutions of the Church of Latter Day Saints* (Cincinnati: Glezen and Shepard, 1840); and John Taylor, *A Short Account of the Murders, Roberies [sic], Burnings, Thefts, and Other Outrages Committed by the Mob and Militia of the State of Missouri* (Springfield, Ill.[?]: n.p., 1839).

30. Thomas J. Kirk, *The Mormons and Missouri: A General Outline of the History of the Mormons* (Chillicothe, Mo.: J. H. Darlington, 1844), 5. See also James H. Hunt, *Mormon-*

ism; Embracing the Origin, Rise and Progress of the Sect (St. Louis: Ustick and Davies, 1844); and Missouri [Fifth] Circuit Court, *Document Containing the Correspondence, Orders, &c. in Relation to the Disturbances with the Mormons* (Fayette, Mo.: Boon's Lick Democrat, 1841).

31. B. H. Roberts, ed., *History of the Church of Jesus Christ of Latter-Day Saints: Period I, History of Joseph Smith, the Prophet, by Himself,* 6 vols. (Salt Lake City: Deseret News, 1902–12), 3:346.

32. Ibid., 6:409.

33. Quoted in Dean Jessee, "Howard Coray's Recollections of Joseph Smith," *BYU Studies* 17 (Spring 1977): 346.

34. The best discussions of the writing, compiling, editing, and publishing of this "history" are in Dean C. Jessee, "The Writing of Joseph Smith's History," *BYU Studies* 11 (Summer 1971): 439–73; Dean C. Jessee, "The Reliability of Joseph Smith's History," *Journal of Mormon History* 3 (1976): 23–46; and Searle, "Early Mormon Historiography," 200–336.

35. For evaluations of Roberts's work, see Searle, "Early Mormon Historiography," 307–36; Truman G. Madsen, *Defender of the Faith: The B. H. Roberts Story* (Salt Lake City: Bookcraft, 1980), 290–93; and Davis Bitton, "B. H. Roberts as Historian," *Dialogue: A Journal of Mormon Thought* 3 (Winter 1968): 25–44. A seventh volume dealing with the first several years of Brigham Young's leadership, 1844–48, was added in 1932.

36. Charles Mackay, *The Mormons; or, Latter-Day Saints, with Memoirs of the Life and Death of Joseph Smith, the "American Mahomet"* (London: Office of the National Illustrated Library, 1851). For background on Mackay, see Leonard J. Arrington, "Charles Mackay and His 'True and Impartial History' of the Mormons," *Utah Historical Quarterly* 36 (Winter 1968): 25–40.

37. London: 1st, 1851; 2d and 3d, 1852; 4th, 1856; 5th, 1857. United States: Auburn, N.Y.: Derby and Miller, 1852, 1853, 1854; New York: Samuel M. Smucker, 1856; and New York: Miller, Orton, 1857, 1858, 1860. France: Amédèe Pichot, *Les Mormons* (Paris: Libraine Hachette, 1854); Germany: Theodor Olshausen, *Geshichte der Mormonen; oder, Jüngsten-Tages Heiligen in Nordamerika* (Göttingen: Bandenhoeck und Ruprecht, 1856); Sweden: *Mormonerna, eller De Yttersta dagarnas heliga . . .* (Stockholm: Trycht a Aftonbladets Trychen, 1853). Later in the century, other editions were issued as well.

38. Mackay, *The Mormons,* 326.

39. John W. Gunnison, *The Mormons; or, Latter-day Saints in the Valley of the Great Salt Lake* (Philadelphia: Lippincott, Grambo, 1852).

40. For additional material on Gunnison, see Brigham D. Madsen, ed., "John W. Gunnison's Letters to His Mormon Friend, Albert Carrington," *Utah Historical Quarterly* 59 (Summer 1991): 264–85; Brigham D. Madsen, "Stansbury's Expedition to the Great Salt Lake, 1849–50," *Utah Historical Quarterly* 56 (Spring 1988): 148–59; and Robert Kent Fielding, *The Unsolicited Chronicler: An Account of the Gunnison Massacre, Its Causes and Consequences* (Brookline, Mass.: Paradigm Publications, 1993).

41. John W. Gunnison to Martha A. Delany Gunnison, 2 February 1850, John W. Gunnison Papers, Henry E. Huntington Library, San Marino, Calif.

42. Gunnison, *The Mormons,* v. See also John W. Gunnison to Martha A. Delany Gunnison, 9 October 1849, John W. Gunnison Papers.

43. Gunnison, *The Mormons,* 89 (first quote), 95, 96 (second and third quotes).

44. Edward Hunter, "Oration Delivered on the South West Corner Stone of the Temple," 7 April 1853, in "Record of Bishops' Meetings," LDS Library-Archives, Salt Lake City, Utah (hereafter LDS Archives). When speaking of the book's supposed inaccuracies, Brigham Young denied that it occasioned widespread anger on the part of the Mormons, though such a claim was made in the eastern press. See Brigham Young to John M. Bernhisel, 31 March 1854, Governor's Letterbook, Volume 1, LDS Archives.

45. Gunnison, *The Mormons,* 129, 165.

46. Nancy Towle, *Vicissitudes Illustrated, in the Experience of Nancy Towle* (Charleston: James L. Burges, 1832); Caswall, *The City of the Mormons;* Josiah Quincy, *Figures of the Past from the Leaves of Old Journals* (Boston: Roberts Brothers, 1883).

47. There was a corollary to these non-Mormon travel accounts. When traveling abroad, the Mormons themselves left their impressions of the world beyond Nauvoo and Deseret, which reveal a great deal of the Mormon, nineteenth-century mind. See, for example, Heber C. Kimball, *Journal of Heber C. Kimball* (Nauvoo: Robinson and Smith, 1840) (travels in Great Britain); Orson Hyde, *A Voice from Jerusalem* (Liverpool: Parley P. Pratt, 1842) (on Palestine); and Erastus Snow, *One Year in Scandinavia: Results of the Gospel in Denmark and Sweden* (Liverpool: F. D. Richards, 1851). In addition to these accounts, numerous letters were published in the *Juvenile Instructor* and the *Millennial Star* by foreign-serving missionaries. For a sampling of material involving Mormons in India, see N. V. Jones, "A Brief History of Calcutta . . . ," *Deseret News* 7 (3 June 1857): 104; Matthew M'Cune, "Chapters on Asia," *Millennial Star* 25 (24 January 1863): 51–52, (28 February 1863): 131–33, (28 March 1963): 196–99, (18 April 1863): 245–48, (23 May 1863): 325–26, (6 June 1863): 357–60; A. M. Musser, "East Indian Mission," *Juvenile Instructor* 6 (February, April, and August 1871): 26, 55, 123; William Fotheringham, "Travels in India," *Juvenile Instructor* (printed serially 1876–84); Hugh Findlay, "Ornaments and Dress in India," *Juvenile Instructor* 17 (15 January 1882): 29; Hugh Findlay, "A Funeral in the East," *Juvenile Instructor* 17 (1 February 1882): 43; and "W" [William Willes?], "The Castes of India," *Juvenile Instructor* 17 (15 July 1882): 221.

48. Richard F. Burton, *The City of the Saints, and across the Rocky Mountains to California* (London: Longman, Green, Longman, and Roberts, 1861); Fitz Hugh Ludlow, *The Heart of the Continent: A Record of Travel across the Plains and in Oregon* (New York: Hurd and Houghton, 1870); Jules Remy and Julius Brenchley, *A Journey to Great-Salt Lake City,* 2 vols. (London: W. Jeffs, 1861).

49. Solomon Nunes Carvalho, *Incidents of Travel and Adventure in the Far West* (New York: Derby and Jackson, 1856); William Chandless, *A Visit to Salt Lake* (London: Smith, Elder, 1857); John Codman, *The Mormon Country: A Summer with the "Latter-day Saints"* (New York: United States Publishing, 1874); William Hepworth Dixon, *New America,* 2 vols. (London: Hurst and Blackett, 1867); Elizabeth Kane, *Twelve Mormon Homes Visited in Succession on a Journey though Utah to Arizona* (Philadelphia: n.p., 1874); Elizabeth Kane, *A Gentile Account of Life in Utah's Dixie, 1872–73* (Salt Lake City: Tanner Trust Fund, University of Utah Library, 1995); Phil Robinson, *Sinners and Saints: A Tour across the States, and Round Them with Three Months among the Mormons* (Boston: Roberts Brothers, 1883). See also Edwina Jo Snow, "British Travelers View the Saints: 1847–1877," *BYU Studies* 31 (Spring 1991): 63–81; Edwina Jo Snow, "William Chandless: British Overlander, Mormon Observer, and Amazon Explorer," *Utah Historical Quarterly* 54 (Spring 1986):

116–36; Edwina Jo Snow, "Singular Saints: The Image of the Mormons in Book-Length Travel Accounts, 1847–1857" (Master's thesis, George Washington University, 1972). Wilfried Decoo's two articles, "The Image of Mormonism in French Literature: Part I and Part II," *BYU Studies* 14 (Winter 1974): 157–75, and 16 (Winter 1976): 265–76, showed the influence of the travel accounts on French nineteenth- and twentieth-century writers, while Michael W. Homer, "The Church's Image in Italy from 1840 to 1946: A Bibliographic Essay," *BYU Studies* 31 (Spring 1991): 83–114, played a similar role for Italian letters. The traveler Richard Burton is discussed in Fawn M. Brodie's "Sir Richard Burton: Exceptional Observer of the Mormon Scene," *Utah Historical Quarterly* 38 (Fall 1970): 295–311; Brodie's introduction to Burton's reissued *City of the Saints,* ed. Fawn M. Brodie (New York: Alfred A. Knopf, 1963); Laura Foster Wilson, "Richard Burton Visits the City of the Saints," *American West* 12 (January 1975): 4–9; and Thomas K. Hafen, "City of Saints, City of Sinners: The Development of Salt Lake City as a Tourist Attraction, 1869–1900," *Western Historical Quarterly* 28 (Autumn 1997): 342–77. For excerpts of nineteenth-century travel accounts, see William Mulder and A. R. Mortensen, eds., *Among the Mormons: Historic Accounts by Contemporary Observers* (New York: Alfred A. Knopf, 1958). During the twentieth century, another travel account of Elizabeth Kane was issued, *A Gentile Account of Life in Utah's Dixie, 1872–73,* preface and notes by Norman R. Bowen and profile of Elizabeth Kane by Mary Karen Bowen Solomon (Salt Lake City: Tanner Trust Fund, University of Utah Library, 1995).

50. Benjamin G. Ferris, *Utah and the Mormons: The History, Government, Doctrines, Customs and Prospects of the Latter-Day Saints* (New York: Harper and Brothers, 1854), 249 (first quote), 298 (second and third quotes). For other highly charged comments about the Saints, see ibid., 41, 47–48, 96, 111, 150, 181, 194, 197–98, and 259.

51. This is the theme of several publications written by Gary L. Bunker and Davis Bitton, including their book *The Mormon Graphic Image, 1834–1914: Cartoons, Caricatures, and Illustrations* (Salt Lake City: University of Utah Press, 1983). See also Terryl L. Givens, *The Viper on the Hearth: Mormons, Myths, and the Construction of Heresy* (New York: Oxford University Press, 1997).

52. For an examination of Bennett's colorful career and a discussion of his book, see Andrew F. Smith, *The Saintly Scoundrel: The Life and Times of Dr. John Cook Bennett* (Urbana: University of Illinois Press, 1997).

53. Orvilla S. Belisle, *Mormonism Unveiled; or, A History of Mormonism* (London: Charles Clarke, 1855); Maria N. Ward, *Female Life among the Mormons* (London: C. H. Clarke, 1855); Austin N. Ward, *The Husband in Utah; or, Sights and Scenes among the Mormons* (London: James Blackwood, 1857); Catherine Waite, *The Mormon Prophet and His Harem; or, An Authentic History of Brigham Young* (Cambridge, Mass.: Riverside, 1866).

54. This literature is treated by Craig L. Foster, "Anti-Mormon Pamphleteering in Great Britain, 1837–1860" (Master's thesis, Brigham Young University, 1989); and Craig L. Foster, "Victorian Pornographic Imagery in Anti-Mormon Literature," *Journal of Mormon History* 19 (March 1993): 115–32.

55. John Hyde, *Mormonism: Its Leaders and Designs* (New York: W. P. Fetridge, 1857). For information on Hyde, see Lynne Watkins Jorgenson, "John Hyde, Jr., Mormon Renegade," *Journal of Mormon History* 17 (1991): 120–44.

56. Fanny Stenhouse, *"Tell It All": The Story of a Life Experience in Mormonism* (Hart-

ford, Conn.: A. D. Worthington, 1874). The American edition of Stenhouse's earlier memoir appeared under the title *Exposé of Polygamy in Utah: A Lady's Life among the Mormons* (New York: American News Company, 1872). For further information on the Stenhouses, see Ronald W. Walker, "The Stenhouses and the Making of a Mormon Image," *Journal of Mormon History* 1 (1974): 51–72.

57. Ann Eliza [Webb] Young, *Wife Number 19; or, The Story of a Life in Bondage* (Hartford, Conn.: Dustin, Gilman, 1875).

58. William Hickman, *Brigham's Destroying Angel, Being the Life, Confession, and Startling Disclosures of the Notorious Bill Hickman* (New York: George A. Crofutt, 1872).

59. John Hanson Beadle, *The History of Mormonism: Its Rise, Progress, Present Condition and Mysteries* (Toronto, Ontario: A. H. Hovey, 1873). For a discussion of Beadle, see Leonard J. Arrington, "Kate Field and J. H. Beadle: Manipulators of the Mormon Past" (American West Lecture, University of Utah, Salt Lake City, 31 March 1971).

60. Hope A. Hilton, *"Wild Bill" Hickman and the Mormon Frontier* (Salt Lake City: Signature Books, 1988).

61. John D. Lee, *Mormonism Unveiled; or, The Life and Confessions of the Late Bishop, John D. Lee* (Philadelphia: Bryan, Brand, 1877).

62. Edward W. Tullidge, *Life of Brigham Young; or, Utah and Her Founders* (New York: Tullidge and Crandall, 1876), *Women of Mormondom* (New York: Tullidge and Crandall, 1877), and *Life of Joseph the Prophet* (New York: Tullidge and Crandall, 1878); Orson F. Whitney, *Life of Heber C. Kimball, an Apostle: The Father and Founder of the British Mission* (Salt Lake City: Kimball Family, 1888); George Q. Cannon, *The Life of Joseph Smith, the Prophet* (Salt Lake City: Juvenile Instructor, 1888); B. H. Roberts, *The Life of John Taylor, Third President of the Church of Jesus Christ of Latter-day Saints* (Salt Lake City: George Q. Cannon and Sons, 1892).

63. Edward W. Tullidge, *History of Salt Lake City* (Salt Lake City: By the author, 1886); Andrew Jenson, *Biographical Encyclopedia* (Salt Lake City: By the author, 1888 [later extended to 4 vols., 1914–36]); Emmeline B. Wells, *Charities and Philanthropies . . . Woman's Work in Utah* (Salt Lake City: George Q. Cannon and Sons, 1893).

64. Orson F. Whitney, *History of Utah*, vol. 4 (Salt Lake City: George Q. Cannon and Sons, 1904); Frank Esshom, *Pioneers and Prominent Men of Utah: Comprising Photographs, Genealogies, Biographies* (Salt Lake City: Utah Pioneers Book, 1913).

65. George H. Callcott, *History in the United States, 1800–1860: Its Practice and Purpose* (Baltimore: Johns Hopkins University Press, 1970), 114–15.

66. Elden J. Watson, ed., *Manuscript History of Brigham Young, 1846–1847* (Salt Lake City: Elden J. Watson, 1971). For information on the "History of Brigham Young," see Searle, "Early Mormon Historiography," 337–57; Howard C. Searle, "Authorship of the History of Brigham Young: A Review Essay," *BYU Studies* 21 (Winter 1981): 101–22; and Dean C. Jessee, "The Writings of Brigham Young," *Western Historical Quarterly* 4 (June 1973): 273–94. At first the quality of this collection held up well; however, after 1858 it deteriorated into a kind of miscellany scrapbook.

67. For a convenient publication list of the various sketches found in the "History of the Twelve," see Searle, "Early Mormon Historiography," 344–45.

68. George A. Smith, *Historical Address Delivered by President Geo. A. Smith* (Salt Lake City: n.p., 1868) and *The Rise, Progress, and Travels of the Church of Jesus Christ of Latter-day Saints* (Salt Lake City: Deseret News, 1869).

69. *New Year's Issue* (Salt Lake City: Deseret News, 1893).

70. *Fifty Years Ago Today* (Salt Lake City: Salt Lake Tribune, 1897).

71. Franklin D. Richards, *A Compendium of the Faith and Doctrines of the Church of Jesus Christ of Latter-day Saints* (Liverpool: O. Pratt, 1857); John Jaques, *The Church of Jesus Christ of Latter-day Saints: Its Priesthood, Organization, Doctrines, Ordinances and History* (Salt Lake City: Deseret News, 1882); Abraham H. Cannon, *A Hand-book of Reference to the History, Chronology, Religion and Country of the Latter-day Saints* (Salt Lake City: Juvenile Instructor, 1884).

72. For more on Jenson, see Davis Bitton and Leonard J. Arrington, *Mormons and Their Historians* (Salt Lake City: University of Utah Press, 1988), 41–55; and Keith W. Perkins, "Andrew Jenson: Zealous Chronologist" (Ph.D. diss., Brigham Young University, 1974), which formed the basis for an article by the same title in *Supporting Saints: Life Stories of Nineteenth-Century Mormons,* ed. Donald Q. Cannon and David J. Whittaker (Provo, Utah: Religious Studies Center, Brigham Young University, 1985), 83–99.

73. Andrew Jenson, *Encyclopedic History of the Church of Jesus Christ of Latter-day Saints* (Salt Lake City: Deseret News, 1941).

74. For more on Tullidge's work, see Ronald W. Walker, "Edward Tullidge: Historian of the Mormon Commonwealth," *Journal of Mormon History* 3 (1976): 55–72. For information on the Godbeite movement, in which Tullidge played a role, see Ronald W. Walker, *Wayward Saints: The Godbeites and Brigham Young* (Urbana: University of Illinois Press, 1998).

75. Edward Tullidge, *Tullidge's Histories, Volume II: Containing the History of All the Northern, Eastern, and Western Counties of Utah; Also the Counties of Southern Idaho* (Salt Lake City: Juvenile Instructor, 1889).

76. Cannon, *The Life of Joseph Smith.*

77. Emily C. Blackman, *History of Susquehanna County, Pennsylvania* (Philadelphia: Remsen and Haffelfinger, 1873); Henry P. Smith, ed., *History of Broome County* (Syracuse, N.Y.: D. Mason, 1885); James H. Smith, *History of Chenango and Madison Counties, New York* (Syracuse, N.Y.: D. Mason, 1880); Orsamus Turner, *History of the Pioneer Settlement of Phelps and Gorham's Purchase* (Rochester, N.Y.: W. Alling, 1851).

78. *The History of Jackson County, Missouri* (Kansas City, Mo.: Union Historical Co., 1881); *History of Caldwell and Livingston Counties, Missouri* (St. Louis: National Historical Co., 1886).

79. Thomas Ford, *A History of Illinois: From Its Commencement as a State in 1818 to 1847* (New York: Ivinson and Phinney, 1854), 252.

80. The expression "synthesis historians" was first offered by Leonard J. Arrington, "The Search for Truth and Meaning in Mormon History," *Dialogue: A Journal of Mormon Thought* 3 (Summer 1968): 56–66.

81. John Hay, "The Mormon Prophet's Tragedy," *Atlantic Monthly* 24 (December 1869): 669–78.

82. Thomas Gregg, *The Prophet of Palmyra* (New York: John B. Alden, 1890), 2–5, 8, 95, 462 (quote). Gregg also wrote a local history that contained important information about the Mormons: *History of Hancock County, Illinois, Together with an Outline History of the State* (Chicago: Chas. C. Chapman, 1880).

83. William A. Linn, *The Story of the Mormons: From the Date of Their Origin to the Year 1901* (New York: Macmillan, 1902), 59, 89, 223, 610–11 (quotes).

84. T. B. H. Stenhouse, *The Rocky Mountain Saints* (New York: D. Appleton, 1873). For more on this point, see Walker, "The Stenhouses and the Making of a Mormon Image"; and Walker, *Wayward Saints,* which gives the larger Godbeite context.

85. Stenhouse, *The Rocky Mountain Saints,* 158.

86. Hubert Howe Bancroft, *History of Utah: 1540–1886* (San Francisco: History Company, 1889). A chapter from Bancroft's book, describing Utah conditions from 1848–50, was published independently. See Hubert Howe Bancroft, "A Chapter from the History of Utah," *Magazine of American History* 22 (November 1889): 358–70.

87. H. H. Bancroft, *Literary Industries* vol. 39 of *The Works of Hubert Howe Bancroft* (San Francisco: History Company, 1890), describes the material the author collected on Utah and the Mormons, as well as quoting several letters exchanged by Bancroft and Mormon leaders during the production of the book. For additional information on Bancroft's methods and sources, see S. George Ellsworth, "Hubert Howe Bancroft and the History of Utah," *Utah Historical Quarterly* 22 (April 1954): 99–124; S. George Ellsworth, comp., "A Guide to the Manuscripts in the Bancroft Library relating to the History of Utah," *Utah Historical Quarterly* 22 (July 1954): 197–247; John Walton Caughey, *Hubert Howe Bancroft: Historian of the West* (Berkeley: University of California Press, 1946); Harry Clark, *A Venture in History: The Production, Publication, and Sale of the Works of Hubert Howe Bancroft* (Berkeley: University of California Press, 1973); and Charles S. Peterson, "Hubert Howe Bancroft: First Western Regionalist," in *Writing Western History: Essays on Major Western Historians,* ed. Richard W. Etulain (Albuquerque: University of New Mexico Press, 1991), 43–70.

88. Quoted in Caughey, *Hubert Howe Bancroft,* 384; see also Bancroft, *Literary Industries,* 592–617.

89. Orson F. Whitney, *History of Utah,* 4 vols. (Salt Lake City: George Q. Cannon and Sons, 1892–1904). For biographical information on Whitney, see his memoir *Through Memory's Halls: The Life Story of Orson F. Whitney as Told by Himself* (Independence, Mo.: Zion's Printing and Publishing, 1930); and Bitton and Arrington, *Mormons and Their Historians,* 56–68. Upon completing his *History of Utah,* Whitney claimed it was "as if an elephant had been lifted from his shoulders. . . . For fourteen years I have been under the harrow of this great undertaking, blamed for things of which I was entirely innocent, and with little more than kicks and cuffs for my labor and pains." Whitney to Heber J. Grant, 13 December 1904, Heber J. Grant Collection, LDS Archives. Whitney later became LDS assistant historian and, in 1906, a member of the LDS Quorum of the Twelve.

90. Orson F. Whitney, *Popular History of Utah* (Salt Lake City: Deseret News, 1916).

2. Traditionalism Meets Modernism, 1900-1950

As the twentieth century began, Mormon society was in the process of rapid change. The major events of the previous decade—the financial panic of 1893, the granting of Utah statehood, and the Spanish-American War—each reflected the economic, political, and cultural forces that were bringing once-isolated Utah into the national mainstream. Brigham Young's Great Basin kingdom, with its emphasis on Mormon peculiarity, was giving way to national aims and more secular ways.

The writing of Mormon history reflected these changes (historiography gauges popular culture as accurately as any branch of intellectual history). While faith claims and polemics continued to characterize and polarize many historians, other writers found common ground in a new kind of history. This "new history" was partly defined by new scholarly institutions that trained historians and facilitated their work: the graduate school, the learned or scholarly journal, and the professional society. The emerging history also was characterized by a less provincial and more national mood. These new writers viewed the Mormon past through such perspectives as *au courant* Pragmatism, hard-nosed Progressive economics, and even imaginative Freudian analysis. Their methods were by no means narrowly historical. Folklore, regional and rural geography, and historical sociology now became tools for studying the past.

Popular and Nonprofessional History

As the new century began, however, old patterns persisted. The most prominent vehicle for presenting Mormon history was the popular journal, full of

sectarian crusade, antiquarianism, and history written by amateurs. Each
shade of Mormon opinion had its own outlet. Mormon opponents had
Goodwin's Weekly (1902–19), founded by James T. Goodwin but dominated
by his septuagenarian father, C. C. Goodwin; the elder Goodwin, a former
editor of the anti-Mormon *Salt Lake Tribune,* continued his long-standing
LDS antagonism.[1] Members of the Midwest-based Reorganized Church of
Jesus Christ of Latter Day Saints (RLDS) read the *Journal of History.*

Far more numerous were the journals of the Utah-based church, which
included four private ventures: *Parry's Magazine* and *Utah Monthly Magazine,* ephemera of the 1880s and 1890s, and the longer-lasting, early twentieth-
century publications, *New West Magazine* and *Utah Educational Review.*
Together these regional journals published more than forty historical pieces
about the Mormons that contained valuable but now overlooked material.
In addition, the Mormon church had its own official and semiofficial publications, including the Sunday Schools' *Juvenile Instructor* (1866–1970), renamed the *Instructor* in 1930; the British mission's *Millennial Star* (1840–
1970); and the women's *Young Women's Journal* (1889–1929) and *Woman's
Exponent* (1872–1914). The best LDS popular history appeared in the *Utah
Genealogical and Historical Magazine* (1910–40) and in the church's main
periodical, the *Improvement Era* (1897–1970).

Two dozen early twentieth-century national magazines also featured articles on Mormonism. These national periodicals included the *Arena, Atlantic
Monthly, Everybody's Magazine, Harper's, Leslie's Monthly, Muncey's Magazine,* and even Elbert Hubbard's controversial *Philistine* (when discussing
Mormon plural marriage, Hubbard upset some traditionalists by suggesting
that most American frontier communities practiced de facto polygamy).
Despite high-sounding titles that suggested in-depth historical treatment,
these national periodicals usually provided only superficial surveys on such
perennially favorite topics as LDS polygamy and supposed Mormon con-
spiracies in the American West. As a result, they were useful not so much for
revealing information about the Mormon past but for demonstrating
Mormonism's national image.

Several "muckrakers" turned their attention on the Mormons. These
popular journalists, who claimed to expose the political and economic mis-
deeds of the nation's elites, explored similar themes in Mormondom. For
instance, Frank J. Cannon and Harvey J. O'Higgins produced nine articles
in *Everybody's Magazine* that strongly indicted church president Joseph F.
Smith (Smith "lives, like the Grand Turk, openly with five wives, against the
temporal law of the state, . . . and in violation of his own solemn covenant
to the country"[2]). Cannon and O'Higgins later enlarged their articles into a

book entitled *Under the Prophet in Utah: The National Menace of a Political Priestcraft.* The book in unflattering words described events that led to Utah statehood and in equally unfavorable terms detailed turn-of-the-century Mormon economic policy. Not unexpectedly, Cannon and O'Higgins's book was dismissed by Mormon defenders as a case of thwarted ambition. Cannon, who had served the state as a U.S. senator, lost local support and a re-election bid partly because of his checkered personal behavior.[3]

Of the various popular journals, the RLDS and LDS presses published the most enduring history. The RLDS *Journal of History,* anxious to draw theological and institutional boundaries, repeatedly published material that set the RLDS Church apart from the plural marriage and theocracy of its "Brighamite" rival in the West. This same institution-defining impulse may have prompted the magazine to run articles on splinter movements founded by Alpheus Cutler, George M. Hinkle, and James J. Strang. There were other *Journal of History* themes. Samuel A. Burgess, Vida E. Smith, Walter W. Smith, and especially Heman C. Smith, an RLDS apostle and church historian, provided biographies of important early church leaders, wrote of the founding events of Mormonism, and discussed a series of particular topics: early LDS hymnals and music, High Council procedures, Iowa's pioneer trails, Nauvoo education, the Mormon practice of baptizing its converts, and the important Philadelphia and St. Louis congregations.

The *Journal of History* also published several diaries and autobiographies that recorded the conversion of LDS members to RLDS belief. Levi Graybill's recollection told of his traveling the emigrant trail to Council Bluffs, Iowa, before turning back to become a member of the Reorganized Church. In another case, Charles W. Wandell, a former Nauvoo church clerk, detailed how LDS elders in California rekindled his Mormon faith only for him to later join the RLDS Church. Still other accounts detailed the conversion of Utah settlers. Although these various diaries and autobiographies were published with a clear religious intent, they also demonstrated the tension and complexity of early Mormon life.

The popular journals of the LDS Church were like-minded. Like the RLDS writers, the popular LDS writers tried to convey the nobility of their religious heritage. They also chose for their subjects small segments of the past, provided little analysis and historical context, and neglected to explain or detail personality when examining the life story of a church leader. Mormon popular history was vignette history, defensive, simple, and, above all else, self-congratulatory.

One of the first to write in this style was Nephi Anderson (1865–1923), editor of the *Utah Genealogical and Historical Magazine.* Arriving in Utah at the age of six from his native Norway, Anderson and his family settled in Summit County and later in Weber County. As a young adult, he served two church missions and began a writing career, which included penning popular literature. His most popular novella for juveniles, *Added Upon,* had more than a dozen editions, and *A Young Folks' History of the Church of Jesus Christ of Latter-day Saints* was directed to the same audience.[4] The history that he wrote and edited for the *Utah Genealogical and Historical Magazine* was similar; straightforward and ardent, it evangelized at a comfortable but middle-brow level of expression.

More significant was the contribution of B. H. Roberts (1857–1933). Born in Lancashire, England, Roberts endured a childhood as difficult as any found in a Dickens novel ("My childhood was a nightmare; my boyhood a tragedy," he later said[5]). In 1866, the nine-year-old Roberts came to Utah, where, during his teenage years, he worked as a field hand, a mining camp roustabout, and a blacksmith apprentice. By his early twenties, Roberts found himself drawn to the world of words and ideas, an interest that led to a University of Utah teaching degree and to a rigorous course of self-education. Soon Roberts himself was writing important books. During his career, he wrote two biographies, eight historical narratives and compilations, and another dozen books dealing with theology and other church themes.

In the late 1890s, Roberts also helped establish the *Improvement Era.* He raised money, selected the journal's name, and framed an editorial policy that featured history (during its seventy-three-year history, the *Improvement Era* printed over eight hundred history-related articles). As its longtime, de facto editor, Roberts used some of the best local talent available: Edward H. Anderson, Joseph J. Cannon, John Henry Evans, Susa Young Gates, Preston Nibley, Joseph Fielding Smith, Junius F. Wells, and John A. Widtsoe. Later such important writers as Juanita Brooks, Richard L. Evans, Bryant S. Hinckley, and William Mulder joined the *Improvement Era* ranks. No one was more prolific than Roberts himself, however. During his thirty-five-year association with the periodical, he averaged three articles a year.[6]

Several of these men and women produced significant books. A half-dozen of the essays Susa Young Gates (1856–1933) wrote for the *Improvement Era* were later incorporated into her biography of her father, *The Life Story of Brigham Young,* coauthored with Gates's daughter, Leah D. Widtsoe.[7] Preston Nibley (1884–1966), a real estate developer and small business entrepreneur, used the same technique; his *Brigham Young: The Man and His Work* had its roots in early articles published in the *Improvement Era.*[8] Nibley followed this biography with a life story of Joseph Smith, a history of the Mormon "exodus" from Nauvoo, and a compilation of essays on the presidents of the LDS Church.[9]

Joseph Fielding Smith (1876–1972) was another of the *Improvement Era*'s promising young writers. Like his father, the Mormon president Joseph F. Smith, young Smith was an unusual combination of church dedication, personal kindness, and combativeness (an early priesthood blessing promised he would "never be confounded" when defending "the evidence of the divinity of the mission of the Prophet Joseph [Smith]").[10] Carrying this theme forward during his career, this "soldier of truth" wrote twenty-five volumes that defended and explicated Mormonism.[11]

Although most of Smith's books were theological, he also wrote one of the most influential LDS historical works of the century, *Essentials in Church History*.[12] Smith's prose was straightforward, and he presented his information in a primer style that made the book extremely popular. It would be reissued twenty-eight times during the middle decades of the century. From the modern point of view, however, the book was not without serious shortcomings. It showed little interest in social or cultural topics, twentieth-century events, or "everyday" people, especially women. Nor did the book reveal much historical analysis or context. Rather, for Smith the "essential" thing about Mormonism (borrowing from the book's title) was its divinity, which was boldly stated.

It was B. H. Roberts, not Smith, who wrote the best history of the time. Despite a busy political and church career, which included service in the LDS First Council of the Seventy, Roberts repeatedly returned to writing history. In 1892, he published a biography of the church president John Taylor.[13] Eight years later, he followed with *The Missouri Persecutions* and *The Rise and Fall of Nauvoo*.[14] Next, the indefatigable Roberts worked on a still more important assignment: republishing in book form the "History of the Church," or, as it was sometimes called, the "Joseph Smith History," earlier printed in serial form in the church's periodicals. Roberts's new, six-volume edition featured critical notes, new documents, sidebar headings for most paragraphs, and extensive interpretive essays that introduced each volume. Unfortunately, Roberts continued the confusing structure of the original, where various documents were spliced together and inaccurately attributed to Joseph Smith. This inaccuracy was preserved in the new series' lengthy title, *History of the Church of Jesus Christ of Latter-day Saints: Period I, History of Joseph Smith, the Prophet by Himself*.[15] In 1932, a similarly formatted seventh volume was added, this one dealing with President Brigham Young's early administration.[16]

Roberts's most important historical labor, however, was a multivolume narrative history of the church. He began the project in 1909 when invited to present the "story of Mormonism" in *Americana*, a monthly magazine published by the American Historical Society. For the next six years, Roberts turned out chapter after chapter, and when the series was concluded in 1915, Mormonism had its most extensive, though not its most easily accessible, historical treatment. Hoping to bring his work to a Mormon audience, during the next seven years Roberts repeatedly asked church leaders to republish his manuscript as a multivolume set, which they declined to do because of the cost.[17] Just as disappointing to Roberts, he was also overlooked when the church authorized Joseph Fielding Smith's one-volume history. At that time, Roberts hoped to condense his *Americana* articles into a single volume.[18]

Almost a decade later, Roberts realized his goal when the church authorized the publication of his *Americana* project as part of its 1930 centennial observation. Despite failing health and a growing petulance ("I am irritable, disappointed, unapproachable, impatient," he admitted[19]), he revised his narrative, added large blocks of new material, and checked footnotes. When he was finished, Roberts grandiloquently pronounced his 3,459-page, 189-chapter, six-volume work a "sermon" and, when presenting the completed volumes to the church, laid it on the Salt Lake Tabernacle pulpit, as if on "an altar." He quietly exulted, "Father, the glory be thine for this work accomplished."[20]

Roberts's *Comprehensive History of the Church of Jesus Christ of Latter-day Saints: Century I* was a monumental achievement.[21] Critics complained that its viewpoint was unabashedly Mormon, that its discussion was generally hierarchical, male, and political, and that its tone was often argumentative, serious-minded, and dramatic in the passé style of the nineteenth-century Romantics. Yet the *Comprehensive History* also had offsetting strengths. It chronicled for the first time (or in some cases for the first time in detail) large blocks of Mormon history, especially late nineteenth-century and early twentieth-century events. It introduced readers to an unprecedented variety of primary and secondary sources; a generation would pass before another work rivaled the *Comprehensive History*'s grasp of documents and published material. Moreover, Roberts disdained the faith-promoting myths that sometimes become attached to religious history. Claiming to be personally refreshed by ridding the record of "the untruth, the spectacular, the bizarre," he swept from his narrative fanciful underbrush and, at several places, acknowledged his people's errors.[22] Roberts was a partisan, not an unquestioning apologist.

Above all, the *Comprehensive History* was a new synthesis. Never before had so much of the Mormon past been integrated in a single work. Indeed, seventy years after its publication, it remains unsurpassed both for its detail and for its comprehensive treatment of many LDS themes.[23] As such, the *Com-*

prehensive History transcended ordinary history. It assured twentieth-century Saints that Mormonism had roots that could be intellectually defended, and when the LDS men and women who came of age in the 1930s and 1940s were polled, they had high praise. According to one important spokesman, Roberts was "the intellectual leader of the Mormon people in the era of Mormonism's finest intellectual attainment."[24]

The Mormon nonprofessionals had other successes, although nothing on the scale of the *Comprehensive History.* Like Americans elsewhere, during the first decades of the twentieth century, the Mormon people celebrated the triumph of Western civilization by focusing on the themes of refinement and youth. Several articles narrated the history of the Primary Association (an organization for preadolescents), the Mutual Improvement Association (for adolescents), and the Sunday School (for all age groups).[25] Still another study focused on the church's broader role in education.[26]

Early LDS writers also recorded their personal achievements by penning autobiographies, some of which became important twentieth-century publications. Two of the best were written by the Mormon pioneers Howard Egan (*Pioneering the West, 1846 to 1878: Major Howard Egan's Diary*) and George W. Bean (*Autobiography of George Washington Bean: A Utah Pioneer of 1847*). In a similar vein, Peter Gottfredson's *History of Indian Depredations in Utah* was a compilation of reminiscences and other source material, which despite its uneven quality remains an important primary document for understanding Mormon-Indian frontier relations.[27]

The impulse to celebrate the past also led to the organization of several lay historical societies, two of which published history. The Sons of Utah Pioneers issued the *Pioneer.* Although its brief sketches lacked substance, by the end of the century the refurbished magazine became more visually attractive and its articles more substantial. The Daughters of Utah Pioneers (DUP) had a greater historical impact, which bore the imprint of its longtime leader, Catherine Vigdus Bearnson (Kate B.) Carter (1892–1976). In 1926, Carter attended a DUP meeting but went away disappointed by the desultory discussion. Carter wanted a regular course of study by which the DUP might formally preserve LDS accomplishments. She eventually had her way.[28]

Under her leadership, the DUP sponsored a program of historical preservation. However, its most significant contribution may have been the collection of several thousand pioneer sketches and reminiscences, which were used for lessons of the kind that Carter championed. At first Carter herself typed and mimeographed these lessons for DUP "camps," but within a decade these readings were being printed and annually bound. The result was five multi-volume sets that spanned much of the century: *Heart Throbs of the West;*

Treasures of Pioneer History; Our Pioneer Heritage; An Enduring Legacy; and *Chronicles of Courage.*[29] In addition, local and national DUP chapters published several dozen pamphlets and even several larger works.

The DUP volumes contained a potpourri of material (sometimes recycled several times) that lacked narrative unity and contained no analysis: there were chronologies, statistics, and lists; text borrowed from other published sources; hundreds of pioneer diaries; and still more historical sketches prepared by DUP members—all linked by the prose of Carter and her successors. While the DUP writing might have been suitable for the organization's informal teaching, scholars were troubled by its loose editorial standards and by its imprecision and occasional inaccuracy. Despite such flaws, the DUP volumes were important. Carter and her successors were especially interested in the details of "everyday" pioneer life—how ordinary settlers lived. Here the huge DUP collection abounded with forgotten lore, and many "common" subjects, often ignored by professional historians and even folklorists, flourished in its pages.

Academic and Professional History

As the twentieth century continued, a new group of scholars became increasingly important. These were full-time scholars, who after securing university graduate degrees often pursued careers in higher education or sometimes government service. They wrote theses, dissertations, scholarly articles, and specialized books; popular and general histories were much less frequent. Their work displayed new interests and techniques. The sense of advocacy and the quest for religious truth—the impulses that so long had characterized Mormon historical writing—seemed less important to them. Instead, the new professionals spoke of "detachment" and pursued the neutral but elusive goal of "scientific objectivity." Reflecting their Progressive and New Deal age, the new scholars also were drawn to practical achievement and activism. This attitude led them to use the new historical tools of the emerging social sciences—rural geography, sociology, and historical economics— to reexamine Mormon nineteenth-century pioneering.

A path-breaking essay by Richard T. Ely in 1903 led the way.[30] Returning from formative study in Germany, where he became an advocate of the positive functions of government, Ely wrote an early draft of the platform of the newly founded American Economic Association. His words, repudiating the prevailing classic Manchester school of economics, helped explain his fascination with Mormonism. "We regard the state as an educational and ethical agency," wrote Ely, "whose positive aid is an indispensable condition of human progress. While we recognize the necessity of individual initiative in industrial life, we hold that the doctrine of laissez faire is unsafe in politics and unsound in morals, and that it suggests an inadequate explanation of the relations between the state and the citizens."[31]

In 1902, Ely visited the LDS First Presidency in Salt Lake City and was in Utah long enough to observe what fifty years of Mormon pioneering had achieved. He found the Mormon community to be an example of the kind of central control and state activism that he wanted to see adopted on a wider scale. Mormonism, his subsequent article maintained, was "the most nearly perfect piece of social mechanism with which I have ever, in any way, come in contact." Calling for an end to controversy over LDS religious doctrine and for the beginning of serious study of Mormonism's "economic and social matters," Ely's article discussed such topics as Utah village life, community irrigation, the sociology of polygamy, and Mormon economic cooperation. It became the text for the next half-century of Mormon scholarship.[32]

The American scholar Edgar Wilson was the first to answer Ely's call to arms, perhaps because of the two men's joint background and approach. Wilson and Ely had both studied under Gustav Schmoller and were disciples of Schmoller's young German historical school of economics, which argued that economic and social phenomena were best explained by historical study, not by theoretical analysis. Following this formula, Wilson's Ph.D. dissertation treated Mormon economics as a series of historical phases that included a "communistic" phase, a "cooperative company" phase, and a "capitalistic" phase. Justifying his interest in a subject so controversial as Mormonism, Wilson quoted Seneca: "For I am accustomed also to go over into alien camps, not so much as a fugitive, but as an explorer."[33]

Ely's article and Wilson's now seldom-read dissertation reflected an emerging climate of scholarly perspective. First, academics were coming to realize that Mormonism could be studied for its own sake, independent of its religious claims. Second, scholars believed that such a study could be best approached by uniting the disciplines of sociology, economics, and history. The approach was characteristic of Progressive Era thinking, which emphasized economic and social forces and argued that the past should be subordinated to the present. In this "presentist" view, history revealed the social and economic forces that shaped the present and suggested, at least by implication, how a better world might be created.[34]

Three important scholars of Mormonism addressed these themes: Ephraim Edward Ericksen (1882–1967), Lowry Nelson (1893–1986), and Nels Anderson (1889–1986). Ericksen began his graduate study at the University of Chicago in 1908, where he hoped to demonstrate the truthfulness of Mormonism to an unsuspecting academic world. However, he soon found his faith changing. No longer able to support the exclusionist claim that the Church of Jesus Christ of Latter-day Saints was the "only one true" church, Ericksen concluded the "true" and "beautiful" of ordinary life manifested God as readily as institutional religion did.[35]

There were other modifications to his Mormonism. Ericksen's dissertation, published in 1922, argued that three historical crises had created the Mormon religion: (1) the conflict between Mormons and "Gentiles," 1830–44; (2) the conflict between Mormons and their Great Basin environment, 1850–1900; and (3) the most recent, the conflict between "new thought and old institutions" as Mormonism encountered modernism. Ericksen believed that the Mormons "functional psychological" response to these crises had largely created their religion. Joseph Smith, by being "highly sensitive to the impulses of his people," became their creation. He was "not only a prophet for them but was made a prophet by them."[36] Later LDS leaders had been equally attentive to their setting.

Such a naturalistic view of Mormonism set aside many of its faith claims or at least did not emphasize them. It also made Ericksen pessimistic about his own times. He believed that contemporary Mormon leaders, reacting to social and economic pressures, were replacing the "radical" and "socialistic" ideals of old LDS group life with an individualism that favored modern corporate capitalism. Moreover, a scholasticism seemed to be enveloping the church. These trends, Ericksen feared, threatened Mormonism's ability to satisfy the social needs of its people. "What Mormonism needs today is the vitalization of its institutions, which need to be put into use rather than merely contemplated," he wrote. "When Mormonism finds more glory in working out new social ideals than in the contemplating of past achievements or the beauty of its own theological system, it will begin to feel its old-time strength."[37]

Ericksen's work, though not widely read, was influential. His emphasis on social process and group life rather than theology; his acceptance of Great Basin pioneering as Mormonism's highest social achievement; his opposition to Mormonism's embrace of twentieth-century corporate capitalism—each of these themes enjoyed a long life in Mormon scholarly circles. Ericksen himself, however, failed to do much writing after his dissertation, preferring instead a teaching and administrative career at the University of Utah. He also served many years on the general board of the LDS Young Men's Mutual Improvement Association, where he sought to implement programs conducive to "well-rounded, moral personalities in a context of social justice and opportunity." The attempt, eventually rejected by church leaders as too theologically neutral, was another sign of Ericksen's social pragmatism.[38]

Lowry Nelson, another scholar of LDS social and group life, spent his formative years in the hamlet of Ferron in east-central Utah. After receiving degrees from Brigham Young Academy and Utah State Agricultural College, Nelson began a career as a country agricultural agent and later joined the Brigham Young University faculty. After church authorities examined his religious views, however, he left BYU to accept a series of New Deal rural relief assignments.[39] He continued his career as a professor of sociology at the University of Minnesota from 1937 to 1958; as a visiting professor at nine universities from 1958 to 1965; and finally as an international consultant specializing in rural land reform. Nelson authored ten books, eight chapters in books, and eighty-one articles and bulletins.[40]

Nelson's most important LDS work, *The Mormon Village: A Pattern and Technique of Land Settlement,* was published at midcentury, although most of its chapters appeared as pamphlet-length articles twenty to twenty-five years earlier.[41] In a series of case studies, the book (or more accurately the published articles that preceded it) described the church's "social invention" of the "Mormon village." Nelson argued that while most American western settlers scattered their homes on the landscape, the Mormons retained the more traditional village pattern that had prevailed in history. In the Mormon case, this included wide streets that were aligned at the cardinal points of the compass and intersected at right angles (an attempt to replicate old Jerusalem, Nelson believed). The Mormon village also encased schools, churches, garden plots, and such structures as barns, chicken coops, pens, and "stack" yards. Outside the village, apart from living quarters and social institutions, settlers worked their farms and grazed their herds.

According to Nelson, the village system promoted small and uniform landholding and therefore homogeneity and unity. The system also encouraged sociability and offered "perhaps the most elaborate mechanism for socialization to be found in any small community of the country"—providing cradle-to-grave recreation, education, and opportunities for self-fulfillment and leadership training. Nelson was more restrained with his major conclusions. While acknowledging that the Mormons' religious devotion and group solidarity made their colonization of the Great Basin a success, Nelson argued that the village system had given these traits a concrete reality and made the Mormons' success "easier" and their achievement in community-building "greater."[42] The role of the village in promoting Mormon success was one of degree.

Although later research qualified some of Nelson's findings and in some cases expanded them, the idea of the Mormon village became an important theme for anthropologists, folklorists, geographers, historians, and sociologists, while literary writers used the concept as a backdrop for essays, short stories, and novels. Clearly, the Mormon village had power as both a historical concept and a symbol. For those anxious about twentieth-century complexity, the Mormon village was not just an example of social Mormonism at its best but also an idealized and nostalgic refuge.

Unlike E. E. Ericksen and Lowry Nelson, who were children of rural Mormon country, Nels Anderson came to study Mormon group life by accident. During the early 1900s, Anderson left the family farm in Michigan for a vagabond life as a self-described "hobo mule skinner." Making his way through southwest Utah, the dispirited Anderson met the family of Lyman L. Woods, a Mormon from the days of Nauvoo. The nineteen-year-old Anderson found the Woods family congenial and remained with them for almost three years. The Woodses became his adopted kin and Mormonism his adopted religion.[43]

"It was not so much Mormon theology that held my interest," Anderson later acknowledged, "it was the story of a people working, often suffering to achieve something."[44] This sense of group life and the high value that Mormons placed on education heavily influenced Anderson. He attended Brigham Young University, studied sociology at the University of Chicago, and later worked for the U.S. government and the United Nations. His career concluded in the Department of Sociology at the University of New Brunswick at Fredericton, Canada. Although he seldom attended Mormon church services, Anderson continued to call himself a Mormon. His church membership, he said, consisted of "personal bonds" with the Mormon families who had given his life purpose. "I will continue to call them my people."[45]

Anderson described his book *Desert Saints: The Mormon Frontier in Utah* as a "thank-you salute in general to all Mormons, but in particular to the Mormon families who took me in as one of their own" (the book begins with the aging patriarch Lyman Woods reminiscing about the past).[46] Apparently Anderson had originally planned to write a regional history of the Mormon towns of Enterprise and St. George in Utah's southwest "Dixie," where he had spent his youth. However, when *Desert Saints* was completed, it had a broader perspective. Using historical examples drawn from the two communities, Anderson told the story of nineteenth-century LDS pioneering from the founding of the church to Utah's acceptance of mainstream national culture at the end of the century. The book remains one of the most literate and informative accounts of Mormon nineteenth-century pioneering.

Ericksen, Nelson, and Anderson were not the only scholars to study Mormon group life. Hamilton Gardner,[47] Joseph A. Geddes,[48] and Feramorz Y. Fox[49] examined the Mormons' cooperative practices. Thomas Lynn Smith began a distinguished career as a historical geographer with an M.A. thesis dealing with Mormon rural culture, while Arden B. Olsen researched Utah's early merchant cooperatives.[50] William J. McNiff's *Heaven on Earth: A Planned Mormon Society,* in turn, was an extended and mature piece of scholarship. Convinced by his graduate school committee to accept Mormonism as a serious intellectual interest, McNiff first completed an Ohio State University dissertation on Mormon culture. A dozen years later, his book followed, which included a sympathetic examination of the Saints' economic cooperation and their centrally managed emigration. But his work was most successful when treating such topics as early Utah drama, education, music, and other aspects of popular culture. On these subjects, it remains an important introductory survey.[51]

LDS scholars studied more than Mormon group life during the Progressive Era. A second strain of the new scholarship was influenced by Frederick Jackson Turner's frontier hypothesis and therefore celebrated Mormon pioneering. Levi Edgar Young (1874–1963) partook of this spirit. A son and grandson of Mormon general authorities, Young showed an early inclination for study, which his mother, Ann Elizabeth Riter, encouraged. "Nothing must interfere with the education of Levi Edgar," a family member recalled.[52] After graduating from the University of Utah, Young studied with the Harvard professors Albert Bushnell Hart, Edward Channing, and Ephraim Emerton, and in 1910 he received a master's degree in history from Columbia University. Still later, he studied the French settlement of Canada at McGill University and Laval University in Montreal. These studies enriched Young's forty-year affiliation with the University of Utah's history department. Young also served for fifty years as a part-time LDS general authority and as a mission president.

Levi Edgar Young published more than two dozen historical articles and five books, two of which treated Mormon themes: *Chief Episodes in the History of Utah* and *The Founding of Utah,* a textbook.[53] Young and his writings were genial, cultured, and intent on building religious bridges in his community. He was part of an era of reconciliation that avoided polemics and hallowed the march of civilization, which was defined as white, Anglo-Saxon, and beneficent.

The work of Andrew Love Neff (1878–1936) had a harder, more theoretical edge, the result of training and personality. His educational pedigree included a bachelor's degree from Stanford University, graduate work at the University of Chicago, and finally a Ph.D. at the University of California at Berkeley. His dissertation, completed at the age of forty under the direction of Herbert E. Bolton, was entitled "The Mormon Migration to Utah." "To my mind," wrote Neff, "the greatest fact in American history is the spread of settlement from the Atlantic seaboard to the Pacific Ocean. And I hope to ascertain the relative part of Mormons in blazing the trail and opening up the continent to settlement."[54] Neff's hope of completing a three-volume history of Utah that would focus Turnerian theory on Mormonism was thwarted by his early death at the age of fifty-eight. Seeking to salvage the project, Leland H. Creer, Neff's colleague at the University of Utah, took the bulk of Neff's preliminary draft, added Neff's dissertation, and at critical gaps inserted 150 pages of his own material. The posthumously published *History of Utah, 1847 to 1869* used an imposing 908 pages to cover the first twenty-two years of Anglo settlement.[55]

Although the *History of Utah* lacked the passion of the writing of Joseph Fielding Smith or even B. H. Roberts (Neff and Creer believed the historian's role was to "tell the truth, not to prove or disprove a pre-determined theory or conclusion"[56]), Neff's research produced a richly detailed manuscript. Moreover, the book explored topics that other historians often overlooked; farming, colonization, business, industry, transportation, government, and education were now examined, while more sensational subjects, such as the Mountain Meadow massacre, received fair but not disproportionate attention. One of Neff's purposes was to re-create the patterns of everyday Utah life, and this sympathy for the rank-and-file settler became one of the book's strengths.

There were other signs of the growing professionalization of Mormon history. From 1930 to 1950, graduate students wrote more than two hundred theses on LDS-related topics, some of lasting consequence.[57] Of the fifty dissertations produced during this same period, those of Leland H. Creer, Dean D. McBrien, Joel E. Ricks, Thomas C. Romney, Milton R. Hunter, and Robert J. Dwyer were published.[58] Generally these works—theses and dissertations alike—emphasized the Utah phase of Mormonism; stressed economic, social, and geographic factors; and had a rural or "frontier history" viewpoint.

Writing in local and scholarly journals was another indication of the ongoing professionalization. During the first fifty years of the twentieth century, many of the nation's local and state history journals featured Mormon history and culture, especially those that had geographical ties with the nineteenth-century LDS movement.[59] Some national social science journals followed suit. Illustrative of the increasing scholarly interest was Utah Agricultural College professor Franklin D. Daines's article, "Separatism in Utah, 1847–1870." Daines argued that the previous fixation with Mormon polygamy had deflected attention from the unusual character of the LDS community, which Daines saw as exclusive, millenarian, and separatist—and deserving further "sociological study."[60]

The early local and national history articles were preliminary; they introduced readers to the Mormon experience and set the stage for further study. The most valuable of them were documentary collections written by men interested in preserving their personal experiences: Edward Overawed, a rifleman from Hancock County, Illinois; Thomas Ford, an Illinois governor; Stephen S. Harding, a New York acquaintance of Joseph Smith and later a Utah governor; William Jennings, a Mormon merchant; William H. Knight and Wilfred H. Munro, overland travelers who interviewed Brigham Young; George Miller, a Mormon bishop who became a dissenter; Hiram S. Rumfield, a mail agent and Utah settler; and John Johnson Davies, a Mormon emigrant.[61]

As the century progressed, the *Utah Historical Quarterly* established itself as the most important state journal publishing LDS history. Begun in 1928 but temporarily suspended during the depression, the *Utah Historical Quarterly* would publish more than five hundred LDS related articles during the century, as editors J. Cecil Alter, A. R. Mortensen, Everett L. Cooley, and Stanley B. Layton encouraged the study of LDS history.[62]

The *Utah Historical Quarterly* suggested a characteristic of the new professional history: much of the new writing was supported by professional or academic organizations. The *Utah Historical Quarterly* received its support from the Utah Historical Society, founded in 1898 as a private institution but, beginning in the late 1920s, financially supported by the state of Utah.[63] Another early patron of LDS professional history was the University of Utah, the academic home of Leland Creer, E. E. Ericksen, Andrew Neff, and Levi Edgar Young. In the 1950s, the University of Utah further aided the new history by supporting the publication of the *Utah Humanities Review,* which issued two dozen articles dealing with the LDS past. Thereafter, work at the university in LDS history began to trail off as it increasingly moved from a local to a regional and national publishing agenda.

As academic studies became more common, new scholarly approaches emerged. One of these was folklore, which studied the language and stories of ordinary people. Several early folklore publications had a historical importance, including Kimball Young's "Story of the Rise of a Social Taboo"; Wayland D. Hand's "Three Nephites in Popular Tradition"; Claire Noall's "Superstitions, Customs, and Prescriptions of Mormon Midwives"; Hector Lee's dissertation, later published as *The Three Nephites: The Substance and Significance of the Legend in Folklore;* and especially a series of articles written in the 1940s and early 1950s by Austin E. Fife, which culminated in *Saints of Sage and Saddle: Folklore among the Mormons,* coauthored with his wife, Alta S. Fife.[64]

Another new approach was psychological analysis, used to explore the life and career of Joseph Smith. I. Woodbridge Riley's *Founder of Mormonism: A Psychological Study of Joseph Smith, Jr.,* published in 1902, was an early example of this method.[65] Riley, a non-Mormon who completed his research at Yale, believed that in-depth analysis of the Book of Mormon revealed that the Mormon prophet had unconsciously taken from his environment the idea of a Hebrew origin of the American Indian. Smith then gave this explanation an evangelical Protestant interpretation and thus produced the Book of Mormon. In Riley's view, Mormonism rose not because Smith was duplicitous but because of the inner workings of his mind.

Other psychological explanations followed, including Walter F. Prince's belief that the vocabulary of the Book of Mormon revealed an unconscious debt to upstate New York's anti-Masonic movement. It was a theory that Prince and Theodore Schroeder debated in a series of exchanges.[66] However, the most influential book to use the technique of psychohistory was Fawn McKay Brodie's landmark 1945 study, *No Man Knows My History.* Reared in the Mormon village of Huntsville, Utah, in circumstances she described as idyllic but parochial, Brodie (1915–81) experienced a mixed Mormon heritage. Her father and uncle served as LDS general authorities (her uncle David O. McKay eventually became president of the LDS Church). Brodie's mother, however, left a different legacy: Brodie described her mother, Fawn Brimhall McKay, as a "quiet heretic" who encouraged her intellectual independence.[67]

Brodie's undergraduate study of psychology, sociology, and especially literature at the University of Utah produced a growing religious estrangement, a process that graduate work at the University of Chicago accelerated. Within weeks of arriving in Chicago, the last remnant of her Mormon faith was gone—like "taking off a hot coat in the summertime," she would later say.[68] But liberation brought no peace. In Brodie's mind, Mormonism's founding prophet was so undeserving of his reputation that her personal redress was required, which by her own admission became cathartic and compulsive. It was "*imperative,*" she believed, that other young Mormons see evidence of Smith's shortcomings.[69]

At first, the vehicle of Brodie's vexation was a projected essay on early Mormon sources, but her fascination with Smith's character and her interest in biography transformed her original plan into a full-scale study of Mormonism's founder. Reflecting her continuing alienation, the early drafts of her book accepted mainline, nineteenth-century anti-Mormonism: Smith was a conscious fraud and impostor who allowed events gradually to recast him into a religious leader.[70] After readers of her early draft suggested a more rounded portrait, however, Brodie softened her interpretation.[71] When

Brodie's book finally appeared, it spoke of Smith's early career as deceiver but also of his natural talent and "genius." It was a begrudging concession. In Brodie's hands, Smith's "genius" owed more to his considerable imagination than to a felt religious mission.[72]

Brodie's naturalism showed little regard for religion as a positive force in the lives of healthy, well-adjusted people. Instead, her probe of Smith and his people found deficiency, if not pathology. For example, Brodie claimed that Mormon temple worship, like plural marriage, had its origin in the affinity between religious and phallic rites that rested in Smith's unconscious. For her, LDS temple endowment ceremony was "essentially fertility worship."[73] Such a startling conclusion was based not on any explicitly stated clinical theory or methodology but on Brodie's personal insight, buttressed by her reading of Freud. For traditionally minded Mormons, such an informal "diagnosis" of Smith's mind was just another item in a consistent pattern of flaws. She used problematic anti-LDS documents, she rejected religion as a positive force, and she seemed uncompromisingly hostile to Joseph Smith. Brodie was excommunicated shortly after the book was published.

For many Mormon intellectuals, particularly those of the rising generation, Brodie's book remained a troubling enigma. Powerfully written, it asked fundamental and largely unanswered questions and had an insistent presence in Mormon studies. It demanded an increased openness about Mormon origins and about Mormon history generally. Non-Mormon readers, however, responded to *No Man Knows My History* with less ambiguity and restraint. For them, the book was a brilliantly written synthesis of the old sources that gained credibility by acknowledging Joseph Smith's ability and creativity.[74] It presented Smith as striving, developing, and, above all else, understandable.

Her watershed book on Smith completed, Brodie continued an interest in psychobiography. Using an increasingly explicit clinical theory, she produced studies of Thaddeus Stevens, the nineteenth-century explorer Richard Burton, Thomas Jefferson, and Richard Nixon, the latter two works receiving mixed reviews.[75] In 1971, she updated and revised her Joseph Smith biography, and she occasionally wrote a paper or gave an interview on a LDS topic. However, these last efforts were aftermath; Brodie's biography of Joseph Smith effectively ended her professional interest in the church of her birth.

Brodie was part of an intellectual generation that some have called "Mormonism's lost generation"—intellectually gifted men and women culturally and religiously alienated from their Mormon roots.[76] In literature, Vardis Fisher, Virginia Sorenson, and Maurine Whipple fit this profile, each of whom had a strong interest in history that led to historical novels. Yet another example was the essayist and historian Bernard A. De Voto (1897–1955). De Voto grew up in Ogden, Utah, a product of mixed Mormon and Catholic parentage (in both cases apostates, said De Voto).[77] Settling in the East, he achieved national literary prominence as a columnist for *Harper's,* an editor for the *Saturday Review,* and the author of three historical books on the American Far West, one of which won the Bancroft and Pulitzer prizes.

A Mormon cultural expatriate and devotee of the curmudgeon style of H. L. Mencken, De Voto at first had little praise for his nativity. "The Mormons were staid peasants whose only distinguishing characteristics were their servility to their leaders and their belief in a low-comedy God," he wrote in his 1926 essay "Utah."[78] In a subsequent essay, "The Centennial of Mormonism," he dismissed Joseph Smith as a "paranoid" and Brigham Young as a "small and paunchy prophet" who was "as American as Jim Fisk or Jay Gould, and his genius was identical with theirs."[79]

When the national image of Mormonism moderated in the 1930s, De Voto became more evenhanded. The Mormon-related passages of his *Year of Decision, 1846* were positive.[80] De Voto was probably correct in describing them as "the most sympathetic treatment of the Mormons ever published by a Gentile."[81] A further indication of his moderation, he formally repudiated his earlier essays on Utah and Mormonism. They were, he now conceded, "ignorant, brash, prejudiced, malicious, and, what is worst of all, irresponsible."[82] Utah's sharped-tongued émigré had taken a step toward coming home.

Dale L. Morgan (1914–71) was another of Mormonism's straying intellectuals. A descendant of the early LDS apostle Orson Pratt and the son of a staunchly Mormon mother, Morgan set aside his Mormonism in early adulthood for what he described as a passive atheism. His outlook carried little accompanying bitterness. Unlike Brodie, Morgan did not feel the need to emphasize his departure from his inherited faith; nor was he, as the early De Voto had been, passionate in his dismissal of Utah's parochialism. Notwithstanding his relative passivity, however, Morgan had been described as bridling at what he saw as Mormonism's tendency toward "myth and symbol" rather than "factual accuracy," at least in historical matters.[83]

At the age of fourteen, Morgan contracted spinal meningitis, leaving him deaf. Seeking work compatible with his disability, he found employment with the New Deal Historic Records Survey and later with the Utah Historical Society and the Utah Writers' Project. These positions gave Morgan the opportunity to collect local Utah records and later to write several articles and books, generally without attribution. The first was a lengthy article on the Mormons' provisional government that was printed in a special issue of the

Utah Historical Quarterly; it was later reissued under the title *The State of Deseret.*[84] He followed with *A History of Ogden* and historical material published in *Utah: A Guide to the State; Provo: Pioneer Mormon City;* and *The Great Salt Lake.*[85] The last volume, Morgan's first book to list his name as author, contained geology and geography as well as a history and revealed the growing depth of his scholarship.

During Morgan's distinguished career, he edited or authored more than forty books and was especially recognized for his contribution to the understanding of the California gold rush, the history of the fur trade, and the Overland Trail.[86] Moreover, his book reviews introduced a generation of readers to western history and fiction, especially after he began writing a series of reviews in the *Saturday Review of Literature* in 1945. Whether in the capacity of editor, author, or editor, Morgan wrote with style. Ray A. Billington praised his work for "poetic imagery and word sense" and for "exactness of expression required by the canons of history," fulsome but deserved praise.[87]

While Morgan found his greatest success as a western regional historian, he occasionally returned to the narrower themes of Utah and Mormon history. His articles addressed such topics as Brigham Young's Indian superintendency, Salt Lake City's social development, and Mormon literature. However, Morgan's two most important LDS projects were never completed. The first was a bibliography of early Mormon printed sources. Morgan published three preliminary listings in the *Western Humanities Review,* but the comprehensive bibliography that he envisioned did not appear until after his death, when Chad J. Flake, a Brigham Young University librarian, greatly expanded Morgan's work and issued *A Mormon Bibliography, 1830–1930.*[88] Morgan's second project, even more ambitious, was a projected multivolume history of Mormonism. Seven draft chapters dealing with Joseph Smith's early years appeared posthumously in *Dale Morgan on Early Mormonism: Correspondence and a New History.*[89] Finally, Morgan influenced Mormon historiography in another way. He was an indefatigable correspondent, whose letters helped shape the writing of several of his contemporaries, including Brodie, whose book under his encouragement became a more rounded biographical portrait and less an indictment.[90]

Juanita Leavitt Brooks (1898–1989), another of Morgan's correspondents,[91] retained the institutional faith that her nativity in the LDS village of Bunkerville, Nevada, bequeathed her. Nevertheless, Brooks shared some of the characteristics of her "lost generation" contemporaries: her historical interests were regional, she was drawn to a rural Mormonism that found expression in the Mormon village, and she sought the intellectual freedom to examine sensitive LDS historical topics.

It was Nels Anderson, then a local U.S. Emergency Relief administrator, who involved Brooks in historical matters. Anderson commissioned Brooks to interview the aging settlers of Utah's Dixie region and to gather their historical manuscripts. Brooks used some of this material for the first article that she wrote, "A Close-Up of Polygamy," published in *Harper's* in February 1934.[92] Seven years later, in another autobiographical piece also published in *Harper's,* she sketched the importance of water in her youthful Bunkerville community.[93]

Picturesque, wry, and good-humored, these essays were good enough to have Dale Morgan suggest a more extended treatment of the Mormons. Brooks worked on the project much of her professional life but never was able to find a publisher. Issued after her death, *Quicksand and Cactus: A Memoir of the Southern Mormon Frontier* unevenly offered both polished and preliminary prose.[94] However, the book's first half was as evocative as any piece of literature about Mormon village life, and these pages remain a classic account of LDS pioneering.

During the 1940s, Brooks continued to write about people and events of her distinctive region. She produced a short biography of her grandfather Dudley Leavitt; edited the diary of Thales Haskell, an early settler and Indian missionary; sketched an account of Mormon-Indian relations on the southern frontier, and wrote two articles dealing with the Mormons' celebrated "apostle" to the Indians, Jacob Hamblin.[95] Each of these ventures drew Brooks to the most compelling event in pioneer southern Utah history: the infamous Mountain Meadows massacre.

The incident was one of the most frightful in Mormon history. In 1857, persecution-scarred and hysterical Mormon settlers had joined Indians in killing more than a hundred California-bound emigrants. In telling this story, Brooks did not want to be branded as "an old apostate." Nor did she want church authorities to tell her to stop working on a project that had fascinated her from early adulthood ("I know I couldn't stop even were I so commanded," she said).[96] While important church records were denied her, by 1950 Brooks had enough information to publish the fullest treatment of the massacre to date, *The Mountain Meadows Massacre.*[97]

The book was understated but unrelenting. Contrary to some explanations, Brooks built a case that local church leaders played a major role in the tragedy, impelled by the frenzy that accompanied the dispatch of federal troops during the so-called Utah War of 1857–58. Moreover, while not charging Brigham Young with the commission of the crime, Brooks held him as an accessory for allegedly attempting to suppress evidence of Mormon involvement and for making John D. Lee, a southern Utah settler, the scapegoat of the affair. Brooks's honest examination of a topic that many considered a taboo made *The Mountain Meadows Massacre,* like Brodie's book, a milestone. Although its research and scholarly perspectives now seem dated, the book helped create a new climate of openness in Mormon studies.

One of Brooks's purposes in writing the book was to better understand the character of John D. Lee. (One of Lee's pleased descendants financially supported the printing of the book.) Brooks continued the process by helping edit Lee's diaries and by publishing a series of articles that resulted in a biography of the controversial southern Utah settler. Brooks also edited the diaries of such other first-generation Utahns as Thomas D. Brown, Martha Spence Heywood, and Hosea Stout.[98] Taken together, Brooks's various publications were an unusual achievement for a scholar whose first major work appeared when she was in her fifties.

Curiously, the three leading historians of Mormonism at midcentury—Brodie, Morgan, and Brooks—were not professionally trained in history, although they were very much a part of the new historical culture. Brodie and Brooks secured graduate degrees in English, and Morgan had no formal training beyond an undergraduate degree. Yet each personified the professional ideal by writing with attempted balance, avoiding antiquarian and polemical interests, and demonstrating a willingness to confront difficult issues.

These qualities suggested the importance of the first fifty years of twentieth-century writing. The ground was shifting in Mormon studies. Old theological and interpretive polarities were narrowing because of the influence of new methods (the graduate school seminar and professional inquiry), new interests (Progressive reform, Turnerianism, Freudian analysis, folklore, and rural sociology), and a new openness (the "lost generation's" detachment and skepticism). In turn, these emerging trends were encouraged by new publishing outlets and by a newer, more educated audience of readers (professional societies and their publications). All this "change" and "preparation" provided nourishing soil for the remarkable growth of LDS historical studies yet to come.

Notes

1. *Goodwin's Weekly,* continuing under the title of the *Citizen,* was published until 1929.

2. Frank J. Cannon and Harvey J. O'Higgins, *Under the Prophet in Utah: The National Menace of a Political Priestcraft* (Boston: C. M. Clark, 1911), 10.

3. Cannon also published a like-minded but less well-known biography of Brigham Young: Frank J. Cannon and George L. Knapp, *Brigham Young and His Mormon Empire* (New York: Fleming H. Revell, 1913).

4. Nephi Anderson, *Added Upon* (Salt Lake City: Deseret News, 1898) and *A Young Folks' History of the Church of Jesus Christ of Latter-day Saints* (Salt Lake City: George Q. Cannon and Sons, 1900).

5. Quoted in Truman G. Madsen, *Defender of the Faith: The B. H. Roberts Story* (Salt Lake City: Bookcraft, 1980), 1.

6. Ibid., 237–38; Heber J. Grant, Typed Diaries, Digest of Correspondence, box 145, folder 1, Heber J. Grant Papers, LDS Library-Archives, Salt Lake City, Utah (hereafter LDS Archives).

7. Susa Young Gates and Leah D. Widtsoe, *The Life Story of Brigham Young* (New York: Macmillan, 1930; London: Jarrolds, 1930).

8. Preston Nibley, *Brigham Young: The Man and His Work* (Salt Lake City: Deseret News, 1936).

9. Nibley Preston, *Joseph Smith the Prophet* (Salt Lake City: Deseret News, 1944), *Exodus to Greatness: The Story of the Mormon Migration* (Salt Lake City: Deseret News, 1947), and *The Presidents of the Church* (Salt Lake City: Deseret Book, 1941).

10. Joseph Fielding McConkie, "Joseph Fielding Smith," in *The Presidents of the Church,* ed. Leonard J. Arrington (Salt Lake City: Deseret Book, 1986), 316.

11. The expression "soldier of truth" is McConkie's, "Joseph Fielding Smith," 321.

12. Joseph Fielding Smith, *Essentials in Church History* (Salt Lake City: Deseret News, 1922).

13. B. H. Roberts, *The Life of John Taylor, Third President of the Church of Jesus Christ of Latter-day Saints* (Salt Lake City: George Q. Cannon and Sons, 1892).

14. B. H. Roberts, *The Missouri Persecutions* (Salt Lake City: George Q. Cannon and Sons, 1900) and *The Rise and Fall of Nauvoo* (Salt Lake City: Deseret News, 1900).

15. B. H. Roberts, ed., *History of the Church of Jesus Christ of Latter-day Saints: Period I, History of Joseph Smith, the Prophet, by Himself* (Salt Lake City: Deseret News, 1902–12).

16. B. H. Roberts, ed., *History of the Church of Jesus Christ of Latter-day Saints: Period II, From the Manuscript History of Brigham Young and Other Original Documents* (Salt Lake City: Deseret Book, 1932).

17. Joseph F. Smith to B. H. Roberts, 29 January 1915, and Heber J. Grant to B. H. Roberts, 13 May 1920, First Presidency Letterbooks, LDS Archives; Heber J. Grant to B. H. Roberts, 16 December 1922, Heber J. Grant Letterbooks, 60:63, LDS Archives.

18. When a church committee authorized Smith, not Roberts, to write the one-volume book, Roberts bitterly complained that a "great injustice" had been done to him. While President Heber J. Grant did not disagree, he refused to reverse the decision. Heber J. Grant, Typed Diary, 3 May 1921, Heber J. Grant Papers.

19. B. H. Roberts to Elizabeth Hinckley, 8 September 1929, quoted in Madsen, *Defender of the Faith,* 359.

20. *One Hundredth Annual Conference of the Church of Jesus Christ of Latter-day Saints* (Salt Lake City: Church of Jesus Christ of Latter-day Saints, April 1930), 49.

21. B. H. Roberts, *A Comprehensive History of the Church of Jesus Christ of Latter-day Saints: Century I,* 6 vols. (Salt Lake City: Deseret News, 1930).

22. Quoted in Madsen, *Defender of the Faith,* 363.

23. Davis Bitton, "B. H. Roberts as Historian," *Dialogue: A Journal of Mormon Thought* 3 (Winter 1968): 25–44, ably critiques Roberts's work, though the emphasis is more on its shortcomings than on its contributions.

24. Leonard J. Arrington, "The Intellectual Tradition of the Latter-day Saints," *Dialogue: A Journal of Mormon Thought* 4 (Spring 1969): 22. For a similar comment, see Sterling M. McMurrin, "B. H. Roberts: Historian and Theologian," foreword in *The Autobiography of B. H. Roberts,* ed. Gary James Bergera (Salt Lake City: Signature Books, 1990), viii.

25. On the Primary, see Marion Belnap Kerr, "The Primary Association Yesterday and Today," *Improvement Era* 38 (April 1935): 244, 272. On the Mutual Improvement Association, see Orson F. Whitney, "The Wasatch Literary Association," *Improvement Era* 28 (September 1925): 1017–24; Susa Young Gates, *History of the Young Ladies' Mutual Improvement Association of the Church of Jesus Christ of Latter-day Saints from November 1869 to June 1910* (Salt Lake City: Deseret News, 1911); Junius F. Wells, "Historical Sketch of the Y.M.M.I.A.," *Improvement Era* 28 (June, July, September, October 1925): 713–29, 873–82, 1069–74, 1149–54; Junius F. Wells, "The Original Y.M.M.I.A., Thirteenth Ward, Salt Lake City," *Improvement Era* 28 (June 1925): 737–40; Clarissa A. Beesley, "The Young Women's Mutual Improvement Association," *Improvement Era* 38 (April 1935): 243, 264, 266, 271; and Clarissa A. Beesley, "Diamond Jubilee of the Young Women's Mutual Improvement Association," *Improvement Era* 47 (November 1944): 664–65. On Sunday School, see Deseret Sunday School Union, *Jubilee History of Latter-day Saints Sunday Schools, 1849–1899* (Salt Lake City: Deseret Sunday School Union, 1900); and A. Hamer Reiser, "Latter-day Saint Sunday Schools," *Improvement Era* 38 (April 1935): 241, 262–63.

26. Milton Lynn Bennion, *Mormonism and Education* (Salt Lake City: Deseret News, 1939).

27. Howard Egan, *Pioneering the West, 1846 to 1878: Major Howard Egan's Diary* (Richmond, Utah: Howard R. Egan Estate, 1917); George W. Bean, *Autobiography of George Washington Bean: A Utah Pioneer of 1847* (Salt Lake City: Utah Printing, 1945); Peter Gottfredson *History of Indian Depredations in Utah* (Salt Lake City: Skelton, 1919).

28. "President Kate B. Carter," in *Our Pioneer Heritage,* comp. Kate B. Carter, 20 vols. (Salt Lake City: Daughters of Utah Pioneers, 1958–77), 20:344.

29. *Heart Throbs of the West,* 12 vols. (Salt Lake City: DUP, 1939–51); *Treasures of Pioneer History,* 6 vols. (Salt Lake City: DUP, 1952–57); *Our Pioneer Heritage,* 20 vols. (Salt Lake City: DUP, 1958–77); *An Enduring Legacy,* 12 vols. (Salt Lake City: DUP, 1978–89); and *Chronicles of Courage* (Salt Lake City: DUP, 1990–present).

30. Richard T. Ely, "Economic Aspects of Mormonism," *Harper's Monthly* 106 (April 1903): 667–78.

31. Quoted in Henry Steele Commager, *The American Mind: An Interpretation of American Thought and Character since the 1880s* (New Haven, Conn.: Yale University Press, 1950), 234.

32. Ely, "Economic Aspects of Mormonism," 668 (first quote), 667 (second quote).

33. Edgar Wilson, "Cooperative Economy and Forms of Enterprise in the Mormon Commonwealth" (Ph.D. diss., University of Berlin, 1906), as cited and translated in Leonard J. Arrington, "Scholarly Studies of Mormonism in the Twentieth Century," *Dialogue: A Journal of Mormon Thought* 1 (Spring 1966): 17. Arrington's discussion of German historical economics and Wilson's study are the basis for our treatment of these topics. The German title for Wilson's dissertation was "Gemeinwirtschaft und Unternehmungsformen in Mormonenstaat" and was published in *Jarbuch für Gesetzgebung, Verwaltung und Volkswirtschaft im Deutschen Reich,* 30 vols. (Leipzig: n.p., 1877–1915), 21:1003–56.

34. For a concise summary of these themes, see Robert Allen Skotheim, *The Historian and the Climate of Opinion* (Reading, Mass.: Addison-Wesley, 1969), 43.

35. These quotations are drawn from uncited references in the Ephraim Edwards Ericksen Papers, privately held, but published in Scott Kenney, "E. E. Ericksen, Loyal Heretic," *Sunstone* 3 (July–August 1978): 17.

36. Ephraim Edward Ericksen, "The Psychological and Ethical Aspects of Mormon Group Life" (Ph.D. diss., University of Chicago, 1918) and *The Psychological and Ethical Aspects of Mormon Group Life* (Chicago: University of Chicago Press, 1922), 28 (quotes).

37. Ericksen, *The Psychological and Ethical Aspects of Mormon Group Life*, 99.

38. Kenney, "E. E. Ericksen, Loyal Heretic," 20.

39. Nelson apparently made more of the BYU orthodoxy incident than the situation required. During the examination, LDS president Heber J. Grant was "very favorably impressed" with the professor, especially after Nelson "announced his absolute faith in the immortality of the soul." Heber J. Grant, Typed Diary, 23 and 24 November 1934, Heber J. Grant Papers.

40. Lowry Nelson, *In the Direction of His Dreams: Memoirs* (New York: Philosophical Library, 1985), esp. 2–3, 248–60, and 334–49.

41. Lowry Nelson, *The Mormon Village: A Pattern and Technique of Land Settlement* (Salt Lake City: University of Utah Press, 1952). For Nelson's earlier publications, see "A Social Survey of Escalante, Utah," *BYU Studies* 1 (1925): 1–44; "The Utah Farm Village of Ephraim," *BYU Studies* 2 (1928): 1–41; "The Mormon Village: A Study in Social Origins," *Proceedings of the Utah Academy of Sciences* 7 (1930): 11–37, reprinted in *BYU Studies* 3 (1930): 11–37; "Some Social and Economic Features of American Fork, Utah," *BYU Studies* 4 (1933): 5–73; and "The Mormon Settlements of Alberta," in *Group Settlement: Ethnic Communities in Western Canada*, ed. Carl A. Dawson (Toronto: Macmillan, 1936).

42. Nelson, *The Mormon Village*, xiii.

43. Nels Anderson, "On My Being a Mormon," *Measuring Mormonism* 6 (Fall 1980): 4–9.

44. Ibid., 9.

45. Ibid., 4, 15.

46. Nels Anderson, *Desert Saints: The Mormon Frontier in Utah* (1942; reprint, Chicago: University of Chicago Press, 1966); Anderson, "On My Being a Mormon," 6 (quote).

47. Hamilton Gardner, "Coöperation among the Mormons," *Quarterly Journal of Economics* 31 (May 1917): 461–99; Hamilton Gardner, "Communism among the Mormons," *Quarterly Journal of Economics* 37 (1923): 134–74. Gardner's broader work, "Economic Activities among the Mormons," undertaken at Harvard, was never published. At the end of his career, Gardner returned to Mormon themes and published several articles on the Mormon nineteenth-century militia, the Mormon Battalion, and the Utah War.

48. Joseph A. Geddes, *The United Order among the Mormons (Missouri Phase): An Unfinished Experiment in Economic Organization* (New York: AMS, 1975), was based on Geddes's similarly titled Ph.D. dissertation completed at Columbia University in 1924. See also "The United Order Answers," *Improvement Era* 35 (October 1932): 724–26, 757, 766; and *Institution Building in Utah*, Eighth Annual Faculty Research Lecture (Logan: Faculty Association, Utah State Agricultural College, 1949).

49. Feramorz Y. Fox, "Cooperation among the Mormons" (Master's thesis, University

of California, 1912); Feramorz Y. Fox, "The Mormon Land System: A Study of the Settlement and Utilization of Land under the Direction of the Mormon Church" (Ph.D. diss., Northwestern University, 1932). Fox subsequently published "The Consecration Movement of the Middle 'Fifties,'" *Improvement Era* 47 (February, March 1944): 80–81, 120–21, 124–25, 146–47, 185, 187–88; "United Order: Discrimination in the Use of Terms," *Improvement Era* 47 (July 1944): 432, 459, 461–62; and "Experiment in Utopia: The United Order of Richfield, 1874–1877," *Utah Historical Quarterly* 32 (Fall 1964): 355–80. Fox's unpublished material later became one of the bases for Leonard J. Arrington, Feramorz Y. Fox, and Dean L. May, *Building the City of God: Community and Cooperation among the Mormons* (Salt Lake City: Deseret Book, 1976).

50. Thomas Lynn Smith, "A Sociological Analysis of Some of the Aspects of Rural Religious Culture as Shown by Mormonism" (Master's thesis, University of Minnesota, 1929); Arden Beal Olsen, "The History of Mormon Mercantile Cooperation in Utah" (Ph.D. diss., University of California, Berkeley, 1935).

51. William J. McNiff, *Heaven on Earth: A Planned Mormon Society* (Oxford, Ohio: Mississippi Valley Press, 1940) and "The Part Played by the Mormon Church in the Cultural Development of Early Utah (1847–1879)" (Ph.D diss., Ohio State University, 1929). See also McNiff's "The Kirtland Phase of Mormonism," *Ohio State Archaeological and Historical Quarterly* 50 (1941): 261–68.

52. S. Dilworth Young, "A Scholar, a Gentle Man, President Levi Edgar Young," *Improvement Era* 67 (January 1964): 17. For other biographical surveys, see G. Homer Durham, "Levi Edgar Young—Senior President: First Council of the Seventy," *Improvement Era* 55 (August 1952): 570–73, 612–15; and Milton R. Hunter, "Levi Edgar Young," *Utah Historical Quarterly* 25 (July 1957): 207–9.

53. Levi Edgar Young, *Chief Episodes in the History of Utah* (Chicago: Lakeside, 1912) and *The Founding of Utah* (New York: Charles Scribner's Sons, 1923).

54. Quoted in Davis Bitton and Leonard J. Arrington, *Mormons and Their Historians* (Salt Lake City: University of Utah Press, 1988), 92.

55. Andrew Love Neff, *History of Utah, 1847 to 1869,* ed. Leland Hargrave Creer (Salt Lake City: Deseret News, 1940).

56. Editor's foreword in ibid., vi.

57. While many of the master's theses were preliminary studies with impossibly broad topics, some were important. See, for example, F. E. Langlois, "The History of Mormonism with Special Reference to the Influence of the Mormon Church on the Economic Development of the Far West" (Master's thesis, University of Idaho, 1926); Gustive O. Larson, "History of the Perpetual Emigrating Fund Company" (Master's thesis, University of Utah, 1926); George S. Tanner, "The Religious Environment in Which Mormonism Arose" (Master's thesis, University of Chicago, 1931); T. Edgar Lyon, "Orson Pratt—Early Mormon Leader" (Master's thesis, University of Chicago, 1932); and Richard D. Poll, "The Twin Relic: A Study of Mormon Polygamy and the Campaign by the Government of the United States for Its Abolition, 1852–1898" (Master's thesis, Texas Christian University, 1939).

58. Leland H. Creer, "Utah and the Nation, 1846–1861" (Ph.D. diss., University of California at Berkeley, 1926); Dean D. McBrien, "The Influence of the Frontier on Joseph Smith" (Ph.D. diss., George Washington University, 1929); Joel E. Ricks, "Forms and

Methods of Early Settlement in Utah and the Surrounding Region, 1847–77" (Ph.D. diss., University of Chicago, 1930); Thomas C. Romney, "The State of Deseret" (Ph.D. diss., University of California at Berkeley, 1930); Milton R. Hunter, "Brigham Young the Colonizer" (Ph.D. diss., University of California at Berkeley, 1936); Robert J. Dwyer, "The Gentile Comes to Utah: A Study in Religious and Social Conflict" (Ph.D. diss., Catholic University of America, 1941).

59. At least seventy-five articles appeared in periodicals published by local, state, and regional historical societies located in California, Illinois, Iowa, Missouri, Nevada, and Ohio.

60. Franklin D. Daines, "Separatism in Utah, 1847–1870," in *Annual Report of the American Historical Association for the Year 1917* (Washington, D.C.: American Historical Association, 1920), 333, 343. Other regional and national journals that showed an interest in Mormon studies included the *American Historical Review, American Journal of Psychology, Proceedings of the American Antiquarian Society, Canadian Geographical Journal, Journal of Geography, Mississippi Valley Historical Review, New England Quarterly, North American Review, Pacific Historical Review,* and *Quarterly Journal of Economics.*

61. Edward Overawed, "Reminiscences of the Mormon War in Illinois," in *Transactions of the Illinois State Historical Society,* Publication No. 10 (Springfield: Illinois State Historical Library, 1906), 183–93; Thomas Ford, "Executive Letter-book of Thomas Ford, 1842–1853," in *Governors' Letter-Books: 1840–1853,* ed. Evarts Boutell Greene and Charles Manfred Thompson (Springfield: Illinois State Historical Library, 1911), 38–128; Stephen S. Harding, "A Letter from Stephen S. Harding to William H. Seward," *Indiana Magazine of History* 26 (June 1930): 157–65; William Jennings, "Carson Valley," *Nevada Historical Society Papers* 1 (1913–16): 178–83; William H. Knight, "Interviewing Brigham Young in 1859," *Journal of American History* 21 (April 1928): 112–17; Wilfred H. Munro, "Among the Mormons in the Days of Brigham Young," *Proceedings of the American Antiquarian Society* 36 (October 1926): 214–30; George Miller, "'De Tal Palo Tal Astilla,'" ed. H. W. Mills, *Publications of the Historical Society of Southern California Annual* 10 (1917): 86–174; Hiram S. Rumfield: "Letters of an Overland Mail Agent in Utah," *Proceedings of the American Antiquarian Society* 38 (October 1928): 227–302; John Johnson Davies, "The Journey of a Mormon from Liverpool to Salt Lake City," ed. Austin L. Venable, *Arkansas Historical Quarterly* 2 (1913): 346–52.

62. "Utah State Historical Society: Sixty Years of Organized History," *Utah Historical Quarterly* 25 (July 1957): 191–92; Gary Topping, "One Hundred Years at the Utah State Historical Society," *Utah Historical Quarterly* 65 (Summer 1997): 223–32.

63. "Utah State Historical Society: Sixty Years of Organized History," 191–92; Topping, "One Hundred Years at the Utah State Historical Society," 200–302.

64. Kimball Young, "A Story of the Rise of a Social Taboo," *Scientific Monthly* 26 (May 1928): 449–53; Wayland D. Hand, "The Three Nephites in Popular Tradition," *Southern Folklore Quarterly* 2 (September 1938): 123–29; Claire Noall, "Superstitions, Customs, and Prescriptions of Mormon Midwives," *California Folklore Quarterly* 3 (April 1944): 102–14; Hector Lee, *The Three Nephites: The Substance and Significance of the Legend in Folklore* (Albuquerque, N.M.: University of New Mexico Press, 1949); Austin E. Fife and Alta S. Fife, *Saints of Sage and Saddle: Folklore among the Mormons* (Bloomington: Indiana University Press, 1956). Fife's early articles included "The Legend of the Three Nephites among the Mormons," *Journal of American Folklore* 53 (January/March 1940): 1–49;

"Popular Legends of the Mormons," *California Historical Quarterly* 1 (April 1942): 105–25; "Folk Belief and Mormon Cultural Autonomy," *Journal of Mormon Cultural Autonomy* 61 (January/March 1948): 19–30; "The Bear Lake Monsters," *Utah Humanities Review* 2 (April 1948): 99–106; and "Folkways of a Mormon Missionary in Virginia," *Southern Folklore Quarterly* 16 (June 1952): 92–123. In addition, Fife coauthored with Alta S. Fife, "Folk Songs of Mormon Inspiration," *Western Folklore* 6 (January 1947): 42–52.

65. I. Woodbridge Riley, *The Founder of Mormonism: A Psychological Study of Joseph Smith, Jr.* (New York: Dodd Mead, 1902).

66. Walter Franklin Prince, "Psychological Tests for the Authorship of the Book of Mormon," *American Journal of Psychology* 28 (July 1917): 373–89. For the Prince-Schroeder exchange, see Theodore Albert Schroeder, "'Authorship of the Book of Mormon,'" *American Journal of Psychology* 30 (January 1919): 66–72; and Walter Franklin Prince, "A Footnote: 'Authorship of the Book of Mormon,'" *American Journal of Psychology* 30 (October 1919): 427–28. Schroeder, a leading early twentieth-century crusader for First Amendment civil liberties, wrote a half-dozen articles on the Mormons. See David Brudnoy, "A Decade in Zion: Theodore Schroeder's Initial Assault on the Mormons," *Historian* 37 (February 1975): 241–56; and David Brudnoy, "Liberty's Bugler: The Seven Ages of Theodore Schroeder" (Ph.D. diss., Brandeis University, 1971).

67. Fawn McKay Brodie, *No Man Knows My History* (New York: Alfred A. Knopf, 1945); "Fawn McKay Brodie: An Oral History Interview," *Dialogue: A Journal of Mormon Thought* 14 (Summer 1981): 102 (quote).

68. "Fawn McKay Brodie: An Oral History Interview," 100. Brodie's biographer is less sure of the immediacy of her religious alienation. See Newell G. Bringhurst, *Fawn McKay Brodie: A Biographer's Life* (Norman: University of Oklahoma Press, 1999), 58.

69. "Fawn McKay Brodie: An Oral History Interview," 106. For a discussion of Brodie's estrangement from the LDS Church, see Mario S. De Pillis, "Fawn McKay Brodie: At the Intersection of Secularism and Personal Alienation," in *Reconsidering No Man Knows My History,* ed. Newell G. Bringhurst (Logan, Utah: Utah State University Press, 1996), 94–126.

70. Bringhurst, *Fawn McKay Brodie,* 107; Bringhurst, "A Biography of the Biography: The Research and Writing of *No Man Knows My History,*" 20.

71. Newell G. Bringhurst, "Fawn M. Brodie, 'Mormondom's Lost Generation,' and *No Man Knows My History,*" *Journal of Mormon History* 16 (1990): 16. Bringhurst's *Fawn McKay Brodie* is the best source on her life and career, but see also Bringhurst's collection of essays on Brodie, *Reconsidering No Man Knows My History.*

72. Fawn McKay Brodie, *No Man Knows My History: The Life of Joseph Smith, the Mormon Prophet,* 2d ed. (New York: Alfred A. Knopf, 1971), ix (quote), 68–70.

73. Ibid., 279.

74. For the reaction to Brodie's book, see Newell G. Bringhurst, "Applause, Attack, and Ambivalence—Varied Responses to Fawn M. Brodie's *No Man Knows My History,*" *Utah Historical Quarterly* 57 (Winter 1989): 46–63.

75. Fawn McKay Brodie, *Thaddeus Stevens: Scourge of the South* (New York: W. W. Norton, 1959); Fawn McKay Brodie, *The Devil Drives: A Life of Sir Richard Burton* (New York: W. W. Norton, 1967); Fawn McKay Brodie, *Thomas Jefferson: An Intimate History* (New York: W. W. Norton, 1974); Fawn McKay Brodie, *Richard Nixon: The Shaping of His Character* (New York: W. W. Norton, 1981).

76. Bringhurst, "Fawn M. Brodie, 'Mormondom's Lost Generation,' and *No Man Knows My History,*" 11–23. The phrase was first used in Edward A. Geary, "Mormondom's Lost Generation: The Novelists of the 1940s," *BYU Studies* 18 (Fall 1977): 89–98. Geary's essay, however, was less concerned with religious commitment than with cultural displacement. Geary argued that many early twentieth-century novelists, while feeling an attraction to the old Mormon village, also understood its stagnation, decline, and irretrievable loss. As a result, these writers felt a "cultural breakdown" and wrote "expatriate" novels.

77. Quoted in Catherine Drinker Bowen, "The Historian," in *Four Portraits and One Subject: Bernard De Voto* (Boston: Houghton Mifflin, 1963), 10.

78. Bernard De Voto, "Utah," *American Mercury* 7 (March 1926): 319.

79. Bernard De Voto, "The Centennial of Mormonism," *American Mercury* 19 (January 1930): 4 (first quote), 10 (second and third quotes).

80. Bernard De Voto, *Year of Decision, 1846* (Boston: Little, Brown, 1943), especially 72–76, 76–98, 137–41, 235–42, 313–20, 431–44, 444–46, 450–54, 462–64, 485–87, 494–95, and 504–6.

81. Bernard De Voto, "A Reevaluation," *Rocky Mountain Review* 10 (Autumn 1945): 9.

82. Ibid., 7.

83. Topping, "One Hundred Years at the Utah State Historical Society," 234. See also Richard Saunders, "'The Strange Mixture of Emotion and Intellect': A Social History of Dale L. Morgan, 1933–42," *Dialogue: A Journal of Mormon Thought* 28 (Winter 1995): 55, 58; and Charles S. Peterson, "Dale Morgan, Writer's Project, and Mormon History as a Regional Study," ibid. 24 (Summer 1991): 50.

84. Dale Morgan, "The State of Deseret," *Utah Historical Quarterly* 8 (April, July, and October 1940): 67–239; Dale Morgan, *The State of Deseret* (Salt Lake City: Utah State Historical Society, 1940).

85. Utah Historical Records Survey Project, Works Project Administration, *A History of Ogden* (Ogden, Utah: Ogden City Commission, 1940); Workers of the Writers' Program of the Works Progress Administration for the State of Utah, comps., *Utah: A Guide to the State* (New York: Hastings House, 1941); Workers of the Writers' Program of the Works Progress Administration for the State of Utah, comps., *Provo: Pioneer Mormon City* (Portland, Ore.: Binfords and Mort, 1942); Dale Morgan, *The Great Salt Lake* (Indianapolis: Bobbs-Merrill, 1947).

86. Richard L. Saunders, *Eloquence from a Silent World: A Descriptive Bibliography of the Published Writings of Dale L. Morgan* (Salt Lake City: Caramon, 1990).

87. Quoted in Peterson, "Dale Morgan," 52.

88. Chad J. Flake, ed., *A Mormon Bibliography, 1830–1930: Books, Pamphlets, Periodicals, and Broadsides relating to the First Century of Mormonism* (Salt Lake City: University of Utah Press, 1978).

89. Dale L. Morgan, *Dale Morgan on Early Mormonism: Correspondence and a New History,* ed. John Phillip Walker (Salt Lake City: Signature Books, 1986).

90. Bringhurst, "Fawn M. Brodie, 'Mormondom's Lost Generation,' and *No Man Knows My History,*" 15–18. For Morgan's correspondence with several midcentury intellectuals, see Morgan, *Dale L. Morgan on Early Mormonism,* 23–216.

91. Morgan, *Dale L. Morgan on Early Mormonism,* 25–33, 49–52, 62–66, 74–78, 84–91, 119–24. For Brooks's life, see Levi S. Peterson, *Juanita Brooks: Mormon Woman Historian*

(Salt Lake City: University of Utah Press, 1988). For a study of the correspondence between Brooks and Brodie, with Morgan often in the middle, see Newell G. Bringhurst, "Juanita Brooks and Fawn Brodie—Sisters in Mormon Dissent," *Dialogue: A Journal of Mormon Thought* 27 (Summer 1994): 105–27.

92. Juanita Leavitt Brooks, "A Close-Up of Polygamy," *Harper's* 168 (February 1934): 299–307. See also Juanita Leavitt Brooks, "I Married a Family," *Dialogue: A Journal of Mormon Thought* 6 (Summer 1971): 19; and Davis Bitton and Maureen Ursenbach [Beecher], "Riding Herd: A Conversation with Juanita Brooks," *Dialogue: A Journal of Mormon Thought* 9 (Spring 1974): 22–23. For Brooks's experience as an interviewer, see Juanita Brooks, "Jest a Copin' Word f'r Word," *Utah Historical Quarterly* 37 (Fall 1969): 375–95.

93. Juanita Leavitt Brooks, "The Water's In!" *Harpers* 182 (May 1941): 608–13. The article was later condensed and reprinted in the *Reader's Digest* 38 (June 1941): 101–3.

94. Juanita Brooks, *Quicksand and Cactus: A Memoir of the Southern Mormon Frontier* (Salt Lake City: Howe Brothers, 1982). For a review, see Levi S. Peterson, "Juanita Brooks's *Quicksand and Cactus:* The Evolution of a Literary Memoir," *Dialogue: A Journal of Mormon Thought* 20 (Spring 1987): 145–55.

95. Juanita Brooks, *Dudley Leavitt: Pioneer to Southern Utah* (St. George, Utah: n.p., 1942); Thales H. Haskell, "Journal of Thales H. Haskell," ed. Juanita Brooks, *Utah Historical Quarterly* 12 (January/April 1944): 68–98; Juanita Brooks, "Indian Relations on the Mormon Frontier," *Utah Historical Quarterly* 12 (January/April 1944): 1–48; Juanita Brooks, "The Southern Indian Mission," *Improvement Era* 48 (April–June): three-part series; Juanita Brooks, "Jacob Hamblin: Apostle to the Indians," *Improvement Era* 47 (April 1944): 210–11, 249, 251–55; Juanita Brooks, "Jacob Hamblin: Apostle to the Lamanites," *Pacific Spectator* 2 (Summer 1948): 315–30; Juanita Brooks, "The First One Hundred Years of Southern Utah History," *Proceedings of the Utah Academy of Sciences, Arts, and Letters* 24 (1947): 71–79.

96. Quoted in Peterson, *Juanita Brooks,* 129.

97. Juanita Brooks, *The Mountain Meadows Massacre* (Stanford, Calif.: Stanford University Press, 1950).

98. John D. Lee, *A Mormon Chronicle: The Diaries of John D. Lee, 1848–1876*, 2 vols., ed. Robert Class Cleland and Juanita Brooks (San Marino, Calif.: Huntington Library, 1955); Juanita Brooks, *John Doyle Lee: Zealot, Pioneer Builder, Scapegoat* (Glendale, Calif.: Arthur H. Clark, 1961); Thomas D. Brown, *Journal of the Southern Indian Mission: Diary of Thomas D. Brown,* ed. Juanita Brooks (Logan: Utah State University Press, 1972); Martha Spence Heywood, *Not by Bread Alone: The Journal of Martha Spence Heywood, 1850–1856,* ed. Juanita Brooks (Salt Lake City: Utah State Historical Society, 1978); Hosea Stout, *On the Mormon Frontier: The Diary of Hosea Stout, 1844–1861,* 2 vols., ed. Juanita Brooks (Salt Lake City: University of Utah Press and Utah State Historical Society, 1964).

3. The New Mormon History: Historical Writing since 1950

IN 1968, MOSES RISCHIN, then a Fulbright professor of history at the University of Uppsala in Sweden, described a "most exciting" development in the writing of Mormon history.[1] According to Rischin, historians seemed willing to put aside Mormon "persistent cohesiveness," its "Old Testament concreteness," and its "cultural isolation" for a new kind of historical writing that was "at home among the *avant garde* Gentiles." Rischin eventually suggested a title for this new development: "new Mormon history."[2]

As the expression caught on, several historians tried to define it more fully. According to Robert Flanders, who wrote an influential essay on the new Mormon history, the school revealed a shift from parochialism and polemics to a more humane and universal history rooted in such "humanistic and scientific disciplines" as "philosophy, social psychology, economics, and religious studies." Flanders also argued that the new history showed a willingness to examine Mormonism's denominational branches, including Flanders's own Reorganized Church of Jesus Christ of Latter Day Saints.[3] Another commentator, Thomas G. Alexander, saw an element of self-discovery in the movement: most of the new Mormon historians were "active" and "devout" Mormons using their professional training to understand their heritage.[4] However, it was Leonard J. Arrington, the dean of the new historians, who may have best captured the spirit of the writing. Arrington believed that he and his contemporaries were investigating the Mormon past in human or naturalistic terms without rejecting its divinity.[5]

During the ensuing decades, the expression "new Mormon history" assumed several connotations, some pejorative. However, the general tendency of the phrase—and the movement that it described—remained the same.

Instead of defending or attacking LDS faith claims—one of the major characteristics of nineteenth-century Mormon historiography—the new historians were more interested in examining the Mormon past in the hope of understanding it—and understanding themselves. Their tools were the same as those of other professionally trained historians: secular or naturalistic historical analysis. But instead of being put off by the study of religion, as the earlier rural agrarians or Mormonism's "lost generation of intellectuals" had been, the new generation believed that Mormonism, in all its diversity, deserved study. They accordingly asked new questions and explored new topics, many of which had nothing to do with the "truth" of the religion. Their hope was to broaden the base for understanding Mormonism's history.

Some of the "new historians" were non-Mormon. Others came from non-Utahn branches of the LDS restoration. Still others were "cultural Mormons," more interested in their heritage than in exploring faith. The largest group of "new Mormon historians" were, however, "believing" Mormons, positioned at various places on a spectrum of belief, who hoped to use new historical methods to interpret their religion. Even these men and women wrote with a quiet interpretive voice that some church leaders found disturbingly detached and passive. Most new Mormon history writers sought a middle ground between the polemical historical literature of the past and the intellectual and "scientific" disapproval of religion that had filled the early twentieth century. Their audience was mainly LDS readers, often college educated, who sought a faith that could be intellectually challenged and explained.

The Beginning of the New History

Because the new history was largely written by Mormons for Mormons, it could be clannish and open to the charge of narcissism. "Every group naturally wants to know its own special story and little more," John Higham wrote in a passage that might be applied to recent Mormon writing.[6] To its credit, at its best the Mormons' new history used the tools current in the broader historical profession: comparative analysis, folklore, geography, local history, material culture study, religious studies, sociology, demography, and women's history. As such, it was part of the academic and secular professional history that the post–World War II generation was writing.

The spirit of the new Mormon history was personified by three young LDS scholars who established an informal network in Logan, Utah, during the early 1950s. S. George Ellsworth (1916–98), fresh from obtaining his Ph.D. degree from the University of California at Berkeley, was beginning an influential teaching career at Utah State University. Ellsworth's dissertation,

"A History of Mormon Missions in the United States and Canada, 1830–1860," plotted Mormonism's first congregations and argued that the new religion, instead of being nurtured in the soil of the American frontier, came from a region rapidly maturing, both socially and economically. Ellsworth followed this important dissertation with more than a dozen essays and edited works and by a popular text on Utah history written for junior high school students.

The second historian was Eugene E. Campbell (1915–86), an associate director of the LDS Institute of Religion, adjacent to Utah State University, who later continued his career in the Department of History at Brigham Young University. Campbell's 1952 dissertation, a history of the Mormon Church in California, foreshadowed a long-term interest in Mormon western pioneering.[7] Most important, he helped edit and contribute to the influential text *Utah's History* and wrote *Establishing Zion: The Mormon Church in the American West, 1847–1869*, published posthumously.[8] Campbell's books and articles had the common characteristic of "setting the record straight," which admirers and critics variously viewed as courageous or sometimes crossgrained, perhaps both.[9]

The third Logan historian was Leonard J. Arrington (1917–99), a native of Twin Falls County, Idaho, who became perhaps the single most important figure to write LDS history. Arrington described his career as going from "chicken farmer to agriculture major; from agriculture to economics; from regional economics to Western economic history; and finally from Western history to Mormon studies."[10] After growing up on his family's irrigated Idaho farm and graduating from the University of Idaho in 1939, Arrington studied at the University of North Carolina at Chapel Hill. This last experience introduced him to the southern agrarian writers of the post–World War I era, whose influence was pivotal. He felt a "burning in my bones" to do for the American West what Howard W. Odum, Rupert B. Vance, Milton S. Heath, and others had done for southern regionalism.[11]

Two men further refined Arrington's sense of mission. The first was Richard T. Ely, whose 1903 essay in *Harper's Monthly* had launched the work of the early twentieth-century Mormon regionalists. In 1939, Arrington met Ely in Philadelphia at the annual convention of the American Economic Association. I "felt it [was] a gift of heaven that I could talk with this short, pink-cheeked, boyish-faced man, who had influenced two generations of economists and economic policy," Arrington later wrote.[12] Ely plied his young acquaintance with stories about the Mormon contribution to western settlement—stories that affected Arrington deeply. Later, Arrington modestly reported that his Ph.D. dissertation was "merely an extension" of Ely's pioneering work.[13]

The other figure who helped direct Arrington's professional interest was the Mormon apostle John A. Widtsoe. After completing his course work at Chapel Hill and serving in World War II as a youthful Allied controller of the Central Institute of Statistics during the American occupation of Italy, Arrington returned to the Intermountain West in 1946, accepting a teaching position in economics at Utah State University in Logan. Hoping to get his professional bearings, Arrington sought Widtsoe's advice. The former president of Utah State University and the University of Utah urged Arrington to narrow his interest in western regionalism to Mormon country. There, Widtsoe perceptively argued, the young scholar would find a unified cultural region ideal to his ambition. Mormon regionalism had abundant and largely untapped historical resources.[14]

The late 1940s and early 1950s were busy for Arrington. He increasingly gained access to the rich but previously restricted sources of the LDS archives in Salt Lake City. In Logan, he joined Ellsworth, Campbell, and another Institute of Religion faculty member, Wendell O. Rich, in monthly study sessions in which the men read papers, many later published, on Mormon culture and history. Ellsworth was especially helpful in introducing Arrington to the methods and standards of historical writing. Then, in 1951, Arrington began to publish in such scholarly journals as *Rural Sociology, Journal of Economic History, Economic History Review, Western Humanities Review, Pacific Historical Review,* and *Business History Review.*[15]

Arrington's early work culminated in the publication of *Great Basin Kingdom: An Economic History of the Latter-day Saints, 1830–1900,* a watershed in the writing of the new Mormon history.[16] The book summarized the sociological and economic literature produced by the rural agrarians earlier in the century. More important, it contained Arrington's own meticulous and pathbreaking research. The result was a fresh and detailed view of Mormon pioneering (despite the book's expansive subtitle, it focused on the Utah era). At the same time, the book reached a larger audience as a case study of "modern" economic planning. Arrington suggested that the Mormons' Great Basin kingdom, more than eighty years before the New Deal or the Fair Deal, was the agent in a vast enterprise of centralized decision making and regulation. Moreover, the theocracy's social ideas of homogeneity, equality, and unity coincided with many of the values urged by Richard Ely, the southern agrarians, and New Deal planners. Arrington's book was a part of the intellectual (and liberal) zeitgeist of its times.

The book was important on another level. It suggested a new approach to how Mormon history, as religious history, could be written. According to an important passage in the book's preface:

The true essence of God's revealed will, if such it be, cannot be apprehended without an understanding of the conditions surrounding the prophetic vision, and the symbolism and verbiage in which it is couched. . . . A naturalistic discussion of "the people and the times" and of the mind and experience of Latter-day prophets is therefore a perfectly valid aspect of religious history, and, indeed, makes more plausible the truths they attempted to convey. While the discussion of naturalistic causes of revelations does not preclude its claim to be revealed or inspired of God, in practice it is difficult, if not impossible, to distinguish what is objectively "revealed" from what is subjectively "contributed" by those receiving the revelation.[17]

It was not that Arrington denied the hand of providence in the unfolding of Mormon events. Rather, he felt uncertain and unwilling to identify it, and so scrupulous was his restraint that some Mormon readers, unused to scholarly writing, assumed that *Great Basin Kingdom* was written by a non-Mormon or an anti-Mormon. In another passage, Arrington suggested the difficulty of writing religious history. "The professional in us fights against religious naiveté," he wrote, while "the religionist in us fights against secular naiveté—believing too little. And if this internal warfare weren't enough, we have a similar two-front war externally—against non-Mormons who think we LDS historians believe too much, and against super-Mormons who think we believe not enough."[18] Arrington's cautious approach to writing religious history—his willingness to give natural explanations, his restrained religious voice, and his attempt to find a middle ground between the extremes of secular and religious feeling—became hallmarks of the new Mormon writing.

His career launched, Arrington came to regard himself not only as an individual scholar but also as a "historical entrepreneur."[19] This new role meant coordinating team efforts and often collaborating with graduate students and colleagues to produce a series of articles and monographs, mostly on western economic history. It also meant mentoring. Several church authorities, impressed with Arrington's professionalism and LDS sympathy, urged Arrington to assist the rising generation of historical scholars.[20]

In 1965, Arrington played a leading role in organizing the Mormon History Association (MHA) and served as its first president. The association was an outgrowth of informal discussion sessions that Arrington and other LDS historians had held at various regional and national professional meetings. Three years later, the MHA began to hold an annual meeting independent of other associations, and within fifteen years the MHA had between seven and eight hundred members, both Mormon and non-Mormons.[21]

As a "historical entrepreneur," Arrington also played a role in the reorganization of the LDS Church Historian's Office (CHO). In January 1966, President N. Eldon Tanner, a counselor in the First Presidency of the church, interviewed Arrington about possible reforms at the CHO. Several years later, Arrington was a member of a committee of historians that advised the CHO to establish a continuing liaison with the historical community, to build a professional staff, to collect new material, to fund research grants for non-CHO personnel, and, most important, to begin an ambitious, multivolume publishing program.[22] These suggestions helped address the growing concern that the Church Historian's Office was not meeting its scriptural obligation to keep "a record . . . among you."[23] Since the publication of B. H. Roberts's multivolume *Comprehensive History of the Church* in the 1930s, the CHO had not published new material. Moreover, the CHO's policy of restricting access to its material had discouraged nonaffiliated historians from writing church history.

In January 1972, Arrington's role was greatly enlarged. In a precedent-breaking move, President Tanner called Arrington to the office of LDS Church historian, the first non–general authority to serve in this position. "We are under obligations to write our history for the benefit of the generations to come, and we want it done in a thoroughly professional way," Tanner explained.[24]

At the time of his selection, Arrington was fifty-four years old. He had published widely and had served as president of the Agricultural History Society, the Western History Association, and the Mormon History Association. Although his appointment was coupled with a half-time professorship at Brigham Young University, his teaching and research duties would increasingly be displaced by overseeing the work of others. There was a compensating advantage, however: as church historian, he could use the research and writing of his associates to enhance his own writing projects.[25]

Arrington's new assignment placed him in charge of the History Division, a newly created section of the renamed LDS Historical Department assigned the responsibility of writing history. Arrington and his superior at church headquarters, Alvin R. Dyer, set high goals for the History Division, several of which had been discussed in previous conversations.[26] The program included publishing a sixteen-volume history of the church that would mark Mormonism's 150-year anniversary in 1980. Arrington and Dyer also saw the need for a new one-volume treatment of church history and proposed two different books: a narrative history designed for church members and a topically arranged and analytical volume for outsiders. Other parts of the proposed publishing program included a "Heritage Series" featuring important diaries and documents; an oral history program; the publication of articles for scholarly journals and church periodicals; and such miscellaneous projects as biographies of church leaders, gender studies, local and regional history, and histories addressing "aspects of ordinary life."[27] It was, of course, an agenda for an entire generation of scholarship.

To meet these goals, Arrington chose two assistants who were leaders in the new history movement. Both had been involved in the discussions relating to the CHO's reorganization, and each, as half-time assistants, played an important role in designing the "Arrington" publishing program. James B. Allen (b. 1927) received his professional training at the University of Southern California, and after serving as an Institute of Religion instructor in the LDS educational system in southern Utah, he accepted a professorship at Brigham Young University. The second was Davis Bitton (b. 1930). Trained in European history at Princeton University, Bitton served on the faculty at the University of Texas, the University of California at Santa Barbara, and the University of Utah. In addition to Arrington, Allen, and Bitton, the History Division at its high tide had eleven full-time "historical associates" slots, which were filled by younger historians beginning their careers.[28] Further expanding its resources, the History Division granted more than five dozen $1,000 grants, many to men and women fresh from graduate school who produced a rich harvest of published articles and books.[29]

During its ten-year history, the History Division completed an impressive tally of work. Its oral history program interviewed 800 people in almost 1,500 interviews. Edyth Romney transcribed 3,000 church documents filling more than 50 volumes. The History Division staff wrote more than 350 articles, book chapters, and published reviews, 70 of which appeared in church periodicals.[30] Still more significant, the History Division published 20 books, several of major importance. Dean C. Jessee, editor of *Letters of Brigham Young to His Sons,* allowed Mormonism's second leader to speak for himself, and as a result Brigham Young emerged as a caring family man.[31] Leonard J. Arrington, Feramorz Y. Fox, and Dean L. May, in *Building the City of God: Community and Cooperation among the Mormons,* clarified the Mormons' communitarian "united order movement" of the 1870s.[32] Davis Bitton's *Guide to Mormon Diaries and Autobiographies* provided information on almost 3,000 LDS diaries.[33] Because the book offered a précis for each entry, it also was important social history.

Perhaps the History Division's most important contributions were two comprehensive histories of Mormonism. In *The Story of the Latter-day Saints,* James B. Allen and Glen M. Leonard offered the first scholarly, one-volume treatment of the church in a half-century.[34] A model example of the new Mormon history, the book summarized past scholarship, placed Mormon events in their wider context, and respectfully (and faithfully) confronted many thorny historical issues. Moreover, it devoted a third of its pages to twentieth-century issues, fresh ground for a Mormon narrative history. It remains the best one-volume treatment of the Mormon past and the place where the beginning student of LDS history should first turn.

Its companion volume, *The Mormon Experience: A History of the Latter-day Saints,* was more analytical, more interested in themes and ideas, and more detached in spirit.[35] Written by Arrington and Bitton and designed for the nonbeliever, the volume displayed a sensitive ear to current academic trends; its topically arranged chapters gave generous treatment to Mormon and Native American relations, the history of LDS women, and the cultural diverseness of nineteenth-century Mormon immigrants. It also spoke of the church's "creative adjustment" and "reinvigoration" during the twentieth century. In short, here was a sophisticated and readable book that placed Mormonism in the mainstream of contemporary culture. It was religious history in the best sense.

Despite the outward success of the History Division, all was not well. Some general authorities disapproved of the kind of history being produced at church headquarters. In 1976, Ezra Taft Benson, president of the Council of the Twelve Apostles, warned of the tendency to humanize church leaders. Such an approach minimized God's ruling hand and undermined "our prophetic history," Benson thought. Moreover, Benson objected to the neutral language employed by some of the historians. Such scholarly expressions as "experimental systems" and "communal life" seemed too foreign to Mormon traditional history and possibly a breach of it.[36]

Apostle Boyd K. Packer was also concerned about the History Division's writing. His address "'The Mantle Is Far, Far Greater Than the Intellect'" cautioned historians about telling too much. Packer wanted a more sympathetic, spiritual, and partisan history. "We are at war with the adversary," he reminded church members.[37] The views of Benson and Packer received support from a widely circulated University of Utah honor's thesis written by Richard Marshall. Marshall saw the threat of "secularism" in such events as the organization of the Mormon History Association and the professionalism of the Historical Department.[38] Although Marshall's study was preliminary in its analysis and depth, it seemed to confirm the growing doubts about the historical community.

Signs of disfavor grew, especially after the issuing of Allen and Leonard's *Story of the Latter-day Saints.* The History Division staff was downsized. Arrington's scriptural title of church historian was replaced by a more bureaucratic one. Still more telling, the flagship sixteen-volume, sesquicentennial series was canceled; church leaders honored author contracts and gave permission for the outside publication of ongoing volumes, but they wanted no further tie to the project. In 1982, Arrington and a core of seven scholars were transferred to Brigham Young University, where they became members of the newly created Joseph Fielding Smith Institute for Church History. In a related move, administrators of the LDS archives restricted access to the church's collection and took steps to control the publication of past and ongoing research completed at the archives.[39]

In announcing the transfer of the History Division's staff, church president Spencer W. Kimball put the best face on the church's decision. "The stature, objectivity, and effectiveness of our fine professional historians will be enhanced by association with the church's university," Kimball said.[40] It was true that BYU offered Arrington and his historians a more congenial home than did the church headquarters, with its consensus and public relations style of management. However, it was also true that the move indicated a longing on the part of church authorities for more traditional, faith-promoting history. "Our great experiment in church-sponsored history has proved to be, if not a failure, at least not an unqualified success," the usually ebullient Arrington privately wrote. He was particularly distressed that the collapse of the History Division might renew critics' charge that historical writing and faith were incompatible.[41] As always, Arrington stood between two fires and felt the heat of each.

Institutional Historians

Arrington served as director of BYU's Joseph Fielding Smith Institute for Church History from 1980 to 1986, retiring from the university the following year. He was replaced by Ronald K. Esplin (b. 1944), a longtime member of his staff. The Smith Institute, perhaps warned by the History Division's experience and only half the size of its predecessor, seemed content to assume a lower profile. While still a center for the new Mormon history, the new research center did not publicly promote historical issues or attempt to mold the rising generation. Arrington's historical entrepreneurship was replaced by the quiet, low-profile writing of history.

Fifteen years after its founding, the Smith Institute (later renamed the Joseph Fielding Smith Institute for LDS History) had the solid record of producing more than forty books and monographs and another three hundred items issued as notes, reviews, chapters, and articles. Some of these works were major, especially nineteenth-century biography. One of the first of these studies, Leonard J. Arrington's *Brigham Young: American Moses,* quickly became the standard biography of Mormonism's second leader.[42]

William G. Hartley (b. 1942), who devoted much of his career to understanding the everyday routines of first- and second-generation LDS lives, wrote several books highlighting the role of "common" Saints, including *"They Are My Friends": A History of the Joseph Knight Family, 1825–1850* and *My Best for the Kingdom: History and Autobiography of John Lowe Butler, a Mormon Frontiersman.*[43] Maureen Ursenbach Beecher issued two books on Eliza Roxcy Snow, the "leading sister" of the Utah founding era: *Eliza and Her Sisters,* a compilation of essays, and the edited *Personal Writings of Eliza Roxcy Snow,* which placed Snow in a theoretical framework that helped readers understand the role of LDS women leaders in pioneer society.[44]

Ronald W. Walker's *Wayward Saints: The Godbeites and Brigham Young* was a collective biography of a group of religious and intellectual dissenters, who during the 1870s resisted Young's theocracy.[45] Walker (b. 1939) argued that these British-born men and women demonstrated not only a classic confrontation between conscience and authority but also the cultural and demographic fissures of nineteenth-century Mormon society. Walker also coedited a collection of essays entitled *Nearly Everything Imaginable: The Everyday Life of Utah's Mormon Pioneers* that described the routines of "ordinary" settlers during the pioneering era of Utah: diet, dress, music, schooling, village life, and worship.[46]

Other Smith Institute historians were also interested in Mormonism's British converts. Richard L. Jensen (b. 1943) and BYU Department of History member Malcolm R. Thorp edited an important anthology of essays, *Mormons in Early Victorian Britain.*[47] Still another Smith Institute collaboration was James B. Allen, Ronald K. Esplin, and David J. Whittaker's *Men with a Mission, 1837–1841: The Quorum of the Twelve Apostles in the British Isles,* which told the story of the introduction of Mormonism to Great Britain.[48] These two carefully researched and written volumes were among the best sources for the nineteenth-century Mormon experience in England.[49]

James B. Allen, who after retiring from BYU's Department of History maintained an association with the Smith Institute, collaborated with Jessie L. Embry and Kahlile Mehr in publishing *Hearts Turned to the Fathers: A History of the Genealogical Society of Utah, 1894–1994.*[50] More than an institutional history of the world's largest repository of genealogical records, the book also contained important information on such diverse topics as technology, Mormon theology, and the role of women in the twentieth-century church. The book was also issued as a volume in the scholarly periodical *Brigham Young University Studies.*[51]

Smith Institute historians Maureen Ursenbach Beecher (b. 1935), Jill Mulvay Derr (b. 1948), and Carol Cornwall Madsen (b. 1930) wrote LDS women's history. Madsen, working on a biography of the feminist and church leader Emmeline B. Wells, edited three books on women's topics: *In Their*

Own Words: Women and the Story of Nauvoo; Journey to Zion: Voices from the Mormon Trail; and *Battle for the Ballot: Essays on Woman Suffrage in Utah, 1870–1896.*[52] Derr and Beecher collaborated with Janath Russell Cannon, a former member of the LDS Relief Society general board and general presidency, to produce *Women of Covenant: The Story of Relief Society.*[53] Presented to the Mormon women's organization as part of its sesquicentennial year celebration, *Women of Covenant* was written in the moderate and restrained voice of official history. Yet, especially in the pages devoted to the nineteenth-century history of the Relief Society, the book was an important synthesis of past scholarship and a source for new information.

One of the Smith Institute's most lasting contributions to LDS scholarship was furnished by Dean C. Jessee (b. 1929), the premier editor of LDS primary documents, who in the 1980s began the task of documenting the life of Joseph Smith. In *The Personal Writings of Joseph Smith,* Jessee presented material that revealed Smith's thought and personality.[54] Later Jessee launched, with official approval, a comprehensive and multivolume series entitled *The Papers of Joseph Smith,* two volumes of which were completed by the late 1990s.[55] For the first time in the lengthy publishing history of Joseph Smith's papers, readers had a text on which they could rely. Jessee carefully identified authorship, preserved original spelling and punctuation, and marked emendations in the printed text. To further help students, Jessee furnished useful chronologies, offered biographical sketches of the men and women mentioned in Smith's writing, and supplied a selection of valuable maps and photographs.

One of the longest and most valuable labors of the Smith Institute was a two-part bibliography of published sources dealing with LDS history. Smith Institute members James B. Allen and Ronald W. Walker, along with David J. Whittaker, curator of the Western and Mormon Manuscripts at BYU's Harold B. Lee Library, worked fifteen years to produce *Studies in Mormon History, 1830–1997: An Indexed Bibliography.*[56] This work listed more than 16,000 books, articles, theses and dissertations, and miscellany by author name and by subject matter. The work was supplemented by "A Topical Guide to Published Social Science Literature on the Mormons," compiled by Armand L. Mauss and Dynette Ivie Reynolds, which included 2,300 social science items. *Studies in Mormon History, 1830–1997,* published in 2000 at the beginning of a new century, demonstrated the vitality of Mormon studies 170 years after the LDS religious movement had begun.

The LDS History Division and the Smith Institute for Church History were not the only church-sponsored institutions to pay attention to Mormon history. BYU's Charles Redd Center for Western Studies was another. Established

in 1972 by a donation from Charles and Annaley Redd, the center was char-
tered to promote the interdisciplinary study of the Intermountain West. That
some of its resources were devoted to Mormon studies no doubt reflected
the interest of its first two directors, Leonard J. Arrington and Thomas G.
Alexander. Arrington, who had received the Redd appointment as a half-time
assignment when named as church historian, yielded the position to
Alexander in 1980.

Thomas Alexander (b. 1935) was a prolific writer and a defender of the new
history. A native of Ogden, Utah, he studied at Weber State College, the University of Utah, and Utah State University. After receiving his Ph.D. at the
University of California at Berkeley, Alexander returned to Utah to accept an
appointment in the Department of History at Brigham Young University. His
selection of BYU reflected a professional ambition: he wanted to write Utah
and western history.[57]

By the end of the 1990s, Alexander had produced three dozen articles, had
edited nine books, and had authored three major books—each dealing with
Utah and Mormon themes and each dedicated to full disclosure. "I resolved
that whatever else I did," he later wrote, "I would try to be honest about the
Church's past."[58] His first major LDS book, *Mormonism in Transition: A
History of the Latter-day Saints, 1890–1930,* pioneered the terrain of post-
Manifesto church history.[59] Once intended as one of the History Division's
sesquicentennial volumes, the book interpreted the four decades as an era
of transition from first-generation religious "other-worldliness" to an increasing accommodation to the modern world. Alexander used social and
intellectual topics as well as the more traditional political and administrative themes to illustrate his narrative.

Alexander's next Mormon book, *Things in Heaven and Earth: The Life and
Times of Wilford Woodruff, a Mormon Prophet,* realized a biographical interest that George Ellsworth had first engendered in Alexander when he was a
student at Utah State University.[60] However, if Mormonism's fourth president had long been a matter of curiosity, Alexander's theoretical approach
was more recent. Accepting a relativistic historicism, Alexander argued that
the realms of secular and religious knowledge could be broached by a methodology that accepted Woodruff's sincerity. When writing his biography,
Alexander therefore tried to understand Woodruff's religious experiences as
Woodruff himself understood them, although Alexander reinterpreted them
for a modern audience.[61] The approach became an influential interpretive
model in new Mormon history.

Alexander's most comprehensive book, *Utah, the Right Place: The Official
Centennial History,* was commissioned by the Utah State legislature as part

of the state's centennial observance.[62] Although devoted to the nondenomi-
national themes of Utah's historical growth, the book also covered Mormon
topics, especially those of the nineteenth century and early twentieth.

Under Alexander's leadership, the Charles Redd Monographs in Western
History series frequently published Mormon topics. The Redd Center also
collected Mormon oral interviews. Its major collections included the LDS
Polygamy Oral History Project (over 250 interviews), the LDS Afro-Ameri-
can Oral History Project (over 200 interviews), and the LDS Family Life Oral
History Project (over 150 interviews). Smaller collections featured the LDS
experience of Asian Americans, Hispanic Americans, Native Americans, and
Polynesian Americans.[63]

Jessie L. Embry (b. 1952), the director of the Redd Center's oral history
program, used the material she collected for several books. *Mormon Polygamous Families: Life in the Principle* described how plural marriage had been
lived—the first major examination of this topic since Kimball Young's work
thirty years earlier. She concluded that Mormon polygamous families were
not much different from their monogamous counterparts—the Mormons
had "simply adapted Victorian ideology to fit their new polygamous life-
style."[64] Embry's subsequent books discussed the challenge that African
Americans, Hispanic Americans, and Asian Americans experienced adapting to the Mormons' middle-class, upwardly mobile culture.[65]

Another BYU unit that paid attention to Mormon history was the Department of History. During the 1960s and 1970s, Eugene E. Campbell, Gustive
O. Larson, and Richard D. Poll wrote history while training a new generation of students. Larson authored a nineteenth-century Utah history text and,
more significant, a survey tracing the cultural and political accommodation
that accompanied Utah's quest for statehood.[66] For his part, Poll coauthored
with Campbell a biography of the LDS Church leader Hugh B. Brown, wrote
articles dealing with the so-called Utah War of 1857–58, and coedited *Utah's
History.*[67]

Newer department members also made significant contributions. R. Lanier
Britsch authored four books detailing the Mormon experience in Oceania,
the Asian Rim, and Asia itself.[68] Marvin S. Hill produced essays on the founding of Mormonism, coedited with James B. Allen an anthology of essays placing Mormonism within the framework of American culture, and published
Quest for Refuge: The Mormon Flight from American Pluralism.[69] Hill's book,
a revision of his 1968 dissertation at the University of Chicago, argued that
Jacksonian America, full of secular social and cultural tumult, had set the
stage for Mormonism's celebrated political theocracy. Other department
members produced a stream of articles and books, although much of this

work was completed under different institutional auspices.[70] By the close of the century, despite abundant available historical sources and an interested student body, the department increasingly was ceding the writing of LDS history to others.

The various divisions of the LDS educational system also had its historians.[71] Although these scholars were restrained by heavy teaching duties and sometimes by administrative constraint, several completed valuable projects. Members of BYU's church history and doctrine faculty at the College of Religious Education were especially active. Richard Cowan produced a pioneering book on twentieth-century Mormonism, and Richard Lloyd Anderson, a colleague working on the beginning of Mormonism, wrote about the Book of Mormon witnesses and Joseph Smith's ancestry.[72] Yet another historian at the College of Religious Education was Bruce A. Van Orden, whose works included a book on the nineteenth-century church secretary George Reynolds.[73] Richard Neitzel Holzapfel brought the canons of professional history to a series of semipopular articles but most important established himself as a leading historian of LDS images; Holzapfel, who often worked with T. Jeffery Cottle, produced books of historical photographs on Mormonism's historic sites, buildings, and people, such as Brigham Young.[74] Finally, Susan Easton Black compiled databases on LDS and RLDS membership and researched the composition of Mormonism's 1847 pioneer migration.[75]

Beginning in the late 1980s and continuing to the present, the College of Religious Education issued more than a half-dozen compilations in the series Regional Studies in Latter-day Saint Church History. Published internally and without peer review, these volumes contained uneven but often important material on the Mormon experience in Arizona, Illinois, New England, New York, Missouri, Ohio, and Great Britain.

One of the most productive scholars of the College of Religious Education was Milton V. Backman Jr., who authored more than a half-dozen books in the traditional faithful style. Backman's *Heavens Resound: A History of the Latter-day Saints in Ohio, 1830–1838,* another volume of the lapsed sesquicentennial series, provided the best one-volume survey of the Kirtland era.[76] The book contained useful population summaries and argued, unlike previous interpretations, that most "faithful Kirtland Saints" did not abandon their faith but continued the Mormon hegira. Kirtland had not hemorrhaged Saints.

Another productive College of Religious Education scholar was Richard E. Bennett, who came to BYU late in his career after serving as the director of the archives and special collections at the University of Manitoba in Canada. Bennett wrote more than twenty articles on LDS history, some dealing with Mormons in Canada. His chief contribution, however, was his detailing of the nineteenth-century Mormon exodus to the West in *Mormons at the Missouri, 1846–52: "And Should We Die"* and *We'll Find the Place: The Mormon Exodus, 1846–1848.*[77]

Grant Underwood, a former member of the Church Education System and later a member of BYU's Joseph Fielding Smith Institute for LDS History, wrote *The Millenarian World of Early Mormonism.* Comfortable with comparative analysis and the history of ideas, Underwood proposed examining the "mental world of early Mormonism" by studying its millenarian thought. His book, based largely on published sources, had a conservative conclusion. "Upon closer examination, the attitudes and behavior of early Mormons seem more mainstream and the alleged radicalism of their marital, economic, and political relations more superficial than has often been assumed," Underwood wrote.[78]

If the work of the church's religious educators was sometimes hesitant and defensive, written in small historical segments and avoiding broad themes, the work of the historians of the Reorganized Church of Jesus Christ of Latter Day Saints was situated on the left end of the intellectual spectrum. Robert B. Flanders (b. 1930) was one of the first and most important. Flanders encountered Arrington's *Great Basin Kingdom* while a student at the University of Wisconsin and was influenced by it. Could a similar book be written for his own RLDS branch of the restoration movement?

The result was a Ph.D. dissertation that Flanders reworked into the book *Nauvoo: Kingdom on the Mississippi.* Here was history after Arrington's model: passages rich in detail and full of human striving (and frailty), historical events placed in a larger, non-Mormon context, and an emphasis on "corporate" or "political" Mormonism. But there was something new, too; Arrington's quiet naturalism became a thoroughgoing secularism. In Flanders's work, Joseph Smith was not so much a religious prophet as a Jacksonian Era "man of affairs"—a "planner, promoter, architect, entrepreneur, executive, politician, filibusterer." Departing still further from RLDS interpretation, which regarded Utah Mormonism as an apostasy, Flanders argued that Joseph Smith's Nauvoo "kingdom" had laid the foundation for Brigham Young's Utah "kingdom." Nauvoo social organization, Nauvoo theocracy, Nauvoo acceptance of Old World immigration, and Nauvoo polygamy had established precedents for what had followed. "Without that seven years' experience in Illinois," Flanders summarized, "the development of the Great Basin, and of the [Mormon] West, would not have been the same."[79]

The book was troubling to RLDS traditionalists, and the controversy that it stirred may have led to Flanders's decision to leave the church and end his

Mormon studies. However, the influence of the book was lasting. It prompted RLDS leaders to begin a reevaluation of their church's teachings and mission, still not fully resolved. It also signaled a change in the relations between RLDS and LDS historians. After its publication, men and women from across the old religious divide appreciated more fully their shared heritage, and friendships were established. "All people of the Restoration Movement have had a common past despite themselves," Flanders reminded.[80]

Richard P. Howard (b. 1920) was another of the new RLDS scholars. Howard was educated at Graceland College, the University of Kansas, the University of California at Berkeley, American University, and the St. Paul School of Theology, studying journalism, history, and theology. Shortly after his appointment as RLDS Church historian in 1965, he explained his approach to history. Although acknowledging the difficult "narrow line" between credulity and disbelief, he spoke of the historian's "moral obligation" to question. "Any statement ought to be doubted as long as a reasonable basis for doubt exists," he said.[81]

Howard quickly became, as W. Grant McMurray put it, "the most controversial of [RLDS official] historians, leaning more to the tools of the secular historians than any of his predecessors."[82] In successive moves, Howard opened the RLDS archives for public use, including research by LDS scholars; subjected Joseph Smith's written revelations to historical analysis; and probed some of the most delicate historical questions facing contemporary Mormonism: Joseph Smith's "First Vision," early LDS plural marriage practices, and the historicity of the Book of Abraham. He capped his writing career by issuing a two-volume history of the RLDS movement, a semiofficial history that couched RLDS revisionism in a restrained voice.[83]

When Howard gave his Mormon History Association presidential address in 1991, he spoke of the historical ecumenicism that had transformed Mormon studies during the past twenty-five years: "Walls" had given way to "windows."[84] The process of RLDS and LDS conciliation, which Howard himself personified, was also reflected in the careers of the RLDS scholars Alma R. Blair, Paul M. Edwards, Roger D. Launius, F. Mark McKiernan, W. Grant McMurray, and William D. Russell. Another indication of cooperation was the publication of *The Restoration Movement: Essays in Mormon History.*[85] The book, edited by McKiernan, Blair, and Edwards, featured five historical essays written by RLDS authors and seven by LDS writers. The work proved so popular within the restoration that Herald House, the RLDS publishing unit, secured the copyright and issued several reprintings during the 1970s and 1980s. While some of these essays were significant in their own right, the book's greater importance was its intercommunion partnership.[86]

Three periodicals reflected the new RLDS scholarly spirit. The first was *Courage: A Journal of History, Thought and Action.* Founded by Graceland faculty members Paul M. Edwards, William D. Russell, and Roy Muir as a reaction to conservative RLDS publishing policies, it took a fresh and often left-of-center look at contemporary RLDS issues, including historical questions. Some of the journal's articles questioned the prophetic quality of Joseph Smith's revelations, the historicity of the Book of Mormon, Joseph Smith's "translation" of the Book of Abraham, and even the value of a modern scriptural canon.[87] The periodical also served the cause of Mormon historical conciliation by reviewing a dozen LDS publications and making this scholarship known to its RLDS readership.[88]

Two other RLDS periodicals were more enduring. *Restoration Studies* was a semiofficial occasional series devoted to publishing short articles dealing with RLDS history, belief, and practices. Since the periodical began in 1980, more than half a dozen volumes have been produced, each containing about twenty articles, some bearing on LDS heritage. The more historically minded *John Whitmer Historical Association Journal* was published by the John Whitmer Historical Association (JWHA). Organized in 1972, the JWHA constituted an independent group of scholars who hoped to "infuse the spirit of renewal" into the Reorganized Church. While "predominantly midwestern" (RLDS) in scope, the organization also sought to continue "the marvelous and fruitful association" already begun with LDS scholars.[89] To accomplish these goals, JWHA began holding an annual convention and publishing a newsletter. In 1980, eight years after its formal organization, JWHA started publishing its journal.

By the end of the twentieth century, the *John Whitmer Historical Journal* had established itself as the organ for RLDS history, although its articles dealing with the early years of the restoration were also of interest to LDS readers. Moreover, the journal frequently reached out to a wider audience. During its first decade, twenty-two of its sixty-one articles were written by LDS authors. The journal also reviewed sixty-four books written by LDS writers—thirty-nine of these were produced by RLDS reviewers, fifteen by LDS reviewers, and ten by non-Mormon reviewers.[90]

Much of the new RLDS history resulted in a new historical and theological formulation that seemed more mainstream and liberal Protestant than restoration Mormon. That was the view of Roger D. Launius (b. 1954), who believed that because RLDS leaders accepted these new views, the church lost its familiar restoration and anti-Utah Mormon identity. It consequently became "adrift, without mission, ideal, or hope for the future.[91] As one of the younger RLDS scholars, Launius seemed less concerned about foundational issues (Was Joseph Smith a polygamist? Was the Book of Mormon an ancient document?) and instead pursued a range of less thorny topics. His writing on restoration themes included biography (Joseph Smith III; Alexander W. Doniphan, a Missouri moderate who was helpful to the Mormons; and James Fletcher, the Mormon administrator of the National Aeronautics and Space Administration); religious dissent; historiography; and early restoration events (Zion's Camp, the Kirtland temple, and the Ohio period).[92]

Historians Not Supported by the LDS or RLDS Churches

Some of the best new Mormon history was written at institutions not supported by either the LDS or RLDS churches, often by non-Mormons. One of the first and ablest of these scholars was Thomas F. O'Dea. Born to Roman Catholic parents of Irish extraction, O'Dea served in World War II and later attended Harvard University, graduating summa cum laude. He encountered the topic of Mormonism while doing graduate work in social relations. His paper on "Mormon values" was so well received that he was selected to do field study under the direction of the anthropologist Clyde Kluckhohn, then participating in the Comparative Study of Values in Five Cultures Project in New Mexico. O'Dea was assigned to examine Mormon culture in the community of Ramah, renamed "Rimrock" in O'Dea's later writing.[93]

O'Dea's fieldwork resulted in a series of publications: a 500-page, two-volume dissertation, four scholarly articles, a monograph on the sociology of Mormonism, and, most important, a book entitled *The Mormons*.[94] This work combined the talents of an anthropologist, sociologist, historian, theologian, and social critic and was one of the most thoughtful "outside" glimpses of the Mormon movement since John W. Gunnison's similarly titled book published a century earlier. Especially important was O'Dea's historical classification of the Mormons. Rising and developing in America, the religion had gone from "near-sect" to "near nation."[95] But was Mormonism more? Citing parallels with the rise of some world religions, O'Dea wondered if Mormonism was not a major new religion in the making—a young Judaism, Christianity, or Islam.[96]

O'Dea also sought to understand how Mormonism had avoided the "sectarian stagnation" common to many new religious movements and why it remained so dynamic. Part of the answer, O'Dea believed, lay with the religion's family and group life: Cumorah and its citizens had a wholesome vitality. Seeking to explain this phenomenon, O'Dea concluded that the Mormon people had taken such classical American routines as daily activity and work, which had been secularized by most Americans, and had "resacralized" them. As one scholar paraphrased O'Dea's thinking, the Mormons "bound sacred and secular so close together that the dividing line between them all but disappeared. Human endeavor . . . became a sacred and eternal reality, a matter of 'eternal progression.'"[97]

When interpreting Mormonism, O'Dea drew on sociological models, placed the Saints within their American setting, and classified and explained them in terms that emphasized their religious energy. Each of these approaches influenced later twentieth-century writing, including that of Klaus J. Hansen (b. 1931). Hansen, a post–World War II German émigré, first published *Quest for Empire: The Political Kingdom of God and the Council of Fifty in Mormon History*.[98] The book sought to explain Mormon kingdom building (the impulse that led O'Dea to make his "near-nation" categorization) by examining the working of a semisecret "Council of Fifty," allegedly responsible for early LDS political activity.[99] Hansen's *Mormonism and the American Experience* was a more complex piece of scholarship.[100] Using insights from such wide-ranging clinicians as Freud, Jung, and Adler and from a half-dozen modern anthropologists and sociologists, Hansen explored Mormonism's place in American culture. One important idea was how turn-of-the-century Mormonism transformed itself from being a defender of a radical and idiosyncratic kingdom of God to becoming a pillar of modern Americanism. Hansen argued that Mormons had experienced a social and intellectual "paradigm shift" similar to that experienced by the seventeenth-century New England Puritans. Mormon Saints, like Puritan saints, had their geographical and psychological "errand into the wilderness" that changed them.[101]

Mark P. Leone's *Roots of Modern Mormonism* was a modern anthropologist's view of the religious movement albeit with a Marxist interpretation. Using historical sources and "ethnographic observations," Leone sought to show how Mormonism, as a religious minority, was "created, maintained, and changed." Like Hansen, Leone was struck by Mormonism's late nineteenth-century transformation, which Leone saw pejoratively. The shift from theocratic Mormonism to modern Mormonism left the movement in a "colonial" state of "memorylessness," adaptable to change but rudderless and forgetful of its past. Having lost touch with their roots, the Mormons became, in Leone's view, culturally eviscerated—a "powerless people in modern society."[102]

Leone drew on the emerging "religious studies" literature—works, like O'Dea's pioneering effort, that often used comparative and behavioral models to describe the rise and development of "new religions." The scholar who led this new tendency in Mormon studies was Jan Shipps (b. 1929), one of the leading non-LDS scholars of Mormonism as the century closed. Shipps, a native of the American rural South, came upon Mormon studies and academia relatively late in life. In 1960, she began studying Mormon culture when her husband accepted an appointment at Utah State University in Logan. "What I knew about Mormonism when I started back to school at Utah State [University] was limited to the knowledge one could gain from reading news magazines and the *Reader's Digest*," she later admitted.[103]

Several years later, Shipps left Logan with a bachelor's degree and a desire to place her growing knowledge of Mormonism into some kind of inclusive design. Could her "kaleidoscopic vision of Mormonism" be transformed into a unified pattern so that "nothing would be left out?"[104] The quest led to M.A. and Ph.D. degrees in history from the University of Colorado, where her thesis and dissertation, which discussed Mormon political involvement, left her unsatisfied. Seeking a wider perspective, Shipps surveyed the sociological literature that dealt with the formation and classification of new religious movements.

Even this new terrain left her dissatisfied. To Shipps, such terms as *sect, denomination,* and *cult,* while descriptive, were not sufficiently comprehensive. Nor did the terms *church* and *religious movement* explain Mormonism's diversity.[105] Eventually Shipps concluded that only a more significant and encompassing concept would do. Shipps finally concluded that Mormonism represented a "new religious tradition." As Judaism spawned Christianity, modern Christianity had given rise to Mormonism with its open canon, living prophets, and a unique religious history.[106]

Shipps presented this insight in *Mormonism: The Story of a New Religious Tradition.*[107] Using the theories and comparative models of contemporary religious studies, Shipps argued that Mormonism followed a pattern typical of the rise of other new religious traditions: it emerged during a time of cultural crisis when many Americans had lost faith in the prevailing Christian institutions, and it proclaimed a new religious dispensation. During the pivotal 1880s and 1890s, it preserved itself by surrendering plural marriage and the political kingdom—impediments to Mormonism's cultural integration and accommodation. Shipps argued that in this last pursuit Mormonism had moved from "sacred time" to "ordinary time"—from the spiritual illusion of a "religious cult" to the practical and conservative reality of an established tradition.

Shipps refused to be drawn into the old faith arguments that had earlier polarized the writing of LDS history. These she "bracketed out." This approach was partly a "conscious scholarly strategy" to provide intellectual distance for study. But a personal equation was also at play. Whether the

"Latter-day Saints are or are not correct when they bear their formulaic testimonies that 'Mormonism is true' is simply not on my agenda of things to
try to find out," she admitted.[108] Nevertheless, the tone of her narrative was
warm. Like other new Mormon history writers, she adopted a behaviorist
historicism that took the faith claims of her historical actors at their word,
to be studied as artifacts, not necessarily to be believed. The technique, she
believed, allowed her to see the restoration movement "*as perceived from the
inside*"—that is, how the Saints themselves thought and believed.[109] Her
method was so thorough (and characteristic of her personality) that she came
to view herself as an LDS "inside-outsider."[110]

By the end of the twentieth century, Mormon studies were using the sophisticated methods of the social sciences, especially those drawn from sociology and religion. The result was the publication of hundreds of articles
and books, many of which were more descriptive of contemporary LDS life
than historical in nature.[111] Armand L. Mauss's *Angel and the Beehive: The
Mormon Struggle with Assimilation* drew on this literature in describing the
development of twentieth-century Mormonism.[112] Like O'Dea and the scholars who had followed him, Mauss understood that successful religious movements must navigate between two contrary impulses, which in their Mormon context Mauss identified as the Angel Moroni and the Beehive (each
statuary located in Salt Lake City near LDS headquarters). The first, which
requires a new religion to maintain its uniqueness, is characterized by "sepa-
rateness, peculiarity, and militance."[113] The second impulse, necessary for a
new religion's preservation, is characterized by the new religion's assimilation of the larger culture and by a desire for respectability. It was the first
impulse, Mauss believed, that dominated post–World War II Mormon history, which, in Mauss's view, threatened to make Mormonism into a narrow
and brittle movement, perhaps like rigid Protestant fundamentalism. The
trend left Mauss, a lifelong Mormon, feeling marginalized.

The historians who treated Utah statehood also discussed the theme of
Mormonism's dramatic change, as the church in the 1890s set aside old practices to secure political acceptance. Yale University's Howard R. Lamar considered Utah statehood in several articles and in a regional study of the
American southwest.[114] Jean Bickmore White, a professor at Weber State
University focused on the process of Utah's constitution making.[115] However,
Leo Edward Lyman's *Political Deliverance: The Mormon Quest for Utah Statehood* provided the fullest treatment.[116] Lyman, a professor of history at Victor Valley College in California, argued that church leaders achieved their
long-sought goal of Utah statehood by clever public relations, political ma-
neuvering, and, most important, unintended policy. Lyman believed that the

Mormon leaders first regarded their retreat from plural marriage and theocracy as tactical and temporary, but as these decisions gained momentum, they became permanent.

The scholars who were affiliated with non-LDS institutions contributed other perspectives besides Mormonism's growth and change. William Mulder, who began his career as an editor for the LDS *Improvement Era* before accepting a position at the University of Utah, insisted on a traditional approach to the craft: history should be a literary art, not simply a science.[117] Mulder proved his point by writing *Homeward to Zion: The Mormon Migration from Scandinavia* and coediting with A. R. Mortensen a collection of first-person accounts describing Mormon society and culture, *Among the Mormons: Historic Accounts by Contemporary Observers.*[118] Both books remain classics in Mormon historical literature, models of artful expression and scholarly research.[119]

Another bequest of the new Mormon history was historical geography. As early as 1960, Donald W. Meinig, a non-Mormon, upbraided his fellow geographers for ignoring history in their study of American regionalism. He cited Arrington's *Great Basin Kingdom* (a "penetrating analysis of regional distinctiveness") as a possible place to begin.[120] Five years later, Meinig produced an essay that was as important to Mormon geographers as Arrington's had been to narrative and economic historians: "The Mormon Culture Region: Strategies and Patterns in the Geography of the American West, 1847–1964."[121] Meinig argued that Mormonism had its own "culture region" consisting of three parts: (1) a dominant "core" area along the Wasatch Oasis, (2) a less dense "domain" covering much of Utah and southeastern Idaho, and (3) a still thinner "sphere" of culture that extended from eastern Oregon to Mexico.[122] Meinig's work suggested that Mormondom's spatial configuration reflected its historical development and that the disciplines of history and geography had much to learn from each other.

Other geographers followed. Lowell "Ben" Bennion (b. 1935), one of Meinig's former students at Syracuse University, was assigned to provide maps for the church's sixteen-volume sesquicentennial series and perhaps to complete a Mormon history atlas. When these projects were abandoned, Bennion turned to his own research and produced more than a dozen articles dealing with Mormon historical geography.[123] Even more productive was the BYU geographer Richard W. Jackson, who was especially interested in the geography of LDS nineteenth-century pioneering.[124] Richard V. Francaviglia's *Mormon Landscape: Existence, Creation, and Perception of a Unique Image in the American West* examined how the rural Mormon village had affected its "landscape," which Francaviglia defined in psychological and material terms.

According to Francaviglia, the material culture included weed-filled irrigation ditches, old Mormon fences, solid brick homes, tall poplars, gray or
brown barns, and half-built hay barns—features that could be seen throughout Mormon country.[125]

By the end of the twentieth century, LDS historical geography contributed
to two important compilations. Wayne L. Wahlquist's *Atlas of Utah* contained
cutting-edge layout design and research, while S. Kent Brown, Donald Q.
Cannon, and Richard H. Jackson's *Historical Atlas of Mormonism* focused
more narrowly on Mormon concerns.[126] Each contained useful maps, graphs,
and short articles that explained the development of the religious movement.

Yet another new historical approach was demography, or the statistical
study of populations. In 1976, the LDS Church established a research unit to
provide sociological and demographic analysis of its membership, which
several BYU professors continued as members of the university's Center for
Studies of the Family. Some of this work resulted in Marie Cornwall, Tim B.
Heaton, and Lawrence A. Young's *Contemporary Mormonism: Social Science
Perspectives,* which was oriented to contemporary social topics.[127] The Mormon Historical Demographic Project, centered at the University of Utah, was
more historically focused. This undertaking aimed at a cross-disciplinary
study of the Mormon past using computer-linked vital records, including
medical histories, death certificates, census records, and especially the LDS
genealogical "family group" sheets that contained data on 170,000 Utah families, or about 1.2 million individuals.[128]

When the Mormon Historical Demography Project was organized in 1973,
scholars hoped to use the statistical data base to study demographic structure and change, nuptiality, polygyny (polygamy), fertility, natural fertility,
mortality, migration, community studies, inheritance, family correlations as
seen in marriage and migration, genetic demography, and sex ratios.[129] In the
intervening years, more than a half-dozen scholars have produced a stream
of articles describing the social contours of Utah and Mormon history.[130]

Dean L. May (b. 1938), a former member of the LDS History Division and
later a professor of history at the University of Utah, was also interested in
statistical studies. His path-breaking article, "A Demographic Portrait of the
Mormons, 1830–1980," provided pre-Utah and Utah population figures, described nineteenth-century Utah ethnicity, and suggested that the "plural-
ization" and assimilation of Utah society began two decades before the supposed watershed of the 1890s. May's article also showed that the "Gentile"
population reached its proportional high tide in the 1920s before receding
because of high Mormon birthrates.[131] In another article, May studied the
southern Utah village of Kanab. He found that Kanab, compared with other

American towns, had an unusually high number of children and an uncommonly equal resource distribution, although like other frontier communities, it experienced a rapid mobility of its population.[132]

May's interest in quantitative and communal history led to his writing *Three Frontiers: Family, Land, and Society in the American West, 1850–1900*.[133] The book compared the Mormon village of Alpine, Utah, located about thirty-five miles south of Salt Lake City, with two other rural western communities—Sublimity, Oregon, and Middleton, Idaho. These "three frontiers" offered a comparative study of American town life. In Alpine, everyone had small fields and was poor, but because of their Mormon ideals and community associations, the villagers enjoyed a community life that bound them together as a people and to Alpine as a place. Uncomfortable with modern America's social fragmentation, May offered Alpine as an antidote to contemporary individualism.[134]

May was interested in examining the forces that had produced modern Americans, and he believed that the relatively fluid communities of the American West, of which Alpine, Sublimity, and Middleton were types, offered a social laboratory. Here, scholars could view "societies in the process of being reborn" as settlers from different backgrounds grappled "with the problems of building (or failing to build) a base of common identity and commitment."[135] May's contrarian interest in the nonurban West (contemporary scholars disdained agrarian and Turnerian frontier studies); his interest in demographic, comparative, and community study; and his interest in examining Mormonism in its wider cultural and historical context made him an important innovator of new Mormon history.[136]

Larry Logue's *Sermon in the Desert: Belief and Behavior in Early St. George, Utah* also used the historical tools of demography and community history.[137] Logue found that the Saints' practices (behavior) closely followed their theology (beliefs). He was also interested in the nineteenth-century Mormon cultural dichotomy that placed side-by-side the opposing forces of Americanism and separatism. But instead of defining separatism solely as political kingdom building, as many previous scholars had done, Logue saw it as having an ideological dimension that was expressed in "antimodern" social practice. During the first years after settlement, the St. George Saints married at a younger age than their American counterparts, had a high rate of plural marriage (in 1880 perhaps two out of five active LDS households were polygamous),[138] and had high levels of childbearing. Yet the Mormons also possessed a latent Americanism that, after the federal prosecutions forced an end to kingdom building, allowed them to enter modern society successfully.[139]

Charles S. Peterson (b. 1927) was another important social historian who was drawn to the study of Mormon community life. Peterson, the director of the Utah State Historical Society, a professor of history at Utah State University, and the editor of the *Western Historical Quarterly,* was a prolific author whose work included *Utah: A Bicentennial History.*[140] The theme that seemed most compelling to Peterson was the village life of his own origins, partly because of his democratic hope that LDS history might increasingly focus on "humble and obscure people" instead of Salt Lake City's governing authorities and elites.[141] Peterson pursued this interest in a series of essays and in his book *Take Up Your Mission: Mormon Colonizing along the Little Colorado River, 1870–1900,* which told the story of Mormon settlement on the Little Colorado River in Arizona.[142] It was in such regions as this, Peterson believed, that Mormon peculiarity peaked, long after Salt Lake City yielded to the forces of cultural accommodation.

As the twentieth century grew to a close, three historians represented the diversity of the institutional outsiders—one was a non-Mormon scholar, another a Mormon conservative, and the third an LDS excommunicate. Lawrence Foster (b. 1947), the first, was the son of overseas Methodist missionaries and a man of earnest religious feeling. "My goal," he later said of his historical writing, "was not so much to convert across faith lines but to encourage others to appreciate and better understand the universal values within their own heritage—to become *better* Methodists, Catholics, Jews, Buddhists, Mormons, or whatever."[143] Although Mormon themes had interested him, it was not until he encountered the human complexities described in modern Mormon historical writing that he found himself "baffled," "challenged," and driven in his study. An internship at the LDS Historical Department during the summer of 1974—a time of new friendships and investigation of sources then readily accessible—was "one of the most exciting and rewarding periods of my life." He left Salt Lake City wanting to show "the most rampant skeptic" the importance of religion generally and Mormonism in particular. Perhaps he could even nudge Mormonism to "see itself more clearly and move toward the development of its full potential as a world religion," he later wrote.[144]

Like so many of his era, Foster sought a cure to modern rootlessness in the social concept of community. More specifically, he explored family and especially marriage relationships in the context of nonmainstream, institutional religion. His book *Religion and Sexuality: Three American Communal Experiments of the Nineteenth Century* and its allied volume, *Women, Family, and Utopia: Communal Experiments of the Shakers, the Oneida Community, and the Mormons,* explored the "enlarged" (read: nonmonogamist), community-unifying family relationships of the Oneida Perfectionists, the

Shakers, and the Mormons.[145] Each book sought to combine an outsider's critical judgment with an insider's sympathy.

The Columbia University professor Richard L. Bushman (b. 1931), a prize-winning historian of early American culture, only occasionally turned to Mormon themes.[146] When he did, it was with the assurance of a settled religious belief. "I do believe," he spoke of his Mormonism. "That is a given of my nature." He also admitted to an intellectual independence ("I have always thought it possible that virtually anything taught and believed in the academy could be wrong.").[147] These traits were manifest in his *Joseph Smith and the Beginnings of Mormonism,* another of the History Division's intended sesquicentennial volumes and the first major treatment of Mormonism's early years since B. H. Roberts's work fifty years earlier.[148] Bushman supported the church's traditional interpretation on many uncertain historical points of young Joseph Smith's life and mission. The book also appeared to respond to Fawn Brodie's naturalistic portrait of Mormonism's founding prophet. In Bushman's view, Joseph Smith and Mormonism were genuinely religious.

While conservative and traditional, Bushman's book also explored difficult issues. On the question of Smith's various versions of his "First Vision," Bushman concluded that the boy first viewed his experience as a religious awakening. Only later, as a seasoned churchman, did he understand the epiphany heralded a new dispensation. On the still more vexing problem of young Smith's treasure hunting, Bushman argued that Smith, once he began his religious mission, outgrew the magic world of his New England countryside. In making this argument, Bushman blurred one of the divides that had hindered an understanding of Mormon origins since the publication of E. D. Howe's *Mormonism Unvailed* 150 years earlier. Adapting providential history, Bushman saw Smith both as a youthful treasure hunter and, later, as a divine prophet.

The third representative noninstitutional historian was D. Michael Quinn (b. 1944), who described his heritage as a "split-identity": his mother was a seventh-generation Mormon, his father a Roman Catholic of Mexican extraction. It was not this birthright that haunted his adolescence, Quinn said, but "an intense personal relationship with God," which he described in the providential language of the third person: "This young man seemed to have constant experience with a presence from God in comfort and revelation 'like a fire burning' within him."[149] Beginning a career as a historian, Quinn joined Arrington's History Division, which gave him access to LDS records. He next secured a Ph.D. at Yale University and prepared himself, according to his own account, to face the opposition that might arise from his controversial research.[150] Upon his graduation, although he labeled himself as "an honest apologist for the Mormon faith and experience," he found himself at odds with church leaders.[151] After making a point-by-point refutation of the anti-new-Mormon-history arguments of the general authorities Ezra Taft Benson and Boyd K. Packer and after exploring other issues to the discomfort of church authorities, Quinn left a teaching position at Brigham Young University. Seven years later, in 1988, he was excommunicated from the church for reasons that were never disclosed.[152]

During his tenure at BYU, Quinn published *J. Reuben Clark: The Church Years,* a biography of an influential member of the LDS First Presidency.[153] Quinn's second book, *Early Mormonism and the Magic World View,* argued that many early Mormons held magical beliefs, including Joseph Smith and his family, the witnesses to the Book of Mormon, and nearly half of the original Quorum of the Twelve. Further, Quinn argued that Smith carried these beliefs into his mature years. Rather than view these conclusions as destructive of the faith, Quinn believed folk magic was a part of Smith's larger religious heritage.[154]

Quinn followed with two volumes loosely devoted to the LDS leadership: *The Mormon Hierarchy: Origins of Power,* which dealt with the church up to 1847, and *The Mormon Hierarchy: Extensions of Power,* focusing on the years from 1847 to the modern era.[155] The books were filled with encyclopedic data that were often new and untraditional. In addition to the narrative passages of each manuscript, Quinn presented extensive notes and appendices, including an impressionistic LDS chronology that reflected his personal interests. While clearly aimed at a radical and more human interpretation of the Mormon experience, the two volumes lacked a unifying thesis or method, even on the central question of Mormon elites. Data often went unexplained or without a context. "My study is primarily descriptive," explained Quinn. "I leave it to others to provide the comparative analysis and new insights."[156]

Quinn's *Same-Sex Dynamics among Nineteenth-Century Americans: A Mormon Example* was devoted to a discussion of Mormon same-sex beliefs and practices (the word *homosexuality* was too recent and too narrow, noted Quinn).[157] The volume shared many characteristics with several of Quinn's earlier works. Once again Quinn was drawn to controversy and showed disdain for the "silence" of traditional, public-relations LDS history. Once more, there were heavy footnotes and a chronology of selected events. And once more, Quinn's conclusions at times overreached his evidence. Yet *Same-Sex Dynamics* was an important book, probably Quinn's best to date. It considered Mormonism's wider American context, had new information and views, and treated a topic that was once taboo.[158]

Quinn suggested that his books were not influenced by any theoretical model. Yet, if only by unconscious sharing of his cultural environment, Quinn had much in common with avant garde, twentieth-century American history. His focus on power structures, nontraditional religion (folk magic), women (plural marriage), and same-sex attraction had several parallels with the new social history being written by the other historians. Specifically, Quinn's work seemed influenced by such theorists as Paul de Man (a powerful presence at Yale while Quinn studied there) and by the postmodern deconstructionists Jacques Derrida and Michel Foucault. Like these thinkers, Quinn conveyed a mistrust of elites and power, examined history's "underside" and people who populated it, highlighted unusual and piecemeal topics rather than general ones, and often appeared unconcerned about traditional narrative form. If not a historical deconstructionist, Quinn clearly hoped to create a new view of the Mormon past—and use new methods in defining that past.

Scholarly "Helps": Reference Works, Professional Organizations, and Publishers

Another mark of the new Mormon history was the ancillary resources that it generated. By the end of the twentieth century, important reference works began to appear. In addition to Davis Bitton's diary guide and the atlases of Utah and Mormonism, already mentioned, two encyclopedias summarized new Mormon history research. *Utah History Encyclopedia,* edited by Allan Kent Powell, provided brief articles and biographical sketches on a wide range of LDS topics.[159] Daniel H. Ludlow edited the five-volume *Encyclopedia of Mormonism,* which contained a half-dozen lengthy articles summarizing church history and scores of shorter topical articles.[160] (Many of the latter had the unusual quality of being written by "lay" authors.) Chad J. Flake's *Mormon Bibliography, 1830–1930* listed the printed material of Mormonism's first century (over 10,000 items) and included valuable tracing information about where these titles, many of them rare, could be found.[161]

Another important reference book was *Mormon Americana: A Guide to Sources and Collections in the United States.*[162] Edited by David J. Whittaker, the book included twenty essays that described the main LDS source repositories in the United States and their Mormon holdings. Whittaker also included a dozen descriptive and bibliographic articles on specialized topics. For neophytes as well as veterans of LDS research, *Mormon Americana* was often the place to begin working on a topic.

The computer age brought electronic tools that provided powerful computer-assisted searching capability. The commercial firm Infobases marketed the CD-ROM *LDS Collectors Library,* a database that contained early LDS newspapers, membership records, general authorities' sermons, and more than a half-dozen standard Mormon reference works. Still more important for historical research was Infobases' CD-ROM *LDS Family History Suite.* This electronic archive had primary and secondary works, including material previously unavailable in printed form: The Utah State Historical Society's *Guide to Archives and Manuscript Collections in Selected Utah Repositories* listed the primary source holdings of Utah's leading libraries and universities; Milton V. Backman Jr.'s *Writings of Early Latter-day Saints and Their Contemporaries* provided edited transcriptions of over two hundred autobiographies, diaries, and journals of Mormonism's pre-Utah, first generation; and Susan Easton Black's six-volume *Early Members of the Reorganized Church of Jesus Christ of Latter Day Saints* and her fifty-volume *Membership of the Church of Jesus Christ of Latter-day Saints: 1830–1848* were valuable collections of biographical data.[163]

Following the lead of Infobases' products, the church-owned Deseret Book Company marketed its own CD-ROM compilation, which it called *Gospe-Link.*[164] This rival collection provided readers electronic access to the rich publishing collection of the Deseret Book Company and to newspapers and magazines, including the *Improvement Era.* By the beginning of the new century, the Infobases and GospeLink rivals were consolidated under the ownership of Deseret Book, which promised a new edition of electronic material drawing upon the strengths of each.

Two other CD-ROM collections appeared. The *Utah History Suite* (the second edition of the *Utah Centennial History Suite*) was issued in 1999 and featured many of the issues of the *Utah Historical Quarterly* (volumes 1–23 [1928–51], 40–50 [1968–78], and 63–66 [1991–94]). The *Utah History Suite* also provided complete runs of *History Blazer,* a series that described various events in Utah history; *Beehive History,* an annual publication intended for high school students; and the electronic text of twenty-nine county histories that the Utah State Legislature had commissioned to mark the state's centennial. Even more important was the *New Mormon Studies CD-ROM: A Comprehensive Resource Library.* This remarkable collection included runs of *Sunstone, Dialogue,* the nonfiction titles of Signature Books, some of the Mormon-related books published by the University of Illinois Press, and such miscellany as early editions of LDS scripture, periodicals, and sermons.[165]

These electronic editions were products "in the making," often fragmentary and inconsistent in the material they included. However, they had the virtue of providing a lot of source material and ease of access. They clearly demonstrated how the face of historical study and research was changing at the end of the twentieth century.

The diverse writers and compilers of the new Mormon history movement, whatever their LDS, RLDS, or non-Mormon inclination, found a common bond in the Mormon History Association.[166] The association's annual three-day convention, usually held near an RLDS or LDS population center, had joint sessions with fifty or more papers—"an abundant smorgasbord with various offerings to fit different tastes," wrote Davis Bitton on the MHA's twenty-fifth anniversary.[167] Most presentations seemed theologically and historically middle-of-the-road.[168] Another feature of the MHA meeting was the endowed Obert C. and Grace A. Tanner lecture delivered annually in a plenary session. The lecture highlighted a prominent non-Mormon scholar who spoke on a LDS topic from the perspective of his or her previous study.

The Mormon History Association attracted a diverse group. An early 1990 survey found that three out of four MHA members were male, although the number of women was on the rise. Most MHA members were middle age: 25 percent were in their forties, and nearly 40 percent were between fifty and sixty-five. Another 15 percent were older than sixty-five. An important characteristic was the mix of professionals and amateurs. Only half of the organization's members could be identified as "professional," and many of these were drawn from business, industry, and government. Only 25 percent of the MHA members were academics, and many of these held positions outside the field of history.[169] The organization, with its wide-ranging clientele, suggested the interest that history held for many LDS and RLDS rank and file.

The Mormon History Association encouraged scholarship, in part by funding an impressive list of awards given at the annual convention—"an embarrassment of riches" for a small professional association, suggested one veteran member.[170] But these annual awards, including those given for the best dissertation, the best article, the best documentary book, and the best general book, encouraged professional standards and often rewarded promising and innovative scholarship.[171] Some MHA members found the organization's bequest to be more informal. The association offered friendship, networking, and acceptance—precisely the kind of emotional space that Mormonism's interwar "lost generation" of intellectuals had been without and, as a result, had been left intellectually bereft. Many MHA members reported that their informal discussions were "the choicest experience of the conventions."[172]

The MHA also promoted scholarship by publishing Mormon history. Its newsletter printed primarily contemporary notices, but it also issued material useful to research. For instance, the newsletter frequently published topical bibliographies, including a dozen compiled by David J. Whittaker. Of greater impact, in 1974 the MHA began publishing the *Journal of Mormon*

History, which established itself as one of the most important periodicals dealing with Mormon historical studies. The journal has printed almost two hundred historical studies and the annual MHA presidential address and Tanner lecture. It is now published twice a year and contains book reviews and occasional review essays.

Brigham Young University Studies was another important outlet for historical studies. First issued in the 1920s as a vehicle for Lowry Nelson's regional monographs, *BYU Studies* was revived in 1959 and has since published four issues annually.[173] During the 1960s, the periodical reserved one issue each year for Mormon history, and although this practice has stopped, its editors continue to show a strong interest in historical material. It has printed more than five hundred history-related articles. The journal also features "The Historians' Corner," an occasional section devoted to short miscellany, especially historical documents. Cautious in content yet often forthright, *BYU Studies* describes itself as "dedicated to the conviction that the spiritual and the intellectual are complementary avenues of knowledge."

If *BYU Studies* represented conservative new Mormon historical literature and the *Journal of Mormon History* the ideological center, another scholarly journal increasingly positioned itself on the liberal left. *Dialogue: A Journal of Mormon Thought* began in 1966 as an "independent national quarterly established to express Mormon culture and examine the relevance of religion to secular life." Could LDS historical and religious heritage be brought to bear on modern experience, especially for those who felt adrift from the "larger world"?[174] Polling readers' preferences, editors discovered that such a "dialogue" often meant history.[175] The magazine published as many history-related articles as did *BYU Studies,* many with an ideological and theoretical edge absent in other Mormon periodicals.

Other scholarly outlets for new Mormon history included *Courage* and the *John Whitmer Historical Journal,* the RLDS publications already discussed. In addition, the Mormon church published the *Improvement Era,* which in 1971 was reconstituted as the *Ensign.* When publishing history, these periodicals specialized in short, devotional pieces. Still another outlet for Mormon history writing was the privately published *Sunstone.* Established in 1977 as a student magazine and taking its name from the "sunstones" that had once decorated the Nauvoo Temple ("Nauvoo temple, light, truth, intelligence, sun/Son," explained the founding editor, Scott G. Kenney[176]), *Sunstone* soon broadened its audience and published many short articles on history, sometimes with a progressive bent. Finally, *Exponent II* specialized in publishing LDS women's history. Taking its name from the Mormon women's magazine of the late nineteenth century and early twentieth, *Exponent II* was a women's forum that navigated between the "dual platforms of Mormonism and Feminism."[177] It was a formula that produced liberal Mormonism and conservative feminism.

A similar number of publishers issued books written from the perspective of new Mormon history, including such university-affiliated presses as Brigham Young University Press, the University of Utah Press, and the Utah State University Press. A newcomer to this group was Brigham Young University Studies, which by the mid-1990s had become a publisher of Mormon book-length material.[178] Still another publisher was Signature Books, owned by George D. Smith, an LDS liberal activist who published material largely in his ideological image. At the other end of the spectrum was the church-owned Deseret Book Company, which continued to print a large number of titles for a popular and semipopular LDS audience. Some of Deseret Book's best historical works were documentary collections, a printing category that minimized controversy.

The most surprising and successful entry into the Mormon publishing market was the geographically distant University of Illinois Press. As Elizabeth Dulany, the former associate director, noted, the press "discovered that there was a market for Mormon history books, [and] that there was a need for them."[179] By the end of the century, the University of Illinois Press had issued more than forty-five LDS titles and had another five in the process of publication. "Simply put," said a University of Illinois Press self-appraisal that seemed accurate, "many of the standard and seminal works in Mormon studies are Illinois publications."[180] Dallin H. Oaks and Marvin S. Hill's *Carthage Conspiracy: The Trial of the Accused Assassins of Joseph Smith* became one of the press's best sellers, with over 28,000 copies in print.[181] The press further added to its Mormon credentials by reissuing several important titles forsaken by other publishers.

Assessment and the "Outsiders' View"

The new Mormon history movement had achieved some noteworthy successes. Mormonism had two new general histories, and gender and topical histories were proliferating. Moreover, for the first time carefully edited primary sources and reference guides were available in print and in electronic format. Even a half-dozen volumes of the canceled sesquicentennial series had been published.

The volume of work was also impressive. In the fifteen years from the end of World War II to 1960, historians produced about as many historical works as had been written during the previous half-century—about 1,200 titles.

Thereafter totals accelerated: almost 1,100 titles during the ten-year period from 1960 to 1969; more than 2,100 from 1970 to 1979; and more than 2,700 from 1980 to 1989. Category totals were also significant. Since 1945, 1,700 graduate degrees had been granted in Mormon-related topics, including more than 450 Ph.D. degrees. At the same time, historians wrote 6,000 articles and chapters in books, and 1,700 books. Mormon history had become a prolific division of western and American history, requiring its own specialists.

More important, however, were the qualitative changes. If the pre-1950 literature was largely devotional, popular, or polemical in nature, the newer writing had the texture of new methods and new interpretations, with some of the best of the writing reflecting important trends in the social sciences and the growing field of religious studies. With major repositories available for use, new facts and new conclusions followed. It is not too much to say that the new Mormon history created a transformed historical landscape.

Of course, the movement's legacy was open to question. Mormon traditionalists had only begrudging praise and more often criticism. After the collapse of the History Division and the public censure of historians by Ezra Taft Benson and Boyd K. Packer, a growing conservative critique began, generally along two fronts. Religious educators, for one, repeated the concerns of Benson and Packer and isolated themselves by publishing in nonrefereed publications and by participating in professional groups of their own making. The process often left them at the intellectual margins.[182]

Second, historians were increasingly attacked by conservative academics led by a few BYU political scientists. In their view, the new Mormon history was a form of secularism, and to prove their point, they claimed the authors were guilty of employing loose working assumptions that were drawn, perhaps unconsciously, from nineteenth-century positivism.[183] This criticism went beyond a debate about methods and philosophy; it implicitly sought to reestablish a faith story that in its most extreme form represented an antihistorism.[184] Stung by these views, some new Mormon historians defended themselves and counterattacked.[185]

Historians did not have to go beyond their own ranks to hear criticism. The comments of fellow historians at times paralleled those of the neotraditionalists. For example, Klaus Hansen was unsettled by the "behavioralism" adopted by Thomas G. Alexander, Richard L. Bushman, and Jan Shipps, perhaps more as a matter of logic than because of his own theology or philosophy. Hansen believed that the behavioral approach of accepting the religious statements of historical figures at face value allowed writers to disregard questions of ultimate "truth." How could Shipps (a nonbeliever) and

Bushman (a believer) "write the same kind of history?" Hansen asked. In making this criticism, Hansen reminded colleagues that Joseph Smith had challenged "modern relativist metaphysical assumptions emphasizing process and consciousness," precisely the kind of thing that some new Mormon historians seemed to be doing.[186]

Bushman outlined his own concerns about the new writing at the beginning of the movement. Bushman believed that the religious faith of Mormon historians was seldom reflected in their writing, and he had an explanation: LDS historians were not just members of the Mormon faith; they were also middle-class American intellectuals trained in the American higher education system. Bushman argued that as a result "the secular, liberal, establishmentarian, status-seeking, decent, tolerant values of the university govern us . . . far more than our faith." Although Bushman understood that these human and secular qualities were "not without merit," he urged Mormons to work to create a "faithful history" in which distinctive Mormon values might have a central role.[187] Although widely quoted, Bushman's essay had little perceptible impact on actual writing.

Bushman continued this theme in another essay. Traditional history had been a battleground where combatants fought over issues of "cosmic significance," Bushman argued, and as a result it aroused passion. In contrast, the new Mormon history was strikingly different. Should citizens of the nineteenth century be transported to the twentieth, Bushman thought that they would certainly view the new writing as "not only dispassionate but insipid and, really, somewhat irrelevant—in short, academic." This last adjective was telling. In Bushman's view, it was the academy, not the church, that had become the historians' nourishing environment.[188] It is not clear whether Bushman meant these observations as criticism, but they were an early articulation of the growing conservative critique. According to this view, the new Mormon history lacked grand themes and failed to excite emotion, including, ironically, religious feeling. Had it lost touch with its main audience—church members—and become an inbred discipline composed of likeminded but relatively few people?

Another critic, Charles S. Peterson, argued that the new history had proven to be a dead-end. Despite its moderate spirit of "acquiescence and well-being," it had failed to gain the support of LDS leaders (not a single Mormon leader spoke publicly in its favor). Peterson believed that it had also failed to engage the interest of mainstream American historians—perhaps because it was "too defensive" and "assertive" and therefore idiosyncratic. Without the support of the Mormon church and isolated from its peers, the new Mormon history had failed, and Peterson seemed ready to lay the blame on its grandsire, Arrington's *Great Basin Kingdom*. Despite the book's great strengths, Peterson believed that it had helped create a nonmainstream, "exceptionalist" history that ultimately was self-defeating. In effect, the *Great Basin Kingdom* was responsible for beginning and ending its own historical movement.[189]

The RLDS historian Roger D. Launius, another late twentieth-century observer, sensed that after more than forty years the new Mormon history suffered a "deceleration" of energy and suggested several reasons to explain this, including "short-sighted and anti-intellectual church officials," "restrictive archival practices," and "aging professionals" who were not being replaced by a new generation of scholars. Launius's main concern, however, was the "ghettoization" of Mormon scholars. Like Peterson, he believed that Mormon studies had become too provincial, and he urged a new research agenda more in line with mainstream historical study—more work involving race, ethnicity, class, and gender and an avoidance of traditional Mormon topics that focused on church origins, lineal development, and elites.[190]

Had the new Mormon history produced a peculiar history for a peculiar people? While its defenders could argue that any major field in history is necessarily exceptionalist, having its own norms and concerns, it was also true that some Mormon writers failed to balance the "exceptions" and "definitions" of their craft with the larger views of their historical profession. The reason was not difficult to find. From the beginning, self-discovery had motivated many of them; they wanted to understand their religious and cultural heritage. This impulse produced a history that was moderate and practical, and it allowed many educated church members to find an intellectually acceptable faith that permitted them to continue as "active" Mormons. But it also produced a kind of history that could be introspective and self-confining.

While some writers of Mormon studies found it difficult to reach beyond their culture, this same tendency was also true of many non-Mormons when they attempted to discuss Mormonism. As early as 1844, Robert Baird's *Religion in America* had divided churchgoers into evangelical and nonevangelical camps and had placed Mormons (along with the equally disfavored Roman Catholics) in the latter category. For the next hundred years, such historians of religion as Philip Schaff, Shirley Jackson Case, and William Warren Sweet used Baird's approach to reveal their preference for frontier, Baptist-Methodist religious groups that seemed "most American."[191] Reflecting this attitude, Melvile Dewey's first books on library classification put the Mormons in a non-Christian category.

The tendency to marginalize Mormonism or at least to be confused by it continued into the twentieth century. For example Sidney Ahlstrom's *Religious History of the American People* asked if Joseph Smith's revelation was "a sect, a mystery cult, a new religion, a church, a people, a nation, or an American subculture." For Ahlstrom, Mormonism appeared to have been "at different times and places . . . all of these."[192] Of the major surveys of American religion published near the turn of the century, only the most recent edition of Winthrop S. Hudson's *Religion in America: An Historical Account of the Development of American Religious Life* seemed to offer Mormonism a more mainline and less prejudicial taxonomy.[193]

Two books published in the 1990s showed the outsider's point of view, and each stressed Mormonism's distinctiveness. The first was Harold Bloom's *American Religion: The Emergence of the Post-Christian Nation*.[194] Unlike many twentieth-century historians who focused on Mormon pioneering and kingdom building, Bloom was drawn to the religious story of Mormonism, which he labeled "*materia poetica*." He was especially interested in the peculiar Mormon doctrines of plural marriage, the literal kingdom of God, baptism for the dead, and the nature of God, some of which Bloom thought had parallels in the Jewish esoteric tradition. He found Joseph Smith to be an authentic "religious genius," who had created a new faith and a "new people," not unlike the Jews or Muslims, and whose future seemed to have a "titanic design." At first glance, it was an unblushing argument that only the most faithful Mormon might have put forth. However, Bloom's context was "post-Christian" religious movements, which, once more, put the Mormons beyond the pale of traditional Christianity.[195] Bloom emphasized Mormonism's Americanism, not its Christian belief.

John L. Brooke's *Refiner's Fire: The Making of Mormon Cosmology, 1644–1944* also looked to unusual byways to explain and define Mormon uniqueness, in this case the hermetic tradition of the Renaissance. Bloom's "selective reinterpretation of the founding story of Mormonism" exposed Brooke to the charge of historical determinism and reductionism.[196] Yet both Brooke and Bloom had the advantage of offering fresh insight while looking beyond old interpretative categories.

What lies ahead? Despite the productivity of new Mormon historians, much remains to be done. Twentieth-century Mormon history awaits the same attention that has been given to that of the nineteenth century. The field still lacks scholarly biographies, especially for those who were not church presidents and those who lived in the last century. The church's expansion beyond Utah's Wasatch Front is another gap. History of the "common people," studies of life stages (childhood, adolescence, parenthood, the elderly), gender and feminist critiques, and the impact of technology on the church and its members are further examples of work that remains. How have Mormons reacted to their civil and cultural setting? Most telling, Mormon studies require synthesis. Since the writing of the Allen and Leonard's *Story of the Latter-day Saints,* first published in 1976 and updated sixteen years later, no similar work has appeared to take advantage of the new Mormon history's fecundity.

Perhaps these and other prospective projects will be completed using the middle-of-the-road methods and views of the new Mormon history, which still has momentum. But other approaches will certainly appear as well. Future writing may reflect the contradictory criticism that has been leveled. New books may be more faithful and devout, less detached, and more scriptural in tone, just like the pattern suggested by the church's conservatives. Or writers may create a more secular, hardheaded, professional, and interdisciplinary history, more like regional and national norms. It is hoped that new approaches will reduce the insular nature that so often has afflicted the study of the LDS past. This much is certain: any departure will reflect the concerns of Mormon society and intellectuals, for every historical generation writes its story in its own image, and that image, as the church enters the new century, is still in the process of becoming.

Notes

1. Moses Rischin, "Beyond the Great Divide: Immigration and the Last Frontier," *Journal of American History* 55 (June 1968): 49.

2. For Rischin's more extended comments, including the material quoted here, see his "The New Mormon History," *American West* 6 (March 1969): 49. See also Moses Rischin, "Beyond the Great Divide: Immigration and the Last Frontier," *Journal of American History* 55 (June 1968): 49. For another early use of the phrase, Robert A. Rees, "'Truth Is the Daughter of Time': Notes toward an Imaginative Mormon History," *Dialogue: A Journal of Mormon Thought* 6 (Autumn–Winter 1971): 15–22.

3. Robert B. Flanders, "Some Reflections on the New Mormon History," *Dialogue: A Journal of Mormon Thought* 9 (Spring 1974): 35. It was Flanders's essay that especially popularized the expression "new Mormon history" for Mormon readers.

4. See especially Thomas G. Alexander, "Toward the New Mormon History: An Examination of the Literature on the Latter-day Saints in the Far West," in *Historians and the American West,* ed. Michael P. Malone (Lincoln: University of Nebraska Press, 1983), 344–68; and Thomas G. Alexander, "Historiography and the New Mormon History: A Historian's Perspective," *Dialogue: A Journal of Mormon Thought* 19 (Fall 1986): 25–49.

5. Leonard J. Arrington, "Scholarly Studies of Mormonism in the Twentieth Century," *Dialogue: A Journal of Mormon Thought* 1 (Spring 1966): 28.

6. John Higham, *Send These to Me: Jews and Other Immigrants in Urban America* (New York: Atheneum, 1975), vii.

7. Eugene E. Campbell, "A History of the Church of Jesus Christ of Latter-day Saints in California, 1846–1946" (Ph.D. diss., University of Southern California, 1952).

8. Richard D. Poll, Thomas G. Alexander, Eugene E. Campbell, and David E. Miller, eds., *Utah's History* (Provo, Utah: Brigham Young University Press, 1978); Eugene E. Campbell, *Establishing Zion: The Mormon Church in the American West, 1847–1869* (Salt Lake City: Signature Books, 1988).

9. As illustration, Campbell's award-winning article "Brigham Young's Outer Cordon— A Reappraisal," *Utah Historical Quarterly* 41 (Summer 1973): 221–53, challenged the long-held idea that Brigham Young established a ring of outer colonies to protect the main core of Mormon settlements. It was simply happenstance, said Campbell.

10. Leonard J. Arrington, "Historian as Entrepreneur: A Personal Essay," *BYU Studies* 17 (Winter 1977): 194.

11. Ibid., 197. For another statement on the importance of southern regionalism, see Leonard J. Arrington, "In Praise of Amateurs," *Journal of Mormon History* 17 (1991): 35–42.

12. Leonard J. Arrington, *Adventures of a Church Historian* (Urbana: University of Illinois Press, 1998), 26.

13. Ibid.

14. Arrington, "Historian as Entrepreneur," 196–98.

15. For a listing of Arrington's writing, see David J. Whittaker, comp., "Leonard James Arrington (1917–1999): A Bibliography," *Journal of Mormon History* 25 (Fall 1999): 11–45.

16. Leonard J. Arrington, *Great Basin Kingdom: An Economic History of the Latter-day Saints, 1830–1900* (Cambridge, Mass.: Harvard University Press, 1958).

17. Ibid., ix.

18. Leonard J. Arrington, "Reflections on the Founding and Purpose of the Mormon History Association, 1965–1983," *Journal of Mormon History* 10 (1983): 101.

19. Arrington, "Historian as Entrepreneur," 200.

20. For Arrington's description of some of these contacts, see "The Founding of the LDS Church Historical Department, 1972," *Journal of Mormon History* 18 (Fall 1992): 41–47.

21. Between 1976 and 1991, MHA membership averaged 736, hitting a peak of 1,042 during 1980, the LDS sesquicentennial year. See Patricia Lyn Scott, James E. Crooks, and Sharon G. Pugsley, "'A Kinship of Interest': The Mormon History Association's Membership," *Journal of Mormon History* 18 (Spring 1992): 155, 170.

22. Impressed by Arrington, Tanner authorized the historian to regard his historical work as the "equivalent in importance to other major [church] assignments you have held." Arrington, "The Founding of the LDS Church Historical Department, 1972," 42.

23. Doctrine and Covenants 21:1, 47:1, 69:2–3, 85:1.

24. Arrington, "The Founding of the LDS Church Historical Department, 1972," 47–48.

25. Embarking on his new assignment, Arrington once more tried to steer a middle course. In August 1972, he wrote in his diary: "As a result of yesterday's meeting with the First Presidency I have been thinking and praying about my calling as Church Historian. . . . On the one hand, I am the *Church* historian and must seek to build testimonies, spread the Word, build the Kingdom. On the other hand, I am called to be a *historian,* which means that I must earn the respect of professional historians. What I write must be craftsmanlike, credible, and of good quality. This means that I stand on two legs— the leg of faith and the leg of reason. . . . May the Lord bless me to be honest, frank, and

fearless, when I must be honest, frank, and fearless; and may He bless me to be diplomatic and understanding when those qualities are required!" Leonard J. Arrington Diary, 8 August 1972, copy in Leonard J. Arrington Archive, Utah State University Library, permission given for use. See also Arrington, *Adventures of a Church Historian,* 94.

26. For an expression of Dyer's enthusiasm, see Alvin R. Dyer, "The Future of Church History," *Ensign* 2 (August 1972): 58–61.

27. "History Is Then—and Now: A Conversation with Leonard J. Arrington, Church Historian," *Ensign* 5 (July 1975): 11.

28. These slots were filled at various times by Maureen Ursenbach Beecher, Bruce D. Blumell, Jill Mulvay Derr, Ronald K. Esplin, William G. Harley, Richard L. Jensen, Gordon Irving, Dean C. Jessee, Glen M. Leonard, Dean L. May, Carol Cornwall Madsen, D. Michael Quinn, Gene A. Sessions, and Ronald W. Walker. For a brief sketch of the History Division's associates, see the preface to *Celebrating the LDS Past: Essays Commemorating the Twentieth Anniversary of the 1972 Founding of the LDS Church Historical Department's "History Division"* (Provo, Utah: Joseph Fielding Smith Institute for Church History, 1992), xi–xv.

29. Even a partial list of "fellows" is impressive: Paul L. Anderson, Danel W. Bachman, Lowell C. (Ben) Bennion, Alfred L. Bush, Lawrence C. Coates, Rebecca Cornwall (Bartholomew), Richard O. Cowan, Eugene England, B. Carmon Hardy, Scott Kenney, John S. McCormick, Max H. Parkin, Richard Sherlock, David J. Whittaker, and Linda P. Wilcox.

30. Arrington, "The Founding of the LDS Church Historical Department, 1972," 54–55. For the History Division's oral history program, see Arrington, "Historian as Entrepreneur," 207. For a list of the History Division's publications, see Davis Bitton, "Ten Years in Camelot: A Personal Memoir," *Dialogue: A Journal of Mormon Thought* 16 (Autumn 1983): 20–33.

31. Dean C. Jessee, ed., *Letters of Brigham Young to His Sons* (Salt Lake City: Deseret Book, 1974).

32. Leonard J. Arrington, Feramorz Y. Fox, and Dean L. May, *Building the City of God: Community and Cooperation among the Mormons* (Salt Lake City: Deseret Book, 1976).

33. Davis Bitton, *Guide to Mormon Diaries and Autobiographies* (Provo, Utah: Brigham Young University Press, 1977).

34. James B. Allen and Glen M. Leonard, *The Story of the Latter-day Saints* (Salt Lake City: Deseret Book, 1976).

35. Leonard J. Arrington and Davis Bitton, *The Mormon Experience: A History of the Latter-day Saints* (New York: Alfred A. Knopf, 1979).

36. Ezra Taft Benson, *The Gospel Teacher and His Message* (Salt Lake City[?]: Church Educational System[?], 1976), 11 ("our prophetic history"), 12 ("experimental systems" and "communal life"); Ezra Taft Benson, "God's Hand in Our Nation's History," in *1976 Devotional Speeches of the Year* (Provo, Utah: Brigham Young University Press, 1977), 310, 313; Benson's criticism was apparently aimed at passages in *Building the City of God* and *The Story of the Latter-day Saints.*

37. Boyd K. Packer, "'The Mantle Is Far, Far Greater than the Intellect,'" *BYU Studies* 21 (Summer 1981): 264, 268.

38. Richard Stephen Marshall, "The New Mormon History" (Senior honor's project summary, University of Utah, 1977).

39. For the insiders' view on the decline of the History Division, see Davis Bitton, "Ten Years in Camelot: A Personal Memoir," *Dialogue: A Journal of Mormon Thought* 16 (Autumn 1983): 9–33; and Arrington, *Adventures of a Church Historian,* 158–226.

40. Quoted in Arrington, "The Founding of the LDS Church Historical Department, 1972," 54.

41. Statement, authors' possession. See also Arrington, *Adventures of a Church Historian,* 149–50.

42. Leonard J. Arrington, *Brigham Young: American Moses* (New York: Alfred A. Knopf, 1985).

43. William G. Hartley, *"They Are My Friends": A History of the Joseph Knight Family, 1825–1850* (Provo, Utah: Grandin, 1986) and *My Best for the Kingdom: History and Autobiography of John Lowe Butler, a Mormon Frontiersman* (Salt Lake City: Aspen Books, 1993).

44. Maureen Ursenbach Beecher, *Eliza and Her Sisters* (Salt Lake City: Aspen Books, 1991); Eliza R. Snow, *The Personal Writings of Eliza Roxcy Snow,* ed. Maureen Ursenbach Beecher (Salt Lake City: University of Utah Press, 1995).

45. Ronald W. Walker, *Wayward Saints: The Godbeites and Brigham Young* (Urbana: University of Illinois Press, 1999).

46. Ronald W. Walker and Doris R. Dant, eds., *Nearly Everything Imaginable: The Everyday Life of Utah's Mormon Pioneers* (Provo, Utah: Brigham Young University Press, 1999).

47. Richard L. Jensen and Malcolm R. Thorp, eds., *Mormons in Early Victorian Britain* (Salt Lake City: University of Utah Press, 1989).

48. James B. Allen, Ronald K. Esplin, and David J. Whittaker, *Men with a Mission, 1837–1841: The Quorum of the Twelve Apostles in the British Isles* (Salt Lake City: Deseret Book, 1992).

49. They replaced Richard L. Evans, *A Century of "Mormonism" in Great Britain* (Salt Lake City: Deseret News, 1937). For other important books dealing with early British Mormonism, see Philip A. M. Taylor, *Expectations Westward: The Mormons and the Emigration of Their British Converts in the Nineteenth Century* (Edinburgh: Oliver and Boyd, 1965); James B. Allen and Thomas G. Alexander, eds., *Manchester Mormons: The Journal of William Clayton, 1840 to 1842* (Santa Barbara, Calif.: Peregrine Smith, 1974); and the popularly written V. Ben Bloxham, James R. Moss, and Larry C. Porter, eds., *Truth Will Prevail: The Rise of the Church of Jesus Christ of Latter-day Saints in the British Isles, 1837–1987* (Solihull, England: Church of Jesus Christ of Latter-day Saints, 1987).

50. James B. Allen, Jessie L. Embry, and Kahlile Mehr, *Hearts Turned to the Fathers: A History of the Genealogical Society of Utah, 1894–1994* (Provo, Utah: BYU Studies, 1994).

51. James B. Allen, Jessie L. Embry, and Kahlile Mehr, "Hearts Turned to the Fathers: A History of the Genealogical Society of Utah, 1894–1994," *BYU Studies* 34 (1994–95): 1–392.

52. Carol Cornwall Madsen, comp. and ed., *In Their Own Words: Women and the Story of Nauvoo* (Salt Lake City: Deseret Book, 1994), *Journey to Zion: Voices from the Mormon Trail* (Salt Lake City: Deseret Book, 1997), and *Battle for the Ballot: Essays on Woman Suffrage in Utah, 1870–1896* (Logan: Utah State University Press, 1997).

53. Jill Mulvay Derr, Janath Russell Cannon, and Maureen Ursenbach Beecher, *Women of Covenant: The Story of Relief Society* (Salt Lake City: Deseret Book, 1992).

54. Dean C. Jessee, ed. and comp., *The Personal Writings of Joseph Smith* (Salt Lake City: Deseret Book, 1984).

55. Dean C. Jessee, ed. and comp., *The Papers of Joseph Smith* (Salt Lake City: Deseret

Book, 1989–). Vol. 1 is *Autobiographical and Historical Writings* (1989); vol. 2, *Journal, 1832–1842* (1992).

56. James B. Allen, Ronald W. Walker, and David J. Whittaker, *Studies in Mormon History, 1830–1997: An Indexed Bibliography,* with "A Topical Guide to Published Social Science Literature on the Mormons," by Armand L. Mauss and Dynette Ivie Reynolds (Urbana: University of Illinois Press, 2000).

57. Thomas G. Alexander, "The Faith of an Urban Mormon," in *A Thoughtful Faith: Essays on Belief by Mormon Scholars,* ed. Philip L. Barlow (Centerville, Utah: Canon, 1986), 60.

58. Ibid., 61.

59. Thomas G. Alexander, *Mormonism in Transition: A History of the Latter-day Saints, 1890–1930* (Urbana: University of Illinois Press, 1986).

60. Thomas G. Alexander, *Things in Heaven and Earth: The Life and Times of Wilford Woodruff, a Mormon Prophet* (Salt Lake City: Signature Books, 1991).

61. Alexander had worked through these concepts earlier in "Wilford Woodruff and the Changing Nature of Mormon Religious Experience," *Church History* 45 (March 1976): 56–69, and in "The Place of Joseph Smith in the Development of American Religion: A Historiographical Inquiry," *Journal of Mormon History* 5 (1978): 17. For Alexander's own account of his intellectual deliberations, see Alexander, "The Faith of an Urban Mormon," 61–63.

62. Thomas G. Alexander, *Utah, the Right Place: The Official Centennial History* (Salt Lake City: Gibbs Smith, 1995).

63. Jessie L. Embry, "Charles Redd Center for Western Studies: The Oral History Program," in *Mormon Americana: A Guide to Sources and Collections in the United States,* ed. David J. Whittaker (Provo, Utah: BYU Studies, 1995), 111–19.

64. Jessie L. Embry, *Mormon Polygamous Families: Life in the Principle* (Salt Lake City: University of Utah Press, 1987), xvi.

65. Jessie L. Embry, *Black Saints in a White Church: Contemporary African American Mormons* (Salt Lake City: Signature Books, 1994); Jessie L. Embry, *"In His Own Language": Mormon Spanish Speaking Congregations in the United States* (Provo, Utah: Charles Redd Center for Western Studies, 1997); Jessie L. Embry, *Asian American Mormons: Bridging Cultures* (Provo, Utah: Charles Redd Center for Western Studies, 1999).

66. Gustive O. Larson, *Outline History of Utah and the Mormons* (Salt Lake City: Deseret Book, 1958) and *The "Americanization" of Utah for Statehood* (San Marino, Calif.: Huntington Library, 1971).

67. Eugene E. Campbell and Richard D. Poll, *Hugh B. Brown: His Life and Thought* (Salt Lake City: Bookcraft, 1975); Poll, Alexander, Campbell, and Miller, eds., *Utah's History.*

68. R. Lanier Britsch, *Unto the Islands of the Sea: A History of the Latter-day Saints in the Pacific* (Salt Lake City: Deseret Book, 1986), *Moramona: The Mormons in Hawaii* (Laie, Hawaii: Institute for Polynesian Studies, 1989), *From the East: The History of the Latter-day Saints in Asia, 1851–1996* (Salt Lake City: Deseret Book, 1998), and *Nothing More Heroic: The Compelling Story of the First Latter-day Saint Missionaries in India* (Salt Lake City: Deseret Book, 1999).

69. Marvin S. Hill and James B. Allen, eds., *Mormonism and American Culture* (New York: Harper and Row, 1972); Marvin S. Hill, *Quest for Refuge: The Mormon Flight from American Pluralism* (Salt Lake City: Signature Books, 1989).

70. Those department members who had worked in the field of Mormon history included Thomas G. Alexander, James B. Allen, Leonard J. Arrington, Martha Sonntag Bradley, R. Lanier Britsch, Eugene E. Campbell, Brian Q. Cannon, R. Kent Fielding, B. Carmon Hardy, William G. Hartley, Marvin S. Hill, Blair R. Holmes, Gustive O. Larson, Carol Cornwall Madsen, Richard D. Poll, David H. Pratt, D. Michael Quinn, Malcolm R. Thorp, Douglas F. Tobler, Ronald W. Walker, and David J. Whittaker.

71. The BYU College of Religious Education had Richard L. Anderson, Milton V. Backman Jr., Alexander L. Baugh, Richard E. Bennett, LaMar C. Berrett, Susan Easton Black, Donald Q. Cannon, Richard O. Cowan, Richard N. Holzapfel, Clark V. Johnson, Paul H. Peterson, Larry C. Porter, and Bruce Van Orden; BYU at Hawaii had Lance D. Chase and Grant Underwood; Ricks College had Lawrence G. Coates; and the LDS Institute System had Danel Bachman, Reed C. Durham Jr., Kenneth W. Godfrey, T. Edgar Lyon, and Max H. Parkin.

72. Richard O. Cowan, *The Kingdom Is Rolling Forth: The Church of Jesus Christ of Latter-day Saints in the Twentieth Century* (Provo, Utah: Brigham Young University Press, 1979); Richard Lloyd Anderson, *Joseph Smith's New England Heritage* (Salt Lake City: Deseret Book, 1971). Cowan's book had its origins in another preliminary work, James B. Allen and Richard O. Cowan, *Mormonism in the Twentieth Century* (Provo, Utah: Extension Publications, Division of Continuing Education, Brigham Young University, 1964).

73. Bruce A. Van Orden, *Prisoner for Conscience' Sake: The Life of George Reynolds* (Salt Lake City: Deseret Book, 1992).

74. Richard Neitzel Holzapfel and T. Jeffery Cottle, *Old Mormon Nauvoo, 1839–1846: Historic Photographs and Guide* (Provo, Utah: Grandin Book, 1990); Richard Neitzel Holzapfel and T. Jeffery Cottle, *Old Mormon Kirtland and Missouri: Historical Photographs and Guide* (Santa Ana, Calif.: Fieldbook Productions, 1991); Richard Neitzel Holzapfel and T. Jeffery Cottle, *Old Mormon Palmyra and New England: Historic Photographs and Guide* (Santa Ana, Calif.: Fieldbook Productions, 1991); Richard Neitzel Holzapfel, *Every Stone a Sermon: The Magnificent Story of the Construction and Dedication of the Salt Lake Temple* (Salt Lake City: Bookcraft, 1992); Richard Neitzel Holzapfel and T. Jeffery Cottle, *A Window to the Past: A Photographic Panorama of Early Church History and the Doctrine and Covenants* (Salt Lake City: Bookcraft, 1993); Richard Neitzel Holzapfel, *Their Faces toward Zion: Pictures and Images of the Trek West* (Salt Lake City: Bookcraft, 1996); Richard Neitzel Holzapfel, *My Servant Brigham: Portrait of a Prophet* (Salt Lake City: Bookcraft, 1997).

75. Susan Easton Black, *Membership of the Church of Jesus Christ of Latter-day Saints, 1830–1848*, 50 vols. (Provo, Utah: Religious Studies Center, Brigham Young University, 1989), *Early Members of the Reorganized Church of Jesus Christ of Latter Day Saints*, 6 vols. (Provo, Utah: Religious Studies Center, Brigham Young University, 1993), and *Pioneers of 1847: A Sesquicentennial Remembrance* (Provo[?], Utah: Religious Studies Center, Brigham Young University[?], 1980[?]). Much of Black's material was later made available in electronic format by LDS Infobases.

76. Milton V. Blackman Jr., *The Heavens Resound: A History of the Latter-day Saints in Ohio, 1830–1838* (Salt Lake City: Deseret Book, 1983).

77. Richard W. Bennett, *Mormons at the Missouri, 1846–52: "And Should We Die"* (Norman: University of Oklahoma Press, 1987) and *We'll Find the Place: The Mormon Exodus, 1846–1848* (Salt Lake City: Deseret Book, 1997).

78. Grant Underwood, *The Millenarian World of Early Mormonism* (Urbana: University of Illinois, 1993), 10.

79. Robert B. Flanders, *Nauvoo: Kingdom on the Mississippi* (Urbana: University of Illinois Press, 1965), vi (first quote), v (second quote).

80. Robert B. Flanders, "Some Reflections on the New Mormon History," *Dialogue: A Journal of Mormon Thought* 9 (Spring 1974): 40.

81. Quoted in W. B. Spillman, "The Historian Looks at Church History," *Saints' Herald*, 15 August 1967, 7.

82. W. Grant McMurray, "'As Historians and Not as Partisans': The Writing of Official History in the RLDS Church," *John Whitmer Historical Association Journal* 6 (1986): 48.

83. Richard P. Howard, *RLDS Beginnings, to 1860*, vol. 1 of *The Church through the Years* (Independence, Mo.: Herald Publishing House, 1992) and *The Reorganization Comes of Age, 1860–1992*, vol. 2 of *The Church through the Years* (Independence, Mo.: Herald Publishing House, 1993). For Howard's historical analysis of early Mormon scripture, see *Restoration Scriptures: A Study of Their Textual Development* (Independence, Mo.: Herald Publishing House, 1969).

84. Richard P. Howard, "The Mormon-RLDS Boundary, 1852–1991: Walls to Windows," *Journal of Mormon History* 18 (Spring 1992): 3–18.

85. F. Mark McKiernan, Alma R. Blair, and Paul M. Edwards, eds., *The Restoration Movement: Essays in Mormon History* (Lawrence, Kans.: Coronado, 1973).

86. Howard, "The Mormon-RLDS Boundary, 1852–1991," 17. Another sign of the cooperation was an article coauthored by RLDS Paul M. Edwards and LDS Douglas D. Alder, "Common Beginnings, Divergent Beliefs," *Dialogue: A Journal of Mormon Thought* 11 (Spring 1978): 18–28. The article explored the origins of their respective churches within their common historical heritage.

87. For reasons prompting the creation of the journal and a description of its content, see William D. Russell, "The Rise and Fall of *Courage*, an Independent RLDS Journal," *Dialogue: A Journal of Mormon Thought* 11 (Spring 1978): 115–19.

88. Howard, "The Mormon-RLDS Boundary, 1852–1991," 17, provides a description of the journal's outreach to LDS historians and literature.

89. "The Origin of the John Whitmer Historical Association," *John Whitmer Historical Association Journal* 1 (1981): 63–64.

90. These are the calculations of Howard, "The Mormon-RLDS Boundary, 1852–1991," 17.

91. Roger D. Launius, "The Reorganized Church, the Decade of Decision, and the Abilene Paradox," *Dialogue: A Journal of Mormon Thought* 31 (Spring 1998): 48.

92. For a sampling of Launius's biographic work, see *Joseph Smith III: Pragmatic Prophet* (Urbana: University of Illinois Press, 1988), *Alexander William Doniphan: Portrait of a Missouri Moderate* (Columbia: University of Missouri, 1997), and "A Western Mormon in Washington D.C.: James Fletcher, NASA, and the Final Frontier," *Pacific Historical Review* 64 (May 1999): 217–41; work on dissent, edited with Linda Thatcher, *Differing Visions: Dissenters in Mormon History* (Urbana: University of Illinois Press, 1994); on historiography, "A Bibliographical Review of the Reorganized Church in the Nineteenth Century," *Mormon History Association Newsletter*, no. 64 (January 1987): 5–8, "The 'New Social History' and the 'New Mormon History': Reflections on Recent Trends," *Dialogue:*

A Journal of Mormon Thought 27 (Spring 1994): 109–27, and, edited with John E. Hallwas, *Kingdom on the Mississippi Revisited* (Urbana: University of Illinois Press, 1966); on early restoration events, *Zion's Camp: Expedition to Missouri, 1834* (Independence, Mo.: Herald Publishing House, 1984), *The Kirtland Temple: A Historical Narrative* (Independence, Mo.: Herald Publishing House, 1986), and "The Latter Day Saints in Ohio: Writing the History of Mormonism's Middle Period," *John Whitmer Historical Association Journal* 16 (1996): 31–57.

93. Letter of M. G. Bradford, printed in *Dialogue: A Journal of Mormon Thought* 9 (Summer 1974): 7–8; Robert S. Michaelsen, "Thomas F. O'Dea on the Mormons: Retrospect and Assessment," *Dialogue: A Journal of Mormon Thought* 11 (Spring 1978): 45, 47. The other "cultures" studied in the project were Anglo-Saxon Protestant, Navajo, Spanish-Catholic, and Zuni. See Evon Vogt and Ethel M. Albert, *People of Rimrock: A Study of Values in Five Cultures* (Cambridge, Mass.: Harvard University Press, 1966).

94. Thomas O'Dea, *The Mormons* (Chicago: University of Chicago Press, 1957).

95. Ibid., 115.

96. For a treatment of this aspect of O'Dea's thought, see Michaelsen, "Thomas F. O'Dea on the Mormons," 49.

97. Ibid.

98. Klaus J. Hansen, *Quest for Empire: The Political Kingdom of God and the Council of Fifty in Mormon History* (East Lansing: Michigan State University Press, 1967).

99. It was a conclusion dismissed by one historian as "indefensible" because it lacked substantiating evidence. See D. Michael Quinn, "The Council of Fifty and Its Members, 1844 to 1945," *BYU Studies* 20 (Winter 1980): 163n.

100. Klaus J. Hansen, *Mormonism and the American Experience* (Chicago: University of Chicago Press, 1981).

101. The phrase "errand into the wilderness" was the Puritan historian Perry Miller's. "The proper metaphor for the Mormon migration," Hansen wrote, "is not a quest for refuge, or manifest destiny, or a quest for empire, but an errand into the wilderness." Hansen, *Mormonism and the American Experience*, 209. Hansen thus successively rejected the interpretations of Marvin Hill, Andrew Love Neff, and his own earlier book, *Quest for Empire.*

102. Mark P. Leone, *Roots of Modern Mormonism* (Cambridge, Mass.: Harvard University Press, 1979), v ("ethnographic" and "created"), 225–26 ("colonial"), 166 ("memorylessness"), vi ("powerless people").

103. Jan Shipps, "An 'Inside-Outsider' in Zion," *Dialogue: A Journal of Mormon Thought* 15 (Spring 1982): 146.

104. Ibid., 149.

105. Earlier Mario De Pillis, a non-LDS scholar with an interest in Mormon roots and Mormon communitarianism, had employed the sociological model of "church." De Pillis's influential essay, "The Quest for Religious Authority and the Rise of Mormonism," *Dialogue: A Journal of Mormon Thought* 1 (Spring 1966): 68–88, had suggested that Mormonism, along with Roman Catholicism, Protestantism, and Judaism, constituted a fourth major religion in American society. Klaus Hansen also had used sociological literature in suggesting that Mormonism paralleled early Christian millennial movements, while in a series of works the sociologist Rodney Stark interpreted Mormonism as a potentially

distinct movement. See especially Stark's "The Rise of a New World Faith," *Review of Religious Research* 26 (September 1984): 18–27.

106. Shipps, "An 'Inside-Outsider' in Zion," 159–60. Fawn Brodie provided antecedents to this. In the preface to her *No Man Knows My History: The Life of Joseph Smith, the Mormon Prophet*, 2d. ed. rev. (New York: Alfred A. Knopf, 1971), Brodie wrote that Mormonism "was a real religious creation, one intended to be to Christianity as Christianity was to Judaism: that is, a reform and a consummation" (viii).

107. Jan Shipps, *Mormonism: The Story of a New Religious Tradition* (Urbana: University of Illinois Press, 1985).

108. Shipps, "An 'Inside-Outsider' in Zion," 143.

109. Shipps, *Mormonism*, xii. Like Alexander, Shipps had been influenced by Robert F. Berkhofer, *A Behavioral Approach to Historical Analysis* (New York: Free Press, 1969).

110. Shipps, "An 'Inside-Outsider' in Zion," 139–61.

111. This important literature is summarized in Armand L. Mauss's essay, herein, and in the bibliography complied by Mauss and Dynette Ivie Reynolds in Allen, Walker, and Whittaker, *Studies in Mormon History*, 1057–1152.

112. Armand L. Mauss, *The Angel and the Beehive: The Mormon Struggle with Assimilation* (Urbana: University of Illinois Press, 1994).

113. Ibid., 5.

114. Howard R. Lamar, "Political Patterns in New Mexico and Utah Territories: 1850–1900," *Utah Historical Quarterly* 28 (October 1960): 363–87; "Statehood for Utah: A Different Path," *Utah Historical Quarterly* 39 (Fall 1971): 307–27; "National Perceptions of Utah's Statehood," *Journal of Mormon History* 23 (Spring 1997): 42–65; and *The Far Southwest, 1846–1912: A Territorial History* (New Haven, Conn.: Yale University Press, 1966).

115. Jean Bickmore White, "The Making of the Convention President: The Political Education of John Henry Smith," *Utah Historical Quarterly* 39 (Fall 1971): 350–69; "Woman's Place Is in the Constitution: The Struggle for Equal Rights in Utah in 1895," in *Essays on the American West, 1973–74*, ed. Thomas G. Alexander, Charles Redd Monographs in Western History, no. 5 (Provo, Utah: Brigham Young University Press, 1975): 81–104; "Political Deliverance—at a Price: The Quest for Statehood," *Journal of Mormon History* 12 (1985): 135–39; "Prelude to Statehood: Coming Together in the 1890s," *Utah Historical Quarterly* 62 (Fall 1994): 300–315; and "So Bright the Dream: Economic Prosperity and the Utah Constitutional Convention," *Utah Historical Quarterly* 63 (Fall 1995): 320–40. These articles were synthesized in Jean Bickmore White, *Charter for Statehood: The Story of Utah's State Constitution* (Salt Lake City: University of Utah Press, 1996).

116. Leo Edward Lyman, *Political Deliverance: The Mormon Quest for Utah Statehood* (Urbana: University of Illinois Press, 1986).

117. William Mulder, "Mormonism and Literature," *Western Humanities Review* 9 (Winter 1954–55): 85–89; "Mormon Angles of Historical Vision: Some Maverick Reflections," *Journal of Mormon History* 3 (1976): 13–22; and "'Essential Gestures': Craft and Calling in Contemporary Mormon Letters," *Weber Studies* 10 (Fall 1993): 7–25.

118. William Mulder, *Homeward to Zion: The Mormon Migration from Scandinavia* (Minneapolis: University of Minnesota Press, 1957); William Mulder and A. R. Mortensen, eds., *Among the Mormons: Historic Accounts by Contemporary Observers* (New York: Alfred A. Knopf, 1958).

119. While Mulder may have been a traditionalist in terms of writing history, his LDS

views were more expansive, as suggested by the leading role he played in the early 1950s with the "Mormon Seminar," or "Swearing Elders." "I think if anything marks the Swearing Elders," Mulder later said, "it was a healthy skepticism about anything that the Brethren [LDS Church leaders]—early or late—uttered, and the last resort was always a sense of rationality, the attempt to be rational about everything." Quoted in Thomas A. Blakely, "The Swearing Elders: The First Generation of Modern Mormon Intellectuals," *Sunstone* 10, no. 9 (1985): 11. Other historians who participated in this group, at least occasionally, included Leonard Arrington, Gustive Larson, Richard Poll, and T. Edgar Lyon. Invited speakers included Juanita Brooks, Carl Carmer, Whitney Cross, Bernard De Voto, and Thomas F. O'Dea.

120. Meinig's remarks were printed in Walter Prescott Webb, "Geographical-Historical Concepts in American History," *Annals of the Association of American Geographers* 50 (June 1960): 96.

121. Donald W. Meinig, "Mormon Culture Region: Strategies and Patterns in the Geography of the American West, 1847–1964," *Annals of the Association of American Geographers* 55 (June 1965): 191–220.

122. Ibid., 190–91.

123. See, for example, Dean R. Louder and Lowell C. Bennion, "Mapping the Mormons across the Modern West," in *The Mormon Role in the Settlement of the West,* ed. Richard H. Jackson (Provo, Utah: Brigham Young University Press, 1978), 135–69; Lowell C. Bennion and Merrill K. Ridd, "Utah's Dynamic Dixie: Satellite of Salt Lake, Las Vegas, or Los Angeles?" *Utah Historical Quarterly* 47 (Summer 1979): 311–27; Lowell C. Bennion, "Mormon Country a Century Ago: A Geographer's View," in *The Mormon People: Their Character and Traditions,* ed. Thomas G. Alexander (Provo, Utah: Brigham Young University Press, 1980), 1–26; Lowell C. Bennion, "The Incidence of Mormon Polygamy in 1860: 'Dixie' versus Davis Stake," *Journal of Mormon History* 11 (1984): 27–42; Lowell C. Bennion, "A Geographer's Discovery of *Great Basin Kingdom,*" in *Great Basin Kingdom Revisited: Contemporary Perspectives,* ed. Thomas G. Alexander (Logan: Utah State University Press, 1991), 109–32; Lowell C. Bennion, "The Geographic Dynamics of Mormondom, 1965–95," *Sunstone* 18 (December 1995): 21–32; and Lowell C. Bennion and Lawrence A. Young, "The Uncertain Dynamics of LDS Expansion," *Dialogue: A Journal of Mormon Thought* 29 (Spring 1996): 8–32.

124. Jackson began a reexamination of LDS pioneering in "Myth and Reality: Environmental Perception of the Mormons, 1840–1865, an Historical Geosophy" (Ph.D. diss., Clark University, 1970) and continued with a series of articles that included "Great Salt Lake and Great Salt Lake City: American Curiosities," *Utah Historical Quarterly* 56 (Spring 1988): 128–47; "The Mormon Village: Genesis and Antecedents of the City of Zion Plan," *BYU Studies* 17 (Winter 1977): 223–40; "Mormon Perception and Settlement," *Annals of the Association of American Geographers* 68 (1978): 317–34; "The Mormon Experience: The Plains as Sinai, the Great Salt Lake as the Dead Sea, and the Great Basin as Desert-cum-Promised Land," *Journal of Historical Geography* 18 (January 1992): 41–58; "The Overland Journey to Zion," in *The Mormon Role in the Settlement of the West,* ed. Jackson, 1–27; "Sacred Space and City Planning: The Mormon Example," *Architecture and Comportment/ Architecture and Behavior* 9 (June 1993): 251–60; and "Utah's Harsh Lands, Hearth of Greatness," *Utah Historical Quarterly* 49 (Winter 1981): 4–25.

125. Richard V. Francaviglia, *The Mormon Landscape: Existence, Creation, and Percep-*

tion of a Unique Image in the American West (New York: AMS, 1978), 34–35. These themes are also discussed in Carol A. Edison, "Material Culture: An Introduction and Guide to Mormon Vernacular," in *Mormon Americana,* ed. Whittaker, 306–35.

126. Wayne L. Wahlquist, ed., *Atlas of Utah* (Provo, Utah: Weber State College and Brigham Young University Press, 1981); S. Kent Brown, Donald Q. Cannon, and Richard H. Jackson, eds., *Historical Atlas of Mormonism* (New York: Simon and Schuster, 1994).

127. Marie Cornwall, Tim B. Heaton, and Lawrence A. Young, eds., *Contemporary Mormonism: Social Science Perspectives* (Urbana: University of Illinois Press, 1994). Most of the research at church headquarters went unpublished. The earlier name for the Center for Studies of the Family was the Family and Demographic Research Institute.

128. Lee L. Bean, Dean L. May, and Mark Skolnick, "The Mormon Historical Demography Project," *Historical Methods* 11 (Winter 1978): 45–53.

129. Ibid., 49.

130. For a sampling of this literature, see Douglas L. Anderton and Rebecca Jean Emigh, "Polygynous Fertility: Sexual Competition versus Progeny," *American Journal of Sociology* 94 (January 1989): 832–55; Lee L. Bean and Geraldine P. Mineau, "The Polygyny-Fertility Hypothesis: A Re-evaluation," *Population Studies* 40 (March 1986): 67–81; Lee L. Bean, Geraldine P. Mineau, and Douglas Anderton, "Residence and Religious Effects on Declining Family Size: An Historical Analysis of the Utah Population," *Review of Religious Research* 25 (December 1983): 91–101; Geraldine P. Mineau, "Utah Widowhood: A Demographic Profile," in *On Their Own: Widows and Widowhood in the American Southwest: 1848–1939,* ed. Arlene Scadron (Urbana: University of Illinois Press, 1988), 140–65; Geraldine P. Mineau, Lee L. Bean, and Douglas L. Anderton, "Migration and Fertility: Behavioral Change on the American Frontier," *Journal of Family History* 14, no. 1 (1989): 43–61; and Geraldine P. Mineau and James Trussell, "A Specification of Marital Fertility by Parents' Age, Age at Marriage and Marital Duration," *Demography* 19 (August 1982): 335–50.

131. May also cited Mormon Historical Demography Project research to show that social behavior began to shift in the 1870s. Utah fertility, for example, slowly changed from "natural fertility" to a pattern more representative of the national practice of limiting and spacing the birth of children. May's essay "A Demographic Portrait of the Mormons, 1830–1980" was first published in *After 150 Years: The Latter-day Saints in Sesquicentennial Perspective,* ed. Thomas G. Alexander and Jessie L. Embry (Provo, Utah: Charles Redd Center for Western Studies, Brigham Young University, 1983): 37–69, and was reprinted in *The New Mormon History: Revisionist Essays on the Past,* ed. D. Michael Quinn (Salt Lake City: Signature Books, 1992), 21–35. For another early demographic study, see Dean R. Louder, "A Distributional and Diffusionary Analysis of the Mormon Church, 1850–1970" (Ph.D. diss., University of Washington, 1972).

132. Dean L. May, "People on the Frontier: Kanab's Families of 1874," *Journal of Family History* 1 (December 1976): 169–92. In an earlier essay, "The Making of Saints: The Mormon Town as a Setting for the Study of Cultural Change," *Utah Historical Quarterly* 45 (Winter 1977): 75–92, May argued for the appropriateness of statistical study of LDS community life.

133. Dean L. May, *Three Frontiers: Family, Land, and Society in the American West, 1850–1900* (New York: Cambridge University Press, 1994).

134. Twice May cited Alexis de Tocqueville's doomsaying about democracy's rootless and isolating impulse, including a passage located in the book's final paragraph. Ibid., 6, 282–83.

135. Ibid., 7.

136. May also completed two other books dealing with Mormon topics. In addition to Arrington, Fox, and May, *Building the City of God,* written at the LDS History Division, he published *Utah: A People's History* (Salt Lake City: University of Utah Press, 1987), a brief but useful survey that grew out of a television series he had written.

137. Larry M. Logue, *A Sermon in the Desert: Belief and Behavior in Early St. George, Utah* (Urbana: University of Illinois Press, 1988).

138. Logue's conclusions about the high incidence of plural marriage reflected a growing revisionism, because the historical literature had previously suggested that plural marriage was marginal in LDS society. Other examples of this revisionism include Bennion, "The Incidence of Mormon Polygamy in 1880: 'Dixie' versus Davis Stake," 27–42; and Marie Cornwall, Camela Courtright, and Laga Van Beek, "How Common the Principle? Women as Plural Wives in 1860," *Dialogue: A Journal of Mormon Thought* 26 (Summer 1993): 139–53.

139. For another similar-minded study of Spring City, Utah, see Michael S. Raber, "Religious Polity and Local Production: The Origins of a Mormon Town" (Ph.D. diss., Yale University, 1978).

140. Charles S. Peterson, *Utah: A Bicentennial History* (New York: W. W. Norton, 1977).

141. Charles S. Peterson, "A Mormon Town: One Man's West," *Journal of Mormon History* 3 (1976): 3–4.

142. Charles S. Peterson, *Take Up Your Mission: Mormon Colonizing along the Little Colorado River, 1870–1900* (Tucson: University of Arizona Press, 1973). For a sampling of some of Peterson's essays, see "A Mormon Town"; "Utah's Regions: A View From the Hinterland," *Utah Historical Quarterly* 47 (Spring 1979): 103–9; "Life in a Village Society, 1877–1920," *Utah Historical Quarterly* 49 (Winter 1981): 78–96; "Winter Feed, Summer Shelter, Tabernacles, and Genealogy: Reflections on Straw-Thatched Cowsheds," *Western Folklore* 41 (April 1982): 145–47; and *"A Utah Moon": Perceptions of Southern Utah,* Juanita Brooks Lecture Series (St. George, Utah: Dixie College, 1984).

143. Lawrence Foster, "A Personal Odyssey: My Encounter with Mormon History," *Dialogue: A Journal of Mormon Thought* 16 (Autumn 1983): 90. Foster spoke of being put off by lukewarm religionists, admiring those possessed of a "true religious consciousness." Ibid. See also Lawrence Foster, "A Radical Misstatement," *Dialogue: A Journal of Mormon Thought* 22 (Summer 1989): 6, which states his religious background. He identified himself as sympathetic to Quaker belief and practice, although he was not a member of that denomination.

144. Foster, "A Personal Odyssey," 91 ("baffled" and "challenged" quotes), 91–92 ("exiting" quote), 92 ("skeptic" quote), 93 ("see itself" quote).

145. Lawrence Foster, *Religion and Sexuality: Three American Communal Experiments of the Nineteenth Century* (New York: Oxford University Press, 1981) and *Women, Family, and Utopia: Communal Experiments of the Shakers, the Oneida Community, and the Mormons* (Syracuse, N.Y.: Syracuse University Press, 1991).

146. Bushman's non-Mormon books included *From Puritan to Yankee: Character and*

the Social Order in Connecticut, 1690–1765 (Cambridge, Mass.: Harvard University Press, 1967), for which he received the Bancroft and Phi Alpha Theta prizes; *King and People in Provincial Massachusetts* (Chapel Hill: University of North Carolina Press, published for the Institute of Early American History and Culture, 1985); and *The Refinement of America: Persons, Houses, Cities* (New York: Alfred A. Knopf, 1992).

147. Richard L. Bushman, "My Belief," in *A Thoughtful Faith,* ed. Barlow, 21, 27.

148. Richard L. Bushman, *Joseph Smith and the Beginnings of Mormonism* (Urbana: University of Illinois Press, 1984).

149. D. Michael Quinn, "On Being a Mormon Historian (and Its Aftermath)," in *Faithful History: Essays on Writing Mormon History,* ed. George D. Smith (Salt Lake City: Signature Books, 1992), 72.

150. When describing his turmoil at Yale, he again used the third-person voice: "This faltering young historian obtained a spiritual witness that it was right to complete his dissertation, despite the so-called 'controversies' and 'sensitive' areas of church history with which it dealt. He then asked for courage and strength to face criticism and consequences which might result from those who were hostile to the kinds of things he was researching and writing. He continued to 'pray into print' everything he published." Ibid., 73–74.

151. Ibid., 107n45.

152. For a draft of his remarks and for their resulting effect, see ibid. 69–111.

153. D. Michael Quinn, *J. Reuben Clark: The Church Years* (Provo, Utah: Brigham Young University Press, 1983).

154. D. Michael Quinn, *Early Mormonism and the Magic World View* (Salt Lake City: Signature Books, 1987). Quinn pursued this line of argument in a passage that he only partly developed: "Like many early Americans, Joseph Smith and his family were religious seekers who did not accept the limits imposed by secular rationalists and mainline Protestant clergymen. The Smiths knew the King James Bible and were also conversant with the lore (and possibly the literature) of the magic world view. . . . Although understandably sensitive to the ridicule of those who rejected this amalgam, Joseph Smith, his family, and other early Mormons evidently saw themselves as simply drawing upon a larger frame of reference in their religious quest." Ibid., 226. For other work pursuing this same line of reasoning, see Ronald W. Walker, "The Persisting Idea of American Treasure Hunting" and "Joseph Smith: The Palmyra Seer," both in *BYU Studies* 24 (Fall 1984 [1986]): 429–59, 461–72.

155. D. Michael Quinn, *The Mormon Hierarchy: Origins of Power* (Salt Lake City: Signature Books, 1994) and *The Mormon Hierarchy: Extensions of Power* (Salt Lake City: Signature Books, 1997).

156. Quinn, *Mormon Hierarchy: Extensions of Power,* ix.

157. D. Michael Quinn, *Same-Sex Dynamics among Nineteenth-Century Americans: A Mormon Example* (Urbana: University of Illinois Press, 1996).

158. The book marked Quinn's "coming out." Near the time of its publication, Quinn was quoted as saying, "I don't define myself as 'bisexual' because I don't have an equal attraction to both genders. I am overwhelmingly attracted to men." Quoted in "Quinn and Controversial Book Come 'Out,'" *Sunstone* 19 (December 1996): 73.

159. Allan Kent Powell, ed., *Utah History Encyclopedia* (Salt Lake City: University of Utah Press, 1994).

160. Daniel H. Ludlow, ed., *Encyclopedia of Mormonism,* 5 vols. (New York: Macmillan, 1992).

161. Chad J. Flake, comp., *A Mormon Bibliography, 1830–1930: Books, Pamphlets, Periodicals, and Broadsides relating to the First Century of Mormonism* (Salt Lake City: University of Utah Press, 1978). Chad J. Flake and Larry W. Draper, comps., *A Mormon Bibliography, 1830–1930: Ten Year Supplement* (Salt Lake City: University of Utah Press, 1989), provided titles missed in Flake's initial survey.

162. David J. Whittaker, ed., *Mormon Americana: A Guide to Sources and Collections in the United States* (Provo, Utah: BYU Studies, 1995).

163. *Infobases Library* [CD-ROM] (Salt Lake City: Bookcraft, 1999); *LDS Family History Suite* [CD-ROM] (Salt Lake City: Infobases, 1996); Utah State Historical Society, *Guide to Archives and Manuscript Collections in Selected Utah Repositories* (Salt Lake City: Utah State Historical Society, 1991); Milton V. Backman Jr., *Writings of Early Latter-day Saints and Their Contemporaries,* 2d. ed., rev. (Provo, Utah: Religious Studies Center, Brigham Young University, 1996); Black, *Early Members of the Reorganized Church of Jesus Christ of Latter Day Saints;* Black, *Membership of the Church of Jesus Christ of Latter-day Saints.*

164. *GospelLink* [CD-ROM] (Salt Lake City: Deseret Book, 1998).

165. *Utah History Suite,* 2d ed. [CD-ROM] (Provo, Utah: Historical Views, 1999); *New Mormon Studies CD-ROM: A Comprehensive Resource Library* (Salt Lake City: Smith Research Associates, 1998).

166. Thirty years after its founding, the Mormon History Association continued to reflect the personality of its leading organizer, Leonard Arrington. RLDS Church member Paul Edwards, after attending one of his first MHA conventions, reported an initial impression: "These were fine scholars . . . who were openly talking about being Mormons, who knew that I wasn't and didn't care. I mean, nobody attacked me, nobody made any attempt to convert me, nobody laughed at my church." Edwards Oral History, quoted in Maureen Ursenbach Beecher, "*Entre Nous:* An Intimate History of MHA," *Journal of Mormon History* 12 (1985): 47. For additional information on the development and functioning of the Mormon History Association, see Arrington, "Reflections on the Founding and Purpose of the Mormon History Association, 1965–1983," 91–103; Davis Bitton, "Taking Stock: The Mormon History Association after Twenty-five Years," *Journal of Mormon History* 17 (1991): 1–27; and Paul M. Edwards, "A Community of Heart," *Journal of Mormon History* 17 (1991): 28–34.

167. Bitton, "Taking Stock," 9. Bitton judged that few of these papers challenged traditional faith, perhaps one in twenty.

168. Ibid., 8–9. Bitton's observation was borne out by the religious experiences of its membership. Replying to an MHA survey question, "What impact has your MHA membership had on your religious faith?" 27 percent of the respondents claimed the MHA had "increased" their faith, while 60 percent reported "no impact." Only 3 percent declared a diminution. On the question of church attendance, 80 percent reported that the MHA had made no difference in their activity, while 11 percent said the MHA had influenced them to be more frequent worshipers. Scott, Crooks, and Pugsley, "'A Kinship of Interest,'" 159.

169. Scott, Crooks, and Pugsley, "'A Kinship of Interest,'" 158–59.

170. Bitton, "Taking Stock," 4.

171. For a listing of MHA officers, council members, conference sites and their chairs,

Tanner lecturers, and annual awards up to 1989–90, see ibid., 13–27. This listing is a valuable source for understanding the history of the MHA and the new Mormon history movement itself.

172. *Mormon History Association Newsletter,* 15 January 1972, quoted in Beecher, "*Entre Nous,*" 47. Said one member, with some embellishment, of the friendly discussion, "I often feel like an emotional vampire, coming to conferences to dig my Draculaian fangs into the professional life-blood of an otherwise healthy association." Edwards, "A Community of Heart," 29.

173. For information on the establishment of the periodical during the 1960s, see Clinton F. Larson, "The Founding Vision of *BYU Studies,*" *BYU Studies* 31 (Fall 1991): 5–9.

174. G. Wesley Johnson, "Editorial Preface," *Dialogue: A Journal of Mormon Thought* 1 (Spring 1966): 6. For a treatment of *Dialogue*'s first years, see Devery S. Anderson, "A History of *Dialogue,* Part One: The Early Years, 1965–1971," *Dialogue: A Journal of Mormon Thought* 32 (Summer 1999): 15–66.

175. Armand L. Mauss, John R. Tarjan, and Martha D. Esplin, "The Unfettered Faithful: An Analysis of the *Dialogue* Subscribers Survey," *Dialogue: A Journal of Mormon Thought* 20 (Spring 1987): 32–33, 42, 52.

176. Scott Kenney, "Sunstone," *Dialogue: A Journal of Mormon Thought* 11 (Spring 1978): 101. See also Lee Warthen, "History of Sunstone, chapter 1: The Scott Kinney Years, Summer 1974–June 1978," *Sunstone* 22 (June 1999): 48–61.

177. Claudia L. Bushman, editorial, *Exponent II* 1 (July 1974): 2. See also Nancy T. Dredge, "The Next Ten Years," *Exponent II* 10 (Fall 1983): 2; and Chris Rigby Arrington, "Voices of Conflict: The Literature of Mormon Sisterism," in *Proceedings of the Symposia of the Association of Mormon Letters, 1978–79* (1979): 95–105.

178. Important titles included Allen, Embry, and Mehr, *Hearts Turned to the Fathers;* Jan Shipps and John W. Welch, eds., *The Journals of William E. McLellin, 1831–1836* (Provo, Utah: BYU Studies, Brigham Young University, 1994; Urbana: University of Illinois Press); B. H. Roberts, *The Truth, the Way, the Life: An Elementary Treatise on Theology,* ed. John W. Welch (Provo, Utah: BYU Studies, 1994); Whittaker, ed., *Mormon Americana;* and Garold N. Davis and Norma S. Davis, *Behind the Iron Curtain: Recollections of Latter-day Saints in East Germany, 1945–1989* (Provo, Utah: BYU Studies, 1996).

179. Elizabeth Dulany, unpublished remarks made at the annual meeting of the Mormon History Association, 1993, transcript in authors' possession.

180. "Mormon Studies at the University of Illinois Press," statement of the University of Illinois Press, in authors' possession.

181. Dallin H. Oaks and Marvin S. Hill, *Carthage Conspiracy: The Trial of the Accused Assassins of Joseph Smith* (Urbana: University of Illinois Press, 1975).

182. For an illustration and defense of this position, see Keith W. Perkins, "Why Are We Here in New England? A Personal View of Church History," in *Regional Studies in Latter-day Saint Church History,* ed. Donald Q. Cannon (Provo, Utah: Department of Church History and Doctrine, Brigham Young University, 1988), 1–13. See also Joe J. Christensen, "The Value of Church History and Historians: Some Personal Impressions," *Proceedings of the Church Education System Church History Symposium* (Provo, Utah: Brigham Young University Press, 1977), 12–17; and Robert Millet, "How Should Our Story Be Told?" in *To Be Learned Is Good, If . . . ,* ed. Robert Millet (Salt Lake City: Bookcraft, 1987), 1–8.

183. For a sampling of these critiques, see the work of David E. Bohn: "No Higher Ground: Objective History Is an Illusive Chimera," *Sunstone* 8 (May–June 1983): 26–32; "Our Own Agenda: A Critique of the Methodology of the New Mormon History," *Sunstone* 14 (June 1990): 45–49; "The Larger Issue," *Sunstone* 16 (February 1994): 45–63; and "Unfounded Claims and Impossible Expectations: A Critique of New Mormon History," in *Faithful History*, ed. Smith, 227–61. See also Neal W. Kramer, "Looking for God in History," *Sunstone* 8 (January–March 1983): 15–17; Gary F. Novak, "Naturalistic Assumptions and the Book of Mormon," *BYU Studies* 30 (Summer 1990): 23–40; Louis C. Midgley, "The Challenge of Historical Consciousness: Mormon History and the Encounter with Secular Modernity," in *By Study and Also by Faith*, 2 vols., ed. John M. Lundquist and Stephen D. Ricks, 2 vols. (Salt Lake City: Deseret Book and Foundation for Ancient Research and Mormon Studies, Brigham Young University, 1990): 2:502–51; and M. Gerald Bradford, "The Case of the New Mormon History: Thomas G. Alexander and His Critics," *Dialogue: A Journal of Mormon Thought* 21 (Winter 1988): 143–50.

184. The neotraditionalist criticism was weakened by a zest for controversy that at times seemed as personal as it was professional. Moreover, none of the neotraditionalists attempted to write history, and as a result their criticism remained abstract and theoretical. On the few occasions that the critics cited books they admired, historians were left wondering if a playful sense of irony was at work. See Neal Kramer, "Looking for God in History," *Sunstone* 8 (January–April 1983): 15–17. On one item the critics certainly erred: few new Mormon historians advocated "scientific" or "objective history," a nineteenth- and early twentieth-century chimera long abandoned by the profession.

185. See, for example, Alexander, "Historiography and the New Mormon History," 25–49; Lawrence Foster, "New Perspectives on the Mormon Past: Reflections of a Non-Mormon Historian," *Sunstone* 7 (January–February 1982): 41–45; and Malcolm R. Thorp, "Some Reflections on New Mormon History and the Possibilities of a 'New' Traditional History," *Sunstone* 15 (November 1991): 39–46. For a useful collection of essays on "faithful history," see Smith, ed., *Faithful History.* The exchange between the neoconservatives and historians was often a confrontation instead of a debate, as each side used specialized definitions that talked past each other.

186. Klaus J. Hansen, "Jan Shipps and the Mormon Tradition," *Journal of Mormon History* 11 (1984): 136–37, 144–45.

187. Richard L. Bushman, "Faithful History," *Dialogue: A Journal of Mormon Thought* 4 (Winter 1969): 16, 25.

188. Richard L. Bushman, "The Historians and Mormon Nauvoo," *Dialogue: A Journal of Mormon Thought* 5 (Spring 1970): 52.

189. Charles S. Peterson, "Beyond the Problems of Exceptionalist History," in *Great Basin Kingdom Revisited*, ed. Alexander, 143–48 (quotes on 143 and 148).

190. Launius, "The 'New Social History' and the 'New Mormon History,'" 109–27. See also Roger D. Launius, "From Old to New Mormon History: Fawn Brodie and the Legacy of Scholarly Analysis of Mormonism," in *Reconsidering No Man Knows My History: Fawn M. Brodie and Joseph Smith in Retrospect*, ed. Newell G. Bringhurst (Logan: Utah State University Press, 1996), 197–99; and Roger D. Launius, "Mormon Memory, Mormon Myth, and Mormon History," *Journal of Mormon History* 21 (Spring 1995): esp. 23–24.

191. Robert Baird. *Religion in America; or, An Account of the Origin, Progress, Relation to the State, and Present Condition of the Evangelical Churches in the United States: With*

Notices of the Unevangelical Denominations (New York: Harper, 1844). For more on this point, see Jerald C. Brauer, "Changing Perspective on Religion in America," in *Reinterpretations in American Church History*, ed. Jerald C. Brauer (Chicago: University of Chicago Press, 1968), 1–28.

192. Sidney Ahlstrom, *A Religious History of the American People* (New Haven, Conn.: Yale University Press, 1972), 508.

193. Winthrop S. Hudson and John Corrigan, *Religion in America: An Historical Account of the Development of American Religious Life*, 6th ed. (Upper Saddle River, N.J.: Prentice Hall, 1999), 187, 194–97, 399, 420.

194. Harold Bloom, *The American Religion: The Emergence of the Post-Christian Nation* (New York: Simon and Schuster, 1992).

195. Ibid., 79 (first quote), 84 (second quote), 95 (third quote), 94 (fourth quote).

196. John L. Brooke, *The Refiner's Fire: The Making of Mormon Cosmology, 1644–1844* (New York: Cambridge University Press, 1994), xvi.

4. The Challenge of Mormon Biography

And he said unto me, Son of man, can these bones live? And I
answered, O Lord God, Thou knowest.
—Ezekiel 37:3

EZEKIEL SAW A VALLEY full of dry and lifeless forms, but they had the promise of becoming something more. The name of Ezekiel's valley is not given,
but in a symbolic sense the prophet may have glimpsed the valley of Mormon biography.[1] Like other forms of Mormon history, Mormon life-writing (an appropriate modern term for biography and autobiography) has
passed through several stages. Until recently, however, it has seldom been well
balanced and "alive," full of human realism and descriptive of the "times"
through which an individual has passed. As S. George Ellsworth wrote in the
introduction to his biography of Samuel Claridge, "The life of one person
may be so representative of his times and the movements in which he participated that his biography becomes a history of those times and events."[2]
The challenge of biography, then, is to tell of such a life, fully and honestly,
and in the process to animate a previous "life" and "age."

The purpose of this chapter is three-fold: (1) to identify the major ingredients that, by modern standards, make up good biography; (2) to review the
history of Mormon biography, suggesting some of its strengths and weaknesses; and (3) to suggest to would-be Mormon biographers the challenges
and opportunities that lie before them. Even though some two thousand
Mormon biographies or biographical sketches have appeared in print since
1830, Mormon life-writing is still in the process of fulfilling its potential.

Modern Life-Writing: A Definition

Life-writing of one sort or another has been with us since human beings
began to record their history, though for centuries most of it was written for

nonbiographical purposes. Instead of seeking to reveal the life of an individual, life-writing was often written to instill a higher or more transcending truth. For instance, Plutarch, considered the father of classical biography, chose leading Greek statesmen and wrote with the instructive purpose of showing what made each man great. In a similar vein, medieval writers wrote hagiography that stressed the religious virtue of their subjects. The result in both cases was didacticism, not biography.

James Boswell brought greater human realism to life-writing. When writing an introduction to his *Life of Samuel Johnson,* Boswell promised that his biography would treat Johnson "as he really was." Boswell did not want to produce a "panegyrick, which must be all praise, but his life; which, great and good as he was, must not be supposed to be entirely perfect."[3] Because Boswell had been Johnson's friend and close observer, he was able to provide telling anecdotes and pithy quotations (genuine quotations, not the well-intended fabrications of earlier writing). As a result, Boswell's portrait of Johnson was real and lifelike, and his book established the precedent, so important to modern writing, of full and honest disclosure.

During the nineteenth century, a growing number of readers were attracted to biography, partly because of the age's fascination with prominent historical figures. Some works, such as Elizabeth Gaskell's *Life of Charlotte Brontë* and Washington Irving's *Life of George Washington,* were finely written and offered rich detail.[4] However, nineteenth-century biography could also be overly long, eulogistic, and sentimental. Worse, it was full of Victorian or nationalistic lessons that sometimes ignored, colored, or even invented "facts." Parson Weems's biography of George Washington fabricated such stories as Washington's famous "cherry tree" in the hope of inspiring the nation's children.[5]

Reacting to such writing, Lytton Strachey, an English biographer and critic whose *Eminent Victorians* did so much to foster modern biography, complained of "those two fat volumes with which it is our custom to commemorate the dead—who does not know them, with their ill-digested masses of material, their slipshod style, their tone of tedious panegyric, their lamentable lack of selection, of detachment, or design? They are as familiar as the *cortége* of the undertaker and wear the same air of slow, funereal barbarism."[6] Such disapproval, levied in 1918, partly anticipated a new definition that modern critics have given to life-writing. Since the middle of the twentieth century, they have viewed biography as a new genre, not quite history and not quite literature but a separate art with its own form and rules.

What, then, are the norms by which the craft of modern biography should be judged? With deceptive simplicity, the *Oxford English Dictionary* defines biography as "the history of the lives of individual men [and women], as a branch of literature." This suggests two important ingredients in the mix: (1) the science, or careful methodology, of history; and (2) literary art. But there is also another essential element: human realism, or, ideally, the accurate simulation of a human life. Unfortunately, few biographers have produced works in which these three elements are successfully mixed, and few biographers of Mormons have even tried.

The first requirement of good biography, maintaining high standards of historical scholarship, presents an overwhelming task. Among other things, it requires time-consuming research with the impossible goal of completeness. Anxious to gain additional source material for his biography, for example, James Clifford won admittance to the vaults of London's Barclay Bank, where he toiled painstakingly over huge and dusty ledgers—all for what became a single sentence in his book on literary biography.[7] At least during an initial stage, life-writers may assume an adversarial relationship with their materials. "The biographer does not trust his witnesses, living or dead," one critic has written. "He may drip with the milk of human kindness, believe everything that his wife and his friends and his children tell him, enjoy his neighbors and embrace the universe—but in the workshop he must be as ruthless as a board meeting smelling out embezzlement [and] as suspicious as a secret agent riding the Simplon-Orient express."[8]

To history's standards of thoroughness, frankness, and tough-minded accuracy, biographers must add the second ingredient of successful life-writing: good literary art. A successful narrative cannot be written by simply piling one fact upon another. Biographers must allow their research to suggest a controlling point of view, passion, or insight, which must be arrived at independently of any preconceived idea of "what ideally should be." Then as the narrative is written, it can be shaped, paced, and perhaps rearranged through flashback. A subject's inner thoughts might be probed through reverie, the subjunctive mood, or a word montage of the subject's psychological feelings. Scene, description, density of detail, idiom, and even authentically obtained dialogue may create the illusion of life.

In this literary re-creation of life, objective "facts" and subjective feelings might work together. Carl Pletsch, for example, refuses to separate the "purportedly weak, feminine, covert knowledge of subjectivity" from the "potent, masculine, and linear knowledge of objectivity." Biography, he observes, is one realm that allows "assimilating subjectivity into a larger concept of knowledge."[9] But if modern biographers are similar to novelists and dramatists as they try to merge fact and feeling, their purposes are dissimilar. Paul Murray Kendall has pointed out that older literary arts "seek to evoke reality from illusion," but "biography hopes to fasten illusion upon reality, to elicit, from the coldness of paper, the warmth of a life being lived."[10] Biographers must never "invent" facts or dialogue for the sake of telling a better story, however, for when life-writers go beyond their documents, they destroy the truth that their craft requires. In short, in biography, truthfulness is a basic law.

The third ingredient of good life-writing, accurately portraying all aspects of a human life, is potentially more trying, even exasperating, to Mormon and other religious-minded readers. Einhard suggested it in his preface to *Charlemagne,* over eleven centuries ago. "Here you have a book containing the life of that great and glorious man," he wrote. "There is nothing for you to wonder at or admire except his deeds."[11] Instead of heavy-handed preaching, the excessive veneration of people and institutions, or the making of simpleminded caricatures of the past, Einhard and his modern successors write about human life as it actually was lived. Their subjects are fallible individuals—complex and contradictory, sometimes torn with tension, pulled periodically heavenward or downward by what Faust described as the two souls working within the breast. Good biography understands that men and women grow and atrophy and that virtue to have any meaning must be tested.

The accurate portrayal of human personality is not easily achieved. Biographers often face pressures to retouch their portraits to create "better" or more pleasing pictures. Though outright lying is infrequent in modern life-writing, a more "satisfactory" or useful character is often created by the careful selection or arrangement of facts and by the clever use of emphasis, with occasional character flaws perhaps squeezed into the text to render apparent balance and truthfulness. The resulting biography usually corresponds to a preconceived view of what the subject should be. Similar results often occur when biography attempts to evangelize. The strong emotions of a writer can not only distort the personality of a biographical subject but also create a book that is no longer a biography. In this case, a religious movement or philosophy replaces the subject-person at center stage, and whatever is harmful to the higher cause is screened from view.

Biography—like the men and women it describes—has the potential for limitless variety. We have sketched but one strain, an ideal hybrid that might be called "literary biography," which has history (science), literature (art), and human realism based on intellectual integrity as its three primary qualities. Strachey and those who followed him in the 1920s had a hand in creating this kind of biography by introducing cleverness and technique into the craft, much to the delight and edification of their readers. Serious-minded historians made the next advance in the middle decades of the century, aware of the contrived and at times unfair techniques of the debunkers of the 1920s and 1930s yet also cognizant of the value of their literary flourishes. At last, by the second half of the twentieth century, modern biography began to take its present form. With the exception of a handful of vintage classics, the best biographies in the English language are now being written. Merely to sample the current work, they include Robert Blake's *Disraeli,* James MacGregor Burns's *Roosevelt: The Lion and the Fox,* Lord David Cecil's *Melbourne,* Leon Edel's *Henry James,* James Flexner's four-volume biography of George Washington as well as his one-volume work, Elizabeth Jenkins's *Elizabeth the Great,* and Dumas Malone's six-volume *Jefferson and His Time.*[12] Through these and other writers, literary biography has been born.

Nineteenth-Century Mormon Life-Writing

How, then, does Mormon life-writing stack up when judged by modern standards of historical method, literary art, and human realism? As one might expect, nineteenth-century works did not do well. Not surprisingly, Mormon life-writers followed the standards of their time, displaying more interest in institutions than in individuals. Men dominated over women as subjects. Literary "art" and style were just beginning to develop, and accuracy and realism were also largely things of the future. Yet it would be a mistake to dismiss this early work out of hand. Nineteenth-century biography made an important contribution by capturing the authentic spirit of the times. If a modern reader wishes to enter that first world of Mormon thought—and all its hopes, desires, and dreams—nineteenth-century biography is one of the best places to start.

Early Mormon writing was influenced by the English Puritans. These sixteenth- and seventeenth-century dissenters from elaborate or high church forms carried with them a strong sense of God's personal and inward dealing, which they felt constrained to document for others and themselves. Puritan biographies were often "faithful" explanation. Like the Hebrews who came before them and the Mormons who followed, the English Puritan writers saw themselves as God's chosen people whose coming to America was an extension or unfolding of divine intention. Their history and biography told the saga of God's dealings as seen in their personal lives. In short, Puritan biography and autobiography were simultaneously scripture as well as history.

This combination of providential history and autobiography filled the first Mormon life-writing ever to be published in book form: Lucy Mack Smith's *Biographical Sketches of Joseph Smith the Prophet and His Progenitors for Many Generations.*[13] Dictated by Joseph Smith's mother in her advanced years, this work at first was unfavorably received by church authorities, who regarded it unreliable in detail (although only a few items were corrected in its "revised" 1902 edition). Lucy Smith's work might be best described as a religious family history. Using family records and personal memory, she told of the faith, dreams, and experiences of the Macks and the Smiths on the New England frontier. But it was also full of important anecdotes about Joseph Smith and the rise of Mormonism. The testament of a believer, this volume revealed the strong sense of religious calling that Lucy Smith and her family came to feel about her son's mission. To read it is to share the first Mormon matriarch's pride in her son's ministry,[14] which makes it an indispensable source for any modern biographer attempting to deal with Joseph Smith and his family.

Not all LDS autobiographers told the story from the perspective of the Utah church. Emily Austin related her experience as one of the first New York Mormon converts in her *Mormonism; or, Life among the Mormons,* but her narrative was colored by her later disaffiliation from the movement.[15] John Corrill, in his *Brief History of the Church of Christ,* wrote a short but matter-of-fact narration of what had drawn him to Mormonism when he lived in the Western Reserve of Ohio, but he also outlined the reasons he left the movement during the tumultuous events in Missouri a few years later.[16]

The former apostle Lyman Wight proclaimed a non-Utah brand of Mormonism. His sixteen-page *Address by Way of an Abridged Account and Journal of My Life,* however, insisted that he had honored Joseph Smith's wishes when founding an independent LDS colony in Texas.[17] Likewise, the peripatetic William Smith, who during his life moved among several branches of the movement, including one led by himself, recorded his memories of Mormonism's beginning in *William Smith on Mormonism.*[18] But no dissenting voice was more important than David Whitmer's in *An Address to All Believers in Christ.*[19] Whitmer was one of Joseph Smith's earliest associates and served as one of the three witnesses to the Book of Mormon plates. His recollections of Mormon origins evoked the spirit of the church's first few years when doctrine and procedure were simple. It was this first "church" to which Whitmer claimed loyalty, long after the various branches of the movement, including Utah Mormonism, had passed him by.

These early Mormon biographies and autobiographies told of the events in New York, Ohio, Missouri, and Illinois. Others told the LDS story from the Utah perspective. Daniel Webster Jones's *Forty Years among the Indians* was meant to be a romance tale and carried the formula language and narrative devices common to that kind of literature.[20] Jones, one of Mormonism's more than a dozen Indian scouts, told of harrowing escapes and dramatic encounters but in the process conveyed the earnestness of men of his stripe. James S. Brown was another hardy Great Basin frontiersman, who had helped discover California gold in 1848 and touched off the "Forty-Niner" onrush the following year. But Brown also had an active Mormon career, negotiating with the Indians and colonizing the Mormon cultural area. His turn-of-the-century *Life of a Pioneer* was full of devotion and served as a fitting epitaph to LDS men and women who had pioneered the West.[21]

The Mormon memoir with the best claim to literary quality was Parley P. Pratt's posthumous *Autobiography*.[22] The energetic and prolific Pratt left his mark as pamphleteer, preacher, poet, hymn-writer, explorer, missionary, and apostle. Many of these activities were recorded in his book, which successfully evoked the spirit of the church's first generation. While Pratt's prose sometimes moralized, at its best it achieved a poignancy that escaped other LDS works of this genre. If Pratt had lived to do some final drafting, this volume might have achieved the status of an American classic.[23]

The first Utah-based writer to turn to life-writing was the English immigrant and intellectual Edward W. Tullidge, who compiled three major biographical works in the 1870s: *Life of Brigham Young; Women of Mormondom;* and *Life of Joseph the Prophet*.[24] In addition, he penned perhaps as many as a hundred sketches, which appeared in the author's two historical and literary journals, *Tullidge's Quarterly Magazine* and the *Western Galaxy,* and in the biographical supplements to his *History of Salt Lake City and Its Founders* and *Tullidge's Histories, Volume II: Containing the History of All the Northern, Eastern, and Western Counties of Utah; Also the Counties of Southern Idaho*.[25]

Tullidge tried to infuse in his biographical writing an emotion in keeping with his view that Mormonism represented a major innovation in the affairs of humankind. To do so, he used Thomas Carlyles's great man theory. Tullidge saw Joseph Smith and Brigham Young as two of history's "men of destiny," who promised to revolutionize world society. His *Women of Mormondom,* filled with praise and idolization, was largely a series of autobiographies loosely tied together by the author's highly stylized epic prose. The religiously quixotic Tullidge (he repeatedly accepted and rejected traditional LDS belief) provided one innovation. Unlike most early Mormon writers, he generally set aside religious devotion for themes of empire building and social movement, for he saw himself as *the* historian and biographer of the Mormon commonwealth.[26]

Other biographies followed. George Q. Cannon, a member of the First Presidency and superintendent of the church's Sunday schools, published several biographies largely for youth in his fourteen-volume "Faith Promoting Series" of journals, histories, biography, and miscellany (after Cannon's death three additional works were added).[27] The biographical materials included extracts from the missionary journals of the apostle Wilford Woodruff and Cannon himself. Also published were the diary of the Mormons' famed "Apostle to the Indians," *Jacob Hamblin: A Narrative of His Personal Experience,* and the diary material of Brigham Young's counselor, *President Heber C. Kimball's Journal.*[28]

Cannon's more ambitious *Life of Joseph Smith, the Prophet* was also written for the church's youth.[29] However, the book's smooth-flowing, integrated narrative allowed it to reach a larger audience and become a church standard. But, like much early Mormon biography, it was panegyric, and its religious devotion prevented in-depth probing.

Even B. H. Roberts's *Life of John Taylor, Third President of the Church of Jesus Christ of Latter-day Saints* bordered on eulogy.[30] Roberts, perhaps Mormonism's ablest historian of the era, had access to Taylor's journals and family papers that have since disappeared, but the final product, written in the aftermath of the anti-Mormon judicial crusade, was defensive in tone. Moreover, the work bore another frailty common to biographical writing of the time: Roberts, obviously drawn to his subject, found objectivity difficult.

Striking a different chord was Fanny Stenhouse. Her *Exposé of Polygamy in Utah: A Lady's Life among the Mormons,* later reworked into the more familiar *"Tell It All": The Story of a Life Experience in Mormonism, an Autobiography,* repudiated Mormonism.[31] Stenhouse, like Tullidge, was associated with the reform movement of William S. Godbe and E. L. T. Harrison, which rejected Brigham Young's religious and economic policies.[32]

Most early Mormon life-writing venerated spiritual and family forebears. This was especially true of the popular vignette biography that emerged throughout the United States during the 1876 Independence centennial. As part of the celebration, many American communities honored their pioneers with local histories, complete with "mug book" biographical sketches that were often financially underwritten by the subjects themselves.[33] On the Mormon scene, this genre was apparent in the brief portraits that Tullidge appended to his historical works written in the 1880s. Andrew Jenson, later the LDS assistant church historian, followed with an 1888 biographical supplement to his periodical series, the *Historical Record.* These and other biographical essays eventually found their way into his four volume *Latter-day Saint Biographical Encyclopedia.*[34] Other Utah authors did likewise. The fourth and final volume of Orson F. Whitney's *History of Utah* was given over to biographical sketches, while Frank E. Esshom's *Pioneers and Prominent Men of Utah* contained over four thousand brief profiles.[35]

Taken together, these works represented the start of the LDS biographical tradition. Seldom, however, did they move beyond chronological summary. Most were one-dimensional views that stressed civic or church activity, and few women passed through the biographical portals. If Mormon life-writing was representative of the time, Mormon society at the turn of the century remained oriented to men, hierarchy, institution, and religion. But these weaknesses had at least one virtue. The best nineteenth-century works, for all their flaws, captured the authentic devotion of the times. Their authors were men and women of the first and second generation, evangels of the new faith, and their writing bore the imprint of their spirit. Though they did not stack up to the best literary biography produced a century later, they are essential sources for those seeking to understand the spirit of their times.

Twentieth-Century LDS Life-Writing

Mormon interest in biography and autobiography greatly increased during the twentieth century. Indeed, life-writing became one of Mormonism's most prominent cultural expressions. Between 1900 and 1997, 320 books, 670 articles, and 115 theses and dissertations with a biographical theme appeared—more than 1,100 titles. Also impressive were the number of autobiographical works: 72 books and 93 article-length manuscripts. These statistics did not include several hundred privately published family biographies, most of which made little attempt at historical or literary craftsmanship. Nor did they include almost 700 brief biographical sketches that were published during the century. Clearly life-writing had a special meaning for Mormons.

Unfortunately, women were woefully underrepresented, and minorities were almost completely ignored. Well over 80 percent of the biographies published during the century had men as their subjects. Moreover, many of these works dwelt with "great men"—church leaders of major or secondary importance. Until nearly the end of the century, ordinary members of the church, whose lives were often just as dynamic and just as revealing of the Mormon experience as those of the leaders, also received lamentably short shrift.

Biographies of Joseph Smith

Still another indication of the traditional approach of Mormon biography, almost one in every four book-length manuscripts had a president of the church as its central figure. Although these writings varied in quality and perspective and some made valuable contributions, only a handful were literary biographies in the sense we have discussed here. At least half were written by people not trained in history or a related scholarly field: family members, journalists, amateur (though sometimes competent) historians, and others who had various reasons for writing. Most of these biographies were bland in their presentation and more bent on adulation and faith promotion than on balance and scholarly analysis. The most prolific producer of presidential biographies, for example, was Francis M. Gibbons, secretary to the First Presidency and later a general authority who served on the Council of the Seventy. Between 1977 and 1996, he produced a book on every president of the church except the most recent incumbents. Written with a church audience in mind, Gibbons's works cast his prophet-heroes in a "faithful" light, as some of the titles of his books suggested: *Joseph Smith: Martyr, Prophet of God; Wilford Woodruff: Wondrous Worker, Prophet of God; Lorenzo Snow: Spiritual Giant, Prophet of God;* and *Heber J. Grant: Man of Steel, Prophet of God.*[36]

Works about Joseph Smith were especially numerous in the twentieth century.[37] One of the first to be published was I. Woodbridge Riley's *Founder of Mormonism: A Psychological Study of Joseph Smith, Jr.*[38] Riley, who completed his research at Yale at the beginning of the century, reflected a new approach to biography: the technical analysis of character based on psychological scrutiny and criteria. His contemporary Gamaliel Bradford called his own character portraits "psychographs," but eventually this genre came to be known as "psychohistory," and its practitioners drew much of their inspiration from Freud. Riley's approach was less analytical than environmental: using the Book of Mormon, which he assumed Smith had written (not translated, as Mormons believe), he concluded that Smith had unconsciously taken the idea of a Hebrew origin of the American Indian and reshaped it according to the prevailing evangelical Protestantism of his neighborhood. In Riley's view, Smith was more an unwitting product of his culture than a conscious deceiver.

Remarkably, it was another thirty years before another book-length biography of Joseph Smith appeared: John Henry Evans's *Joseph Smith, an American Prophet.* Evans, a religiously active Mormon, nevertheless rejected traditional LDS hagiography. Instead of emphasizing Joseph Smith's prophetic office, he repeatedly commented on Smith's humanity. Young Smith could be "uncouth," "quiet," and "lowspeaking." Moreover, the mature Smith was a "good hater," who erred in suppressing the *Nauvoo Expositor,* which led to his assassination. Nor did Evans believe that Smith was a spiritual automaton who possessed a "divine pipeline" to revelatory truth. Rather, in Evans's view, the Mormon prophet often took ideas from his environment and then reshaped them in unexpected and exciting ways.[39]

Evans understood that Smith's limitations and mistakes were part of the inevitable pattern of human life. As a biographer, he also understood that human qualities and foibles, usually inserted in the text as subordinate clauses, were useful literary devices that gave credence to his more frequent praise of the Mormon prophet. For example, Evans commended Smith for energizing modern Christianity and called him "the most compelling personality" in American religious history. Smith's mission was so creative that Evans viewed him as an enigma defying normal historical explanation.[40]

For non-Mormons, some of Evans's judgments may have seemed sweeping, yet his book was important. Despite its out-of-date research, over sixty years after its publication *Joseph Smith, an American Prophet* remains one of the few biographies of Joseph Smith that takes the Mormon prophet seriously as an important religious figure while placing him in his larger American cultural context.[41]

Fawn McKay Brodie's *No Man Knows My History: The Life of Joseph Smith, the Mormon Prophet* carried a very different spirit. Like Evans, Brodie found Joseph Smith puzzling. But for Brodie, who, unlike Evans, was alienated from her inherited faith, the riddle of Smith involved his supposed disreputable past. She accepted the arguments of such anti-Mormon writers as Eber D. Howe and Doctor Philastus Hurlbut that Smith began his career as an impostor. However, seeking a more balanced and nuanced interpretation, Brodie added the idea that Smith's natural talent, imagination, and genius eventually transformed him into the "Lord's prophet" despite himself. Brodie's approach allowed Smith to grow and develop as a human being, but it was also an interpretation that allowed Smith little sincere religious feeling.[42]

A landmark in Mormon historical writing, *No Man Knows My History* was examined in greater depth in chapter 2, but this much may be said here: her book brilliantly displayed the cares and techniques of a novelist and achieved an emotional depth unusual in Mormon writing. Under Brodie's hand, Smith became a multidimensional, flesh-and-blood man, striving and growing. For those willing to overlook its naturalism and its implicit sense of exposé, Brodie's book was one of Mormon culture's most creative literary biographies. It succeeded as art.[43]

Other Joseph Smith biographers were more open to religious discussion. Daryl Chase's *Joseph Smith the Prophet: As He Lives in the Hearts of His People* was more interpretive and analytical, arguing that Smith and Mormonism were not alone in asserting such things as the need for apostles and prophets and the sacramental ordinance of baptism for the dead.[44] In turn, the New York regionalist Carl Carmer studied Joseph Smith within the framework of the cultural and religious setting of upstate New York. Written in popular style and designed to appeal to the masses, *The Farm Boy and the Angel* was well received by Mormon and non-Mormon audiences alike.[45]

Two books came closer to putting Smith at center stage of good biography. The first was Donna Hill's *Joseph Smith, the First Mormon*, the first major biography of Joseph Smith since Brodie's. The book had the advantage of thirty years of additional research, some of which was provided by Donna Hill's brother, the LDS historian Marvin Hill, who apparently had been a prepublication collaborator. Rich in data and tending toward the modern disciplines of history, sociology, and the study of religion, *Joseph Smith, the First Mormon* was more a history of Smith than a literary biography. His personality, drives, and ambition seemed less well defined than the outward mosaic of his life. Perhaps this was the reason many readers overlooked this important book. Or perhaps its pages tended to be too affirming for a non-Mormon audience: Hill readily confessed a sympathy for Smith, whom she regarded as "an inspired spiritual leader."[46]

The second of these two books was Richard L. Bushman's *Joseph Smith and the Beginnings of Mormonism,* which became one of the best sources for Smith's background and early career. Bushman argued that Smith was influenced by "traditional supernaturalism," which included the folk practices of upstate New York. Contesting this influence was Enlightenment rationalism. Bushman believed that Smith eventually outgrew both of these cultural influences and produced something unique. "We can understand Mormonism better," Bushman wrote, "if it is seen as an independent creation, drawing from its environment but also struggling against American culture in an effort to realize itself."[47] If Bushman's conclusion confirmed traditional Mormon belief, he also brought youthful Smith's treasure hunting into the mainstream of LDS scholarship.

Biographies of Brigham Young

In the twentieth century alone, nearly fifty articles, theses, dissertations, and books were devoted to Brigham Young, the second president of the LDS Church. Some were written by non-Mormons. For instance, Morris R. Werner, a journalist and popular historian, wrote a *Ladies Home Journal* series that became the basis for his biography, *Brigham Young.*[48] Werner's book was both a history of Mormonism and a biography of Young; almost a third of his manuscript focused on early Mormonism and Joseph Smith. Unfortunately, Werner's sources were limited to secondary works and to Young's published sermons, which prevented in-depth discussion. Werner's judgments, which seemed to waver between ironic detachment and genuine admiration for his subject, were superficial.

Stanley P. Hirshson, at the outset of his book *The Lion of the Lord: A Biography of Brigham Young,* claimed to believe that Young was an "unusual man" of wide interests.[49] In fact, he gave Young little praise, partly because of his choice of source materials. Arguing that the key to Young's life was not to be found in Utah sources—Young's own voluminous papers and allied church primary documents housed in the church's Salt Lake City archives—Hirshson turned to the nineteenth-century accounts of contemporaneous journalists and Utah observers, notorious for their lack of sympathy for the LDS leader. The result was not balanced biography but caricature. At best, Hirshson's book provided the useful service of indexing Young's nineteenth-century eastern image.[50]

In the first part of the century, two Mormon church workers also produced biographies of Young. Preston Nibley, the son of Charles W. Nibley, a wealthy businessman and general authority, published more than a half-dozen articles on Young in the church-owned *Improvement Era.* These articles became the basis for Nibley's book *Brigham Young: The Man and His Work.* For source material, Nibley drew heavily on Young's reminiscent statements contained in his published sermons. As a result, his narrative—more by implication than by argument—revealed how the church leader viewed himself. Nibley, however, was not a biographer in the modern sense. He made no effort to examine Young's complexity and avoided controversy. He managed to write his 550-page manuscript without even mentioning Young's celebrated polygamy. The result was distortion by omission.[51]

The second church worker was Susa Young Gates, who had much in common with Nibley. Like Nibley, she served on important churchwide committees, had a distinguished general authority father (Brigham Young), and possessed a desire to write ("All my life, I have wanted to do great deeds, speak mighty words, write powerful books," she said).[52] She published preliminary material on Young in the *Improvement Era.* Finally, late in life, Gates and her daughter Leah D. Widtsoe coauthored a biography by using the material Gates had already written, adding additional narrative, and wielding scissors to cut and paste together a large collection of haphazardly gathered anecdotes. A condensed and edited version was published in London as *The Life Story of Brigham Young* in 1930 and an American edition followed within the year.[53]

The Gates and Widtsoe biography helped readers understand Brigham Young's personality, especially in a private setting. They created a warmer portrait than previous historians had given the church leader, but, like Nibley, Gates and Widtsoe were guarded in their writing. Gates excused her selectivity of facts by explaining that her father's enemies had so magnified his faults that there was "small need" for his friends to paint "personal shadows."[54] *The Life Story of Brigham Young*, then, was a family biography, important for its contribution but without the complexity of a full-scale biography.

During the century, several important though more modest works appeared. *Here Is Brigham: Brigham Young, the Years to 1844* was written by S. Dilworth Young, a family member who was a general authority; it contained fine writing and helpful insights.[55] Eugene England's *Brother Brigham* was a series of personal and often affectionate essays in which the negative in Young's life was subordinated to the positive. On Young's platform manner, for example, he wrote that Young "used his voice and example in ways that were picturesque, abrasive (though acceptably so to most), marvelously motivating to almost every one, and at times tenderly spiritual."[56] Susan Easton Black and Larry C. Porter edited sixteen essays for a book entitled *Lion of the Lord: Essays on the Life and Service of Brigham Young.*[57] Though unevenly edited, some of these articles contained information on previously neglected topics. Newell G. Bringhurst's *Brigham Young and the Expanding American Frontier* used the research notes of Donald R. Moorman, whose projected Brigham Young biography was cut short by Moorman's early death.[58] Bringhurst emphasized the western movement and Mormon-U.S. relations, effectively placing Young in a larger historical context. His book remains the best short biography of the Mormons' second leader.

Leonard J. Arrington, dean of Mormon historians, wrote the first full-scale modern biography of Young, *Brigham Young: American Moses*. Arrington took advantage of the years that he had served as director of the History Division at LDS headquarters to examine the extensive collection of Young papers. He had also directed several members of his staff to write a series of articles, monographs, and edited works dealing with Young. This research and writing became the basis for Arrington's book, the first to make extensive use of Young's private material and official documents. The result was a historian's biography, full of detail, with an emphasis on Young's life and times. However, the book also sought to reveal Young's character. Navigating between the interpretative extremes of Young as saint and Young as devil, Arrington found a man of complexity and contradiction: "He shared with most public men the subtleties of policy that give every appearance of duplicity, yet he acted again and again in ways that could have been fueled only by deep sincerity."[59] Generally, however, Arrington's portrait was favorable.

Biographies of Other Church Leaders

No other LDS leader received the biographical attention given to Joseph Smith and Brigham Young, and often work done on other figures was preliminary. Nevertheless, signs of solid biography began to appear. Samuel W. Taylor, a professional writer who knew how to develop a scene, wrote successive biographies of his father and grandfather. The fictionalized *Family Kingdom* had the colorful, defrocked LDS apostle John W. Taylor as its central character.[60] The more history-minded *The Kingdom or Nothing: The Life of John Taylor, Militant Mormon* presented the life story of the LDS Church's third president.[61] Although this biography had enough Strachey-like, against-the-grain comment to offend many Mormons (not to mention errors of fact and interpretation), the work did succeed in portraying Taylor's personality and life as few LDS biographies were able to do.

Thomas G. Alexander produced a biography of the fourth prophet, seer, and revelator, *Things in Heaven and Earth: The Life and Times of Wilford Woodruff, a Mormon Prophet.*[62] This fact-filled work, which considered Woodruff's family background, was a model of scholarly research and analysis. The book's conclusions, moreover, seemed unassailable: the long-lived Woodruff was a transitional figure who helped usher his church into the modern times. Milo J. Pusey used a multigenerational theme in his book *Builders of the Kingdom: George A. Smith, John Henry Smith, George Albert Smith.*[63] Pusey, who had won a Pulitzer Prize and a Bancroft Prize for non-Mormon biography, traced the careers of a father, son, and grandson, each of whom served in the LDS First Presidency; the last, George Albert Smith, became the eighth president of the church in the middle of the twentieth century.

J. Reuben Clark, a staff member in the U.S. Department of State, an ambassador to Mexico, and a counselor in three LDS first presidencies, was the subject of two exemplary biographies: Frank W. Fox's *J. Reuben Clark: The Public Years* and D. Michael Quinn, *J. Reuben Clark: The Church Years.*[64] Both of these well-written volumes had a frankness unusual for institutional biography, which was probably the result of the insistence of Marion G. Romney, a former protégé of Clark who became a First Presidency counselor himself. "Any biographer of President Clark must write the truth about him," insisted Romney. "An account of his life should tell of his decisions and indecisions, sorrows and joys, regrets and aspirations, reverses and accomplishments, and, above all, his constant striving."[65] Romney's statement provided an important guideline for all LDS biography.

Other prominent LDS leaders were also the subjects of biographies. Sidney Rigdon, one of Joseph Smith's counselors, received preliminary treatment in F. Mark McKiernan's *Voice of One Crying in the Wilderness: Sidney Rigdon, Religious Reformer, 1793–1876* and fuller attention in Richard S. Van Wagoner's *Sidney Rigdon: A Portrait of Religious Excess.*[66]

Several of Brigham Young's close associates also received attention. Stanley B. Kimball's biography, *Heber C. Kimball: Mormon Patriarch and Pioneer*, surveyed the life of his great-great-grandfather, one of Young's closest friends and Young's counselor in the LDS First Presidency. Kimball painted a portrait of an unsophisticated "guileless Nathaniel," revered as much for his foibles as for his strengths.[67] Claire Noall's *Intimate Disciple: A Portrait of Willard Richards* was the life story of another of Young's influential counselors.[68] Unfortunately, the value of Noall's highly readable book was reduced by its use of "creative" dialogue that mingled fact and fiction.

One of the best Mormon biographies was the life story of George Q. Cannon, another colleague of Brigham Young whose career as an apostle and councilor in the church's First Presidency lasted until 1901. Davis Bitton's *George Q. Cannon: A Biography* argues that except for Joseph Smith and Brigham Young "no one surpassed Cannon as a leader, shaper, and defender of nineteenth-century Mormonism."[69] In truth, Cannon was an important immigrant, pioneer, missionary, publisher, educator, entrepeneur, politician, and especially churchman, whose diaries Bitton ranked with those of Samuel Pepys. In telling this life story, Bitton has the advantage of being the first to publish from this important source as well as from other pristine material; he also brings to the task his background as one of Mormonism's senior and most experienced scholars. The result is a richly detailed and well-told biography that is essential reading for students of late nineteenth-century Mormonism. Regretfully, because the book is commissioned biography, it smooths Cannon's edges and minimizes or deletes some items of controversy from his career.

Several able biographies examined the lives of nineteenth-century apostles. Breck England's *Life and Thought of Orson Pratt* treated the life of the scholarly and sometimes intellectually recalcitrant church leader.[70] Andrew Karl Larson's *Erastus Snow: The Life of a Missionary and Pioneer for the Early Mormon Church* surveyed the life of the LDS apostle who led Mormon proselytizing to Scandinavia and later directed the settlement of Utah's southwest "Dixie" region.[71] Fair-minded and generous, Snow was also known for his rambling sermons, unintentionally memorialized by Larson's discursive writing style. Leonard Arrington produced a series of commemorative biographies. One of the best of these was *Charles C. Rich: Mormon General and Western Frontiersman*, which gave the history of the LDS apostle who directed church colonization in southern California and later in the Bear Lake region on the Utah-Idaho border.[72]

Biographies of twentieth-century church leaders were harder to come by. Preparing for a book-length manuscript, Ronald W. Walker produced a series of articles on the family and life of Heber J. Grant, the church's long-tenured president during the first half of the century,[73] but the full biography is still in the making. Eugene E. Campbell and Richard D. Poll's *Hugh B. Brown: His Life and Thought* was a workmanlike survey of one of twentieth-century Mormonism's most interesting general authorities.[74] Highly gifted as a speaker, Brown had liberal-leaning social and political views that set him apart from his conservative counterparts. David S. Hoopes and Roy Hoopes's *Making of a Mormon Apostle: The Story of Rudger Clawson* reviewed the life of a longtime apostle, who although he allegedly took a post-Manifesto plural wife was never disciplined for the act.[75]

Truman Madsen's *Defender of the Faith: The B. H. Roberts Story* was in many ways an artful rendering of one of the church's most important historians and intellectuals. Recorded are Roberts's early struggles with alcohol (it "would not only beat him to his knees but to his elbows and chin"), his well-intentioned but maladroit attempts at husbandhood and fatherhood, and his unremitting cycles of pugnacity and reconciliation.[76] Yet much of this information was conveyed in nonchalant sentences and paragraphs that might have been expanded in a more rounded and frank portrait.

One of the most interesting developments in the writing of LDS biography was the rise of popular institutional biography of living church leaders. This genre owed a great deal to two well-crafted books about church president Spencer W. Kimball and his wife, Camilla Eyring Kimball: Edward L. Kimball and Andrew E. Kimball Jr.'s *Spencer W. Kimball: Twelfth President of the Church of Jesus Christ of Latter-day Saints* and Caroline Eyring Miner and Edward L. Kimball's *Camilla: A Biography of Camilla Eyring Kimball*.[77] Written by family members, these volumes boldly cast Mormondom's "first brother and sister" into the texture of real life. Here was struggling personality, the depiction of genuine emotion, and details that were at times stark (for example, during President Kimball's subdural hematoma operation, Miner and Kimball wrote, "the pressure [on his skull] was so great that fluid spurted out two feet").[78]

Such realism and honesty departed from the eulogistic formulas of the time and made the Kimball biographies best-sellers. Their popularity established a precedent: since the Kimball presidency concluded in 1985, popular biographies have been issued for each succeeding church president and for several prominent general authorities. While lacking the detachment, complexity, and analysis required of more enduring biography, these warmly written and anecdote-filled books have acquainted church members more fully with their leaders.[79] Their shorter counterparts were the biographical sketches published by such popular, institutionally oriented magazines as the

Ensign, This People, and the briefly published *Mormon Heritage Magazine.* More substantial was *Presidents of the Church,* an anthology of essays dealing with the lives of Mormon presidents that was edited by Leonard J. Arrington.[80]

Outside the Ranks of the General Authorities

Contemporary LDS biography showed an increasing interest in men and women who were not church leaders, though some were particularly close to the centers of Mormon power and played important roles in Mormon history. Some were prominent in business, education, or other professions, while others were notable primarily for how well their lives reflected the rank-and-file experience. Donald Q. Cannon and David J. Whittaker's *Supporting Saints: Life Stories of Nineteenth-Century Mormons* collected more than a dozen biographical essays of nineteenth- and twentieth-century figures, most of whom never held major ecclesiastical office.[81]

Among the noteworthy full-length biographies of non–general authorities was another of Leonard Arrington's commemorative biographies. *From Quaker to Latter-day Saint: Bishop Edwin D. Woolley* detailed the life of the long-standing bishop of Salt Lake City's Thirteenth Ward, one of the most prominent congregations of the pioneer era. Arrington also wrote books on the Utah governor William Spry, the industrialist David Eccles, the entrepreneur Harold F. Silver, and the cattleman Charles Redd.[82] Martin B. Hickman's *David Matthew Kennedy: Banker, Statesman, Churchman* told the story of a small-town Mormon who became a leading national banker, a U.S. Federal Reserve officer, a cabinet member in the Nixon administration, and, finally, the LDS Church's political "ambassador" in its effort to establish relationships with many foreign governments.[83] Mary Lythgoe Bradford's *Lowell L. Bennion: Teacher, Counselor, Humanitarian* was the biography of an honored educator and community worker.[84] Lythgoe traced Bennion's service as an influential instructor at the LDS Institute of Religion adjacent to the University of Utah as well as his later humanitarian work in the Salt Lake City community.

James B. Allen's *Trials of Discipleship: The Story of William Clayton, a Mormon* examined the life of an important associate of Joseph Smith and a later Utah pioneer. Because Clayton served as one of Smith's secretaries, his career helped illuminate the church's Nauvoo era, including the development of its semisecret plural marriage. It also showed the crosscurrents of Utah society. Allen intended his book as an example of how the study of a "disciple" (he used this term as a methodological device) could have greater importance than just the telling of a single person's life story. Clayton's "problems were often community problems," Allen wrote, "his attitudes reflected those of many other Mormons, and his frustrations dramatically illustrate the diversity of frustrations that were possible inside the Mormon community."[85]

S. George Ellsworth's *Samuel Claridge: Pioneering the Outposts of Zion* presented the life history of another pioneer whose life was intertwined with many of the defining events of nineteenth-century Mormon history: settlement in central Utah, participation in the especially difficult Muddy mission in southern Nevada, later settlement in southern Utah, participation in the well-known economic enterprise known as the United Order, missionary work in England, pioneering and leadership roles in Arizona, and participation in plural marriage.[86]

Nineteenth-century Mormon culture produced more than its share of frontiersmen, Indian fighters, and adventurers, whose colorful lives attracted the attention of biographers. Paul Bailey wrote lively but thinly researched books on Sam Brannan, Jacob Hamblin, and Walter Murray Gibson.[87] Hope A. Hilton produced a biography of "Wild Bill" Hickman, one of her ancestors. Hickman, who lived on the margins of Mormonism's pioneer life, eventually authored a "tell-all" account of early pioneer conditions that claimed to implicate Brigham Young in extralegal killing.[88] Perhaps the best and most meticulously researched example of the "adventure" genre was Juanita Brooks's *John D. Lee: Zealot—Pioneer Builder—Scapegoat.* Brooks, who had written earlier on the infamous Mountain Meadows massacre, provided additional information on the man traditionally held responsible for the affair but who Brooks believed was a scapegoat.[89] Finally, Harold Schindler's *Orrin Porter Rockwell: Man of God, Son of Thunder* described the life of early Utah's most famous lawman and the alleged "enforcer" of Brigham Young's secret will.[90] Schindler's book contained well-crafted writing and controversial research.

More often than not, the growing body of biographical literature was commissioned biography and therefore required writers to separate familial celebration from honest reporting, a delicate and difficult task. Richard D. Poll, who wrote a biography of the life of the Michigan banker Howard J. Stoddard, was forthright about the problems this kind of biography presented. This book "accents the positive," Poll unblushingly admitted, although he also noted that "the reader will have no difficulty discovering why Howard Stoddard was a controversial figure."[91] Davis Bitton provided an important look at the human side of Mormon history with his readable *Redoubtable John Pack: Pioneer, Proselyter, Patriarch,* which argued the case for Mormonism's rank-and-file. According to Bitton, Pack was a loyal, hardworking, but uncelebrated Saint, who had met the test of "difficult challenges" and therefore helped determine Mormonism's growth and success.[92]

Another historian who produced several commissioned, rank-and-file biographies but avoided the myopic tendency to overlook "problems" was Brigham Young University's William G. Hartley. His book *"They Are My Friends": A History of the Joseph Knight Family, 1825–1850* traced the career and family of one of Joseph Smith's first converts. Another Hartley biography, *My Best for the Kingdom: History and Autobiography of John Lowe Butler, a Mormon Frontiersman,* featured a church member whose life embodied many of the important events of first-generation Mormonism: the exodus from Illinois, Utah colonization and settlement, Native American relations, plural marriage relationships, and local church governance. A strong narrative style and attention to the broader historical context were characteristics of Hartley's several books.[93]

Women: Too Often Neglected

Women, so long neglected as a subject of Mormon biography, slowly increased in importance. Most work was preliminary and therefore appeared in articles rather than in books. However, some of these articles indicated important ongoing projects. For instance, Carol Cornwall Madsen produced more than half a dozen articles on Emmeline B. Wells, a nineteenth-century feminist, suffragist, and later president of the church's Relief Society.[94] Maureen Ursenbach Beecher used the articles-to-book approach as she worked on a study of Eliza Roxcy Snow, perhaps the most influential LDS woman during the last half of the nineteenth century. Beecher reprinted her essays in *Eliza and Her Sisters.*[95]

Essay-length biography took other forms. Such publications as the *Utah History Encyclopedia,* edited by Allan Kent Powell; the *Encyclopedia of Mormonism,* edited by Daniel H. Ludlow; and Richard S. Van Wagoner and Steven C. Walker's *Book of Mormons* had sketches of important LDS women and men.[96] Leonard Arrington and his daughter Susan Arrington Madsen published a volume dealing with the mothers of LDS Church presidents.[97] Janet Peterson and LaRene Porter Gaunt wrote three books that sketched the women who presided over the church's three female organizations—the children's Primary Organization, the teenagers' Young Women's Mutual Improvement Association, and the adults' Relief Society.[98] Still another collection of women's biography, edited by Collen Whitley, featured nine prominent Utah women.[99] Perhaps the most substantive of these biographical collections was Vicky Burgess-Olsen's edited anthology, *Sister Saints.* This volume featured almost two dozen essays written by leading LDS women scholars, many of whom were beginning their careers when the book was first published.[100]

Gradually book-length studies of women began to appear. John A. Widtsoe penned an affectionate sketch of his mother, Anna K. G. Widtsoe.[101] Juliaetta Bateman Jensen's biography of her mother, Marinda Allen Bateman, told of pioneer midwifery, plural marriage on the "underground," and the routines of early Utah existence.[102] Leonard J. Arrington's *Madelyn Cannon Stewart Silver: Poet, Teacher, Homemaker* presented the life story of a woman who both reflected twentieth-century female norms and, because of her ability, exceeded them.[103] Juanita Brooks wrote the biography of Emma Lee, a plural wife of John D. Lee.[104] Brooks herself became a subject of a major biography written by Levi S. Peterson, which confirmed Brooks's place as a leading twentieth-century LDS historian and woman intellectual.[105] Linda King Newell and Valeen Tippetts Avery's book, *Mormon Enigma: Emma Hale Smith,* was a series of episodal chapters that dealt sympathetically with Joseph Smith's first wife and challenged traditional assumptions about Joseph Smith, plural marriage in Nauvoo, and Mormonism itself.[106]

At the end of the century, another competent woman's biography appeared, Newell G. Bringhurst's *Fawn McKay Brodie: A Biographer's Life.*[107] In preparing his manuscript, Bringhurst used the article-to-book approach; more than half a dozen articles preceded his published book. Conceptually, Bringhurst realized the biographer's need to understand the self and noted the parallels between Brodie and him. Both shared a Mormon family heritage that no longer seemed religiously compelling. Both wished to probe their biographical subjects beyond the surface: "I have tried to present the whole individual, emphasizing not only. . . . [Brodie's] varied accomplishments and contributions as a preeminent biographer but also assessing her frailties, frustrations, and failures—all reflective of the complex, compelling individual she was."[108] The result was a rounded and balanced portrait, including the irony that Brodie had the same sexual repression that she found in her own biographical subjects.

Dissenters and Schismatics

Yet another new biographical topic involved dissenters—those men and women who departed from the orthodox path as defined by Utah Mormonism. Lyndon W. Cook's *William Law* sought to place William Law, Joseph Smith's counselor at Nauvoo, in a larger context. Cook saw Law as a Jefferson Democrat who opposed Smith for many of the same reasons that other nineteenth-century citizens opposed strong-willed if not "autocratic" rule elsewhere in the United States.[109] Andrew F. Smith's *Saintly Scoundrel: The Life and Times of Dr. John Cook Bennett* told of the adventures of one of Mormonism most problematic (although talented and ambitious) figures.[110] Bennett rose to brief prominence in Nauvoo before his excommunication led him to write an anti-Mormon exposé. Smith concluded that Bennett was "Barnumesque" in his interests, more scoundrel than saint. Another dissenter, the idiosyncratic and colorful James J. Strang, was the subject of several biographies, including the recently published work by Roger Van Noord, *King of Beaver Island: The Life and Assassination of James Jesse Strang.*[111] Strang, who established a schismatic headquarters at Beaver Island, Michigan, and for several years contested Brigham Young's succession, was later killed by two malcontents of his group.

Members of the Reorganized Church of Jesus Christ of Latter Day Saints—those who followed the religious policies of Joseph Smith's son Joseph Smith III—also received biographical attention. Roger D. Launius produced two studies of Joseph III, most important, *Joseph Smith III: Pragmatic Prophet.*[112] Launius described the founder of the Reorganized Church of Jesus Christ of Latter Day Saints as both principled and practical—someone who used "patience and compromise" in seeking worthy goals.[113] Another of Joseph Smith's sons, David Smith, was the subject of Valeen Tippetts Avery's *From Mission to Madness: Last Son of the Mormon Prophet.* Avery suggested that Smith, viewed as a man of promise by members of the restoration's various branches, became instead a tragic figure.[114] While naturally endowed as a musician, poet, and preacher, Smith eventually succumbed to a mental instability that came at least partly from the religious and sexual tension existing in his life.

Two books dealing with dissent had a larger perspective. Roger D. Launius and Linda Thatcher edited *Differing Visions: Dissenters in Mormon History,* which focused on sixteen dissenters drawn from the restoration movement—fundamentalists, intellectuals, would-be prophets, and still others who were alienated because of political, religious, and sexual issues.[115] Ronald W. Walker's collective biography, *Wayward Saints: The Godbeites and Brigham Young,*[116] on one level discussed the intellectual schism of William S. Godbe and E. L. T. Harrison (and associate dissenters Fanny Stenhouse, T. B. H. Stenhouse, Henry W. Lawrence, and Edward W. Tullidge), who sought to "liberalize" Brigham Young's theocractic Great Basin kingdom. However, Walker also used the Godbeite dissent to examine the cultural, economic, and ethnic divisions that beset nineteenth-century Utah Mormonism, including the influence that large-scale British immigration had on Mormon society.[117]

Autobiography

Twentieth-century life-writing also included many autobiographies. Like its sister genre of biography, autobiography, to be literature, required a frank depiction of human experience as well as an artful style of expression. One LDS autobiography that approached this ideal was written by the early twentieth-century general authority John A. Widtsoe, who titled his memoir *In a Sunlit Land: The Autobiography of John A. Widtsoe.* But even the Widtsoe autobiography, for all its merit, suffered from well-intentioned obscurantism. "After some reflection, personalities, hundreds of which have entered my life, have been almost entirely omitted," Widtsoe warned his readers in his preface. "If mentioned, comments would probably follow. That might hurt the feelings of some."[118]

The hesitant quality of Mormon autobiography was also often accompanied by a moral tone that filtered out conflicting emotions. Thus, many autobiographies, especially of Mormonism's pioneer generation, emphasized heroic deeds and correspondingly downplayed such personal aspects as religious doubt, social conflict, and even individuality. Still, valuable autobiographies were produced that provided a great many details of early Mormonism, including the reminiscences of George W. Bean, James S. Brown, John Brown, Joseph Fish, Christopher Layton, Mary Elizabeth Rollins Lightner, Louisa Barnes Pratt, and Aurelia Spencer Rogers.[119] In addition, the many journals and memoirs kept by pioneer men and women provide powerful, first-person accounts that, when skillfully edited, make important contributions to the growing field of autobiographical literature. A recent example of such a work is *Mormon Odyssey: The Story of Ida Hunt Udall, Plural Wife,* edited by Udall's granddaughter Maria S. Ellsworth.[120] Bringing together several memoirs and journals and over 170 letters, Ellsworth gave new life to Udall's experience in plural marriage as well as to other aspects of the nineteenth-century Mormon experience.

Shorter autobiographical statements of pioneer women were recorded in *Women's Voices: An Untold History of the Latter-day Saints, 1830–1900,* edited by Kenneth W. Godfrey, Audrey M. Godfrey, and Jill Mulvay Derr, and in materials published by the Daughters of the Utah Pioneers.[121] A more specialized collection of autobiographical excerpts was edited by Joyce Kinkead and titled *A Schoolmarm All My Life: Personal Narrative from Frontier Utah.*[122]

Pioneer women's autobiography will no doubt be furthered by the Life Writing of Frontier Women series to be published by the Utah State University Press under the direction of Maureen Ursenbach Beecher. To date, four volumes in this series have been issued.[123]

Twentieth-century autobiographical life-writing was richer. Several LDS general authorities produced autobiographies. In addition to Widtsoe's book, there were autobiographies written by George P. Lee, a Navajo educator and general authority who later became an excommunicant; Helvécio Martins, a Brazilian convert who was the church's first black general authority; Russell M. Nelson, a heart surgeon and apostle; Charles W. Nibley, a businessman, presiding bishop, and member of the First Presidency; B. H. Roberts, an intellectual and member of the Council of the Seventy; Sterling W. Sill, an insurance salesman and member of the Council of the Seventy; and Orson F. Whitney, an author and apostle.[124] In addition, some Mormons who served in the public sector completed manuscripts: U.S. Secretary of Agriculture (and later LDS president) Ezra Taft Benson; New Dealer and U.S. Federal Reserve chairman Marriner S. Eccles; Utah governors Herbert B. Maw and Calvin L. Rampton; and turn-of-the-century territorial delegate and later senator Joseph L. Rawlins.[125]

Some scholars and writers eagerly wrote their reminiscences: Ephraim E. Ericksen, LeRoy R. Hafen and Ann F. Hafen, Andrew Jenson, Andrew Karl Larson, Lowry Nelson, Hugh W. Nibley, and Obert C. Tanner.[126] Especially noteworthy was Leonard J. Arrington's *Adventures of a Church Historian.* Arrington, a former LDS Church historian and the dean of the "new Mormon history," provided one of the most important twentieth-century memoirs of LDS intellectual life.[127] The book successively presented Arrington as churchman, university teacher, administrator who dueled with church leaders, defender of the historical movement that he came to lead, and chronicler of a troubled historiographical past.

By the end of the twentieth century, the body of LDS autobiographies was large and growing. However, two twentieth-century titles especially stood out as literature that had the possibility of transcending their own time. Annie Clark Tanner's *Mormon Mother: An Autobiography* related the experience of a plural wife married to the insensitive educator John M. Tanner.[128] Told in a matter-of-fact style, Annie Clark Tanner's story was a poignant indictment of her personal experience while at the same time evidence of her own character and ability. More affirming to Mormon belief was the recollection of Juanita Brooks, published posthumously as *Quicksand and Cactus: A Memoir of the Southern Mormon Frontier.*[129] Although Brooks did not live to polish the final half of her memoir, the first part strongly evoked the spirit of

Mormon community life. In these pages, Brooks wrote about her childhood in a Mormon village in eastern Nevada.

Challenges and Opportunities

There are, of course, many kinds of life-writing. This essay focused on the modern narrative biography, with its three criteria of the science of modern historical method, the art of literature, and the intellectual integrity of truth-telling. To fulfill all these requirements and produce more high-quality literary biographies, future Mormon life-writers face numerous challenges, but they also have many opportunities.

One of the strengths of Mormon biography has been its historical content. Most biographies have been written by academic historians (in contrast to academics in other disciplines and professional writers) who based their biographies in solid (sometimes stolidly expressed) research. While informative and franker than earlier writing, this kind of biography has often lacked literary distinction. Moreover, it has frequently failed to probe much past a chronological outline of a subject's life.

"Full truth" requires the investigation into personality, psychology, physiology and health, and sexuality. It may also mean examining human weakness, human relationships, and the influence of political, social, and economic contexts. Many Mormon biographers have been wary of such questions. The closer LDS subject-characters have been to the locus of power, the less likely biographers have engaged in careful examination. Sometimes this tendency to conceal is revealed in the "art of telling," that is, putting disturbing facts into the record without offending conservative-minded readers. While a few stylists, such as John Henry Evans and Leonard Arrington, have managed to handle controversial topics with fine phrasing, other writers have been less successful. Their caution has often produced simple and harmonious portraits where simplicity and harmony were out of place.

Mormon biography often lacks the telling anecdote, the offhand comment, the characteristic trivia that great biographers have sized upon to reveal their subjects. It might be the excited platform style of an introverted Daniel H. Wells—struggling to control his flinging arms as they move perilously close to the scriptures stacked beside him on the podium. Or it could be the self-confident Charles Nibley cracking a salty joke as he lay dying. What could be more descriptive of Brigham Young than his motto: "I have got the grit in me, and I will do my duty any how"? And what better way to summarize the saintly and otherworldly life of Wilford Woodruff than by speaking of his favorite hymn: "God Moves in a Mysterious Way"?[130] This sense of detail and anecdote is not a part of the Mormon tradition, partly because of the failure of many biographers to pay attention to literary art but also because of a hesitancy to penetrate the inner person and sometimes even a lack of interest in doing so.

As LDS biography matures in research, technique, and realism, it will confront additional challenges. The massive bulk of today's manuscript collections, once a life-writer's fondest reverie, has become an illusory nightmare— an embarrassment of riches. The Joseph Smith material is stored in the LDS Library-Archives in six boxes occupying several feet of shelving. In contrast, the papers of Mormonism's seventh president, Heber J. Grant, required almost two hundred boxes and one hundred linear feet, while the David O. McKay collection, which is three times larger, ran the length of a football field.[131]

Even as Mormon biographers search into the behemoth manuscript collections now at hand, they have never been so unsure of themselves. Non-Mormon writers no longer ask "How much should be told?" but pose the more perplexing questions, "How much in fact can be known" and "What is truly important?"[132] The problem lies not in establishing a chronicle but in grasping the intimacy of a life in its totality, sensing the interior and sometimes the hidden aspects of a career. Dostoyevsky's observation in *Notes from Underground* is relevant: "In the reminiscences of every man there are some things that he does not reveal to anyone except possibly to friends. Then there are some that he will not even reveal to friends, but only to himself, and even so in secret. But finally there are some that a man is afraid to reveal even to himself."[133]

Fortunately, Mormon life-writers are not left empty-handed in their quests. "All sorts of keys to human behavior have been handed to the biographer," Paul Murray Kendall observed, "Which, it is true, he has sometimes used to open the wrong door, or has thrown away, or has played with like a small boy, uttering squeals of delight."[134] With Marxists vying with Freudians, and preachers with philosophers, biographers ask which key they should grasp—and some Mormon biographers grasp none at all. I. Woodbridge Riley's *Founder of Mormon: A Psychological Study of Joseph Smith, Jr.* (1903) began the psychological treatment that Brodie continued a half-century later. Her work was explicitly psychoanalytical, but the era that vaunted technical analysis in biography has largely given way. It is difficult enough to pronounce a diagnosis with the patient emitting a stream of consciousness on the couch, let alone write a biography separated from a subject by time and distance.

Nevertheless, the twentieth century speaks of defense mechanisms, inferiority complexes, repressions, rationalizations, and sublimations, and these insights have an important and unfulfilled role in Mormon biography. James Clifford's advice is probably best: "Be sensitive to possible psychological quirks of character, and give all of the relevant evidence, but make no attempts at technical analysis."[135] Robert Gittings offers a further piece of advice: Since biographers often interpret biographical subjects in their own image or at least as a reflection of their own concerns, "the first method of modern biography . . . is self-analysis."[136] By seeking to understand their own personal motivations in subject, thesis, and fact selection—in short, by psychoanalyzing the self—writers may avoid distortions in interpretation. Had Brodie analyzed herself, she might have softened her portrait of Joseph Smith and perhaps those of her non-LDS biographical subjects as well.

But of all the challenges facing LDS biographers—both Mormon and non-Mormon—none is as tormenting as how they should treat their own religious faith—if at all. While richly variegated, the fabric of most modern biography is decidedly secular, nonjudgmental, and more than faintly skeptical. In contrast, religious passion fills Mormon life-writing, as polarized Mormon and anti-Mormon jousting often continues as the order of the day. "This for-or-against mentality permeates the consciousness of everyone connected with Mormon studies," one critic held about two decades ago. "It helps explain why the historiography of Mormonism, vast as it is, contains little worth reading."[137] There is still much truth in what he said, but there are also signs of progress.

At stake is the question of "faithful biography." The expression is a contradiction in terms if *faithful* is taken to mean gilding the lily, tracing grand theological designs, ignoring historical context, or supplanting characterization with religious ends and emotions—apt characterizations of many Mormon, run-of-the-mill biographies.

Richard Bushman noted that "virtually everyone who has shown the 'human side' of the church and its leaders has believed the enterprise was strictly human." Of course this need not be so. Bushman suggested that historians are needed "who will mourn the failings of the Saints out of honor for God instead of relishing the warts because they show the church was earthbound after all."[138] Perhaps a clever biographer will manage this highly sophisticated task, though arguing God's cause or even mourning in his behalf is filled with hagiographic dangers. Other biographers may take a safer course. They will want to give the transcendent its proper due, and while providing historical context for such phenomena, they will largely allow biographical subjects and their peers to speak for themselves. Judgment of such an event will be left to those with spiritual eyes to see, with readers, not authors, mourning God's cause. Such an unobtrusive and unassuming manner may offend many. Gone will be the thunderous undulations of the nineteenth-century stylist who with Olympian sureness described the pattern of God's hand. Left to biographers is a more discrete task, freer from conceit and hubris, of describing earthly events as caring mortals fully aware of their own fallibility.

Even on this limited stage, biographers have scope for their virtuosity, for life-writing is the stage of everyday life, where the abstract forces of the social scientist, the philosopher, and the theologian come to center in the existence of a human being. Susan Hendricks Swetnam affirmed this in her recent study of seven thousand pages of regional, personal, and family history held at Idaho State University and the Idaho State Historical Library. She argued, "For anyone interested in the settlement of the Intermountain West, in nineteenth century women's history, in the region's agricultural history, and in the sociology of the pioneer family, to name just a few topics, LDS pioneer life stories are an invaluable resource." Her conclusion that "LDS pioneer life story writing ought to be taken seriously, and that it represents an important resource for both scholarly and generally curious readers" reminds her readers of the universal quality of biography.[139] That is why every Utah public library has long rows of shelves of biography and why, at least in part, the Kimball biographies were an LDS marketing phenomena and Schindler's *Orrin Porter Rockwell* remains one of the all-time best-sellers at the University of Utah Press.

At the end of the twentieth century, there was much to do. Future Mormon life-writing must be more concerned with the lives of the rank and file. It must deal more with women. Even within the category of "elites," the genre must provide scholarly biographies for more LDS leaders. The writing of LDS autobiographies is just getting started, yet the prognosis is not bleak. The biographical craft has made progress since the nineteenth century, especially in the last decades as authors have begun to fuse investigation, technique, and openness—the three essentials of biography—and to make use of the social sciences. With these qualities increasingly in place, the dry bones in the valley of Mormon biography may begin to feel the breath of life, and the men and women of the Mormon past may be reconstituted as real and believable human beings.

Notes

Parts of this chapter first appeared in Ronald W. Walker, "The Challenge and Craft of Mormon Biography," *BYU Studies* 22 (Spring 1982): 179–92.

1. Leonard Arrington used this metaphor with reference to Mormon history in "'Clothe These Bones': The Reconciliation of Faith and History" (unpublished address delivered on Salt Lake City's historic Ensign Peak, 23 June 1978, in authors' possession).

2. S. George Ellsworth, *Samuel Claridge: Pioneering the Outposts of Zion* (Logan, Utah: S. George Ellsworth, 1987), vii.

3. James Boswell, *The Life of Samuel Johnson, LL.D*, 5th ed. rev., 4 vols. (London: Printed for T. Cadwell and W. Davies, 1807), 1:6.

4. Elizabeth Greghorn Gaskell, *The Life of Charlotte Brontë* (London: Smith, Elder, 1857); Washington Irving, *Life of George Washington* (New York: G. P. Putnam, 1855).

5. For a twentieth-century version of this often printed and expanded work, see Mason Locke [Parson] Weems, *The Life of Washington*, ed. Marcus Cunliffe (Cambridge, Mass.: Belknap Press of Harvard University Press, 1962).

6. Lytton Strachey, *Eminent Victorians* (Garden City, N.Y.: Garden City Publishing, 1918), vi–vii. Although Mormon biography is largely ignored as a critical study, there are signs of growing interest. See James B. Allen, "Writing Mormon Biographies," in *World Conference on Records: Preserving Our Heritage* (Salt Lake City: World Conference on Records, 1980), 1–15; Gary James Bergera, "Toward 'Psychologically Informed' Mormon History and Biography," *Biography: An Interdisciplinary Quarterly* 4 (Winter 1981): 1–16; Davis Bitton, "Mormon Biography," *Biography: An Interdisciplinary Quarterly* 4 (Winter 1981): 1–16; Susan Hendricks Swetnam, "Turning to the Mothers: Mormon Women's Biographies of Their Female Forebears and the Mormon Church's Expectations for Women," *Frontiers: A Journal of Women Studies* 10, no. 1 (1988): 1–6; Susan Hendricks Swetnam, *Lives of the Saints in Southeast Idaho: An Introduction to Mormon Pioneer Life Story Writing* (Moscow: University of Idaho Press, 1991); and David J. Whittaker, "The Heritage of Tasks of Mormon Biography," in *Supporting Saints: Life Stories of Nineteenth-Century Mormons*, ed. Donald Q. Cannon and David J. Whittaker (Provo, Utah: Religious Studies Center, Brigham Young University, 1985), 1–16.

7. James L. Clifford, *From Puzzles to Portraits: Problems of a Literary Biographer* (Chapel Hill: University of North Carolina Press, 1970), 62–64.

8. Paul Murray Kendall, *The Art of Biography* (New York: W. W. Norton, 1965), 22–23.

9. Carl Pletsch, "Subjectivity and Biography," in *Introspection in Biography: The Biographer's Quest of Self-Awareness*, ed. Samuel H. Baron and Carl Pletsch (Hillsdale, N.J.: Analytical Press, 1985), 360.

10. Kendall, *The Art of Biography*, 28.

11. A. J. Grant, ed. and trans., *Early Lives of Charlemagne by Einhard and the Monk of St. Gall* (New York: Cooper Square, 1966), 6.

12. Robert Blake, *Disraeli* (London: Eyre and Spottiswoode, 1966); James MacGregor Burns, *Roosevelt: The Lion and the Fox* (New York: Harcourt, Brace, 1956); David Cecil, *Melbourne* (Indianapolis, Ind.: Bobbs-Merrill, 1954); Leon Edel, *Henry James* (Minneapolis: University of Minnesota Press, 1960); James Thomas Flexner, *George Washington*, 4 vols. (Boston: Little, Brown, 1965–72); Elizabeth Jenkins, *Elizabeth the Great* (London: Gollancz, 1958); Dumas Malone, *Jefferson and His Time*, 6 vols. (Boston: Little, Brown, 1948–81).

13. Lucy Mack Smith, *Biographical Sketches of Joseph Smith the Prophet and His Progenitors for Many Generations* (Liverpool: S. W. Richards, 1853). The Reorganized Church of Jesus Christ of Latter Day Saints reissued the book in 1880. For the LDS "revised" edition, see *History of the Prophet Joseph by His Mother Lucy Smith as Revised by George A. Smith and Elias Smith* (Salt Lake City: Improvement Era, 1902).

14. For more on this point, see Howard C. Searle, "Early Mormon Historiography:

Writing the History of the Mormons, 1830–1858" (Ph.D. diss., University of California at Los Angeles, 1979), 358–428; and Richard L. Anderson, "His Mother's Manuscript: An Intimate View of Joseph Smith" (Forum address, Brigham Young University, 27 January 1976).

15. Emily Austin, *Mormonism; or, Life among the Mormons* (Madison, Wis.: M. J. Cantwell, 1882).

16. John Corrill, *A Brief History of the Church of Christ* (St. Louis: By the author, 1839).

17. Lyman Wight, *An Address by Way of an Abridged Account and Journal of My Life* (Austin, Tex. [?]: n.p., 1848).

18. William Smith, *William Smith on Mormonism* (Lamoni, Iowa: Herald Steam Book and Job Office, 1883).

19. David Whitmer, *An Address to All Believers in Christ* (Richmond, Mo.: David Whitmer, 1887).

20. Daniel Webster Jones, *Forty Years among the Indians* (Salt Lake City: Juvenile Instructor Office, 1890).

21. James S. Brown, *Life of a Pioneer: Being the Autobiography of James S. Brown* (Salt Lake City: George Q. Cannon and Sons, 1900).

22. Parley P. Pratt, *Autobiography* (New York: Russell Brothers, 1874). For commentary on Pratt, see Dean L. May, "The Millennial Hymns of Parley P. Pratt," *Dialogue: A Journal of Mormon Thought* 16 (Spring 1983): 145–50; Peter Crawley, "Parley P. Pratt: Father of Mormon Pamphleteering," *Dialogue: A Journal of Mormon Thought* 15 (Autumn 1982): 13–26; Dale L. Morgan, "Literature in the History of the Church: The Importance of Involvement," *Dialogue: A Journal of Mormon Thought* 4 (Autumn 1969): 26–32; and David J. Whittaker, "Early Mormon Pamphleteering," *Journal of Mormon History* 4 (1977): 35–49.

23. R. A. Christmas, "The Autobiography of Parley P. Pratt: Some Literary, Historical, and Critical Reflections," *Dialogue: A Journal of Mormon Thought* 1 (Spring 1966): 33–43.

24. Edward W. Tullidge, *Life of Brigham Young* (New York: Tullidge and Crandall, 1876), *Women of Mormondom* (New York: Tullidge and Crandall, 1877), and *Life of Joseph the Prophet* (New York: Tullidge and Crandall, 1878).

25. Edward W. Tullidge, *History of Salt Lake City and Its Founders* (Salt Lake City: Edward W. Tullidge, 1883) and *Tullidge's Histories, Volume II: Containing the History of All the Northern, Eastern, and Western Counties of Utah; Also the Counties of Southern Idaho* (Salt Lake City: Juvenile Instructor, 1889).

26. Ronald W. Walker, "Edward Tullidge: Historian of the Mormon Commonwealth," *Journal of Mormon History* 3 (1976): 55–72.

27. The "Faith-Promoting Series" was published by the *Juvenile Instructor* beginning in 1879, and one or more volumes were annually added until 1887. George Cannon Lambert added three more selections in 1914 and 1915.

28. Jacob Hamblin, *Jacob Hamblin: A Narrative of His Personal Experience,* ed. James A. Little (Salt Lake City: Juvenile Instructor, 1881); Heber C. Kimball, *President Heber C. Kimball's Journal* (Salt Lake City: Juvenile Instructor Office, 1882).

29. George Q. Cannon, *The Life of Joseph Smith, the Prophet* (Salt Lake City: Juvenile Instructor Office, 1888). Ironically, the book was partly researched and perhaps written by Cannon's son Frank, who later strongly attacked the church.

30. B. H. Roberts, *The Life of John Taylor, Third President of the Church of Jesus Christ of Latter-day Saints* (Salt Lake City: George Q. Cannon and Sons, 1892).

31. Fanny Stenhouse, *Exposé of Polygamy in Utah: A Lady's Life among the Mormons* (New York: American News, 1872); *"Tell It All": The Story of a Life Experience in Mormonism, an Autobiography* (Hartford, Conn.: A. D. Worthington, 1874).

32. Ronald W. Walker, "The Stenhouses and the Making of a Mormon Image," *Journal of Mormon History* 1 (1974): 51–72. For Stenhouse's connection with the attempt to reform nineteenth-century Mormonism, see Ronald W. Walker, *Wayward Saints: The Godbeites and Brigham Young* (Urbana: University of Illinois Press, 1998).

33. John Walton Caughey, *Hubert Howe Bancroft: Historian of the West* (Berkeley: University of California Press, 1946), 314–29; Scott E. Casper, *Constructing American Lives: Biography and Culture in Nineteenth-Century America* (Chapel Hill: University of North Carolina Press, 1999), 292–97.

34. Andrew Jensen, *Latter-day Saint Biographical Encyclopedia,* 4 vols. (Salt Lake City: Andrew Jenson History Company, 1901–36).

35. Orson F. Whitney, *History of Utah,* 4 vols. (Salt Lake City: George Q. Cannon and Sons, 1904); Frank E. Esshom, *Pioneers and Prominent Men of Utah* (Salt Lake City: Utah Pioneers Book, 1913).

36. Francis M. Gibbons, *Joseph Smith: Martyr, Prophet of God* (Salt Lake City: Deseret Book, 1977), *Wilford Woodruff: Wondrous Worker, Prophet of God* (Salt Lake City: Deseret Book, 1988), *Lorenzo Snow: Spiritual Giant, Prophet of God* (Salt Lake City: Deseret Book, 1982), and *Heber J. Grant: Man of Steel, Prophet of God* (Salt Lake City: Deseret Book, 1979).

37. The Mormon historical literature, including biography, that deals with Joseph Smith is summarized in Thomas G. Alexander, "The Place of Joseph Smith in the Development of American Religions: A Historiographical Inquiry," *Journal of Mormon History* 5 (1978): 3–17; and Davis Bitton, *Images of the Prophet Joseph Smith* (Salt Lake City: Aspen Books, 1996), 171–96.

38. I. Woodbridge Riley, *The Founder of Mormonism: A Psychological Study of Joseph Smith, Jr.* (New York: Dodd, Mead, 1902).

39. John Henry Evans, *Joseph Smith, an American Prophet* (New York: Macmillan, 1933), 37 (first quotes), 8 (second quote), 360 (third quote).

40. Ibid., 10, 15 (quote), 19, 145, 155, 428.

41. In addition to his biography of Joseph Smith, Evans produced several biographical articles and two books: John Henry Evans, *Charles C. Rich: Pioneer Builder of the West* (New York: Macmillan, 1936); and John Henry Evans and Minnie Egan Anderson, *Ezra T. Benson: Statesman, Saint* (Salt Lake City: Deseret News, 1947). None of this work, however, approached the distinction of his Joseph Smith biography.

42. Fawn McKay Brodie, *No Man Knows My History: The Life of Joseph Smith, the Mormon Prophet* (New York: Alfred A. Knopf, 1945; 2d. ed., 1971). For background on Brodie and her work, see the useful collection of essays in Newell G. Bringhurst, ed., *Reconsidering No Man Knows My History: Fawn M. Brodie and Joseph Smith in Retrospect* (Logan: Utah State University Press, 1996). For an examination of Brodie and her work, see Newell G. Bringhurst, *Fawn McKay Brodie: A Biographer's Life* (Norman: University of Oklahoma Press, 1999).

43. For an examination of Brodie's biographical skills, see Lavina Fielding Anderson,

"Literary Style in *No Man Knows My History: An Analysis*," in *Reconsidering No Man Knows My History,* ed. Bringhurst, 127–53; and Bitton, "Mormon Biography," 4–5. Historians, however, have been much more critical of Brodie's historical method. For an example of such criticism, see Marvin S. Hill, "Brodie Revisited: A Reappraisal," *Dialogue: A Journal of Mormon Thought* 7 (Winter 1972): 72–85; and Marvin S. Hill, "Secular or Sectarian History? A Critique of *No Man Knows My History,*" *Church History* 43 (March 1974): 78–96.

44. Daryl Chase, *Joseph Smith the Prophet: As He Lives in the Hearts of His People* (Salt Lake City: Deseret Book, 1944).

45. Carl Carmer, *The Farm Boy and the Angel* (New York: Doubleday, 1970). Yet another Joseph Smith work was Preston Nibley, *Joseph Smith, the Prophet* (Salt Lake City: Deseret News, 1944), which reverted to the nineteenth-century style of defense and apologia, with little interpretation and a high degree of religious adulation. Although avoiding controversial issues (such as plural marriage), it provided a useful outline of Smith's life. Nibley's career and approach is discussed at greater length later in this chapter.

46. Donna Hill, *Joseph Smith, the First Mormon* (Garden City, N.Y.: Doubleday, 1977), ix-x.

47. Richard L. Bushman, *Joseph Smith and the Beginnings of Mormonism* (Urbana: University of Illinois Press, 1984), 7–8.

48. Morris R. Werner, *Brigham Young* (New York: Harcourt, Brace, 1925).

49. Stanley P. Hirshson, *The Lion of the Lord: A Biography of Brigham Young* (New York: Alfred A. Knopf, 1969), x.

50. In the preface to his book, Hirshson implied that he had been denied access to the LDS collection of material. This assertion brought a warm rejoinder from the LDS historian Leonard J. Arrington. See *BYU Studies* 10 (Winter 1970): 240–45.

51. Preston Nibley, *Brigham Young: The Man and His Work* (Salt Lake City: Deseret News, 1936). During his career, Nibley wrote a similar work on Joseph Smith; a volume dealing with the Book of Mormon witnesses Oliver Cowdery, David Whitmer, and Martin Harris; and a best-selling collection of articles treating LDS Church presidents.

52. Susa Young Gates to Heber J. Grant, 29 December 1899, box 116, folder 15, Heber J. Grant Papers, LDS Library-Archives (hereafter LDS Archives).

53. Susa Young Gates and Leah D. Widtsoe, *The Life Story of Brigham Young* (London: Jarrolds, 1930; New York: Macmillan, 1930). For a discussion of the work, see R. Paul Cracroft, "Susa Young Gates: Her Life and Literary Work" (Master's thesis, University of Utah, 1951), 108–9.

54. Gates and Widtsoe, *The Life Story of Brigham Young,* 238.

55. S. Dilworth Young, *Here Is Brigham: Brigham Young, the Years to 1844* (Salt Lake City: Bookcraft, 1964).

56. Eugene England, *Brother Brigham* (Salt Lake City: Bookcraft, 1980), 78.

57. Susan Easton Black and Larry C. Porter, *Lion of the Lord: Essays on the Life and Service of Brigham Young* (Salt Lake City: Deseret Book, 1995).

58. Newell G. Bringhurst, *Brigham Young and the Expanding American Frontier* (Boston: Little, Brown, 1986).

59. Leonard J. Arrington, *Brigham Young: American Moses* (New York: Alfred A. Knopf, 1985), xvi.

60. Samuel W. Taylor, *Family Kingdom* (New York: McGraw-Hill, 1951).

61. Samuel W. Taylor, *The Kingdom or Nothing: The Life of John Taylor, Militant Mormon* (New York: Macmillan, 1976).

62. Thomas G. Alexander, *Things in Heaven and Earth: The Life and Times of Wilford Woodruff, a Mormon Prophet* (Salt Lake City: Signature Books, 1991).

63. Milo J. Pusey, *Builders of the Kingdom: George A. Smith, John Henry Smith, George Albert Smith* (Provo, Utah: Brigham Young University Press, 1981).

64. Frank W. Fox, *J. Reuben Clark: The Public Years* (Provo, Utah: Brigham Young University Press and Deseret Book, 1980); D. Michael Quinn, *J. Reuben Clark: The Church Years* (Provo, Utah: Brigham Young University Press, 1983).

65. Marion G. Romney, foreword to Fox, *J. Reuben Clark,* xi.

66. F. Mark McKiernan, *The Voice of One Crying in the Wilderness: Sidney Rigdon, Religious Reformer, 1793–1876* (Lawrence, Kans.: Coronado, 1971); Richard S. Van Wagoner, *Sidney Rigdon: A Portrait of Religious Excess* (Salt Lake City: Signature Books, 1994).

67. Stanley B. Kimball, *Heber C. Kimball: Mormon Patriarch and Pioneer* (Urbana: University of Illinois Press, 1981), xii.

68. Claire Noall, *Intimate Disciple: A Portrait of Willard Richards* (Salt Lake City: University of Utah Press, 1957).

69. Davis Bitton, *George Q. Cannon: A Biography* (Salt Lake City: Deseret Book, 1999), ix. The Cannon biography presages a publishing plan to explain the man and his diaries. For the first diary of the series, see George Q. Cannon, *To California in '49,* ed. Michael J. Landon, vol. 1 of *The Journals of George Q. Cannon* (Salt Lake City: Deseret Book, 1999).

70. Breck England, *The Life and Thought of Orson Pratt* (Salt Lake City: University of Utah Press, 1985).

71. Andrew Karl Larson, *Erastus Snow: The Life of a Missionary and Pioneer for the Early Mormon Church* (Salt Lake City: University of Utah Press, 1971).

72. Leonard J. Arrington, *Charles C. Rich: Mormon General and Western Frontiersman* (Provo, Utah: Brigham Young University Press, 1974).

73. Ronald W. Walker, "Young Heber J. Grant and His Call to the Apostleship," *BYU Studies* 18 (Fall 1977): 121–26; "Crisis in Zion: Heber J. Grant and the Panic of 1893," *Arizona and the West* 21 (Autumn 1979): 257–78; "Jedediah and Heber Grant," *Ensign* 9 (July 1979): 46–52; "Heber J. Grant and the Utah Loan and Trust Company," *Journal of Mormon History* 8 (1981): 21–36; "Rachel R. Grant: The Continuing Legacy of the Feminine Ideal," *Dialogue: A Journal of Mormon Thought* 15 (Autumn 1982): 105–21; "A Mormon 'Widow' in Colorado: The Exile of Emily Wells Grant," *Arizona and the West* 25 (Spring 1983): 5–22; "Young Heber J. Grant: Entrepreneur Extraordinary," in *The Twentieth Century American West: Contributions to an Understanding,* ed. Thomas G. Alexander and John F. Bluth (Provo, Utah: Charles Redd Center for Western Studies, Brigham Young University, 1983), 85–113; "Young Heber J. Grant's Years of Passage," *BYU Studies* 24 (Spring 1984): 131–49; "Strangers in a Strange Land: Heber J. Grant and the Opening of the Japanese Mission," *Journal of Mormon History* 13 (1986–87): 20–43; and "Heber J. Grant's European Mission, 1903–1906," *Journal of Mormon History* 14 (1988): 16–33.

74. Eugene E. Campbell and Richard D. Poll, *Hugh B. Brown: His Life and Thought* (Salt Lake City: Bookcraft, 1975).

75. David S. Hoopes and Roy Hoopes, *The Making of a Mormon Apostle: The Story of Rudger Clawson* (Lanham, Md.: Madison Books, 1990).

76. Truman Madsen, *Defender of the Faith: The B. H. Roberts Story* (Salt Lake City: Bookcraft, 1980), 70.

77. Edward L. Kimball and Andrew E. Kimball Jr., *Spencer W. Kimball: Twelfth President of the Church of Jesus Christ of Latter-day Saints* (Salt Lake City: Bookcraft, 1977); Caroline Eyring Miner and Edward L. Kimball, *Camilla: A Biography of Camilla Eyring Kimball* (Salt Lake City: Deseret Book, 1980).

78. Miner and Kimball, *Camilla*, 203.

79. See, for example, Sheri L. Dew, *Ezra Taft Benson: A Biography* (Salt Lake City: Deseret Book, 1987); Eleanor Knowles, *Howard W. Hunter* (Salt Lake City: Deseret Book, 1994); and Sheri L. Dew, *Go Forward with Faith: The Biography of Gordon B. Hinckley* (Salt Lake City: Deseret Book, 1996). Lucile C. Tate has written three popular biographies dealing with members of the Council of the Twelve: *LeGrand Richards: Beloved Apostle* (Salt Lake City: Bookcraft, 1982), *David B. Haight: The Life Story of a Disciple* (Salt Lake City: Bookcraft, 1987), and *Boyd K. Packer: A Watchman on the Tower* (Salt Lake City: Deseret Book, 1995).

80. Leonard J. Arrington, ed., *Presidents of the Church: Biographical Essays* (Salt Lake City: Deseret Book, 1986).

81. Donald Q. Cannon and David J. Whittaker, eds., *Supporting Saints: Life Stories of Nineteenth-Century Mormons* (Provo, Utah: Religious Studies Center, Brigham Young University, 1985). Biographical subjects included Truman O. Angell, Richard Ballantyne, Angus M. Cannon, Martha Cragun Cox, Lucy Hanna White Flake, Rachel R. Grant, William Howells, Andrew Jenson, Edward Hunter, John Lyon, Elijah F. Sheets, Jacob Spori, and Emmeline B. Wells.

82. Leonard Arrington, *From Quaker to Latter-day Saint: Bishop Edwin D. Woolley* (Salt Lake City: Deseret Book, 1976); William L. Roper and Leonard J. Arrington, *William Spry: Man of Firmness, Governor of Utah* (Salt Lake City: Utah State Historical Society and University of Utah Press, 1971); Leonard J. Arrington, *David Eccles: Pioneer Western Industrialist* (Logan: Utah State University Press, 1975); Leonard J. Arrington and John R. Alley, *Harold F. Silver: Western Inventor, Businessman and Civic Leader* (Logan: Utah State University Press, 1992); Leonard J. Arrington, *Utah's Audacious Stockman: Charlie Redd* (Logan: Utah State University Press, 1995).

83. Martin B. Hickman, *David Matthew Kennedy: Banker, Statesman, Churchman* (Salt Lake City: Deseret Book, in cooperation with the David M. Kennedy Center for International Studies at Brigham Young University, 1987).

84. Mary Lythgoe Bradford, *Lowell L. Bennion: Teacher, Counselor, Humanitarian* (Salt Lake City: Dialogue Foundation, 1995).

85. James B. Allen, *Trials of Discipleship: The Story of William Clayton, a Mormon* (Urbana: University of Illinois Press, 1987), x.

86. S. George Ellsworth, *Samuel Claridge: Pioneering the Outposts of Zion* (Logan, Utah: S. George Ellsworth, 1987).

87. Paul Bailey, *Sam Brannan and the California Mormons* (Los Angeles: Westernlore, 1943), *Jacob Hamblin: Buckskin Apostle* (Los Angeles: Westernlore, 1948), and *Hawaii's Royal Prime Minister: The Life and Times of Walter Murray Gibson* (New York: Hastings House, 1980).

88. Hope A. Hilton, *"Wild Bill" Hickman and the Mormon Frontier* (Salt Lake City: Sig-

nature Books, 1988); William A. Hickman, *Brigham's Destroying Angel,* ed. John Hanson Beadle (New York: George A. Crofutt, 1872).

89. Juanita Brooks, *John D. Lee: Zealot—Pioneer Builder—Scapegoat* (Glendale, Calif.: Arthur H. Clark, 1961).

90. Harold Schindler, *Orrin Porter Rockwell: Man of God, Son of Thunder* (Salt Lake City: University of Utah Press, 1966).

91. Richard D. Poll, *Howard J. Stoddard: Founder, Michigan National Bank* (East Lansing: Michigan State University Press, 1980), vii.

92. Davis Bitton, *The Redoubtable John Pack: Pioneer, Proselyter, Patriarch* (Salt Lake City: John Pack Family Association, 1982), ix.

93. William G. Hartley, *"They Are My Friends": A History of the Joseph Knight Family, 1825–1850* (Provo, Utah: Grandin Book, 1986) and *My Best for the Kingdom: History and Autobiography of John Lowe Butler, a Mormon Frontiersman* (Salt Lake City: Aspen Books, 1993). Hartley's additional biographies included *Kindred Saints: The Mormon Immigrant Heritage of Alvin and Kathryne Christenson* (Salt Lake City: Eden Hill, 1982) and *"To Build, to Create, to Produce": Ephraim P. Ellison's Life and Enterprises, 1850–1939* ([Salt Lake City]: Ellison Family Organization, 1997).

94. Carol Cornwall Madsen's major pieces on Wells include "Mormon Women and the Struggle for Definition: The Nineteenth Century Church," *Sunstone* 6 (November/December 1981): 7–11; "Emmeline B. Wells: A Voice for Mormon Women," *John Whitmer Historical Association Journal* 2 (1982): 11–21; "Emmeline B. Wells: 'Am I Not a Woman and a Sister?'" *BYU Studies* 22 (Spring 1982): 161–78; "A Bluestocking in Zion: The Literary Life of Emmeline B. Wells," *Dialogue: A Journal of Mormon Thought* 16 (Spring 1983): 126–40; "Emmeline B. Wells: Romantic Rebel," in *Supporting Saints,* ed. Cannon and Whittaker, 305–41; and "'The Power of Combination': Emmeline B. Wells and the National and International Council of Women," *BYU Studies* 33, no. 4 (1993): 646–73.

95. Maureen Ursenbach Beecher, *Eliza and Her Sisters* (Salt Lake City: Aspen Books, 1991). Beecher eventually abandoned the Eliza Roxcy Snow biography, but her colleague Jill Mulvay Derr continues working on the project.

96. Allan Kent Powell, ed., *Utah History Encyclopedia* (Salt Lake City: University of Utah, 1994); Daniel H. Ludlow, ed., *Encyclopedia of Mormonism,* 5 vols. (New York: Macmillan, 1992); Richard S. Van Wagoner and Steven C. Walker, *A Book of Mormons* (Salt Lake City: Signature Books, 1982).

97. Leonard J. Arrington and Susan Arrington Madsen, *Mothers of the Prophets* (Salt Lake City: Deseret Book, 1987). The book contained short essays on Lucy Mack Smith, Abigail Howe Young, Agnes Taylor, Beulah Thompson Woodruff, Azubah Hart Woodruff, Rosetta Leonora Pettibone Snow, Mary Fielding Smith, Rachel Ridgeway Grant, Sarah Farr Smith, Jennette Eveline Evans McKay, Julia Lambson Smith, Louisa Emeline Bingham Lee, Olive Woolley Kimball, and Sarah Dunkley Benson.

98. Janet Peterson and LaRene Porter Gaunt, *The Children's Friends: Primary Presidents and Their Lives of Service* (Salt Lake City: Deseret Book, 1996), includes biographies of Louie Boulton Felt, May Anderson, May Green Hinckley, Adele Cannon Howells, LaVern Watts Parmley, Naomi Maxfield Shumway, Dwan Jacobsen Young, Michaelene Packer Grassli, and Patricia Peterson Pinegar. Janet Peterson and LaRene Porter Gaunt, *Keepers of the Flame: Presidents of the Young Women* (Salt Lake City: Deseret Book, 1993), includes

biographies of Bertha Stone Reeder, Florence Smith Jacobsen, Elmina Shepard Taylor, Martha Horne Tingey, Ruth May Fox, Lucy Grant Cannon, Ruth Hardy Funk, Elaine Cannon, Ardeth Greene Kapp, and Janette Callister Hales. Janet Peterson and LaRene Porter Gaunt, *Elect Ladies: Presidents of the Relief Society* (Salt Lake City: Deseret Book, 1990), includes biographies of Emma Hale Smith, Eliza R. Snow, Zina Diantha Huntington Young, Bathsheba Wilson Bigler Smith, Emmeline B. Wells, Clarissa Smith Williams, Louise Yates Robison, Amy Brown Lyman, Belle Smith Spafford, Barbara B. Smith, and Barbara W. Winder.

99. Colleen Whitley, ed., *Worth Their Salt: Notable but Often Unnoted Women of Utah* (Logan: Utah State University Press, 1996). Biographical subjects included Patty Bartlett Sessions, Jane Manning James, Sarah Elizabeth Carmichael, Elizabeth Ann Claridge McCune, Mary Teasdel, Maud May Babcock, Alice Merrill Horne, Maude Adams, and Ivy Baker Priest.

100. Vicky Burgess-Olsen, *Sister Saints* (Provo, Utah: Brigham Young University Press, 1978). Carol Cornwall Madsen and David J. Whittaker's review essay, "History's Sequel: A Source Essay on Women in Mormon History," *Journal of Mormon History* 6 (1979): 123–45, described the published woman's biographies and autobiographies that had appeared by the end of the 1970s. For other article-length biographies dealing with LDS women, see Claudia L. Bushman, ed., *Mormon Sisters: Women in Early Utah* (Cambridge, Mass.: Emmeline, 1976); and Maureen Ursenbach Beecher and Lavina Fielding Anderson, eds., *Sisters in Spirit: Mormon Women in Historical and Cultural Perspective* (Urbana: University of Illinois Press, 1987).

101. John A. Widtsoe, *In the Gospel Net: The Story of Anna K. G. Widtsoe* (Independence, Mo.: Zion's Printing and Publishing, 1941).

102. Juliaetta Bateman Jensen, *Little Gold Pieces: The Story of My Mormon Mother's Life* (Salt Lake City: Stanway, 1948).

103. Leonard J. Arrington, *Madelyn Cannon Stewart Silver: Poet, Teacher, Homemaker* (Salt Lake City: Publishers Press, 1998).

104. Juanita Brooks, *Emma Lee* (Logan: Utah State University Press, 1975).

105. Levi S. Peterson, *Juanita Brooks: Mormon Woman Historian* (Salt Lake City: University of Utah Press, 1988).

106. Linda King Newell and Valeen Tippetts Avery, *Mormon Enigma: Emma Hale Smith* (Garden City, N.Y.: Doubleday, 1984).

107. For articles leading to this, see his "Applause, Attack, and Ambivalence—Varied Responses to Fawn M. Brodie's *No Man Knows My History*," *Utah Historical Quarterly* 57 (Winter 1989): 46–63; "Fawn Brodie and Her Quest for Independence," *Dialogue: A Journal of Mormon Thought* 22 (Summer 1989): 79–95; "Fawn M. Brodie, 'Mormondom's Lost Generation,' and *No Man Knows My History*," *Journal of Mormon History* 16 (1990): 11–23; "Fawn M. Brodie—Her Biographies as Autobiography," *Pacific Historical Review* 59 (May 1990): 203–30; "Fawn M. Brodie as a Critic of Mormonism's Policy toward Blacks—A Historiographical Reassessment," *John Whitmer Historical Association Journal* 11 (1991): 34–46; "'The Renegade' and the 'Reorganites': Fawn Brodie and Her Varied Encounters with the Reorganized Church of Jesus Christ of Latter Day Saints," *John Whitmer Historical Association Journal* 12 (1992): 16–30; "Fawn Brodie's *Thomas Jefferson: The Making of a Popular and Controversial Biography*," *Pacific Historical Review* 62 (November 1993): 433–54; "Fawn McKay Brodie: Dissident Historian and Quintessential Critic of Mormon-

dom," in *Differing Visions: Dissenters in Mormon History*, ed. Roger D. Launius and Linda Thatcher (Urbana: University of Illinois Press, 1994), 279–300; "Juanita Brooks and Fawn Brodie—Sisters in Mormon Dissent," *Dialogue: A Journal of Mormon Thought* 27 (Summer 1994): 105–27; "A Biography of the Biography: The Research and Writing of *No Man Knows My History*," in *Reconsidering No Man Knows My History*, ed. Bringhurst, 7–38; and "Fawn McKay Brodie (1915–1981)," in *Dictionary of Heresy Trials in American Christianity*, ed. George H. Shriver (Westport, Conn.: Greenwood, 1997), 65–74.

108. Bringhurst, *Fawn McKay Brodie*, xv.

109. Lyndon W. Cook, *William Law* (Orem, Utah: Grandin Book, 1994).

110. Andrew F. Smith, *The Saintly Scoundrel: The Life and Times of Dr. John Cook Bennett* (Urbana: University of Illinois Press, 1997).

111. Roger Van Noord, *King of Beaver Island: The Life and Assassination of James Jesse Strang* (Urbana: University of Illinois Press, 1988). For earlier and still valuable studies, see Milo Quaife, *The Kingdom of Saint James: A Narrative of the Mormons* (New Haven, Conn.: Yale University Press, 1930); and O. W. Riegel, *Crown of Glory: The Life of James J. Strang, Moses of the Mormons* (New Haven, Conn.: Yale University Press, 1935).

112. Roger D. Launius, *Joseph Smith III: Pragmatic Prophet* (Urbana: University of Illinois Press, 1988), which was based on Launius's Ph.D. dissertation completed at Louisiana State University in 1982; and *Father Figure: Joseph Smith III and the Creation of the Reorganized Church* (Independence, Mo.: Herald Publishing House, 1990).

113. Launius, *Joseph Smith III*, xii.

114. Valeen Tippetts Avery, *From Mission to Madness: Last Son of the Mormon Prophet* (Urbana: University of Illinois Press, 1998).

115. Roger D. Launius and Linda Thatcher, eds., *Differing Visions: Dissenters in Mormon History* (Urbana: University of Illinois, 1994). Biographical subjects included Stephen Post, Joseph Musser, Fawn M. Brodie, William Smith, Maurine Whipple, Jerald and Sandra Tanner, Frank J. Cannon, James and George Dove, William E. McLellin, Alpheus Cutler, Henry W. Lawrence, Sonia Johnson, David Whitmer, Francis Gladden Bishop, James Colin Brewster, and John Corrill.

116. Walker, *Wayward Saints*.

117. Other biographies dealing with dissent included Rupert J. Fletcher and Daisy Whiting Fletcher, *Alpheus Cutler and the Church of Jesus Christ* (Independence, Mo.: Church of Jesus Christ, 1974); Marjorie Newton, *Hero or Traitor: A Biographical Study of Charles Wesley Wandell* (Independence, Mo.: Independence, 1992); C. LeRoy Anderson, *For Christ Will Come Tomorrow: The Saga of the Morrisites* (Logan: Utah State University Press, 1981) (later reprinted under the title *Joseph Morris and the Saga of the Morrisites*); and Ben Bradless Jr. and Dale Van Atta, *The Prophet of Blood: The Untold Story of Ervil LeBaron and the Lambs of God* (New York: G. P. Putnam's Sons, 1981). Russell R. Rich's two compilations also contain brief but useful material on restoration schisms and their leaders: *Those Who Would Be Leaders . . .* (Provo, Utah: Division of Continuing Education, Extension Publications, Brigham Young University, 1959) and *Little Known Schisms of the Restoration* (Provo, Utah: Division of Continuing Education, Extension Publications, Brigham Young University, 1962).

118. John A. Widtsoe, *In a Sunlit Land: The Autobiography of John A. Widtsoe* (Salt Lake City: Deseret News, 1952), viii.

119. George W. Bean, *Autobiography of George W. Bean, a Utah Pioneer of 1847*, comp.

Flora Diana Bean Horne (Salt Lake City: Utah Printing, 1945); Brown, *Life of a Pioneer;* John Brown, *Autobiography of Pioneer John Brown, 1820–1895,* arranged by John Zimmerman Brown (Salt Lake City: Stevens and Wallis, 1941); Joseph Fish, *The Life and Times of Joseph Fish, Mormon Pioneer,* ed. John H. Krenkel (Danville, Ill.: Interstate, 1970); Christopher Layton, *Autobiography of Christopher Layton,* ed. John Q. Cannon (Salt Lake City: Christopher Layton Family Organization, 1966); Mary Elizabeth Rollins Lightner, *The Life and Testimony of Mary Lightner* (Salt Lake City: Kraut's Pioneer, 1982); Louisa Barnes Pratt, *Mormondom's First Woman Missionary, Louisa Barnes Pratt: Life Story and Travels Told in Her Own Words,* ed. Kate B. Carter (n.p.: Nettie Hunt Rencher, [c.] 1950); Aurelia Spencer Rogers, *Life Sketches of Orson Spencer and Others, and History of Primary Work* (Salt Lake City: George Q. Cannon and Sons, 1898).

120. Maria S. Ellsworth, ed., *Mormon Odyssey: The Story of Ida Hunt Udall, Plural Wife* (Urbana: University of Illinois Press, 1992).

121. Kenneth W. Godfrey, Audrey M. Godfrey, and Jill Mulvay Derr, eds., *Women's Voices: An Untold History of the Latter-day Saints, 1830–1900* (Salt Lake City: Deseret Book, 1982); see especially the Daughters of the Utah Pioneers' five multivolume sets: Kate B. Carter, comp., *Heart Throbs of the West,* 12 vols. (Salt Lake City, 1939–51); Kate B. Carter, comp., *Treasures of Pioneer History,* 6 vols. (Salt Lake City, 1952–57); Kate B. Carter, comp., *Our Pioneer Heritage,* 20 vols. (Salt Lake City, 1958–77); *An Enduring Legacy,* 12 vols. (Salt Lake City: 1978–89); and *Chronicles of Courage* (Salt Lake City, 1990–present).

122. Joyce Kinkead, *A Schoolmarm All My Life: Personal Narrative from Frontier Utah* (Salt Lake City: Signature Books, 1996).

123. Mary Haskin Parker Richards, *Winter Quarters: The 1846–1848 Life Writings of Mary Haskin Parker Richards,* ed. Maurine Carr Ward, Life Writings of Frontier Women, vol. 1 (Logan: Utah State University Press, 1996); Patty Bartlett Sessions, *Mormon Midwife: The 1846–1888 Diaries of Patty Bartlett Sessions,* ed. Donna Toland Smart, Life Writings of Frontier Women, vol. 2 (Logan: Utah State University Press, 1997); Louisa Barnes Pratt, *The History of Louisa Barnes Pratt: Being the Autobiography of a Mormon Missionary Widow and Pioneer,* ed. S. George Ellsworth, Life Writings of Frontier Women, vol. 3 (Logan: Utah State University Press, 1998); Effie Marquess Carmack, *Out of the Black Patch: The Autobiography of Effie Marquess Carmack, Folk Musician, Artist, and Writer,* ed. Noel A. Carmack and Karen Lynn Davidson, Life Writings of Frontier Women, vol. 4 (Logan: Utah State University Press, 1999). Earlier, Beecher issued Eliza R. Snow, *The Personal Writings of Eliza Roxcy Snow,* ed. Maureen Ursenbach Beecher (Salt Lake City: University of Utah Press, 1995), which has been reprinted in the Life Writings of Frontier Women series.

124. George P. Lee, *Silent Courage, an Indian Story: The Autobiography of George P. Lee, a Navajo* (Salt Lake City: Deseret Book, 1987); Helvécio Martins, with Mark L. Grover, *The Autobiography of Elder Helvécio Martins* (Salt Lake City: Aspen Books, 1994); Russell Nelson, *From Heart to Heart: An Autobiography* (Salt Lake City: Quality, 1979); Charles W. Nibley, *Reminiscences of Charles W. Nibley, 1849–1931* (Salt Lake City: Nibley Family, 1934); B. H. Roberts, *The Autobiography of B. H. Roberts,* ed. Gary James Bergera (Salt Lake City: Signature Books, 1990); Sterling W. Sill, *The Nine Lives of Sterling W. Sill: An Autobiography* (Bountiful, Utah: Horizon, 1979); Orson F. Whitney, *Through Memory's Halls: The Life Story of Orson F. Whitney as Told by Himself* (Independence, Mo.: Zion's Printing and Publishing, 1930).

125. Ezra Taft Benson, *Crossfire: The Eight Years with Eisenhower* (Garden City, N.Y.: Doubleday, 1962); Marriner S. Eccles, *Beckoning Frontiers: Public and Personal Recollections,* ed. Sidney Hyman (New York: Alfred A. Knopf, 1951); Herbert B. Maw, *Adventures with Life* (Salt Lake City: By the author, 1978); Calvin L. Rampton, *As I Recall,* ed. Floyd A. O'Neil and Gregory Thompson (Salt Lake City: University of Utah Press, 1989); Joseph L. Rawlins, *"The Unfavored Few": The Autobiography of Joseph L. Rawlins,* ed. and amplified by Alta Rawlins Jensen (n.p.: 1956).

126. Ephraim E. Ericksen, *Memories and Reflections: The Autobiography of E. E. Ericksen,* ed. Scott G. Kenney (Salt Lake City: Signature Books, 1987); LeRoy R. Hafen, "A Westerner, Born and Bred," *Western Historical Quarterly* 3 (April 1972): 128–35; LeRoy R. Hafen and Ann W. Hafen, *The Joyous Journey of LeRoy R. and Ann W. Hafen: An Autobiography* (Glendale, Calif.: Arthur H. Clark and Old West, 1973); Andrew Jenson, *Autobiography of Andrew Jenson: Assistant Historian of the Church of Jesus Christ of Latter-day Saints* (Salt Lake City: Deseret News, 1938); Andrew Karl Larson, *The Education of a Second Generation Swede: An Autobiography* (St. George, Utah: By the author, 1979); Lowry Nelson, *In the Direction of His Dreams: Memoirs* (New York: Philosophical Library, 1985); Hugh W. Nibley, "An Intellectual Autobiography," in *Nibley on the Timely and the Timeless: Classic Essays of Hugh W. Nibley* (Salt Lake City: Publishers Press, 1978), xix–xxviii; Obert C. Tanner, *One Man's Journey: In Search of Freedom* (Salt Lake City: Humanities Center, University of Utah, 1994).

127. Leonard J. Arrington, *Adventures of a Church Historian* (Urbana: University of Illinois Press, 1998). Before embarking on his autobiography, Arrington wrote several preliminary essays: "Historian as Entrepreneur: A Personal Essay," *BYU Studies* 17 (Winter 1977): 193–209; "Recalling a Twin Falls Childhood," *Idaho Yesterdays* 25 (Winter 1982): 31–40; and "Why I Am a Believer," *Sunstone* 10 (January 1985): 36–38.

128. Annie Clark Tanner, *A Mormon Mother: An Autobiography* (Salt Lake City: Tanner Trust Fund, University of Utah Library, 1969).

129. Juanita Brooks, *Quicksand and Cactus: A Memoir of the Southern Mormon Frontier* (Salt Lake City: Howe Brothers, 1982). For a discussion of the evolution of the manuscript, see Levi S. Peterson, "Juanita Brooks's *Quicksand and Cactus:* The Evolution of a Literary Memoir," *Dialogue: A Journal of Mormon Thought* 20 (Spring 1987): 145–55.

130. On Wells, see Heber J. Grant to Hannah C. Wells, 25 February 1902, Letterpress Copy Book, 35:55, Heber J. Grant Papers, LDS Archives; on Nibley, see Heber J. Grant to W. W. Wilson, 14 December 1931, Letterpress Copy Book, 69:274, LDS Archives; on Young, see Brigham Young, sermon, 2 August 1857, in *Journal of Discourses,* 26 vols. (Liverpool, England: F. D. and S. W. Richards, 1854–86), 5:98; on Woodruff, see Heber J. Grant to Ed[ward?] H. Snow, 22 January 1915, Letterpress Copy Book, 50:606–7, LDS Archives.

131. We are indebted to Jeffery O. Johnson, formerly of the LDS Archives and now director of the Utah State Archives, who undertook an informal survey of some of the principal Mormon and Mormon-related manuscript collections. His computations are in linear feet. In the LDS Archives: Joseph F. Smith, 50 feet; Hugh B. Brown, 50 feet; Henry D. Hoyle, 50 feet; Brigham Young, 80 feet; Heber J. Grant, 100 feet; Joseph Fielding Smith, 50 feet; John A. Widtsoe, 140 feet; and David O. McKay, 320 feet; at the University of Utah: Sherman Lloyd, 65 feet; George Albert Smith, 85 feet; and Frank Moss, 380 feet; at Brigham Young University: Reed Smoot, 80 feet; J. Reuben Clark, Jr., 250 feet; and Wallace F. Bennett, 500 feet.

132. Alan Shelston, *Biography* (London: Methuen, 1977), 8–9.

133. Fyodor Dostoyevsky, *Notes from Underground,* ed. Robert G. Durgy, trans. Serge Shishkoff (New York: Thomas Y. Crowell, 1969), 37–38.

134. Kendall, *The Art of Biography,* 116.

135. Clifford, *From Puzzles to Portraits,* 131.

136. Robert Gittings, *The Nature of Biography* (Seattle: University of Washington Press, 1978), 42–43.

137. Mario S. De Pillis, "Bearding Leone and Others in the Heartland of Mormon Historiography," *Journal of Mormon History* 8 (1981): 91.

138. Richard L. Bushman, "Faithful History," *Dialogue: A Journal of Mormon Thought* 4 (Winter 1969): 18.

139. Swetnam, *Lives of the Saints in Southeast Idaho,* 3–4 (first quote), 5 (second quote).

5. Flowers, Weeds, and Thistles: The State of Social Science Literature on the Mormons

ARMAND L. MAUSS

THE ORIGIN OF social science literature[1] on the Mormons might reasonably be traced to a 1903 article by Richard T. Ely, a prominent Wisconsin economist, social scientist, and teacher of such early American sociologists as Albion Small and E. A. Ross.[2] Writing not in an academic journal but in a popular (if highbrow) magazine, Ely made the declaration, which now seems so startling, that the "organization of the Mormons is the most nearly perfect piece of social mechanism with which I have ever . . . come in contact, excepting alone the German army."[3] Much has happened, in both Mormondom and Germany, since Ely's visits to the two around the end of the nineteenth century. More than a hundred years later, comparisons to the German army no longer evoke much admiration; and Utah is now neither so Mormon nor so well organized as it was at the end of the nineteenth century. The strong theocratic and cooperative rural communities of nineteenth-century Utah, which Ely so much admired, have long given way to a thoroughgoing Americanization and secularization; and Mormons, in Utah and elsewhere, have generally embraced competitive capitalism with enthusiasm. Ely could see the changes starting even then, but his article was to be a harbinger of the kind of social science literature on the Mormons that was to predominate for decades: historical and contemporary studies of social geography, rural sociology, and agricultural economics.

Leonard Arrington traced such preoccupations in the early literature on the Mormons partly to the influence of the German social and historical economists of Ely's time, with whom Ely had studied (and where, presumably, he got his impressions about the German army firsthand).[4] Among the more prominent of these German scholars was Gustav Schmoller, whose student wrote a doctoral dissertation at Berlin University as early as 1906 on Mormon economic and community life. By midcentury many other unpublished dissertations on similar or related Mormon themes had been completed at major American universities.[5] The same general focus can be seen in the published social scientific literature on the Mormons from the beginning of the century, not only in such journals as *Economic Geography, Journal of Economic History, Journal of Economic Sociology,* or *Rural Sociology,* where one might expect it, but often in the *Western Humanities Review* and the more "mainline" journals of the social sciences and the humanities.

Hamilton Gardner, Joseph Geddes, Gustive O. Larson, William J. McNiff, and Lowry Nelson were particularly important up to about midcentury in the development of this emphasis on rural economy, sociology, and geography.[6] The works of Gardner, Geddes, and McNiff focused primarily on the unique communitarian experiments in early Mormon history. Under the auspices of the USDA's "social anatomy" research program, Lowry Nelson did pioneering studies of three Utah villages during the 1920s and 1930s, which eventually appeared in his well-known *Mormon Village.*[7] Nels Anderson, justly renowned for his sociological study of hoboes during his University of Chicago days, was not as well known for equally perceptive studies of the Mormons that grew out of his pre-Chicago life in Utah.[8]

Beyond these rural community studies, a second prominent theme in the early literature on the Mormons was family life. The most notorious aspect of traditional Mormon family life had, of course, been polygamy (or, more accurately, polygyny), which had generated an enormous body of polemical literature. The Mormons, however, had largely abandoned polygamy by 1910 or so (officially much earlier) and were trying hard to change their public image. This fact might help account for the sparsity of scholarly literature on Mormon polygamy up to midcentury. James E. Hulett Jr., who had written a dissertation in 1939 at the University of Wisconsin on the topic, published two derivative articles in distinguished journals, but Kimball Young's work, which was based on Hulett's data, was probably better known.[9] In recent years, there has been a revival of scholarly interest in early Mormon polygamy by non-Mormon social historians and by a younger generation of Mormon scholars with more emotional detachment from the topic.[10] In general, however, social science literature on Mormon family life, even the early literature, has not been preoccupied with polygamy. The major themes from the beginning have been fertility, child-spacing, and spousal relationships.[11]

Until the 1950s, then, the social science literature on the Mormons tended to concentrate on rural economic, community, and family life. Much less studied was the sociology or anthropology of the Mormon religion itself, though passing references and observations about the religion could hardly be avoided in the community and family literature.[12] There had always been an abundance of partisan, polemical literature on the Mormon religion, from both inside and outside the Mormon community, but few scholarly works existed. Yet the lack of such a literature was not unique to Mormonism. It must be understood within the context of the historical development of the sociology of religion more generally and the intellectual history of the Mormon culture itself.

The Sociology of Religion and the Social Science of Mormons

In the first half of the twentieth century, there was an enormous void in the sociology or social science of religion more generally—not just in Mormon studies—especially in the United States.[13] Among the reasons for this void was the general unavailability in English of the early classics on religion by Durkheim, Weber, Troeltsch, and the like.[14] The works of several English anthropologists were available, of course, but these tended to deal with so-called primitive forms of religion rather than with those of modern or Western societies. Moreover, despite (or perhaps because of) their own rather heavily religious backgrounds, early American sociologists tended to adopt one of two stances. Some cultivated a deliberate aloofness from such "unscientific" subjects as religion; others appropriated a secularized Protestant heritage and pressed it into the service of the "social gospel movement" or a mild kind of "Christian socialism." The latter was frequently advocated in the name of sociology even in the pages of the *American Journal of Sociology.*[15] These early American sociologists seemed to think that religion either should be made useful in a humanistic sense or should be abandoned as mere superstition in such an enlightened age. It was not to be taken seriously as a subject for scientific investigation, least of all in the case of the disreputable Mormons. A few quasi-scholarly attempts can be identified from this early period, though.[16]

Meanwhile, during the first half of the century, Mormonism itself underwent a period of rapid transformation from a remote, unpopular sect to a more assimilated regional denomination. For the first time, young Mormon scholars sought graduate education in the more prestigious universities outside Utah and the Intermountain West. Many of these were responsible for the early literature (mentioned above) on Mormon rural communities and family life, and some gained distinction for accomplishments in other fields of endeavor as well.[17] Yet within Mormon culture, there has always been the classical ambivalence toward scholarship and intellectuals found in all revealed religions, especially in Mormonism, which has only lay clergy and theologians.[18]

On the one hand, religious institutions need loyal intellectuals, and the Mormon church actually sponsored the advanced education of selected young scholars at distinguished universities outside of Utah for a brief period in the 1920s and 1930s.[19] On the other hand, scholarship often threatens the underlying cultural and religious shibboleths of a people when scholars depart from mundane studies of the family, the community, and economic life and turn instead to the sociology or psychology of religious participation itself. It is not difficult to understand, then, why only a few of the early Mormon social scientists were willing to focus on their religion. There simply was not much of a market for such work in those early days, either among Mormons or in academia itself. Those few early Mormons who did undertake social science–oriented investigations of the nature and origins of their religion soon encountered difficulties in their relationships with their coreligionists, ranging from perpetual unease to open rupture, as did early Mormon novelists and other literati.[20] In any case, whatever the reasons, the fact remains that, although there were some important social scientific studies on Mormons by midcentury, few of them dealt much with the *religious* life of the Mormon people.[21]

A New Generation of Scholarship on the Mormons

Since the 1950s, there have been some very important developments, both qualitatively and quantitatively, in social science scholarship on the Mormons. One might even speak of a flowering of such scholarship, though, as will be seen, the flowers are interspersed with many weeds and thistles. Quantitatively, there has been a burgeoning of historical, sociological, and humanistic literature written mostly (but not only) by scholars of Mormon background. Their work has often appeared in respectable professional journals and books. The most recent bibliography makes clear that the overwhelming majority of this literature appeared during the final decades of the twentieth century, at least where the social sciences are concerned (probably also true of the strictly historical literature).[22]

Qualitatively, the sociology of religion in general and of the Mormon religion in particular became more detached and academic. The debunking tone so prominent in the early literature is now rare. The psychohistory approach to the study of the origins of Mormonism, which Fawn Brodie once used to such acclaim in her biography of the founding prophet, and other similar approaches were undermined by subsequent criticism.[23] Both Mormon and non-Mormon scholars in religious studies came to understand that religious experiences, myths, and commitments should be taken seriously as *data* rather than dismissed as pathological or primitive. This more respectful yet detached stance on the origins and nature of the Mormon religion can be seen in the more recent work of both Mormon and non-Mormon scholars in history and the social sciences.[24]

The Nature and Quality of Social Science Literature on the Mormons

Whatever aspects of Mormon life have been featured or ignored in the accumulated social science literature, what sort of literature is it in general? Is it mainly empirical or impressionistic? Is it based mainly on field observations or on social surveys? Is it generally of reliable quality, or is it seriously flawed by weaknesses in methodology, by manifest bias, or by other problems? To what extent is the late twentieth-century "flowering" beset with weeds and thistles?

It is important to recognize at the outset the variety of disciplines and genres covered by the term *social science.* Sometimes the discipline of history is included in that term, and sometimes it is not. Anthropology, psychology, and sociology, though sometimes taken to constitute a separate field of "behavioral sciences," are usually covered also by the designation "social sciences." Political science, economics, social geography, and demography are typically included too, as are a number of "applied" social sciences, such as organizational behavior. For purposes of this essay, works authored by historians or dealing almost entirely with historical aspects of Mormon social life have mostly (but not entirely) been omitted from consideration, for they are duly considered in sister essays. Works representing the other disciplines mentioned here, however, have been considered.

The methodologies of the social sciences are also varied. In both method and content, the social sciences straddle the space between the humanities, on the one side, and the "hard" sciences, on the other. Social science scholars have thus tended to draw on the methods of both the humanistic and the scientific traditions. Accordingly, some of the work cited here uses quantitative, experimental, and statistical methods. At the other extreme are essays based on expert, informed, or even impressionistic observations and opinions offered by presumably knowledgeable authors. Such works would not pass muster as "social science" in the more restricted "scientific" sense, but they have some value to scholars searching the literature for general background and ideas. Falling in between these two extremes are works based on careful empirical observations of individual and collective behavior, the methods typically used by cultural anthropologists in the field and sometimes called "ethnography." The more systematic and thorough these observations are (as opposed to informal and haphazard), the more they approach the ideal of "science."

Any survey of the social science literature on Mormons must conclude that the overwhelming majority of it is on the "soft" side of the continuum between the humanities and the sciences. Just how thin a slice of the literature is to be found in the "hard" social science category was made abundantly clear over a decade ago in an important critical essay by Howard M. Bahr and Renata Tonks Forste, both in the Department of Sociology at Brigham Young University.[25] Their thorough and detailed review of the social science literature for the period between 1970 and 1985 led them to declare that "most published research on Mormons does not pass the test of truth in labelling."[26] The verdict would doubtless be even worse for the period before 1970 and only slightly better for the period since 1985. Their survey demonstrated that (1) very little of that literature was the product of truly empirical findings; (2) very little of it could be generalized to the entire LDS population of the United States, to say nothing of LDS populations elsewhere; and (3) very few factual assertions were justified about Mormons anywhere because of the flaws in data and methodology in most of the studies. Bahr and Forste offered a list of no more than fourteen factual assertions that could be justified, even about Mormons in the U.S. West, plus perhaps half that many "probabilistic" assertions.[27]

As one reviews the few factual and probabilistic assertions acceptable to Bahr and Forste, it is immediately apparent that the overwhelming majority of them are derived from *demographic* studies on fertility, morbidity, and mortality and that the data for these studies come either from the University of Utah's Historical Demography Project or from a small number of systematic surveys sponsored by the church's Research Information Division. In other words, the great majority of all the published empirical studies on Mormons, namely those done *without* the funding or sponsorship of church or university, have yielded no reliable empirical facts about Mormons, owing to stringently limited populations, flaws in the samples, shortcomings in the research methods or analyses, or all these factors. Of particularly dubious utility, in the judgment of Bahr and Forste, have been the numerous studies of LDS college and university students over the years, which have served well enough to produce graduate theses and dissertations but have usually been based on "opportunity samples" representing no identifiable populations (usually not even general student populations)—far more "weeds" than "flowers," in other words. This situation led Bahr and Forste to call for a moratorium on studies of LDS students.[28]

Another common resort for theses and dissertations can be seen in the large number of surveys on Mormon family life, again with samples and methods that render factual assertions and generalizations problematic. Bahr and Forste support this observation by quoting the verdict of the prominent LDS family sociologist Darwin Thomas: "Most of the information about Mormon families comes from a variety of relatively small, nonrepresentative samples and from census data for the state of Utah compared to national averages," the latter being rather problematic because (among other reasons) "no one is sure what percentage of the state of Utah is Mormon."[29] The resort to *Utah* data, as surrogate for Mormon data, is all too common in much of the social science literature generally, understandable as that might be. Even if we can be fairly sure of the Mormon proportion of the state of Utah, the nature and extent of the Mormon/non-Mormon mix lying behind any conclusion are very complicated issues, sure to produce many "weeds" and "thistles."

Furthermore, the traditionally strong studies by rural sociologists and agricultural economists of Mormon community life have not been continued;[30] in any case, they would largely have lost their relevance as Mormons have become primarily an *urban* people. Yet very few studies of urban Mormons appear in the social science literature, and even those, strictly speaking, would not permit generalizations beyond the specific cities studied. Particularly lacking are studies of Mormons in cities where they are small minorities, as opposed to cities in Utah or the Intermountain West.[31] Finally, Bahr and Forste correctly deplore the lack of published social research, especially of a quantitative nature, on Mormons *outside* the United States.[32]

In summarizing the state of social science literature on the Mormons, Bahr and Forste review the gaps and problems noted above and point to four areas in the study of Mormon religious life that seem to have been especially conspicuous by their absence: the nature and consequences of church growth outside North America; missionary work and the conversion process; personal religious experiences and testimonies; and the attribution and management of charisma in the church as an organization.

Bahr and Forste recommend that researchers make a greater effort to use various kinds of public directories as sampling frames, especially in cities with large (but minority) Mormon populations, and national census records in Canada, Britain, and other foreign countries, which often include data on religious preference or affiliation. In the United States, large national survey samples have been accumulating in various archives around the country (e.g., the NSF/NORC General Social Surveys), many of which include enough Mormon cases to make quantitative comparisons feasible.[33] Bahr and Forste's critique must be taken seriously in assessing both the nature and the quality of social science literature on the Mormons, but the field would be much more sparsely planted (if less cluttered) were it not for the sheer quantity of work by social scientists since midcentury. (Even weeds and thistles might serve some useful purposes; at least they help the field resist erosion.)

New Mormon Historians and Social Scientists

Though Mormons were well represented during most of the twentieth century in certain scientific and academic fields (see note 17), professional historians and social scientists of Mormon background were not so common until the later decades. Eventually, a new and larger generation of Mormon scholars, maturing professionally during the 1960s and 1970s, gained increasing visibility for research and publication on the Mormon religious heritage. These scholars received their postgraduate education after midcentury, often outside the Mormon heartland, and were thus trained in the secular canons of meticulous and responsible scholarship. Many of them were reared or lived significant portions of their lives outside Utah. Accordingly, they were somewhat more removed and liberated from the historic controversies and polemics surrounding Mormon history. Yet they were more successful (collectively speaking) than earlier generations in maintaining their spiritual and intellectual ties to Mormonism.[34]

To some extent, the sheer size of this scholarly cohort must be attributed to the extensive opportunities for advanced education provided by the federal government for war veterans, along with the contemporaneous opportunities for new academic careers as teachers of the "baby-boomers" reaching college age in the 1960s. To understand more fully the extraordinary growth in scholarly studies of the Mormons, however, we must look to explanations more institutional than demographic.

The New Mormon Studies in the Broader American Context

First came a post–World War II flowering of the sociology of religion in the United States more generally. Several scholars who were to become internationally visible in the sociology and anthropology of religion began building their careers in the 1950s and 1960s (e.g., Robert Bellah, Joseph Fichter, Charles Glock, Guy ["Ed"] Swanson), especially at such centers as Harvard, Columbia, and Berkeley.[35] The work of such scholars, much of it now regarded as "classic," acquired a well-deserved aura of respectability that gradually extended to the social scientific study of religion as a new subdiscipline.[36] A second and obviously related development during the same general period was the rise of a number of national scholarly societies devoted to the scientific study of religion. The three most important of these have been the Association for the Sociology of Religion, originally called the American Catholic Sociological Association; the Religious Research Association, founded largely through the efforts of professional researchers at the National Council of Churches; and the Society for the Scientific Study of Religion, originally organized mainly by academics at Harvard and Columbia but now by far the largest of the three societies. All three of these societies have thrived and have for decades published important scholarly journals.[37]

A new social scientific focus on the Mormons in particular was a by-product of the anthropologist Clyde Kluckhohn's large Harvard project during the 1950s (the Comparative Study of Values in Five Cultures), which focused largely on the area in and around the Mormon village of Ramah (called "Rimrock" in project reports and publications). Several of the non-Mormon graduate students in that project produced doctoral dissertations and important publications on the Mormons. Probably the best known of these was Thomas F. O'Dea.[38] Meanwhile, a few sociologists of Mormon background also began to publish pioneering work on Mormon life and religion in major journals of the discipline. The earliest of these were Harold T. Christensen and Glenn M. Vernon, who might be considered the "founding fathers," within the Mormon fold, of the new social science of Mormon life after midcentury. Christensen's work mainly continued the earlier focus on Mormon family life, fertility, and sexual mores (but with more scientific sophistication), while Vernon's work concentrated on the social psychology of religious beliefs and commitments.[39]

Certainly other individual social scientists of Mormon background also made important contributions to the new and growing body of Mormon studies after midcentury, through their graduate theses or dissertations and through their published work. Most were appreciably younger than Christensen or Vernon, and a few (like them) sustained career-long interests in Mormon studies to the end of the century or even beyond. It is no exaggeration, however, to say that the upsurge in the social scientific study of the Mormons is partly an unintended consequence of two institutional creations of the Mormon church itself: the expansion and reorganization of the church's Historical Department in 1972 and the establishment of the Research Information Division a few years later.[40]

Camelot Days in the Church Historical Department

Leonard J. Arrington was clearly the dean of the new Mormon historical scholarship. An economic historian with a distinguished publication record in Mormon and western studies dating from the early 1950s, Arrington was appointed church historian in 1972, the first professional to hold that post.[41] During the next decade, Arrington and his colleagues in the Historical Department published an enormous array of scholarly books and articles on Mormon history and collected from church archives the notes and materials for a great deal more. However, the program aroused the misgivings of some conservative church leaders, so it was truncated and reconfigured in 1982.[42] More important for the present discussion, however, this new corps of sponsored scholars constituted a focal point or nucleus with which many of the postwar generation could identify, forming a larger "critical mass" of Mormon scholars, who believed in the ecclesiastical (as well as the scholarly) legitimacy of their enterprise. The energies and products of these new historians and social scientists provided crucial nourishment also to private, unsponsored organizations, such as the Mormon History Association (already organized in 1965), and to such other intellectual enterprises and publications as *Dialogue* and *Sunstone,* which emerged during that same general period.

Church Sponsorship of Social Science Research

Scarcely less important as an impetus to Mormon studies has been the Research Information Division of the Church (RID), as it is now called. Established in the mid-1970s and known by various names since then, RID is a very sophisticated research operation staffed by professional social scientists with graduate degrees, usually doctorates, in such fields as sociology and psychology. Under the direct supervision of a committee of top church authorities, RID conducts evaluations of church programs, basic research for program planning, and periodic general surveys of various segments of the membership.[43] Early in its history, for example, RID undertook a study of inactive church members, with the purpose of eventually enhancing activation and retention efforts. It also conducted a longitudinal study of potential converts, in various stages of the proselyting program, to ascertain the most important factors in the conversion process. Before the establishment of RID, various agencies of the church (especially the Presiding Bishop's Office) had conducted social research or evaluations on a limited and ad hoc basis, but RID provided for the first time in church history a centralized, coordinated, and truly professional social research operation.[44]

RID has retained the sponsorship and goodwill of even the most conservative church leaders by scrupulously guarding its data and permitting few releases outside its in-house project reports to the leaders themselves. Some of the RID staff members are active participants in such professional societies as the Society for the Scientific Study of Religion and the Religious Research Association, and occasionally they have received permission to share some of their research results in oral presentations at meetings of those societies. A small amount of the work of RID has eventually found its way into the public domain through theses, dissertations, and published professional articles, and occasionally the official church magazine and newspaper have contained short pieces based on RID research.[45] In all cases, though, such releases require advance church clearance.

Although such strict proprietary control has kept this operation largely invisible, even to church members, RID has made an important contribution to the social science of Mormonism in two distinct ways: (1) by training younger social scientists in Mormon-specific religious research, and (2) by according a degree of legitimacy to the social scientific perspective on religion, always suspect in the minds of conservative church leaders and members. When it was first established, RID had a relatively small regular staff, which depended largely on temporary consultants and part-time professional personnel. These tended to be recruited as needed from among Mormon social scientists employed elsewhere and increasingly from the faculties of the social science departments at Brigham Young University. With the passage of time, however, the regular staff increased in size, so that much less of the work came to involve "outside" consultants. Meanwhile, for almost two decades, many Mormon social scientists "passed through" RID as consultants or part-time staff or became former staff. Many of these were at early stages of their careers and would undoubtedly never have gotten involved in Mormon studies without the training, sponsorship, and church legitimation provided by their RID participation. Even though these social scientists were not able to publish much from their RID work itself, they still gained much research experience and general knowledge about church programs, the church's inner workings, and membership characteristics of the church. Some of them have been able to use this knowledge in later research and publication based on public data sets.[46]

Institutional Developments Apart from the Church

In addition to these important institutional developments within the church, but not unrelated to them, was the establishment of the Mormon Historical Demography Project at the University of Utah in the 1970s. This project was made possible financially by extensive federal funding, but it was scientifically feasible only because of two venerable practices within the Mormon religion itself: genealogy and nineteenth-century polygamy. Cooperation between the church and the university has given demographers and medical researchers access to huge family data sets maintained by the church across many generations. These data sets have made possible scores of published studies on Mormon marriage, fertility, morbidity, mortality, and derivative topics. Many of these studies are historical in nature, but they also have implications for contemporary Mormon life and make use of sophisticated techniques in demographic analysis.

University presses have also played an important part in promoting Mormon-related work in history, the humanities, and the social sciences. As one might expect, this has been particularly the case for the university presses in Utah, and the University of Utah Press was especially noteworthy in this regard for many years, having published several truly distinguished works in Mormon studies. However, as the University of Utah, including its faculty and its press, became increasingly sensitive about the appearance of domination by Mormons or the Mormon church, it became increasing vigilant (some would say excessively so) about maintaining its separate identity as a major *state* university in the West. Accordingly, its press by the end of the century became very reluctant to publish works on the Mormons, preferring to focus instead on other regional peoples and places. Brigham Young University for a decade or so in the 1970s and 1980s tried unsuccessfully to create a university press up to conventional standards and even started a series on LDS history, which was soon aborted. Fortunately for the cause of Mormon scholarship, however, the University of Illinois Press decided in the 1970s, for its own purposes, to build a major list in Mormon studies. As a result, many distinguished and prize-winning books on Mormon topics were published in history and later in the social sciences as well. In the 1980s, Signature Books was privately established in Salt Lake City as another press devoted primarily to work in historical and social scientific studies on the Mormons, producing some of the most important books of the 1990s. As the century ended, a scholarly press was being revived at Brigham Young University, and the Utah State University Press was starting to fill the vacuum left by the University of Utah Press in Mormon studies.

Finally, some important societies and periodicals for the promotion of Mormon studies in history, the social sciences, and the humanities emerged. *Brigham Young University Studies* first appeared in 1959–60. Though based at BYU, this scholarly journal is largely independent of church control and has published some important articles throughout the years. More fully independent, sometimes quite stridently so, is *Dialogue: A Journal of Mormon Thought,* begun in 1965 by Mormon academics and intellectuals based at Stanford University in California. Both of these interdisciplinary quarterlies contain many more articles in history and the humanities than in the social sciences. The *Journal of Mormon History* has been published since 1974 by the Mormon History Association, itself a society of more than a thousand members organized in 1965. Both the society and the journal are fully independent of the church. *Sunstone* was founded in 1975 by younger Mormon intellectuals based at the Graduate Theological Union in Berkeley, California. Its articles tend to be shorter and less ponderous than those in the other journals mentioned here, but they often deal with contemporary social issues and thus tend to have more social science content than do the other publications mentioned here. Most of these journals are now based in Utah. None of them can be considered "social science" publications as such, but they often contain articles of considerable social science significance, usually well refereed and edited.

More fully devoted to the social science perspective is the Mormon Social Science Association (MSSA, formerly the Society for the Sociological Study of Mormon Life), founded in 1976 with Glenn M. Vernon as its first president and guiding light. With a membership of barely a hundred, the MSSA publishes only a periodic newsletter, not a professional journal. However, it has joint annual meetings as part of the formal program of the nationwide Society for the Scientific Study of Religion, and it funds the biennial Vernon Lecture Series as part of that program. The Association of Mormon Counselors and Psychologists (AMCAP), also founded in the 1970s, has annual meetings and publishes the *AMCAP Journal.* With its well-articulated commitment to integrating counseling psychology with Mormon religious values, this journal contains a mixture of articles ranging from sound academic psychology to manifestly devotional literature (sometimes in the same article).

In summary, at midcentury, and beginning especially in the mid-1960s, a new generation of scholars and scholarship emerged to produce a body of social science literature on the Mormons, which is unprecedented, at least in its sheer quantity. The quality of this literature, however, has varied with the resources available to its authors. In general, the historical literature has benefited more than the strictly social science literature from material support, particularly from the church but also from various foundations and fellowships. Social scientists, especially those striving to do quantitative studies based on large-scale surveys, have generally been forced to depend on relatively small and unsystematic samples, so that few reliable findings can be generalized to the entire Mormon population in North America, to say nothing of the rest of the world. Such limitations have not applied to the research done under church auspices, but the results of that research have generally not been available to the public. Despite the limitations under which they have worked, however, some social scientists have been able to publish reliable studies with some general applicability, and more will probably appear in the future as useful religious variables are increasingly included in large, public, national data sets.

Several conditions have contributed to the emergence of this new social science literature on the Mormons. Some of these had nothing to do with developments peculiar to the Mormons: the greatly increased access to postgraduate education for aspiring historians and social scientists (as well as others), the mushrooming opportunities for their academic employment, and the flowering of the sociology and anthropology of religion as subdisciplines in the nation as a whole. Other conditions fostering the new social science literature were more unique and institutional: certain university-based programs, such as Harvard's Comparative Study of Values in the 1950s and the Historical Demography Project at the University of Utah starting in the 1970s; and the establishment of professional research programs within the LDS Church, first in history and then in social research. A few key presses, starting with the University of Utah Press and more recently the University of Illinois Press and Signature Books, have done much to disseminate and give respectability to books on the Mormons. Scholarly societies and periodicals, some devoted to social scientific studies of religion generally and others limited to the Mormon scene, have also given unprecedented visibility to scholarly work on the Mormons.

Principal Directions and Topics in the New Social Science on Mormons

Whatever the quality of the new social science literature on the Mormons, the conditions that nourished it, or the agencies instrumental in its increasing publication, it is still necessary to discuss the major preoccupations of this literature and how these have differed from earlier foci. The first relevant observation is that much of the new literature simply continued and expanded on some of the topics from the past.

Continuities with Earlier Research

Social science research on the geography, ecology, economy, and family life among the Mormons continued to some extent to the end of the twentieth century, though such studies declined as new interests emerged. There was also some shift in focus for these studies, corresponding to the dispersion and transformation of the Mormon population into a predominantly urban and industrial people, but this shift was in no way commensurate with the extent of urbanization of the modern Mormon communities.

In the years following World War I, especially the depression years, a large-scale Mormon "diaspora" out of Utah occurred, which began to slow down (or even to reverse somewhat) only very late in the century. Numerous conversions of new members after midcentury, combined with the outmigration from the West, produced important Mormon population centers where they had never existed before, primarily in the more highly urbanized areas on either coast of the United States (to say nothing of Mormon growth in other parts of the world). Accordingly, some of the later geographic and ecological literature focused on the dimensions, configuration, and consequences of this dispersion, with continuing interest in the earlier rural community focus as well. Somewhat paradoxically, these studies by geographers have demonstrated both the greatly accelerated dispersion of Mormons throughout the hemisphere and the continuing importance of the Intermountain West as the center of gravity for Mormonism, numerically and culturally.[47]

While historians continued to show some interest in nineteenth-century Mormon economic life, including communitarian experiments, social scientists generally shifted their interest to the more contemporary period. Contemporary Mormon ideas and practices in industrial capitalism, social welfare, and labor relations all received some attention (but not much) in the later literature.[48] Somewhat surprisingly, however, little attention has been given specifically to social stratification among the Mormons or to comparisons between Mormons and others in this respect. The rapid improvement in the average socioeconomic status of Mormons (compared with other Americans) after midcentury has sometimes been noted in passing, but as the century closed there were no studies of the educational and occupational routes preferred by Mormons in achieving their improved status or of the nature and consequences of social class divisions among Mormons.

Mormon family life has continued as a major thrust of social science research, just as in the earlier period. This general topic constitutes one of the most extensive segments of the sociological literature on the Mormons, virtually all of it having been produced by Mormon scholars. (This generalization would probably be even more applicable to the unpublished literature—dissertations and theses—than to the published literature.) It is well known that Mormon families tend to be relatively large, even though polygamy has long since been abandoned. A unique theology of the family lies behind both the fertility of the Mormons and the church's major concern with wholesome family life. An academic expression of this same concern is the Family and Demographic Institute at Brigham Young University, which has sponsored, supported, or fostered much of the family literature that has appeared since midcentury. In addition, Mormons (whether BYU-based or not) have been especially prominent among contemporary family sociologists in the United States.

Published work, however, has focused more on spousal and courting relationships than on parenting and child-rearing. Together with the growing literature on women's roles in Mormon culture, the family literature on spousal relations has partly reflected the influence of the feminist movement of recent decades.[49] Studies of the sexual aspect of spousal relations have usually been limited to the issues of fertility, contraception, and child-spacing, in which the generally pronatal attitude of Mormon couples has expressed itself in the seeming paradox of relatively large families despite regular contraceptive use.[50] Mormon fertility has long been a topic of interest to demographers and family sociologists, but research in that field was greatly augmented by the work of scholars connected with the Historical Demography Project at the University of Utah. Also, although family sociologists generally no longer regard premarital or other nonmarital forms of sexual behavior as part of family sociology, Mormon family sociologists have done a fair amount of research among Mormons on this topic, especially where adolescents are concerned.[51] However, the unmarried condition more generally, including single-parenting, is a topic that has received very little attention, despite a large and growing category of singles among the Mormons, as among most other people.

A somewhat ironic development in family research on the Mormons has been a return to the study of polygyny, a topic all but ignored during most of the twentieth century except, of course, for the polemical literature. A revived interest in polygyny as a social science endeavor was made possible partly by the academic detachment of a new cohort of Mormon scholars two or three generations removed from the conflict and controversy of the nineteenth century. One impetus for the renewed interest in polygamy was the research (again) of the Historical Demography Project at the University of Utah into the contemporary *genetic* consequences of early Mormon family (including polygamous) connections. This research has greatly expanded our understanding of the part played by family relationships, past and contemporary, in *morbidity,* particularly the heritability of cancers and other pathological traits and tendencies. For many Mormon scholars, though, the later studies of polygamy reflect a persistent and largely unfulfilled quest for understanding by modern Mormons, especially feminists, of an institution that was at once so formative for early Mormon culture and yet so ironic for a religion with strong New England roots. This quest has extended also to an interest in the contemporary schismatic polygynous sects of Mormonism, which apparently came to comprise many thousands of adherents throughout Utah and the Intermountain West by the end of the century.[52]

Newly Developing Research Directions and Interests

During the early decades of the twentieth century, historians and social scientists studying the Mormons tended to look at the past itself or at the persistence of nineteenth-century Mormon institutions and beliefs into the new century (village or community organization, economic cooperation, family life, and so on). In midcentury, however, scholars began to focus more on how Mormons were changing, or at least being seriously challenged to change, as a natural and inevitable outcome of having finally engaged the modern world. Although some studies continued to focus on O'Dea's discovery of "incipient nationality" or emergent "ethnicity" in early Mormondom or otherwise stressed Mormon peculiarities, most social science literature has reflected the struggle of the Mormons with "Americanization," which began with the campaign for Utah statehood in the 1890s and greatly accelerated thereafter.

Using such concepts as assimilation, accommodation, secularization, and modernization for this process, many social scientists have identified both its symptoms and its consequences, while at the same time recognizing various Mormon efforts to resist the process.[53] In anthropology, the main exemplar of the study of changing Mormon life in the twentieth century was John L. Sorenson, beginning with his 1961 dissertation on the transformation of two Utah agricultural communities under the impact of a new steel plant in the vicinity.[54] Somewhat later, Erik G. Schwimmer's and Mark P. Leone's anthropological work also emphasized the theme of transformation.[55] In general, however, the implications and consequences of modernization and assimilation receiving the most scholarly attention have been values, politics, racial and ethnic relationships, and the role(s) of modern women.

VALUES   This is a broad and amorphous category that encompasses all social life and institutions. In classical sociological theory, new religions that survive tend to interact with their surrounding societies in such a way that they are transformed from "sects" to "churches." This process typically involves some erosion of the otherworldly values on which the sect was founded, as succeeding generations of believers prosper and increasingly compromise with the world in the process of achieving greater public acceptance. In general, both the Mormon church as an institution and the Mormon people as Americans seem to have trod that time-honored path of assimilation.[56] After midcentury, however, there was growing evidence of a turning back or a "retrenchment" in an effort to recover some of the earlier Mormon sectarian distinctiveness, contrary to the usual unidirectional assumptions of the sect-to-church theory.[57] The assimilation process for Mormons was thus fraught with ambivalence and conflict, both inside and outside the church, as was apparent to O'Dea already in the 1950s.[58] Among the conflicts receiving special attention by scholars more recently are individual agency versus ecclesiastical authority;[59] competitive economic achievement and mobility versus egalitarian simplicity and cooperation;[60] modern scientific rationalism versus traditional dogma and folklore;[61] and patriarchal versus egalitarian family ideals and values.[62]

POLITICS   In any discussion of the political aspects of Mormon assimilation, it is necessary to distinguish the institutional or *ecclesiastical* level from the *popular* level. For all practical purposes, nineteenth-century Mormonism was a theocracy, the dissolution of which was one of the conditions for Utah statehood.[63] During the twentieth century, the church generally maintained a low profile in national politics, even if its vital interests were involved (as at both the beginning and the end of Prohibition). That is, the church tended to limit its involvement to occasional public pronouncements or to the informal prompting of its members in certain elections or legislative actions, at least when it saw "moral" (as opposed to "political") issues. Of course, in Utah state politics, the church has always been a major presence, since three-fourths of the state's population was Mormon even at the end of the century. Yet even there the levers of political power tended to be held by loyal Mormons who understood church interests well enough that they rarely needed prodding from the prophets.[64] Certainly in its official posture, the church has embraced the American ideal of church-state separation by explicitly prohibiting the use of its facilities, its meetings, or its membership lists in favor of one side or another in any political issue or election. However, there have been a few occasions since the 1960s (perhaps as part of the retrenchment reaction mentioned earlier) when church leaders have directly or covertly intervened to influence national or state laws or policies, probably crossing the traditional "wall of separation." By the end of the twentieth century and early in the twenty-first, LDS Church intervention in political campaigns had become noticeably more overt in opposition to same-sex marriage legislation proposed in several states.[65]

At the popular level, Mormons during most of the twentieth century, when their assimilation was so much in evidence, tended to vote with the national majority in almost every presidential election. Coming out of the nineteenth century, most Mormons had tended to favor the Democratic party, since they blamed the Republicans for most of the anti-Mormon legislation of that century. By the mid-twentieth century, however, Mormon voters were about evenly divided between the two major parties.[66] Meanwhile, for peculiar historical reasons having to do with the "deal-making" around the achievement of Utah statehood, most top Mormon leaders allied themselves with the Republicans, a process accelerated by the disaffection of these leaders with Franklin Roosevelt and the New Deal.[67] By the end of the twentieth century, the Mormon popular vote, too, had become disproportionately Republican, although that development must be considered in the context of an increasingly Republican electorate throughout the western United States, especially the mountain states.[68]

All in all, one might summarize the social science evidence on Mormons and politics by saying that during most of the century Mormons assimilated well to the national political consensus, with, however, a noticeably conservative turn late in the century, perhaps reflecting a growing resistance to further assimilation.[69] At the same time, the church has continued to show a great sensitivity to public criticism and to maintain a large and highly professional public affairs department, promoting the image of Mormons as loyal, decent, patriotic citizens and friendly neighbors.[70]

RACIAL AND ETHNIC RELATIONSHIPS   Until 1978, the Mormon church retained an anachronistic nineteenth-century policy of excluding members of black African ancestry from its male lay priesthood. Though no other American denominations had ever had more than minuscule proportions of black clergy either (except, of course, for the so-called black churches), they all had pretty well abandoned racial discrimination as a formal policy during the height of the civil rights movement. This situation left the Mormons conspicuously unique among major denominations in their policy toward African Americans. Given its otherwise highly egalitarian heritage, including a lay clergy, the church's racial policy was all the more anomalous in the 1970s. To keep some historical perspective, however, it must be remembered that Mormons did not have a large number of African Americans either in the church or in its traditional geographic heartland to help raise racial consciousness. Even such astute non-Mormon observers as O'Dea failed in his 1957 book to mention the racial issue among his "sources of strain and conflict" in the Mormon church, despite Mormon sociologist Lowry Nelson's stinging (but not widely noticed) criticism of the racial policy in the pages of the *Nation* magazine as early as 1952.[71]

In any case, this ecclesiastical discrimination proved a source of considerable anguish to the rapidly growing new generation of Mormon scholars and intellectuals, especially those living outside Utah. Particularly in the pages of *Dialogue,* but in other publications as well, they wrote extensive and well-researched articles questioning both the historical and the canonical bases of the policy that barred blacks from the priesthood and tracing the vagaries and consequences of that policy up until its eventual demise in 1978.[72]

In addition, there is a small literature on modern Mormon relationships with Native Americans, toward whom the church has had a somewhat ambivalent policy despite a unique and mildly favorable theological outlook, and also on relationships with Jews, about whom Mormons have traditionally had a very favorable (and somewhat Zionist) theology and relatively low rates of anti-Semitism.[73]

ROLES OF MODERN WOMEN   The revival of feminism in the United States in the 1960s had its impact on the Mormon subculture as well, despite the obstinately patriarchal image that the church had acquired in the mass media. Mormon women in the United States are generally vocal, articulate, and well educated, and they have been well represented among recent generations of Mormon scholars. Female Mormon scholars, in particular, have occasionally come into conflict with the church leadership, which tends to regard the traditional domestic and maternal roles for women as indispensable to the survival (or the restoration) of wholesome family life.[74]

Even in the younger generations, however, few Mormon women have ever shown much inclination to join in the feminist critique of the patriarchal tradition, although a new consciousness of the predicament of the modern Mormon woman can be seen in two grassroots publications. The first of these, published since 1974, is *Exponent II,* an independent quarterly magazine (in tabloid format) that features a variety of personal essays and articles of special interest to women. Deliberately named in memory of the *Woman's Exponent,* an independent nineteenth-century Utah journal that supported the early feminist movement, *Exponent II* is published by Mormon Sisters, Inc., a network of women based on the East Coast. The most obvious of the themes in this publication are the struggles of women with the sometimes harsh realities of modern life, especially family life; celebration of the variety of roles and modalities available to modern women; and the multiplicity of ways in which one can be a devout Mormon woman outside the traditional mold. A decade or so later, a younger generation of Mormon feminists based in Utah founded the *Mormon Women's Forum,* which publishes a quarterly with a kind of newsletter format and has a noticeably more strident tone than *Exponent II.*

Although there was an occasional piece about Mormon women in the scholarly literature of the prefeminist days, the closing decades of the twentieth century presented us with an unprecedented and growing body of literature in the social sciences and humanities on Mormon women, their roles, their needs, their challenges, and their predicaments.[75] Much of this literature has been written by female scholars and intellectuals, who have criticized and resisted some of the noncanonical and Victorian cultural aspects of traditional Mormon patriarchal doctrine and ecclesiology. In their critique, they have made use of (among other things) a unique and little-known Mormon doctrine about a female deity or Heavenly Mother, much to the consternation of church authorities, who have been reluctant to see that doctrinal idea developed outside their control or applied to modern issues.[76] The actual role behavior of modern Mormon women, as opposed to official ecclesiastical prescriptions, has also been studied in recent years, with the usual finding that Mormon women, married or single, live and behave in ways not so different from those of non-Mormon women in the United States and that the patriarchal rhetoric in Mormon culture is paradoxically accompanied by a high degree of egalitarianism in actual relationships between spouses.[77]

The Religious Life of Mormons

Aside from topics deriving from the process of Mormon assimilation, such as those just discussed, an important focus of contemporary social science on the Mormons has been religiosity in its various aspects. In his landmark studies of American Protestants and Catholics, Charles Y. Glock conceived of "religiosity" (or religiousness) in five "dimensions"; in other words, he saw five different ways of being religious: belief, knowledge, practice, experience, and consequences. These five might be correlated, but they are distinct. For example, one might be highly religious in belief (hold very orthodox beliefs) but not attend church regularly or pray very often (practice), and vice versa. Glock also distinguished between the *nature* of religiosity (i.e., its five dimensions) and the *sources* of religiosity (where religiosity comes from or why some people are religious and others are not).[78]

Since theoretical conceptualization in the social science of religion more generally was only just beginning at midcentury, it is not surprising that studies of Mormon religiosity did not occur until the pioneering work of Glenn

M. Vernon in the 1950s. The work of Vernon and other early investigators was more often descriptive than analytical, but the later work of Marie Cornwall and others has proved more informative on the nature, sources, and consequences of Mormon religiosity. In particular, the main institutions of religious socialization among the Mormons appear to be quite effective as sources of religiosity, and the dimensions of religiosity that seem strongest among the Mormons are belief and practice. The consequences of religiosity are reflected much more in the personal habits and family life of the Mormons than in any unique social, civic, or political attitudes or behavior.[79] However, the meaning and importance of religious symbols, rituals, and charismatic experiences to Mormons are largely neglected topics.

Much of the later research on Mormon religiosity benefited from the early collaboration of some of its authors with the church's Research and Information Division, and the RID has continued to collect and analyze a veritable gold mine of reliable and representative data on the nature, sources, and consequences of religiosity among Mormons, as well as on the processes of conversion and defection. Almost none of these data, unfortunately, are accessible to those outside the RID, church members or not.[80] Aside from the more formal expressions of religiosity, popular or folk forms of religiosity have been common among Mormons, as among others. Research since midcentury has produced an especially rich literature on Mormon folk religion, from the work of Austin Fife and Alta Fife and Claire Wilcox Noall in the 1940s and Wilfrid Bailey in the 1950s to the work of William A. Wilson, Richard C. Poulsen, Wayland Hand, and others later in the century.[81]

In summary, social science studies of the Mormons since midcentury have, first of all, continued to some extent the earlier interests in geography, demography, rural sociology, and family life. New thrusts and themes in these areas have appeared, however, in response to the increasing dispersion and urbanization of Mormon community life. Demographic studies have been enriched enormously by the work of the publicly funded Historical Demography Project at the University of Utah and its analysis of church genealogical records. The nineteenth-century institution of Mormon polygyny (and some of its later schismatic derivatives) has also come in for renewed scholarly scrutiny.

Beyond these continuities with the earlier literature, much of the social science relating to Mormons since midcentury has focused on the various aspects and consequences of their assimilation or "Americanization," with particular reference to their values, their politics, their racial and ethnic relationships, and the roles of modern Mormon women. The various sources, dimensions, and consequences of Mormon religiosity also received considerable attention in the social science literature of the later twentieth century, not only in such formal respects as orthodoxy, practice, and conversion but also in folk varieties at the grassroots. There remain, however, many potentially interesting and important aspects of Mormon social life that have not received much attention from social scientists.

Some Neglected Topics in the Social Science Literature on Mormons

If much of even the recent "social science" literature on Mormons is notable more for its quantity than for its quality, there are many important topics on which we have little or no published work. To some extent any catalogue of "neglected" topics (whether on Mormons or anything else) will reflect the criteria and priorities of the person constructing the catalogue. Furthermore, any number of potential topics might be identified, given the scope of the eclectic discipline called "social science." Yet a few candidates for a list of "neglected topics" would seem especially conspicuous in the light of recent developments among the Mormons.[82]

Mormon Missiology

Considering how important and formative the missionary enterprise is in the LDS Church, it has generated relatively little scholarly literature, at least in published form.[83] Among the important aspects of the Mormon missionary experience calling for systematic study are the preparation and training of missionaries and mission presidents; the manifest and latent functions of missions, for both the church and the missionary; the determinants of differential success for missionaries in different missions, from different backgrounds, and with different kinds and degrees of religious socialization; and the various degrees of sophistication and success that the missionaries and their leaders have in bridging cultural boundaries in exotic locales while still containing the tendency toward syncretism with native traditions. The Research Information Division of the church has conducted internal studies on some of these topics.[84]

Consequences of the Exportation of the Mormon Religion

During 1996, the proportion of LDS Church members living outside North America passed the half-way mark. Public comments by church leaders indicated that they recognized some of the consequences of this internationalization of the religion, including the potential clashes of culture.[85] The

Research Information Division has also conducted studies on how the LDS religion is faring in various parts of the world, but, again, these studies are not open to the public. Most of the published research on Mormons outside the United States has been historical or devotional in nature, with little focus on the contemporary period and almost no analysis of prospects or problems involved in the establishment of durable Mormon communities in exotic locales.[86]

Throughout the nineteenth century, the official policy and program of the church was "Zionist" in nature, with thousands of Mormon converts from Europe and elsewhere called to gather in Utah. As the American frontier began to close and new immigration laws were imposed by the U.S. government, the policy of the church was gradually reversed, and Mormon converts overseas were encouraged to remain and help build up the church in their own countries. However, the depressions, wars, and other depredations in Europe and elsewhere during the first half of the twentieth century kept the incentives strong for Mormon converts everywhere to leave their homelands for a better life in Zion. It was not until well after midcentury that most of the world's Mormons were content to remain at home so that stakes could finally be created in large numbers outside North America.

At least two consequences of major sociological importance have resulted from this change. First, the direction of the assimilation process has been reversed. No longer are Mormon converts from other countries coming to the United States for assimilation into the Utah church; rather, the church must now find ways to adapt to many other cultures. Second, for the first time in Mormon history, a second and a third generation of Mormons— the children and grandchildren of the converts who had joined the church starting about 1960—have begun to reach maturity outside of North America.

All sorts of important research questions arise from these two major developments. What is happening to Mormonism as it passes through two or more generations of families in various cultures, and how does the Mormon experience seem to compare in this respect with that of early Islam or Roman Catholicism? In which cultures is the adaptation of the religion working best, and why? How is the American leadership dealing with the constant strain toward syncretism? Is Mormonism changing the "natives" more than the natives are changing Mormonism? How much are they really changing? Are they keeping the faith of their convert parents and grandparents, or are they defecting back into their local societies in large numbers? What accounts for the different rates of retention or defection in different locales? On these and similar questions, there is scarcely any social science literature in any language, either by American scholars or by local ones.[87]

Social Stratification and the Church

Various observers have periodically noted the homogeneous, middle- and upper-middle-class composition of the modern Mormon church in the United States, quite in contrast to its primarily rural and working-class composition at midcentury.[88] To some extent, this change is merely characteristic of the assimilation and "bourgeoisification" usually accompanying the evolution of a new religion from "sect" to "church." Yet one wonders to what extent contemporary recruitment to Mormonism (conversion) is systematically *selective* along social class lines and how that selectivity differs from one society to another. From what strata of society do most Mormon converts come in the United States, and how would the answer to that question differ in, say, Mexico or Argentina or Belgium or Japan? What are the implications and consequences of such selective conversions both within a given country and across national boundaries? To what extent must proselytization, indoctrination, governance, and programs be adapted not only to different cultures but also to different class settings *within* those cultures? Is retention also selective by social class? To what extent is the future of Mormonism in the world dependent on its elective affinity with certain class "carriers" of the religion in various parts of the world? How is the distribution of office and power within the church affected by social class? How is governance within the church affected by social class differences between leaders and laity or between different levels of leadership? The social science literature so far remains virtually silent on all such questions.

Organizational Studies

Among its other attributes, the Mormon church is a large, complex, bureaucratic organization subject to all the strains, stresses, drifts, and contradictions found in other such organizations. The organizational literature on Mormons has grown fairly large, but most of it deals, in one way or another, with methods of control and governance by the ecclesiastical authorities rather than with more general organizational analyses—especially analyses of unintended and unanticipated organizational developments. In any religion, one recurring issue is the ongoing tension between the need to perpetuate and enhance charismatic elements, on the one hand, and the organizational imperative to contain charisma, on the other hand.[89] Of special potential interest to scholars in sociology or organizational behavior was the implementation, starting in about 1960, of the so-called Correlation Program that was intended to centralize and standardize all church policies, programs, indoctrination, and budgeting under the control of the priesthood hierarchy. How well has "correlation" worked in achieving its original goals of simplifying the control of a massive organization by a relatively few top leaders? How well has this system facilitated two-way communication, as opposed to top-down communication only? What has been the impact on organizational morale? How has the distribution of actual power (as opposed to ostensible power) been shifted in the process? How appropriate and effective has the prevalent organizational model been in countries outside the United States? What unintended consequences have resulted from correlation, and how have these been managed? In the meantime, what has happened to the traditional charismatic features of Mormonism? Again, there is only the beginning of a social science literature on such questions.

Deviance, Discipline, and Social Control

Every community and society, religious or otherwise, maintains some system of social control by which to reward conformity and compliance with social norms and to punish violations of those norms. The more stringent and conspicuous the normative boundaries around the community, the less the tolerance for the normative violations (deviance). Mormons, like members of other religious communities, live simultaneously with one normative system for the society in general and another, usually more restrictive, normative system for their religious community. In large part, these two normative systems overlap (e.g., robbery is deviant in both normative systems). In many other respects, though, the religious norms are specific to the religious community (e.g., the Mormon proscription against alcoholic beverages). Deviance in *both* kinds of normative systems is of considerable interest to social scientists, but there is not a large literature on either kind for Mormons. Such as there is tends to focus mainly on juvenile delinquency. Much more remains to be learned about Mormon deviance in general.

Most empirical research shows that religious participation in nearly any denomination or church reduces the likelihood of deviant behavior in the society at large. Religious people, in other words, are more likely than others to be law-abiding and generally to keep out of trouble. The same is true for their children: juvenile delinquency, premarital sex, use of alcohol and drugs, and other normative violations are all less common among religiously active youth than among others. Furthermore, cities, neighborhoods, and communities that have more religious participation in an aggregate, average sense also seem to have less deviant behavior, even among nonparticipants in religion. There is, however, some reason to believe that religious restraints have greater independent impact on "vices" (drugs, alcohol, sex) than on "crimes" (murder, robbery), which are already under heavy sanctions from the justice system and the general normative order.[90]

While we can probably assume that these same generalizations would apply to Mormons and to predominantly Mormon communities, there is very little social science literature on crime and deviance among Mormons (except juveniles) or on how key features of the Mormon religion might uniquely affect such behavior (if at all).[91] Because of the work of Harold Christensen and a few other sociologists, we have earlier research literature on how Mormon premarital sexual behavior has compared with that of others;[92] but since premarital (even nonmarital) sex after age eighteen is no longer generally sanctioned as deviant in most American and European settings, it has come to be an issue only for the more conservative religious communities, such as the Mormons. Other kinds of behavior still problematic in the society at large (including homosexuality) have been little studied among Mormons in particular.[93]

Since journalists and others have periodically claimed that Mormons have relatively high incidences of certain crimes (e.g., financial scams and child-abuse), it would be useful to have some reliable studies on which to rely for the empirical facts. Ever mindful of the Mormon public image, church leaders themselves are not inclined to welcome (to say nothing of sponsor) studies of deviant behavior, even if the studies are done with academic detachment. It is somewhat surprising that with major law schools at the two largest Utah universities, there are no departments of criminal justice, no academic programs in deviance or criminology at either of these universities, and scarcely a research criminologist of any kind to be found.

Whatever problems of social control might be presented by Mormons (religious or not) in the society at large, there is also the question of social control *within* the Mormon church and community (noted above as an organizational issue). To some extent, of course, this question overlaps with the one of defection, for a failure to keep Mormon members participating in church life and observing church norms is the ultimate failure in social control. Far short of the issue of defection, however, is the more common and mundane issue of *selective conformity*. In nearly any religious community, many members pick and choose the norms with which they comply, inventing rationalizations that still permit them to identify themselves as loyal members despite selective compliance. Presumably there are different "normative constituencies" among Mormons, as among others—segments of the membership that generally share their "selections" of what to observe or not to observe and reinforce each other's rationalizations. These constituencies can occur on either side of the "normal curve." On the one side, there might

be a "constituency" of coffee-drinking Mormons (or even "social drinkers"),
while on the other side there might be a constituency of health fanatics who
avoid not only coffee and wine but also white sugar, white flour, and all other
foods that have not been grown or processed "naturally." Both constituencies might claim at least "virtual conformity" to the LDS way of life. Of considerable sociological interest would be studies of these kinds of constituencies, their social compositions, their social constructions of conformity, and
the parts that they play in normative and cultural changes in the larger Mormon arena.

At the institutional level, especially in an authoritarian organizational
structure, what social control mechanisms, incentives, and disciplinary measures are used to keep Mormons within the fold and to ensure adequate loyalty and conformity among those who stay? What offenses are most likely to
bring disciplinary action or even excommunication and how has the list of
heavily sanctioned offenses changed over time? What are the organizational
costs and benefits of heavy sanctions against some offenses and light sanctions against others? There is perhaps some informed social commentary
dealing with some of these questions, but there is no systematic social science research. Much of the interest in such questions lies in what the answers
could tell us about the effectiveness of symbolic and otherworldly incentives
and disincentives, not only to define and maintain normative boundaries but
also to construct the public image and identity of Mormons as a people, both
inside and outside the church.[94]

Conclusion

The body of literature on Mormons that might be regarded as "social
scientific" in nature has flowered since the middle of the twentieth century.
Very little of it, however, is "scientific" in the sense of systematic, quantitative, or even empirical findings that can be generalized to the Mormon people
as a whole—or even to Mormons outside of Utah. Yet in a broader sense, this
literature, despite its many "weeds," is rich in its cumulative observations,
ideas, and hypotheses and in such facts that it does offer us. Its offerings are
especially noteworthy in such demographic topics as fertility, migration, dispersion, morbidity, and mortality and to perhaps a lesser extent in family
relationships and community life.

At the same time, many important aspects of Mormon life and culture have
been badly neglected, especially in parts of the world outside the United States
or even outside the Intermountain West. Despite the highly urbanized nature of social life for most Mormons, the literature reveals little about urban

Mormons, especially where they are in the minority. Furthermore, Mormons, like all other peoples, are stratified in the distribution of wealth, power, and prestige among them, and we know almost nothing about the parts played by stratification either within the Mormon world or in its selective and differential impact on conversion and retention across cultures. Organizational studies of governance, decision making, and the management of charisma, both inside the Mormon church and in comparison with other organizations, also are lacking. Mormon religiosity, including the meaning and importance for different Mormons of different ways of being religious, is another arena that social scientists have only just begun to study. Finally, in the face of growing evidence or at least credible allegations that Mormons have shared in the national breakdown of institutions and mechanisms of social control in the United States, we have yet to learn much about crime and deviant behavior among Mormons.

All researchers would probably agree, however, that reliable, definitive social research on the Mormons will continue to be difficult as far as we can see into the future. The definitive social science literature that has accumulated and especially its rapid growth in recent decades have been made possible primarily by various kinds of *institutional* support, since there are neither many opportunities nor many incentives for private research on Mormons. One can thus hope that the cooperation between the church genealogy archives and the medical and social scientists at the University of Utah will continue, with funding, although even that fruitful institutional collaboration is limited to biological and demographic research and is not likely to last indefinitely.

It is the church itself that stands to gain the most from continued social research of high quality. In the final decade or so of the twentieth century, however, the intellectual environment within Mormondom became somewhat less hospitable to the work of historians and social scientists not under church control. The Research Information Division will likely continue as the principal locus and organ of the best social science research on Mormons, but scholars in general can expect little, if any, of that work to be released to the public for the foreseeable future. It is rare also for either governments or foundations to provide large-scale funding for research on religion. Historians have a great advantage in this respect, because much of the data they need for solid and reliable studies of the Mormon past can now be found in public depositories.[95]

Social scientists, however, will always be forced to continue relying on dubious samples or use their ingenuity in exploiting opportunities for secondary analysis of data gathered by others for other purposes. The future of reliable and sophisticated social science research on Mormons in the United States thus will probably depend on large, publicly funded surveys with adequate Mormon subsamples (always problematic) or on universities' occasional and limited support of dissertations and other small projects carried out by graduate students and faculty (even more problematic). All things considered, it seems unlikely that the first decades of the twenty-first century will see the same rate of growth in social science literature on the Mormons that occurred in the final decades of the twentieth century.

Notes

This chapter incorporates parts of my 1984 essay on a similar topic, with appropriate updating for developments in the literature since then. See Armand L. Mauss, "Sociological Perspectives on the Mormon Subculture," *Annual Review of Sociology* 10 (1984): 437–60. I gratefully acknowledge the permission of Annual Reviews, Inc., of Palo Alto, California, for the right to incorporate the earlier material into this chapter.

   1. Social science literature is distinguished here from literature that is mainly historical in nature.
   2. William H. Swatos Jr., "The Faith of the Fathers: On the Christianity of Early American Sociology," *Sociological Analysis* 44 (Fall 1983): 33–52.
   3. Richard T. Ely, "Economic Aspects of Mormonism," *Harper's Monthly* 106 (April 1903): 668. A somewhat Marxist interpretation of the Mormon economy, particularly the relationship between that economy and the general American economy, was published in England in 1912 and republished in 1994: Ruth Kauffman and Reginald Wright Kauffman, *The Latter Day Saints: A Study of the Mormons in the Light of Economic Conditions* (1912; reprint, Urbana: University of Illinois Press, 1994).
   4. Leonard J. Arrington, "Scholarly Studies of Mormonism in the Twentieth Century," *Dialogue: A Journal of Mormon Thought* 1 (Spring 1966): 15–32.
   5. Ibid.; Marvin S. Hill, "Survey: The Historiography of Mormonism," *Church History* 28 (December 1959): 418–26.
   6. See, for example, Hamilton Gardner, "Cooperation among the Mormons," *Quarterly Journal of Economics* 31 (May 1917): 461–99; Hamilton Gardner, "Communism among the Mormons," ibid. 37 (November 1923): 134–74; Joseph Geddes, *The United Order among the Mormons (Missouri Phase): An Unfinished Experiment in Economic Organization* (1924; reprint, New York: AMS, 1975); Gustive O. Larson, *Prelude to the Kingdom: Mormon Desert Conquest* (1946; reprint, Westport, Conn.: Greenwood, 1978); William J. McNiff, *Heaven on Earth: A Planned Mormon Society* (1940; reprint, Philadelphia: Porcupine, 1972); and Lowry Nelson, *The Mormon Village: A Pattern and Technique of Land Settlement* (Salt Lake City: University of Utah Press, 1952). Leonard J. Arrington, "Property among the Mormons," *Rural Sociology* 16 (1951): 339–52; and *Great Basin Kingdom: An Economic History of the Latter-day Saints* (Cambridge, Mass.: Harvard University Press, 1958) continued this same tradition and overlapped chronologically somewhat with it, but Arrington really belonged to the post–World War II generation of scholars described later in this chapter. For an interesting essay on early Mormon settlement patterns and the various structures

and artifacts concomitant with those patterns, see Carol A. Edison, "Material Culture: An Introduction and Guide to Mormon Vernacular," in *Mormon Americana: A Guide to Sources and Collections in the United States,* ed. David J. Whittaker (Provo, Utah: BYU Studies, 1995), 307–35.

7. Nelson's work on Utah and the Mormons, along with that of many other sociologists, anthropologists, and others, is discussed in John L. Sorenson's valuable essay accompanying his "A Bibliography of Anthropological Studies on Mormons" (unpublished, 1996).

8. Nels Anderson, "The Mormon Family," *American Sociological Review* 2 (October 1937): 601–8; and *Desert Saints* (1942; reprint, Chicago: University of Chicago Press, 1966).

9. James E. Hulett Jr., "Social Role and Personal Security in Mormon Polygamy," *American Journal of Sociology* 45 (January 1940): 542–53; James E. Hulett Jr., "The Social Role of the Mormon Polygamous Male," *American Sociological Review* 8 (June 1943): 279–87; Kimball Young, *Isn't One Wife Enough?* (1954; reprint, Westport, Conn.: Greenwood, 1970). See also Stanley S. Ivins, "Notes on Mormon Polygamy," *Western Humanities Review* 10 (Summer 1956): 229–39.

10. See, for example, Lawrence Foster, *Religion and Sexuality: Three Communal Experiments of the Nineteenth Century* (New York: Oxford University Press, 1981); Lawrence Foster, *Women, Family, and Utopia: Communal Experiments of the Shakers, the Oneida Community, and the Mormons* (Syracuse, N.Y.: Syracuse University Press, 1991); Louis J. Kern, *An Ordered Love: Sex-Roles and Sexuality in Victorian Utopias* (Chapel Hill: University of North Carolina Press, 1981); Richard S. Van Wagoner, *Mormon Polygamy: A History* (Salt Lake City: Signature Books, 1986); Jessie L. Embry, *Mormon Polygamous Families: Life in the Principle* (Salt Lake City: University of Utah Press, 1987); and B. Carmon Hardy, *Solemn Covenant: The Mormon Polygamous Passage* (Urbana: University of Illinois Press, 1992).

11. Representative of the earliest studies of Mormon family and fertility are Anderson, "The Mormon Family," 601–8; Harold T. Christensen, "The Time Interval between Marriage of Parents and the Birth of Their First Child in Utah County, Utah," *American Journal of Sociology* 44 (January 1939): 518–25; Harold T. Christensen, "Mormon Fertility: A Survey of Student Opinion," *American Journal of Sociology* 53 (January 1948): 270–75; Victor A. Christopherson, "An Investigation of Patriarchal Authority in the Mormon Family," *Marriage and Family Living* 18 (November 1956): 328–33; William A. DeHart, "Fertility in Mormons in Utah and Adjacent Areas," *American Sociological Review* 6 (December 1941): 818–29; William G. Dyer and Dick Urban, "The Institutionalization of Equalitarian Family Norms," *Marriage and Family Living* 20 (February 1958): 53–58; Lowry Nelson, "Education and the Changing Size of Mormon Families," *Rural Sociology* 17, no. 4 (1952): 335–42; and Roy A. West, "The Mormon Village Family," *Sociology and Social Research* 23 (March/April 1939): 353–59.

12. Exceptions to this generalization might be seen in some examples of early attempts at social science treatises on the Mormon religion more generally, including work by I. Woodbridge Riley and by Walter F. Prince (see Arrington's "Scholarly Studies of Mormonism in the Twentieth Century," 15–32). A serious scholarly effort was made in Europe by Eduard Meyer with his 1912 *Ursprung und Geschichte der Mormonen* (published in English as *The Origin of the Mormons, with Reflections on the Beginnings of Islam and Chris-*

tianity [Salt Lake City: University of Utah Press, 1961]), but this work was flawed by the same kind of condescending "social science" as the work of the American scholars on whom Meyer largely relied. By modern standards, the social science in all these works was quite primitive, but probably no more so than that reflected in other studies of unconventional religions during that period. The best social science work on the Mormon religion in this early period (perhaps the only one) was a Chicago dissertation by Ephraim E. Ericksen, eventually published as a book and even reprinted in more recent years: *The Psychological and Ethical Aspects of Mormon Group Life* (1922; reprint, Salt Lake City: University of Utah Press, 1975). Nels L. Nelson, a professor of English at Brigham Young University, published *Scientific Aspects of Mormonism* (1904; reprint, Chicago: Hillison and Etten, 1918), attempting to integrate and reconcile the Mormon religion with selected elements of the biological and social sciences of the time, with the promise (321) of a later book to be entitled *Social Aspects of Mormonism*, which apparently was never published. Both Ericksen and Nelson were Mormons educated outside of Utah. Fawn M. Brodie's well-known biography of Joseph Smith, *No Man Knows My History: The Story of Joseph Smith, the Mormon Prophet* (New York: Alfred A. Knopf, 1945; 2d ed., 1971), might also be considered an early exercise in social science because of its "psychohistory" theoretical framework. The work of G. Homer Durham, a Mormon political scientist, on church administration and politics, also dates back (just barely) to the first half of the century (e.g., G. H. Durham, "Coordination by Special Representatives of the Chief Executive: Administrative Organization of the Mormon Church," *Public Administration Review* 8 [Summer 1948]: 176–80), as does the earliest work on Mormon folklore by Austin E. Fife, "The Legend of the Three Nephites among the Mormons," *Journal of American Folklore* 53 (January–March 1940): 1–49; and Claire W. Noall, "Superstitions, Customs, and Prescriptions of Mormon Midwives," *California Folklore Quarterly* 3 (April 1944): 102–14.

13. On this topic, see a pair of articles by Meyer S. Reed Jr.: "An Alliance for Progress: The Early Years of the Sociology of Religion in the United States," *Sociological Analysis* 42 (Spring 1981): 27–46; "After the Alliance: The Sociology of Religion in the United States from 1925 to 1949," *Sociological Analysis* 43 (Fall 1982): 189–204. The history of the psychology of religion generally parallels that of sociology but is probably even more anemic. One contemporary psychologist of religion claims that after World War I the psychology of religion became "almost extinct," especially with the emergence of behaviorism: Richard L. Gorsuch, "Psychology of Religion," *Annual Review of Psychology* 39 (1988): 201–21. See also Ralph W. Hood Jr., "Psychology of Religion," in *Encyclopedia of Religion and Society,* ed. William H. Swatos Jr., 388–91 (Walnut Creek, Calif.: Alta Mira, 1998).

14. Interestingly enough, an early (perhaps the earliest) interpretation of Weber's work was a doctoral dissertation at the University of Strasbourg by the Mormon sociologist Lowell L. Bennion, a work published as *Max Weber's Methodology* (Paris: Les Presses Modernes, 1933). Though not focused on religion specifically, this work did use Mormons to illustrate some of Weber's ideas. Bennion's work on Weber unfortunately remained little recognized in the United States because of its foreign publication and because Bennion did not pursue a career in mainstream academia but opted instead for a career in the LDS Church Education System. See Laurie Newman DiPadova and Ralph S. Brower, "A Piece of Lost History: Max Weber and Lowell L. Bennion," *American Sociologist* 23 (Fall 1992):

37–51; and Mary Lythgoe Bradford, *Lowell L. Bennion: Teacher, Counselor, Humanitarian* (Salt Lake City: Dialogue Foundation, 1995), esp. chapter 3.

15. See Swatos, "The Faith of the Fathers," 33–52.

16. Sorenson, "Bibliography of Anthropological Studies," would include as examples here the work of such social commentators as Dyer D. Lum and Clifton Johnson. He cites Lum's *Social Problems of Today; or, The Mormon Question in Its Economic Aspects* (1886; reprint, New York City: Gordon, 1973); and Johnson's "Life in a Mormon Village," *Highways and Byways of the Rocky Mountains* (New York: Macmillan, 1910), 158–76. To this could perhaps be added the work of Kauffman and Kauffman, *Latter Day Saints,* and others mentioned in note 12.

17. On the early overrepresentation of Mormons and Utahns in various scholarly fields, see Edward L. Thorndike, "The Origins of Superior Men," *Scientific Monthly* 56 (May 1943): 424–33; and Kenneth R. Hardy, "Social Origins of American Scientists and Scholars," *Science* 185, no. 4150 (1974): 497–506. Hardy also makes clear the notable increase in the number of Mormon scholars entering the social sciences between about 1920 and 1970.

18. See Leonard J. Arrington, "The Intellectual Tradition of the Latter-day Saints," *Dialogue: A Journal of Mormon Thought* 4 (Spring 1969): 13–26; and Richard J. Cummings, "Quintessential Mormonism: Literal-Mindedness as a Way of Life," *Dialogue: A Journal of Mormon Thought* 15 (Winter 1982): 92–102.

19. Leonard J. Arrington, "The Founding of the LDS Institutes of Religion," *Dialogue: A Journal of Mormon Thought* 2 (Summer 1967): 137–47; Russell Swensen, "Mormons and the University of Chicago Divinity School," *Dialogue: A Journal of Mormon Thought* 7 (Summer 1972): 37–47.

20. On the ambivalence among Mormons toward modern social, scientific, and intellectual currents, see Thomas G. Alexander, *Mormonism in Transition: A History of the Latter-day Saints, 1890–1930* (Urbana: University of Illinois Press, 1986); Armand L. Mauss, *The Angel and the Beehive: The Mormon Struggle with Assimilation* (Urbana: University of Illinois Press, 1994); and Erich Robert Paul, *Science, Religion, and Mormon Cosmology* (Urbana: University of Illinois Press, 1992). Richard F. Haglund Jr. and Erich Robert Paul, "Resources for the Study of Science, Technology, and Mormon Culture," in *Mormon Americana,* ed. Whittaker, 559–606, offer a very helpful overview of sources for studying the tensions between Mormonism and various fields of science and engineering over time. On the struggle of mid-twentieth-century Mormon literati, see Edward A. Geary, "Mormondom's Lost Generation: The Novelists of the 1940s," *BYU Studies* 18 (Fall 1977): 89–98. A more extensive review of the relation between Mormonism and literature over time is Eugene England, "Mormon Literature: Progress and Prospects," in *Mormon Americana,* ed. Whittaker, 455–505.

21. Ericksen, *Psychological and Ethical Aspects,* and Nelson, *Scientific Aspects,* might constitute exceptions to this generalization.

22. See Armand L. Mauss and Dynette Ivie Reynolds, "A Topical Guide to Published Social Science Literature on the Mormons," in *Studies in Mormon History, 1830–1997: An Indexed Bibliography,* by James B. Allen, Ronald W. Walker, and David J. Whittaker (Urbana: University of Illinois Press, in cooperation with the Smith Institute for LDS History, Brigham Young University, 2000).

23. Brodie's psychohistorical method was not so well received by Jefferson partisans

when she applied it to her biography of the third president. On this point, see Louis Midgley, "The Brodie Connection: Thomas Jefferson and Joseph Smith," *BYU Studies* 20 (Fall 1979): 59–67. Other critical discussions of psychohistory in Mormon studies are Hill, "Historiography of Mormonism," 418–26; and T. L. Brink, "Joseph Smith: The Verdict of Depth Psychology," *Journal of Mormon History* 3 (1976): 73–83.

24. Examples from the work of non-Mormon scholars would include Thomas F. O'Dea, *The Mormons* (Chicago: University of Chicago Press, 1957); Foster, *Religion and Sexuality;* Jan Shipps, *Mormonism: A New Religious Tradition* (Urbana: University of Illinois Press, 1984); Rodney Stark, "The Rise of a New World Faith," *Review of Religious Research* 26 (September 1984): 18–27; and Harold Bloom, "The Religion-Making Imagination of Joseph Smith," *Yale Review* 80 (April 1992): 26–43.

25. Howard M. Bahr and Renata Tonks Forste, "Toward a Social Science of Contemporary Mormondom," *BYU Studies* 26 (Winter 1986): 73–121.

26. Ibid., 83

27. Ibid., 84–94.

28. Ibid., 95–98, 115. To these criticisms, one could add (though Bahr and Forste do not) that much of the research done on Mormons by Mormons has reflected an implicit goal of vindicating the Mormon belief system or way of life. This has been especially conspicuous in theses and dissertations done at BYU, but it has appeared also in the work of those entirely independent of church employment, not only in the written presentation of their research but in the very selection of the topics for research.

29. Ibid., 98–99.

30. It must be noted, however, that several important *historical* studies of early Mormon communities were published late in the century.

31. Ibid., 99–100. Bahr and Forste note that recent social impact studies associated with energy development, migration, and population booms have sometimes included small Utah towns, but these have not covered the religious life of the people in the way that the earlier community studies did. Among the few studies of urban Mormons, Bahr and Forste appropriately acknowledge my mid-1960s surveys in Salt Lake City and in the California Bay area, but they mischaracterize them as based on "nonrepresentative respondents" (100). My Salt Lake City survey (with the help of the LDS Presiding Bishop's Office) was fully representative of all Mormons living in greater Salt Lake City (i.e., between the state capitol and "the point of the mountain"); and the San Francisco survey was representative of all Mormons living in the eastern half of the city (everyone living east of Golden Gate Park), the half selected deliberately to cover the most urbanized and transient part of the city. See the description of my methods in the appendix of Mauss, *The Angel and the Beehive.*

32. Bahr and Forste, "Toward a Social Science of Contemporary Mormondom," 101–2.

33. Ibid., 102–10, 114–17. Examples of the few published works that have made use of large national data sets in the public domain are Tim B. Heaton, Kristen L. Goodman, and Thomas B. Holman, "In Search of a Peculiar People: Are Mormon Families Really Different?" and Stephen J. Bahr, "Religion and Adolescent Drug Use: A Comparison of Mormons and Other Religions," both in *Contemporary Mormonism: Social Science Perspectives,* ed. Marie Cornwall, Tim B. Heaton, and Lawrence A. Young (Urbana: University of Illinois Press, 1994), 87–117, 118–137; and Mauss, *The Angel and the Beehive,* chap-

ters 8, 9, and 10. A few others can be found here and there in the professional social science journals.

34. The reference here is to the earlier "lost generation" mentioned in note 20.

35. On the flowering of the sociology of religion during this period, see Reed, "After the Alliance."

36. Among the family of disciplines considered "social sciences" by a strict definition, only sociology has generated a sizable subdiscipline in the study of religion. Obviously, there are important works and scholars in the psychology of religion and in the anthropology of religion, but they are far less prominent, both in number and in disciplinary visibility, than are the sociologists of religion. For good overviews of the psychology of religion, see Gorsuch, "Psychology of Religion"; Hood, "Psychology of Religion"; and Ralph W. Hood, Bernard Spilka, Bruce Hunsberger, and Richard Gorsuch, *The Psychology of Religion: An Empirical Approach,* 2d ed. (New York: Guilford Publications, 1996). Both the American Sociological Association and the American Psychological Association have subdisciplinary sections or divisions for religious studies. Of course, the boundaries in these various disciplines are often unclear, so that much of the scholarly work in psychology and anthropology could just as well be considered sociology, and vice versa. The boundaries were even less salient at the beginning of the twentieth century, so that Durkheim's work was as much anthropology as sociology (or even more), and Weber's (or Ely's) was as much economics or political science as sociology. The discipline of history, which is sometimes considered a social science and other times the humanities, can overlap with any of the social sciences, depending on the theory, data, and methods used in a given historical work. It would be fair to say that no subdiscipline for the special study of religion has ever gained recognition in either political science or economics.

37. The oldest of these three societies is the Association for the Sociology of Religion (ASR), founded in 1939; the other two were organized about a decade later. The members of all three are disproportionately sociologists, despite the strong commitments of at least the Religious Research Association (RRA) and the Society for the Scientific Study of Religion (SSSR) to interdisciplinary memberships and research. The ASR publishes the *Sociology of Religion* (formerly *Sociological Analysis*); the RRA publishes the *Review of Religious Research;* and the SSSR publishes the *Journal for the Scientific Study of Religion.* There are, of course, many other religion-oriented scholarly societies representing disciplines in the humanities, literature, biblical criticism, and the like, which for the present discussion I would not consider fields of "social science."

38. See, for example, O'Dea's *Mormons;* and his "Mormonism and the Avoidance of Sectarian Stagnation: A Study of Church, Sect, and Incipient Nationality," *American Journal of Sociology* 60 (November 1954): 285–93. See also Evon Z. Vogt and Thomas F. O'Dea, "A Comparative Study of the Role of Values in Social Action in Two Southwestern Communities," *American Sociological Review* 18 (December 1953): 645–54; and Evon Z. Vogt and Ethel M. Albert, *The People of Rimrock: A Study of Values in Five Cultures* (1966; reprint, New York: Atheneum, 1970). See Sorenson, "A Bibliography of Anthropological Studies on Mormons," for more information on the work and authors associated with Kluckhohn's project.

39. Christensen's work, much of which appeared in the best journals of the discipline, goes back to the 1930s but became especially visible in the 1950s and 1960s. See, for ex-

ample, his "Time Interval between Marriage of Parents and the Birth of Their First Child in Utah County, Utah," 518–25; "Mormon Fertility," 270–75; "Cultural Relativism and Premarital Sex Norms," *American Sociological Review* 25 (February 1960): 31–39; "Children in the Family: Relationship of Number and Spacing to Marital Success," *Journal of Marriage and the Family* 30 (May 1968): 283–89; and (with George R. Carpenter), "Value-Behavior Discrepancies regarding Premarital Coitus in Three Western Cultures," *American Sociological Review* 27 (February 1962): 66–74. All of these works and many others by Christensen involved comparing Mormon samples with others. Vernon was a less prolific author, at least in Mormon studies, but he was a pioneer in empirical research on Mormon beliefs and attitudes about religion per se, as contrasted with the religion-behavior connection of such interest to Christensen. See, for example, Vernon's "An Inquiry into the Scalability of Church Orthodoxy," *Sociology and Social Research* 39 (May/June 1955): 324–27; "Background Factors related to Church Orthodoxy," *Social Forces* 34 (March 1956): 252–54; and "Religious Self-Identifications," *Pacific Sociological Review* 5 (Spring 1962): 40–43, all of which involved studies of Mormon samples. Vernon was also the founding president of the Society for the Sociological Study of Mormon Life, later renamed the Mormon Social Science Association. Certainly other social scientists of Mormon background had noteworthy publications on Mormon life before either Christensen or Vernon (e.g., Nels Anderson, Lowry Nelson, and Kimball Young), but they were of an earlier generation whose work generally did not persist into the second half of the century, and who did not sustain a career-long interest in Mormon studies, as did Christensen and Vernon.

40. Somewhat less directly, a third institutional development might also be cited for its encouragement (not always intended) of social scientific research and teaching on Mormons: a renewed church commitment, during the 1970s and 1980s, to upgrade the professional and academic quality of Brigham Young University, a process associated especially with the administration of BYU's President Dallin H. Oaks (1971–1980). As part of this process, such academic departments as sociology were rapidly strengthened by adding talented new faculty who were encouraged to include Mormonism and other religions in their professional research and to become active in the affairs of such scholarly societies as the Society for the Scientific Study of Religion. Similar encouragement has been conspicuously lacking since the mid-1980s. See Gary J. Bergera and Ronald Priddis, *Brigham Young University: A House of Faith* (Salt Lake City: Signature Books, 1985), esp. 32–45.

41. Arrington established his professional credentials early with the publication of his now classic *Great Basin Kingdom*. Though ostensibly retired in 1982, he remained an active and productive scholar until his death in 1999.

42. See the account of Davis Bitton (an assistant church historian during this period) in his "Ten Years in Camelot: A Personal Memoir," *Dialogue: A Journal of Mormon Thought* 16 (Fall 1983): 9–32. The Arrington operation was actually transferred, in somewhat truncated form, to Brigham Young University as the Joseph Fielding Smith Institute for Church History. Arrington's own account of the rise and fall of this "Camelot" period occupies much of the memoir he published just before he died: *Adventures of a Church Historian* (Urbana: University of Illinois Press, 1998).

43. See Marie Cornwall and Perry H. Cunningham, "Surveying Latter-day Saints: A Review of Methodological Issues," *Review of Religious Research* 31 (December 1989): 162–72.

44. Rodney Stark, a nationally prominent sociologist of religion with much experience in the use of survey and archival data, offered the following judgment about the work of the RID in 1984: "I have consulted with many denominational research departments and have read countless reports of their results. . . . Yet, [their] research efforts . . . shrink to insignificance when compared with the quality, scope, and sophistication of the work of the Mormon social research department." Stark, "The Rise of a New World Faith," 26.

45. Examples of work done under RID auspices and available to the public are Linda A. Charney, "Religious Conversion: A Longitudinal Study" (Ph.D. diss., University of Utah, 1986); Kristin L. Goodman and Tim B. Heaton, "LDS Church Members in the U.S. and Canada: A Demographic Profile," *AMCAP Journal* 12, no. 1 (1986): 88–107; Marie Cornwall, "Personal Communities: The Social and Normative Bases of Religion" (Ph.D. diss., University of Minnesota, 1985); Marie Cornwall, "The Social Bases of Religion: A Study of Factors Influencing Religious Belief and Commitment," *Review of Religious Research* 29 (September 1987): 44–56; Marie Cornwall, "The Determinants of Religious Behavior: A Theoretical Model and Empirical Test," *Social Forces* 68 (December 1989): 572–92; Marie Cornwall, Stan L. Albrecht, Perry H. Cunningham, and Brian L. Pitcher, "The Dimensions of Religiosity: A Conceptual Model with an Empirical Test," *Review of Religious Research* 27 (March 1986): 226–44; and Stan L. Albrecht, Marie Cornwall, and Perry H. Cunningham, "Religious Leave-Taking: Disengagement and Disaffiliation among Mormons," in *Falling from the Faith: Causes and Consequences of Religious Apostasy,* ed. David G. Bromley (Beverly Hills, Calif.: Sage Publications, 1988), 62–80.

46. See Cornwall, Heaton, and Young, eds., *Contemporary Mormonism,* in which many of the contributing authors have been closely associated with the Research Information Division at one time or another.

47. The nature and extent of Mormon geographic dispersion is well documented and explained in, for example, Donald W. Meinig, "The Mormon Culture Region: Strategies and Patterns in the Geography of the American West, 1847–1964," *Annals of the Association of American Geographers* 55 (June 1965): 191–220; Donald W. Meinig, "The Mormon Nation and the American Empire," *Journal of Mormon History* 22 (Spring 1996): 33–51; Jerald R. Izatt and Dean R. Louder, "Peripheral Mormondom: The Frenetic Frontier," *Dialogue: A Journal of Mormon Thought* 13 (Summer 1980): 76–89; and Lowell C. Bennion and Lawrence A. Young, "The Uncertain Dynamics of LDS Expansion, 1950–2020," *Dialogue: A Journal of Mormon Thought* 29 (Spring 1996): 8–32. The nature of community life itself as part of this diaspora is less often discussed, but see, for example, Ralph B. Brown, H. Reed Geertsen, and Richard S. Krannich, "Community Satisfaction and Social Integration in a Boomtown: A Longitudinal Analysis," *Rural Sociology* 52 (Winter 1989): 568–86; Mario S. De Pillis, "The Persistence of Mormon Community into the 1990s," *Sunstone* 15 (October 1991): 28–49; Richard H. Jackson and Lloyd E. Hudman, "Border Towns, Gambling, and the Mormon Culture Region," *Journal of Cultural Geography* 8 (Fall/Winter 1987): 35–48; Carole L. Seyfrit, "Migration Intentions of Rural Youth: Testing an Assumed Benefit of Rapid Growth," *Rural Sociology* 51 (Summer 1986): 199–211; and William F. Stinner, Mollie Van Loon, Seh-Woong Chung, and Yongchan Byun, "Com-

munity Size, Individual Social Position, and Community Attachment," *Rural Sociology* 55 (Winter 1990): 494–521, which still deal mostly with Utah.

48. Continuing interest in nineteenth-century Mormon economic life can be seen in much of Arrington's work, of course, but also in that of others, such as James Kearl, Clayne Pope, and Larry Wimmer. See, for example, Leonard J. Arrington, Feramorz Y. Fox, and Dean L. May, *Building the City of God: Community and Cooperation among the Mormons* (Salt Lake City: Deseret Book, 1976); James R. Kearl and Clayne L. Pope, "Wealth Mobility: The Missing Element," *Journal of Interdisciplinary History* 13 (Winter 1983): 461–88; and James R. Kearl, Clayne L. Pope, and Larry T. Wimmer, "Household Wealth in a Settlement Economy: Utah, 1850–1870," *Journal of Economic History* 40 (September 1980): 477–96. A somewhat Marxist analysis of the economic evolution of the Mormons had already been produced by the Kauffmans in their 1912 *Latter Day Saints* and by Mark P. Leone, *Roots of Modern Mormonism* (Cambridge, Mass.: Harvard University Press, 1979), which had a similar theoretical framework. A less ideological perspective on this process can be seen in J. Kenneth Davies, "The Accommodation of Mormonism and Politico-Economic Reality," *Dialogue: A Journal of Mormon Thought* 3 (Spring 1968): 42–54. Studies of more recent economic institutions among the Mormons can be seen in Leonard J. Arrington, "Origin of the Welfare Plan of the Church of Jesus Christ of Latter-day Saints," *BYU Studies* 5 (Winter 1964): 67–85; Albert L. Fisher, "Mormon Welfare Programs Past and Present," *Social Science Journal* 15 (April 1978): 75–100; and Garth L. Mangum and Bruce D. Blumell, *The Mormons' War on Poverty: A History of LDS Welfare, 1830–1990* (Salt Lake City: University of Utah Press, 1993). For relations with organized labor, see Garth L. Mangum, "The Church and Collective Bargaining in American Society," *Dialogue: A Journal of Mormon Thought* 3 (Summer 1968): 106–11; and Richard B. Wirthlin and Bruce D. Merrill, "The LDS Church as a Significant Political Reference Group in Utah: Right to Work," *Dialogue: A Journal of Mormon Thought* 3 (Summer 1968): 129–33.

49. See, for example, Stan L. Albrecht, Howard M. Bahr, and Bruce A. Chadwick, "Changing Family and Sex Roles: An Assessment of Age Differences," *Journal of Marriage and the Family* 41 (February 1979): 41–50; Howard M. Bahr, "Religious Contrasts in Family Role Definitions and Performances: Utah Mormons, Catholics, Protestants, and Others," *Journal for the Scientific Study of Religion* 21 (September 1982): 200–217; Tim B. Heaton, "Four Characteristics of the Mormon Family: Contemporary Research on Chastity, Conjugality, Children, and Chauvinism," *Dialogue: A Journal of Mormon Thought* 20 (Summer 1987): 101–14; and Laurence R. Iannaccone and Carrie A. Miles, "Dealing with Social Change: The Mormon Church's Response to Change in Women's Roles," in *Contemporary Mormonism,* ed. Cornwall, Heaton, and Young, 265–86.

50. Examples include Lester E. Bush, "Birth Control among the Mormons: Introduction to an Insistent Question," *Dialogue: A Journal of Mormon Thought* 10 (Summer 1976): 12–44; Tim B. Heaton and Sandra Calkins, "Family Size and Contraceptive Use among Mormons, 1965–1975," *Review of Religious Research* 25 (Fall 1983): 102–13; and Tim B. Heaton, "Religious Influences on Mormon Fertility: Cross-National Comparisons," *Review of Religious Research* 30 (June 1989): 401–11.

51. As indicated earlier, the pioneering work in this line of research, starting at midcentury, was done by Harold Christensen and his colleagues (see note 39). A few more recent social scientists have studied premarital sex norms and behavior among Mormon

youth, but it is not a popular topic. See, for example, Brent C. Miller and Terrance D. Olson, "Sexual Attitudes and Behavior of High School Students in Relation to Background and Contextual Factors," *Journal of Sex Research* 24, special issue (1988): 194–200; and Bruce A. Chadwick and Brent L. Top, "Religiosity and Delinquency among LDS Adolescents," *Journal for the Scientific Study of Religion* 32 (March 1993): 51–67. A critique of the validity of some survey data on premarital sex among Mormon adolescents has been offered by Dynette I. Reynolds in "Religious Influence and Premarital Sexual Experience: Critical Observations on the Validity of a Relationship," *Journal for the Scientific Study of Religion* 33 (December 1994): 382–87; and in "Youth, Sex, and Coercion: The Neglect of Sexual Abuse Factors in LDS Data and Policy on Premarital Sex," *Dialogue: A Journal of Mormon Thought* 29 (Summer 1996): 89–102.

52. See, for example, Embry, *Mormon Polygamous Families;* Van Wagoner, *Mormon Polygamy;* and Hardy, *Solemn Covenant.* While the largest schismatic Mormon sects are polygynous, some of the smaller ones clearly are not. For example, the Order of Aaron, founded at midcentury, is definitely not polygynous but has instead attempted to follow the abandoned early Mormon communitarian way of life. See Hans A. Baer, *Recreating Utopia in the Desert: A Sectarian Challenge to Mormonism* (Albany: State University of New York Press, 1988).

53. On the assimilation process and its various implications, see, for example, O'Dea, *The Mormons;* Gordon Shepherd and Gary Shepherd, *A Kingdom Transformed: Themes in the Development of Mormonism* (Salt Lake City: University of Utah Press, 1984); Alexander, *Mormonism in Transition;* O. Kendall White, *Mormon Neo-Orthodoxy: A Crisis Theology* (Salt Lake City: Signature Books, 1987); and Mauss, *The Angel and the Beehive.* On the persistence of certain Mormon peculiarities, see Jan Shipps, "Making Saints: In the Early Days and the Latter Days," and Heaton, Goodman, and Holman, "In Search of a Peculiar People," both in *Contemporary Mormonism,* ed. Cornwall, Heaton, and Young, 64–83, 87–117.

54. See John L. Sorenson's "Industrialization and Social Change: A Controlled Comparison of Two Utah Communities" (Ph.D. diss., University of California at Los Angeles, 1961) and several other works cited in his "Bibliography of Anthropological Studies on Mormons." Unfortunately, much of Sorenson's valuable work appears in publications not readily accessible outside of Utah. See, however, his "Mormon World View and American Culture," *Dialogue: A Journal of Mormon Thought* 8 (Summer 1973): 17–29; "Ritual as Theology," *Sunstone* 6 (May 1981): 11–14; and "Science and Mormonism as Traditions," in *Science and Religion: Toward a More Useful Dialogue,* vol. 1, ed. Wilford M. Hess and Raymond T. Matheny (Geneva, Ill.: Paladin House, 1979), 11–15. At the end of his career, Sorenson published these, along with several other previously unpublished essays, in a collection of his works entitled *Mormon Culture: Four Decades of Essays on Mormon Society and Personality* (Salt Lake City: New Sage Books, 1997). Still looking for a publisher in 1999 was *Mindful of Every People: Anthropological Perspectives on the Mormons,* a collection of essays by various authors and edited by John L. Sorenson and Mark Leone.

55. Erik G. Schwimmer was among the first to study Mormons outside of the United States. See his "Mormonism in a Maori Village: A Study in Social Change" (Masters thesis, University of British Columbia, 1965) and "The Cognitive Aspect of Culture Change," *Journal of the Polynesian Society* 74 (June 1965): 149–81. Leone is best known for his *Roots*

of Modern Mormonism, a somewhat Marxist analysis of the transformation of Mormons from agricultural people to "dominated colonials" within the United States. More recently, the anthropologist Hans Baer examined an important modern schismatic reaction to the transformation of Mormonism in *Recreating Utopia in the Desert.*

56. See, especially, Alexander, *Mormonism in Transition;* Mauss, *The Angel and the Beehive;* and Shepherd and Shepherd, *A Kingdom Transformed.*

57. For evidence, see Armand L. Mauss and Philip L. Barlow, "Church, Sect, and Scripture: The Protestant Bible and Mormon Sectarian Retrenchment," *Sociological Analysis* 52 (Winter 1991): 397–414; and Mauss, *The Angel and the Beehive,* chapters 6–8.

58. O'Dea, *The Mormons,* chapter 9.

59. See, for example, Lavina Fielding Anderson, "Leaders and Members: The General Handbook of Instructions," *Dialogue: A Journal of Mormon Thought* 28 (Winter 1995): 145–58; James E. Chapman, "Dissent in the Church: Toward a Workable Definition," *Dialogue: A Journal of Mormon Thought* 26 (Spring 1993): 121–33; Armand L. Mauss, "Authority, Agency, and Ambiguity: The Elusive Boundaries of Required Obedience to Priesthood Leaders," *Sunstone* 19 (March 1996): 20–31; and L. Jackson Newell, "Personal Conscience and Priesthood Authority," *Dialogue: A Journal of Mormon Thought* 13 (Winter 1980): 81–87.

60. See, for example, Vogt and O'Dea, "A Comparative Study of the Role of Values in Social Action in Two Southwestern Communities"; Leone, *Roots of Modern Mormonism;* Warner P. Woodworth, "Third World Strategies toward Zion," *Sunstone* 14 (October 1990): 13–23; and John D. Peters, "Reflections on Mormon Materialism," *Sunstone* 16 (March 1993): 17–21.

61. See, for example, the special issue on science and religion, *Dialogue: A Journal of Mormon Thought* 8 (Fall/Winter 1973); Paul, *Science, Religion, and Mormon Cosmology;* Gene A. Sessions and Craig J. Oberg, eds., *The Search for Harmony: Essays on Mormonism and Science* (Salt Lake City: Signature Books, 1993); and Lester E. Bush Jr., *Health and Medicine among the Latter-day Saints: Science, Sense, and Scripture* (New York: Crossroad, 1993).

62. See, for example, Albrecht, Bahr, and Chadwick, "Changing Family and Sex Roles"; Heaton, "Four Characteristics of the Mormon Family"; Margaret M. Toscano, "Beyond Matriarchy, beyond Patriarchy," *Dialogue: A Journal of Mormon Thought* 21 (Spring 1988): 32–57; Tim B. Heaton, "Role Remodeling in the Mormon Family," *Sunstone* 11 (November 1987): 6; and Lavina Fielding Anderson, "A Voice from the Past: The Benson Instructions for Parents," *Dialogue: A Journal of Mormon Thought* 21 (Winter 1988): 103–13.

63. Edward Leo Lyman, *Political Deliverance: The Mormon Quest for Utah Statehood* (Urbana: University of Illinois Press, 1986).

64. For more on this point, see Frank H. Jonas, "Utah—The Different State," in *Politics in the American West,* ed. Frank H. Jonas (Salt Lake City: University of Utah Press, 1969), 327–89; Robert Gottlieb and Peter Wiley, *America's Saints: The Rise of Mormon Power* (New York: G. P. Putnam, 1984); John Aloysius Ferrell, *Utah: Inside the Church State* (Denver, Colo.: Denver Post, 1982), a series of articles combined in one tabloid; Dennis L. Lythgoe, "A Special Relationship: J. Bracken Lee and the Mormon Church," *Dialogue: A Journal of Mormon Thought* 11 (Winter 1978): 71–87; and Q. Michael Croft, "The Influence of the LDS Church on Utah Politics, 1945–1984" (Ph.D. diss., University of Utah, 1985).

65. Examples of overt church intervention in national political issues late in the twen-

tieth century are discussed at some length in Richard N. Ostling and Joan K. Ostling, *Mormon America: The Power and the Promise* (San Francisco: HarperSanFrancisco, 1999); Gottlieb and Wiley, *America's Saints;* Matthew Glass, *Citizens against the MX: Public Languages in the Nuclear Age* (Urbana: University of Illinois Press, 1993); Dixie Snow Huefner, "Church and Politics at the Utah IWY Conference," *Dialogue: A Journal of Mormon Thought* 11 (Spring 1978): 58–75; Linda Sillitoe, "Off the Record: Telling the Rest of the Truth," *Sunstone* 14 (December 1990): 12–26; O. Kendall White, "Mormonism and the Equal Rights Amendment," *Journal of Church and State* 31 (Spring 1989): 249–67; and Byron W. Daynes and Raymond Tatlovich, "Mormons and Abortion Politics in the United States," *International Review of History and Political Science* 23 (May 1986): 1–13.

66. See Alexander, *Mormonism in Transition,* chapters 2 and 3; and Mauss, *The Angel and the Beehive,* chapter 7.

67. Alexander, *Mormonism in Transition.*

68. Ronald J. Hrebenar, "Utah: The Most Republican State in the Union," *Social Science Journal* 18 (October 1981): 103–14; Mauss, *The Angel and the Beehive,* chapters 7 and 9.

69. Mauss, *The Angel and the Beehive,* chapter 7.

70. See the entire special issue of *Dialogue: A Journal of Mormon Thought* 10 (Fall 1977) on LDS public relations efforts; and Stephen W. Stathis, "Mormonism and the Periodical Press: A Change Is Underway," *Dialogue: A Journal of Mormon Thought* 14 (Summer 1981): 48–73.

71. O'Dea corrected this oversight in a later article, "Sources of Strain in Mormon History Reconsidered," in *Mormonism and American Culture,* ed. Martin S. Hill and James B. Allen (New York: Harper and Row, 1972), 147–68. Lowry Nelson's attack on the LDS policy toward blacks can be found in "Around the U.S.A.: Mormons and the Negro," *Nation* 174 (May 24, 1952): 488.

72. See the collection of articles from *Dialogue: A Journal of Mormon Thought* in Lester E. Bush and Armand L. Mauss, eds., *Neither White nor Black: Mormon Scholars Encounter the Race Issue in a Universal Church* (Salt Lake City: Signature Books, 1984). The definitive book-length treatment of this issue is Newell G. Bringhurst, *Saints, Slaves, and Blacks: The Changing Place of Black People within Mormonism* (Westport, Conn.: Greenwood, 1981).

73. Examples of the literature on modern relationships between Mormons and Native Americans are in a special issue of *Dialogue: A Journal of Mormon Thought* 18 (Fall 1985), devoted entirely to that topic; and Bruce A. Chadwick and Stan L. Albrecht, "Mormons and Indians: Beliefs, Policies, Programs, and Practices," in *Contemporary Mormonism,* ed. Cornwall, Heaton, and Young, 287–309. The historical literature on relations between the early Mormons and Native Americans is much larger. Examples of the literature on modern relations between Mormons and Jews are Seymour Cain, "Judaism and Mormonism: Paradigm and Supersession," *Dialogue: A Journal of Mormon Thought* 25 (Fall 1992): 57–65; Armand L. Mauss, "Mormon Semitism and Anti-Semitism," *Sociological Analysis* 29 (Spring 1968): 11–27; and Douglas F. Tobler, "The Jews, the Mormons, and the Holocaust," *Journal of Mormon History* 18 (Spring 1992): 59–92.

74. Examples of feminist reactions to the patriarchal tradition in Mormonism can be seen in three special issues of *Dialogue: A Journal of Mormon Thought* 6 (Summer 1971),

14 (Winter 1981), and 27 (Summer 1994), in which an increasingly strident tone is perceptible over time; and Maxine Hanks, ed., *Women and Authority: Re-emerging Mormon Feminism* (Salt Lake City: Signature Books, 1992).

75. For an extensive bibliography of late twentieth-century works by and about Mormon women, only some of it clearly inspired by feminism, see Karen Purser Frazier, *Bibliography of Social, Scientific, Historical, and Popular Writings about Mormon Women* (Provo, Utah: Brigham Young University Women's Research Institute, 1990). During the 1980s and 1990s, an annual "Women's Conference" was held at BYU, at first totally under the auspices of BYU but eventually with joint sponsorship from the church's Relief Society and its leaders. Most of these conferences have yielded annual volumes of selected essays from the conference proceedings, edited by the conference organizers and published by the church's Deseret Book Company. See the review and description of the first nine of these volumes in Kathryn H. Shirts, "BYU Women's Conference Books: The Series," *BYU Studies* 35, no. 2 (1995): 176–89. An interesting and probably not entirely coincidental complementarity can be seen over time between these conference volumes and the unsponsored feminist literature described in the note 74. That is, as the unsponsored literature seemed to increase in stridency, the content of the women's conference volumes gradually changed from a rather academic and analytical (even somewhat critical) tone to a greater proportion of essays with a devotional and experiential nature, reflecting an increasing effort to avoid offending church leaders and the more conservative LDS women.

76. For explanations of the Mormon concept of the Heavenly Mother, see Linda P. Wilcox, "The Mormon Concept of a Mother in Heaven," *Sunstone* 5 (September/October 1980): 9–15; and John Heeren, Donald B. Lindsey, and Marylee Mason, "The Mormon Concept of Mother in Heaven: A Sociological Account of Its Origin and Development," *Journal for the Scientific Study of Religion* 23 (December 1984): 396–411. Official sensitivity about unauthorized expounding on this topic (and perhaps about "cutting-edge" feminism in general) can be inferred from the excommunication of Maxine Hanks, the editor of the *Women and Authority,* and especially from the excommunication of Janice Allred for her "Toward a Mormon Theology of God the Mother," *Dialogue: A Journal of Mormon Thought* 27 (Spring 1994): 15–39. See accounts of church disciplinary action in D. Michael Quinn, "Dilemmas of Feminists and Intellectuals in the Contemporary LDS Church," *Sunstone* 17 (June 1994): 67–73; and his "Mormon Feminist Disciplined," *Sunstone* 18 (April 1995): 80–84.

77. Howard M. Bahr discusses evidence for the gap between patriarchal rhetoric and actual attitudes or behavior of LDS women in "The Declining Distinctiveness of Utah's Working Women," *BYU Studies* 19 (Summer 1979): 525–43; and his "Religious Contrasts in Family Role Definitions and Performance."

78. Glock's chief ideas on the nature, origin, and consequences of religiosity are explained and measured empirically in Rodney Stark and Charles Y. Glock, *American Piety: The Nature of Religious Commitment* (Berkeley: University of California Press, 1968).

79. Vernon's early work is cited in note 39. An application of Glock's conceptualization and measurement of religiosity to Mormons across time is in Mauss, *The Angel and the Beehive,* chapters 3 and 9. Using somewhat different conceptualizations of religiosity, Cornwall and her colleagues have provided the most thorough and sophisticated measurements of religiosity among Mormons (see citations in note 45). An overview of the

state of empirical knowledge on the "consequential" dimension of religiosity is in Stan L. Albrecht, "The Consequential Dimension of Mormon Religiosity," *BYU Studies* 29 (Spring 1989): 57–108.

80. See, however, examples in note 45 of work originating in RID and now available to the public.

81. See examples in Austin E. Fife and Alta S. Fife, *Saints of Sage and Saddle: Folklore among the Mormons* (1956; reprint, Salt Lake City: University of Utah Press, 1980); Noall, "Superstitions, Customs, and Prescriptions of Mormon Midwives"; Wilfrid C. Bailey, "Folklore Aspects in Mormon Culture," *Western Folklore* 10 (July 1951): 217–25; William A. Wilson, "The Study of Mormon Folklore: An Uncertain Mirror for Truth," *Dialogue: A Journal of Mormon Thought* 22 (Winter 1989): 95–110; Richard C. Poulsen, "Fate and the Persecutors of Joseph Smith: Transmutations of an American Myth," *Dialogue: A Journal of Mormon Thought* 11 (Winter 1978): 63–70; Richard C. Poulsen, "Some Botanical Cures in Mormon Folk Medicine: An Analysis," *Utah Historical Quarterly* 44 (Fall 1976): 379–88; Richard C. Poulsen, "'This Is the Place': Myth and Mormondom," *Western Folklore* 36 (July 1977): 246–52; and Wayland D. Hand, "Magic and the Supernatural in Utah Folklore," *Dialogue: A Journal of Mormon Thought* 16 (Winter 1983): 51–64. For a thorough bibliographic essay on studies of Mormon folklore, see William A. Wilson, "Mormon Folklore: Cut from the Marrow of Everyday Experience," *BYU Studies* 33, no. 3 (1993): 521–40, which appears also as "Mormon Folklore," in *Mormon Americana*, ed. Whittaker, 437–54. An especially valuable feature of this essay is the introduction of an indexing system for the organization and management of open-ended folklore collections.

82. Some of these have already been identified by Bahr and Forste and briefly in an earlier essay of my own ("Sociological Perspectives on the Mormon Subculture"); other neglected topics have already been mentioned as part of the discussion in the previous section.

83. There is considerably more unpublished literature in the form of documents, diaries, and other manuscripts. Much of this literature is, of course, devotional in nature rather than scholarly. See two helpful reference works by David J. Whittaker: "Missions and Missionaries: A Bibliographical Guide to Published and Manuscript Sources," 1993, Special Collections and Manuscript Section, Harold B. Lee Library, Brigham Young University, Provo, Utah; and "Mormon Missiology: An Introduction and Guide to the Sources," in *The Disciple as Witness: Essays on Latter-day Saint History and Doctrine in Honor of Richard Lloyd Anderson,* ed. Stephen D. Ricks, Donald W. Parry, and Andrew H. Hedges (Provo, Utah: Foundation for Ancient Research and Mormon Studies, Brigham Young University, 2000), 459–538.

84. For a rare public glimpse into one of the RID research projects on the determinants of proselyting success, see Charney, "Religious Conversion."

85. An official awareness of the need to make international Mormonism independent of any particular human culture is apparent from the remarks of members of the First Presidency of the church in their sermons during the April 1995 General Conference and published in the May 1995 issue of the official church magazine, *Ensign.* See, for example, James E. Faust, "Heirs to the Kingdom of God," 61–63, and Gordon B. Hinckley, "This Work Is Concerned with People," 51–53.

86. Among those few to appear later in the century with somewhat more analytical

content are Frederick R. Brady, *The Japanese Reaction to Mormonism and the Translation of Mormon Scripture into Japanese* (Tokyo: Sophia University Press, 1979); F. LaMond Tullis, *Mormons in Mexico: The Dynamics of Faith and Culture* (Logan: Utah State University Press, 1987); Brigham Y. Card, Herbert C. Northcott, John E. Foster, Howard Palmer, and George K. Jarvis, eds., *The Mormon Presence in Canada* (Edmonton: University of Alberta Press; Logan: Utah State University Press, 1990); Marjorie Newton, *Southern Cross Saints: The Mormons in Australia* (Laie, Hawaii: Institute for Polynesian Studies, 1991); and Derek A. Cuthbert, *The Second Century: Latter-day Saints in Great Britain, 1937–1987* (Cambridge: Cambridge University Press, 1987). The final two decades of the century also produced a much larger periodical literature than ever on international aspects of Mormonism in various scholarly journals, although, again, much of it was strictly historical in nature. Note that all the published work referred to is in the English language. Comparable publications in other languages are not covered here, but they are few and far between.

87. A good start near the end of the century in addressing such questions can be found in a special issue of *Dialogue: A Journal of Mormon Thought* 28 (Spring 1996), which is devoted to the theme of Mormons and Mormonism in the twenty-first century and contains candid essays on Mormon prospects in various locales around the world by Mormon scholars of different nationalities.

88. On the rapid upward socioeconomic mobility of Mormons after midcentury, see comparisons across time in W. Clark Roof and William McKinney, *American Mainline Religion: Its Changing Shape and Future* (New Brunswick, N.J.: Rutgers University Press, 1987), 110. For a representative "snapshot" of Mormon social and economic backgrounds in Salt Lake City and in northern California at midcentury, see Mauss, *The Angel and the Beehive*, 46–48.

89. Examples of the few analytical organizational studies of the Mormon church late in the century include F. Reed Johnson, "The Mormon Church as a Central Command System," *Review of Social Economics* 37 (April 1979): 79–94; Jill Mulvay Derr and C. Brooklyn Derr, "Outside the Mormon Hierarchy: Alternative Aspects of Institutional Power," *Dialogue: A Journal of Mormon Thought* 15 (Winter 1982): 21–43; Peter Wiley, "The Lee Revolution and the Rise of Correlation," *Sunstone* 10, no. 1 (1984–85): 18–22; John R. Tarjan, "Goal Displacement in the Church: Or, Why Did They Carpet the Gym?" *Sunstone* 14 (February 1990): 20–25; and Warner P. Woodworth, "Brave New Bureaucracy," *Dialogue: A Journal of Mormon Thought* 20 (Fall 1987): 25–36.

90. On the general relationship between delinquency and various measures of religious influence, see, for example, Rodney Stark, "Religion as Context: Hellfire and Delinquency One More Time," *Sociology of Religion* 57 (Summer 1966): 163–73; and the various references cited in that article.

91. On the religion/deviance relationship among Mormons in particular, see Stan L. Albrecht, Bruce A. Chadwick, and David S. Alcorn, "Religiosity and Deviance: Application of an Attitude-Behavior Contingent Consistency Model," *Journal for the Scientific Study of Religion* 16 (September 1977): 263–74, which is based on data from Utah and Idaho. Of course, much more information is available from various sources on deviance, delinquency, and crime in Utah (e.g., various essays in Tim B. Heaton, Thomas A. Hirschl, and Bruce A. Chadwick, eds., *Utah in the 1990s: A Demographic Perspective* [Salt Lake City: Signature Books, 1996]), but generalizing from Utah to Mormons is dubious at best. Far

more useful are such studies as Bahr, "Religion and Adolescent Drug Use: A Comparison of Mormons and Other Religions," which has comparative data on Mormons and others; but such studies are unfortunately very rare. The relative paucity of work on deviant behavior among the Mormons might well be attributable partly to the recurring preference among Mormon researchers for work that has the effect of vindicating the religion (see note 28).

92. See note 39.

93. However, a variety of scientific and social commentary on homosexuality began to appear late in the twentieth century. See, for example, the collection of essays in Ron Schow, H. Wayne Schow, and Marybeth Raynes, eds., *Peculiar People: Mormons and Same-Sex Orientation* (Salt Lake City: Signature Books, 1994). A much larger literature has appeared in recent years on general "mental health" among the Mormons, largely because of the work of Allen Bergin and others at BYU. Much of this work is summarized in Allen E. Bergin, I. Reed Payne, Paul H. Jenkins, and Marie Cornwall, "Religion and Mental Health: Mormons and Other Groups," in *Contemporary Mormonism*, ed. Cornwall, Heaton, and Young, 138–58.

94. Some of these issues have been discussed in the articles cited in note 45. One primary source for studying changes over time in the *official* church catalogue of punishable offenses is the *General Handbook of Instructions: Book 2, Priesthood and Auxiliaries* (Salt Lake City: Church of Jesus Christ of Latter-day Saints, 1989), with counterparts under somewhat different titles at different points throughout the twentieth century. A cursory comparison of the 1989 version with earlier versions points to the hypothesis that various forms of dissent and heresy tended to displace such "ordinary" sexual violations as fornication and adultery over time as the most strongly sanctioned offenses. If confirmed, such a finding would suggest some very interesting additional hypotheses about other symbolic and cultural changes among the Mormons.

95. See for example, Whittaker, ed., *Mormon Americana.*

APPENDIX A
Mormon Imprints as Sources for Research: A History and Evaluation

THIS APPENDIX DESCRIBES the development and nature of Mormon imprints, which we define as official and semi-official matter printed by or for the church and its representatives, whether one-page broadsides or books of several hundred pages. This overview has two purposes. First, students of Mormonism will want to understand these important sources for their own sake; many research topics in Mormon history require their use. Second, Mormon imprints provide a window into LDS culture, revealing a great deal about such things as Mormon proselyting and Mormon literary culture. In providing this survey, we emphasize nineteenth-century imprints, especially those up to about midcentury. It was during this period that printed material was especially important in defining church doctrines and traditions.[1]

The discussion that follows is primarily historical, but it is also topical. The historical overview describes the setting that produced the Mormon imprints and suggests how they developed over time.[2] Throughout Mormon history, various kinds of printed material have been produced, comprising the following categories: scripture; proclamations and warnings; doctrinal treatises; scriptural guides and helps; histories and petitions for redress; accounts of the martyrdoms of Joseph and Hyrum Smith; exposés by former members; replies to anti-Mormon attacks; newspapers; hymnals and poetry; almanacs; and other special publications. Since these various categories are represented most fully in the earliest historical periods, they are not all discussed separately or systematically in each successive period. We begin with the scriptures and missionary literature of the first few years.

Mormon Imprints through the Middle of the Nineteenth Century

BRIEF OVERVIEW OF LATTER-DAY SAINT SCRIPTURES

Logically, if not always chronologically, the subject of Mormon imprints must begin with the LDS scriptures, canonical and extracanonical. The official canon of the church comprises four "standard works."

The Book of Mormon, in print since it was first published in March 1830, is the most historically significant of these sacred scriptures. A key missionary text from the beginning of Mormonism, it continues to have a wide readership. By the end of the twentieth century, more than 100 million copies had been printed.[3] Its textual history (main editions were published in 1830, 1837, 1840, 1879, 1920, and 1981) has been widely studied, including an extensive critical text project currently underway by Royal Skousen at Brigham Young University.[4] The Foundation for Ancient Research and Mormon Studies at Brigham Young University has produced an extensive listing of printed work dealing with the Book of Mormon: *A Comprehensive Annotated Book of Mormon Bibliography,* edited by Donald W. Parry, Jeanette W. Miller, and Sandra A. Thorne, which lists 6,300 items, including works by such authors as Hugh W. Nibley and John L. Sorenson.[5]

Doctrine and Covenants was first issued in 1833 as A Book of Commandments. A mob largely destroyed this first edition while it was still unbound, making it one of the rarest LDS imprints. Its sixty-five chapters (later called "sections"), containing revelations given to Joseph Smith, were republished in 1835 as Doctrine and Covenants, with textual emendations and additions, including a series of theological "Lectures on Faith." Various subsequent editions have been issued, most recently in 1982. Smith seems to have thought of this work as a kind of handbook of instructions, which he periodically expanded and updated as the church grew. The corrections and emendations made during and since his lifetime continue to create problems for scholars. Each new edition has retained the date of first recording, thus complicating attempts to anchor specific drafts to particular points in Smith's life and thought. The most helpful textual study of the Doctrine and Covenants is by Robert J. Woodford; the best available historical and biographical commentary is by Lyndon W. Cook.[6] A useful edition of all the Joseph Smith revelations is H. Michael Marquardt's *Joseph Smith Revelations, Text and Commentary.*[7]

The Pearl of Great Price, smallest of the four standard works, was first issued as a mission tract in 1851 and was canonized in 1880.[8] Its original purpose was to gather under one cover a variety of Joseph Smith's inspired writings that had appeared in print by about 1844. Today it contains the Book of Moses (including material describing the ministry of the ancient prophet Enoch); the Book of Abraham; Smith's revision of Matthew 24; and excerpts from Smith's "History," including his well-known summary of LDS beliefs, "The Articles of Faith." Although the Book of Abraham has been a source of controversy since some of its original papyri resurfaced in the twentieth century, it has retained its canonical status.[9]

The Holy Bible, King James Version (KJV), has always been considered scripture by the Mormons, with the understanding that it contains errors of accident, intention, or omission, thus requiring modern revelation for a definitive interpretation. Early in Joseph Smith's prophetic ministry, he received a revelation instructing him to revise the KJV, which he partly completed. The large majority of his revisions and emendations occurred in Genesis and in the four Gospels, including Smith's reworking of Matthew 24, which, as mentioned, now appears in the Pearl of Great Price.[10]

The manuscript of Smith's revision remained with his heirs in the Reorganized Church of Jesus Christ of Latter Day Saints (RLDS) and became available to Mormon scholars in the 1970s, in time to be consulted for the church's 1981 LDS edition of the KJV.[11] At that time, many emendations and revisions from the Smith manuscript were added as explanatory footnotes. Perhaps the most important result of Smith's revision was the impetus it gave to his personal Bible study and to the Doctrine and Covenants revelations that came as a result. These Doctrine and Covenants selections include, in whole or in part, sections (or chapters) 74, 76, 77, 84, 86, 88, 91, 93, 102, 107, 113, and 132—the last section providing the textual basis for early Mormon polygamy.

Noncanonical scriptures came to Joseph Smith's attention very early. During his revision of the Bible, he was told in a specific revelation (Doctrine and Covenants 91) that he did not need to revise the fourteen books of the Vulgate Apocrypha, for they contained both truth and error that ought to be approached carefully and prayerfully. However, because of the idea of new and continuous revelation, exemplified by the Book of Mormon and Smith's revision of the Bible, Mormons have shown an interest in works that claimed to have an inspired message, including such apocryphal works as the Book of Enoch, the Book of Jasher, and the Book of the Twelve Patriarchs. In the twentieth century, Mormons also showed an interest in such newly discovered libraries as the Dead Sea Scrolls and the Nag Hammadi collection of early Coptic works.[12]

EARLIEST MISSIONARY PROCLAMATIONS AND WARNINGS

While the Book of Mormon was the most important imprint used in early church proselyting, other works soon followed. These works often had similar characteristics. They usually proclaimed Mormonism as the restoration of New Testament Christianity. They asserted Mormonism as the sole repository of God's authority or priesthood. They were millennial in tone, warning the wicked of coming destruction. These works also reflected prevailing circumstances. They were often issued in response to the anti-Mormonism of the time, and they reflected early Mormonism's loose institutional nature by being published by "free lance" missionaries who neither sought nor received official church sanction. During Mormonism's formative stage, missionary work was an uncoordinated responsibility of discipleship, and church authorities only gradually moved to control or even coordinate these workers in the vineyard.

These first imprints were usually broadsides and pamphlets, and although slight in form, they were important historically. Their pages contained the church's first teaching as well as its first approach to proselytizing and scripture use, such as proof texting. As such, they help illustrate the doctrinal understanding, religious feeling, and education of Mormonism's first generation. They also reveal that missionaries turned to the press when they moved from the villages and hamlets of their nativity to the larger cities where they preached.

One of the first Mormon imprints was Orson Hyde's 1836 *Prophetic Warning to*

All the Churches. This influential work was a one-page broadside that carried the news that the ancient church and priesthood had been restored and warned of the need for repentance and baptism.[13] Another early LDS broadside was the text of Joseph Smith's translation of Matthew 24—that portion of the Savior's Olivet Discourse that told of the end of times.[14] Such broadsides were inexpensive to produce and could be displayed almost anywhere.

PARLEY P. PRATT: MORMON LITERARY PATHFINDER

Parley P. Pratt was especially noteworthy among early Mormon publicists, earning the cognomen "Father of Mormon Pamphleteering."[15] Converted in 1830 from the Disciples of Christ by reading the Book of Mormon, Pratt devoted his career to promoting Mormonism. As a missionary to England in 1840, he became the founding editor of the *Latter-day Saints' Millennial Star.* During another mission to the eastern United States in the middle 1840s, he issued the newspaper the *Prophet,* and a decade later he published the first Mormon tract in Spanish, prompted by his service as one of the first LDS missionaries to the nation of Chile. Made a member of the Quorum of the Twelve Apostles when that body was organized in 1835, Pratt was killed in 1857 while proselytizing in Arkansas.[16]

Pratt's *Voice of Warning and Instruction to All People* may have been the most important book published in early Mormonism outside of the LDS scriptures.[17] As the first volume after the publication of the Book of Mormon and A Book of Commandments to spread the Mormon message, *Voice of Warning* determined the "formula for describing Mormonism's basic doctrines."[18] By 1860, it had been issued in eight editions, and even in the twentieth century it continued in print.

Voice of Warning's first two chapters reviewed past and future biblical prophecies, including those of a new covenant with a latter-day Israel to be gathered out of the world in preparation for the return of Christ. Chapter 3 discussed a church, established in the latter days as the Kingdom of God, ruled by a royal priesthood and properly entered into by baptism. Chapter 4 reviewed the contents of the Book of Mormon and offered some of the first arguments made in print for its authenticity. Chapter 5 provided a cosmic history of the earth and its inhabitants from the beginning to the last days, in which the fall and restoration of the earth are paralleled by the fall and restoration of human beings. In this section, Pratt envisioned the rebuilding of Old Jerusalem and the rise of New Jerusalem in America, as well as the future inheritance of the righteous. The sixth chapter argued that Christ's church must be based on modern revelation embodied by authorized, living prophets. Chapter 7 gave a parallel-column comparison of the doctrines of Christ with the "false doctrines of the nineteenth century." In short, the book's wide-ranging scope and its nineteenth-century literalism made it an ideal pocket companion for missionaries and their converts.[19]

Voice of Warning began the literary defense of Mormonism. Chapter 4 responded to previous attacks made on the Book of Mormon, and subsequent passages in the book attempted to marshal archaeological evidence in behalf of the new scripture.[20]

An even clearer example of Pratt's willingness to engage the church's critics was his forty-seven-page pamphlet published in 1838, *Mormonism Unveiled: Zion's Watchman Unmasked, and Its Editor, Mr. L. R. Sunderland, Exposed: Truth Vindicated: The Devil Mad, and Priestcraft in Danger!*[21] Perhaps the first explicit work of disputation in early Mormon printing, it defended Joseph Smith's character from Sunderland's attack, upheld the principle of contemporary, prophetic revelation, and supported the divine claims of the Book of Mormon, partly by refuting the anti-LDS Spaulding theory of the Book of Mormon's origins. It also expressed the frustration that many Mormon missionaries felt because of the anti-Mormon torrent they encountered ("no sooner are our enemies detected in one falsehood, than a thousand more are put in circulation").[22] Later in his career, Pratt would follow this defense with a stream of other works aimed at rebutting the arguments of the anti-Mormon writers.[23]

In 1835, Pratt published the first book of Mormon poetry, *The Millenium: A Poem, to Which Is Added Hymns and Songs.*[24] The title poem was later reissued as part of a larger collection, *The Millenium and Other Poems, to Which Is Annexed a Treatise on the Regeneration and Eternal Duration of Matter.*[25] The last work—the first substantial essay on the topic of Mormon materialism—was reprinted in *The World Turned Upside Down* in 1841 and 1842 and was expanded in "Immortality and Eternal Life of the Material Body" and "Intelligence and Affection," both published in Pratt's *Appeal to the Inhabitants of the State of New York* in 1844.[26]

During his publishing career, the prolific Parley P. Pratt authored more than twenty-five books and pamphlets, many of which would be recycled time after time, in small and large segments, sometimes without attribution.[27] His model for proclamations, for example, was used by Heber C. Kimball and Wilford Woodruff in *The Word of the Lord to the Citizens of London;* Erastus Snow and Benjamin Winchester in *An Address to the Citizens of Salem and Vicinity;* and Jesse Haven in *A Warning to All.*[28] Pratt's voice, in LDS proclamations alone, was heard in Australia, England, South Africa, India, South America, and the United States.

Another way Parley Pratt's ideas were disseminated in early Mormonism was through the work of his younger brother Orson, also an apostle and a frequent "mission" president, who acknowledged his debt to his brother. "There are no writings in the church with the exception of the revelations, which I esteem more highly than yours," Orson wrote to Parley in 1853.[29] Orson's first effort was his influential 1840 pamphlet, *An Interesting Account of Several Remarkable Visions.*[30] During the years that followed, much of Orson's pamphleteering occurred in two remarkable periods of activity. In 1848–51, he issued fifteen pamphlets, including his widely circulated tract *The Absurdities of Immaterialism.*[31] In 1856–57, he produced an additional eight titles.[32] While Orson's works contained little that was new in Mormon doctrine (again, Parley's works were more seminal), they did define what came to be recognized as "basic Mormonism"—the essential beliefs of the nineteenth-century church. Orson's pamphlets also gave these beliefs the extended arguments and biblical proofs that became important in shaping the message that the Mormon missionaries carried to the world. No doubt Orson's ability for thoughtful and systematic delivery was the reason he was chosen in 1852 to make the first public announcement of plural marriage—and the reason he made the first lengthy defense of plural marriage in print.[33]

The writings of Parley Pratt and Orson Pratt suggest the spectrum of early and even later Mormon thought. Parley's expression was often malleable and literary, even poetical. He was at home with the century's Romantic philosophers. In contrast, Orson personified precision and science, evidenced by his interest in astronomy, his delight with such practical tasks as surveying, and his embrace of the mechanistic philosophy of the Enlightenment scientists. Parley's work suggested an organic, expanding view of human beings and the universe; Orson's clock-work universe was more easily measured and defined. One of Parley's leading publications was *Key to the Science of Theology;* Orson published *The Key to the Universe.*[34] Together, they suggest the richness of early Mormon writing.

EARLY DOCTRINAL TREATISES

Proclamations and pamphlets were designed to capture the attention of potential converts. Doctrinal treatises had another purpose. These works aimed at informing and educating the Mormon disciple. Once more Parley P. Pratt's work took the lead. Not only was his *Voice of Warning* important, but *The Key to the Science of Theology,* begun in San Francisco in 1851 and finally published in Liverpool in 1855, strongly influenced the first generation of Mormonism. Pratt himself considered this last work "altogether the choicest, and most perfect specimen, [yet] from my pen."[35] The book set out and explicated Mormon doctrines that had earlier appeared only in bits and pieces. Pratt treated Mormon theology systematically and comprehensively, indicating that by the mid-1850s the church's theology had become more formal and systematic. The problem was that most of Joseph Smith's teachings were in oral form, recorded only at the time of his death in scattered talks, revelations, journal entries, editorials, and observations by contemporaries. It was up to such men as Pratt to transform this rich material into an organized body of understandable theology.[36]

Other important early doctrinal treatises included Orson Pratt's *Interesting Account of Several Remarkable Visions, and the Late Discovery of Ancient American Records Giving an Account of the Commencement of the Work of the Lord in This Generation,* which contained the first published account of Joseph Smith's celebrated "First Vision"; Moses Martin's *Treatise on the Fulness of the Everlasting Gospel . . . ;* Benjamin Winchester's *History of the Priesthood . . . ;* David Candland's *A Fireside Visitor; or, Plain Reasoner,* the first attempt at a series of Mormon tracts; and Orson Spencer's *Letters Exhibiting the Most Prominent Doctrines. . . .*[37]

SCRIPTURAL GUIDES AND AIDS

In addition to doctrinal treatises and the scriptures themselves, the church's growing missionary force required other tools, for its own training and the teaching of converts. One useful tool was the guide to the scriptures, which conveniently arranged important verses by topic. LDS scriptural guides began to appear in the 1840s, and these led to still other teaching aids, such as the catechism. Together, these early publications offer insights into early LDS exegesis, the formalization of doctrines, and how the first Mormon missionaries used the scriptures when presenting their message.

An example of the church's first scriptural guides was Lorenzo D. Barnes's *References to Prove the Gospel in Its Fulness,* originally published in the final issue of Philadelphia's *Gospel Reflector* and later issued separately under other titles.[38] Still other guides were Charles Blancher Thompson's *Evidences in Proof of the Book of Mormon;* Robert P. Crawford's *Index; or, Reference to the Second and Third Editions of the Book of Mormon . . . ;* Benjamin Winchester's *Synopsis of the Holy Scriptures, and Concordance . . . ;* and John Routledge's *Companion for the Bible or Important References. . . .*[39] Foreshadowing church lesson manuals of more recent times, John Jaques's *Catechism for Children* suggested that by midcentury Mormon teaching was sufficiently formalized to permit an orderly presentation of doctrines to children as well as converts.[40]

EARLY HISTORIES AND PETITIONS FOR REDRESS

Another early print genre was the historical narrative, which, because of the emotions surrounding Mormonism's beginning, was often defensive in tone. This tendency was exacerbated by the fact that the first LDS histories were written in the late 1830s after church members had been driven from western Missouri. Early Mormon histories also emphasized documents at the expense of narrative development, since they were part of the "documania" tradition of the time. They therefore constitute an important source for historians, both as expressions of their time and as source collections. Examples of the first LDS histories include Joseph Smith's "History," begun in 1838. Less monumental but important were such works as Francis Gladden Bishop's *Brief History of the Church;* John Corrill's *Brief History of the Church of Christ . . . ;* and John Whitmer's "History," although Whitmer's work was not published until the twentieth century.[41]

The history of early Mormonism is also conveyed by many personal accounts. These personal histories were often written by men who had played a major role in the expansion of the church (or were written by others working under their direction). These include Heber C. Kimball's *Journal of Heber C. Kimball, an Elder of the Church . . . Giving an Account of His Mission to Great Britain and the Commencement of the Work of the Lord in That Land;* Orson Hyde's *Voice from Jerusalem; or, A Sketch of the Travels and Ministry of Elder Orson Hyde, Missionary of the Church . . . to Germany, Constantinople, and Jerusalem . . . ;* Lorenzo Snow's *Italian Mission;* James B. Meynell's *Few Incidents of Travel in England . . . ;* Orson Spencer's *Prussian Mission;* and Erastus Snow's *One Year in Scandinavia: Results of the Gospel in Denmark and Sweden.*[42] As such, these were the earliest efforts at missiology.

The redress petitions and redress histories were also part of this genre, and they reflected Missouri persecutions. While still incarcerated in a Missouri jail, Joseph Smith counseled his followers to keep a record of their experiences, and on 6 May 1839, a church conference urged members to prepare an account of their difficulties and to seek redress for lost property and violated civil rights.[43] The result was the creation of more than a thousand unpublished written petitions as well as a series of published individual and church committee accounts of the Mormon experience in Missouri. Because of the circumstances of their authorship, these works were often defensive and angry in tone. They documented—and perhaps even strengthened—the mood of persecution that pervaded much of nineteenth-century Mormonism.[44]

Again, one of Parley P. Pratt's works provided a leading example of this kind of imprint. His *History of the Late Persecution Inflicted by the State of Missouri upon the Mormons . . .* was issued in October 1839, and less than a year later it was republished under the title *Late Persecution of the Church of Jesus Christ of Latter Day Saints.*[45] The second edition contained a change that set it apart from the other recitals of the Missouri persecution: Pratt added a summary of basic LDS beliefs that became the church's first short testament of faith. Slightly reworked, this material became the basis for two other titles intended for two different geographical audiences: *An Address by Judge Higbee and Parley P. Pratt . . . to the Citizens of Washington, and to the Public in General* and *An Address by a Minister of the Church of Jesus Christ of Latter-Day Saints, to the People of England.*[46]

Other published works inspired by the Missouri redress movement include John P. Greene's *Facts Relative to the Expulsion of the Mormons from the State of Missouri;* John Taylor's *Short Account of the Murders . . . ;* Ephraim Owen Jr.'s *Mormons, Memorial of . . . ;* Sidney Rigdon's *Appeal to the American People . . . ;* and James Mulholland's *Address to Americans. . . .*[47]

ACCOUNTS OF THE MARTYRDOM

Mormon anger and frustration over the conflict they had experienced with their neighbors reached a peak with the assassination of Joseph Smith and his brother Hyrum in 1844. The result was another series of imprints that combined the defensiveness of the post-Missouri writing with an element of hagiography, which particularly celebrated the career of Joseph Smith. Examples of these accounts are Thomas A. Lyne's *True and Descriptive Account of the Assassination of Joseph and Hyrum Smith . . . ;* Freeman Nickerson's *Death of the Prophets Joseph and Hyrum Smith . . . ;* and William M. Daniels's *Correct Account of the Murder . . . ,* a volume actually written and published by Lyman O. Littlefield.[48] Such works in "martyrology" have even emerged in the twentieth century; N. B. Lundwall's popular *Fate of the Persecutors of the Prophet Joseph Smith,* published in 1952, revisited many of the themes of earlier works.[49]

EXPOSÉS

Like many new religions, Mormonism left few people neutral about its claims. Among the earliest opponents were Abner Cole, who in 1830 wrote in the *Palmyra Reflector;* Ezra Booth, whose 1832 letters were published in the *Ohio Star* (Ravenna, Ohio); and Eber D. Howe, who authored a seminal anti-Mormon tract, *Mormonism*

Unvailed.[50] Some of these writers had once been defenders of the new faith, only to write ardent exposés later in their careers. In this category was John C. Bennett, whose *History of the Saints; or, An Exposé of Joe Smith and the Mormons* focused on the Nauvoo era of the church's history.[51] Such "apostate" literature has been a regular staple of Mormon literature to the present day. Such writers as John Hyde, T. B. H. and Fanny Stenhouse, Frank J. Cannon, Fawn M. Brodie, and Jerald and Sandra Tanner left Mormonism to write uncomplimentary works, but this type of literature, while persistent and important, has received little serious scholarly study.[52] Leonard J. Arrington suggested that one approach scholars might take to this material is to use it to measure Mormonism's "centrifugal tendencies."[53]

REPLIES TO ANTI-MORMON ATTACKS

A genre closely related to apologetic history and petitions for redress were the replies that Mormons wrote in response to their critics. These "responses" revealed the teaching and spirit of the new church, while at the same time they suggested how the early Mormon missionaries presented their message. For instance, Mormon "response literature" is a case study of the ways early missionaries used scripture, including their general tendency toward proof texting.

Parley P. Pratt's reply to L. R. Sunderland in *Mormonism Unveiled* was one of the first works of this type to appear, but many major LDS pre–Civil War writers issued at least one such reply, often using Pratt's work as a prototype.[54] The "response tradition" of Mormon literature has continued in the twentieth century with works by B. H. Roberts, Joseph Fielding Smith, Ben E. Rich, Hugh Nibley, and others and in articles published in the semiannual *FARMS Review*.[55]

NEWSPAPERS

The first publishing effort of the Latter-day Saints after printing the Book of Mormon was the establishment of a religious newspaper, *The Evening and the Morning Star* (June 1832–July 1833). Joseph Smith's revelations were first made public in its pages. This newspaper, along with a more secular counterpart, the *Upper Missouri Advertiser* (1832–33), was first issued at the Mormons' new settlement at Independence, Missouri. After its press was destroyed and its editors tarred and feathered, the newspaper was transferred to Kirtland, Ohio, where it was published with the abbreviated title, *Evening and Morning Star* from December 1833 to September 1834. This second run included material from the Independence, Missouri, printing, although this reissued information was sometimes rearranged and edited, including some textual emendations to Joseph Smith's previously published revelations.[56]

The *Latter Day Saints' Messenger and Advocate* was issued at Kirtland from October 1834 to September 1837. An important source for both New York and Ohio history, this newspaper printed the first history of the church, which "Second Elder" Oliver Cowdery wrote using the literary device of a series of personal letters.[57] The church also issued the secular *Northern Times* in 1835, which complemented the religious-minded *Latter Day Saints' Messenger and Advocate*. Few copies of this periodical have survived.[58] Finally, in October and November 1837, LDS officials at Kirtland issued the *Elders' Journal.* Following the transfer of church headquarters to western Missouri, this newspaper continued for another two issues, July and August 1838, but anti-Mormon conflict forced its suspension.

Once the Saints were established in western Illinois, they resumed the publication of their dual newspapers. From November 1839 to February 1846, the *Times and Seasons* included reports of church conferences, descriptions of church growth, and new church doctrine and new scripture, including the Book of Abraham. Beginning with the March 1842 issue, editors launched the serial publication of the path-breaking "History of Joseph Smith." These various items made the newspaper an important historical source of Joseph Smith's final years.[59] Its secular counterpart, the *Wasp,* begun in 1842, devoted itself increasingly to the deflection of the anti-Mormon parries of Thomas Sharp's *Warsaw Signal.* Perhaps hoping to reduce tension, in May 1843 church officials replaced the acerbic William Smith as editor, and the newspaper was transformed into the *Nauvoo Neighbor.* During its two-year run, the *Nauvoo Neighbor* treated a range of topics, including a subject of great interest to the about-to-emigrate Mormons—conditions existing in the American West.[60]

Other newspapers began publication in the 1840s. These included such little-known and now seldom-researched journals as Benjamin Winchester's *Gospel Reflector,* published in Philadelphia in 1841, and John E. Page's *Gospel Light,* probably published in Pittsburgh from 1843 to 1844.[61] The church's first foreign language newspaper, *Prophwyd y jubili* (*Prophet of the Jubilee*) appeared in Merthyr Tydfil, Wales, from July 1846 to December 1848; it recently has been translated into English.[62] In contrast to these ephemeral publications was the *Latter-day Saints' Millennial Star,* printed in Liverpool, England. First issued in May 1840, this newspaper continued until 1970. During its period of greatest influence, in the middle decades of the nineteenth century, the *Millennial Star* not only was the main source of LDS news and events in the British Empire but also issued a great deal of information about Mormon events in the United States, especially in Utah. Its pages included conference minutes, emigration matters, church financial information, general authority and member correspondence, as well as other items. Its twentieth-century career was less distinguished, because church leaders reduced its role from being a general church newspaper to a press serving as a "mission" or regional publication.[63]

Newspapers are a valuable but seldom-used source for understanding the LDS westward migration and other events of the late 1840s and the early 1850s. The *Prophet* (May 1844–May 1845) and its successor, *New York Messenger* (July–December 1845), were both published in New York City and contained information exchanged between LDS members living on the East Coast and those journeying in the church's main camp to the west.[64] However, the main newspaper of the Mormon exodus was the *Frontier Guardian* (February 1849–February 1852). Edited by Orson Hyde at Kanesville in western Iowa (later renamed Council Bluffs by non-Mormons), the *Frontier Guardian* was a journalistic bridge between the *Times and Seasons* and the church's later Utah-based periodicals. As such, the newspaper documented far more church activities than just migration.[65]

Once established in Utah, the Mormons began issuing the *Deseret News.* Begun in 1850, the newspaper has been published under a variety of sometimes overlapping daily and weekly formats and with several descriptive titles, including the *Deseret Weekly,* the *Deseret News Weekly,* and the *Deseret Evening News.* Since April 1931, the *Church News Section,* a weekly supplement, has reported the church's activities.[66] The *Deseret News* claims to be the oldest continuously issued newspaper in the western United States, but its importance goes beyond its longevity. Undoubtedly the most important LDS newspaper since Mormonism's founding, it is a particularly important source for nineteenth-century Utah and Mormon history, detailing the settlement of the Great Basin and the religious history of the LDS people.[67]

Four newspapers recorded the church's early evangelizing. T. B. H. Stenhouse issued *Le Réflecteur* from January to December 1853; although Geneva, Switzerland, was listed as the place of publication on its title page, the issues of this Swiss mission newspaper were printed at Lausanne. Richard Ballantyne and Robert Sketon published the *Latter-day Saints Millennial Star and Monthly Visitor* in Madras, India, from March to November 1854.[68] Mormon missionaries "down under" published *Zion's Watchman* in Sydney, Australia, from August 1853 to May 1856, with a publishing gap in 1855. This newspaper included information about LDS proselytizing in the Pacific Rim.[69] Finally, the *Western Standard* was published by George Q. Cannon in San Francisco (February 1856–November 1857); the newspaper fulfilled the early plans of Parley P. Pratt, who envisioned but never produced a Pacific Coast "Mormon Herald."[70]

After the public announcement of plural marriage in 1852, the church dispatched several able leaders to defend the practice and soften the expected national outcry. While unsuccessful in turning the public relations tide in the Mormon's favor, Orson Pratt published the *Seer* in Washington, D.C. (1853–54); Erastus Snow issued the *Saint Louis Luminary* (November 1854–December 1855); and John Taylor printed the *Mormon* in New York City (February 1855–September 1857).[71]

Closer to church headquarters, Salt Lake City's *Mountaineer* (August 1859–July 1861) dueled with the virulently anti-Mormon *Valley Tan.* For its secular voice, the nineteenth century depended on the semiprivate *Salt Lake Telegraph* (1864–70) and its successor, the *Salt Lake Herald* (1870–1909). Although the *Telegraph* was owned and edited by T. B. H. Stenhouse, an LDS advocate who later dissented from Mormonism, the newspaper's purpose was to publish secular news and to defend the church in a nonreligious manner.[72]

POETRY AND HYMNS

Emotions not readily accessible to historians in ordinary prose are often expressed in poetry. Early LDS poetry included the already mentioned work of Parley P. Pratt and such collections as John Lyon's *Harp of Zion;* Eliza R. Snow's *Poems: Religious, Political, and Historical;* and Orson F. Whitney's *Poetical Writings of Orson F. Whitney.*[73] Contemporary LDS poetry is illustrated in Carol Lynn Pearson's *Beginnings* and Clinton F. Larson's *Counterpoint: A Book of Poems.*[74]

When studying LDS poetry, scholars should not overlook the church's early hymnals, which were poetry or lyric collections without musical notation. The first of these was prepared in 1835 by Joseph Smith's wife Emma, who was given the task by a revelation recorded in the Doctrine and Covenants 25:10–112 (1830). Emma Smith's preliminary work received "corrections" at the hands of W. W. Phelps, an early convert. This hymnal contained ninety hymns or poems, thirty-five of which were written by Mormons.[75] Three years later, David White Rogers produced another hymnal, but this work was criticized as an unauthorized competition to the Smith standard. A third hymnal, drawing heavily on the first two, was compiled by Benjamin C. Elsworth in 1839, but Elsworth's excommunication lessened its influence.[76] The first hymnal published outside of the United States, *A Collection of Sacred Hymns,* was published by W. R. Thomas in Manchester, England, in 1840. This influential hymnal was issued by the Quorum of the Twelve Apostles during their important mission to Britain, and it served as the model for subsequent works printed in the United States. Although musical text/notes were added to another edition in 1844, no other LDS hymnal contained "music" until the end of the nineteenth century. During the twentieth century, the church issued several major editions of hymns, each suggesting the larger LDS culture of the time. The most recent was published in 1985.[77]

ALMANACS

When Mormonism was established in the first part of the nineteenth century, the publication of almanacs was already a firmly established New England tradition.[78] These popular books combined traditional lore with the practical agricultural information required by Yankee farmers. Mormon almanacs followed suit. Among the first were two issued by Orson Pratt in 1845 and 1846. But the chief LDS compiler of these specialized imprints was William W. Phelps, who, from 1851 to 1864, published fourteen editions. While both Pratt's and Phelps's almanacs expressed their personal astronomical and meteorological interests, the bulk of their volumes contained the advice, recipes, and miscellaneous items that were of interest to rural Mormons.[79] As a result, they offer modern readers a glimpse of the agrarian world of the Mormon pioneers. More recently, the annual *Deseret News Church Almanac,* published by the Deseret News Press, has served a different purpose and clientele. Intended as a quick and useful reference guide, this twentieth-century version of an old printing tradition contains information about the preceding year's events as well as data about church leaders, church growth, and administration.

SPECIAL PUBLICATIONS

During the first decades of Mormonism, the church issued a variety of official and semiofficial miscellany. One of the most unfortunate was Sidney Rigdon's inflammatory *Oration Delivered by Mr. Rigdon on the 4th of July, 1838, at Far West, Caldwell Co., Missouri.*[80] Meant to show Mormon resolve at a time of increasing persecution in Missouri, the publication of Rigdon's speech increased hostilities instead of quieting them. *General Joseph Smith's Views of the Power and Policy of the Government of the United States* was prepared by William W. Phelps to support Smith's 1844 political campaign for the U.S. presidency.[81] Still another example was the proclamation of 1845 announcing the death of Joseph Smith and Hyrum Smith, which ended Joseph Smith's brief candidacy.[82] Official proclamations of this type have been issued periodically by church officials and remain an important source for contemporary church policy and opinion.[83]

Joseph Smith's death also introduced a new kind of church document. In December 1847, the Quorum of the Twelve Apostles issued its first "general epistle" to the church. Two years later, with the reorganization of the LDS First Presidency under the direction of Brigham Young, this practice continued. Between April 1849 and December 1856, fourteen additional "general epistles" were printed, usually in the *Millennial Star,* with overlapping printings in the *Frontier Guardian* and the *Deseret News.*[84] Among the most important documents in early Mormon history for the presentation of detailed advice and news, these general epistles helped unite the church's scattered membership.

Church authorities also issued other kinds of directives, some of which appeared in print. Periodic "Circulars" or "Instructions" contained information on such topics as church and state relations, colonization, emigration, gambling, missionary activity, plural marriage, and other economic and spiritual concerns. For instance, Brigham Young's last such directive, "Circular of the First Presidency to Stake Presidents, Bishops, and Members," issued 11 July 1877, reorganized the priesthood quorums of the church and put the church in order shortly before his death.[85] During the Utah territorial era, leaders periodically issued "Instructions to Bishops" as well as other miscellaneous letters intended for a broader church readership. The territorial press also issued a variety of other items, including ephemera not fully identified.[86]

At first, the church printed reports of its annual and semiannual conferences in its newspapers. However, as the need for a more permanent and wider public record became apparent, the church printed the *Journal of Discourses* (1855–86). This publication contained the edited stenographic reports of church leaders' sermons (rarely were early LDS sermons written in advance and read before a congregation) and emphasized the sermons delivered at the church's general conference. Brigham Young's teachings were especially highlighted in this collection. Of the more than one thousand extant Brigham Young sermons, one-third appear in the *Journal of Discourses;* the rest may be found in contemporary newspapers or at the LDS Library-Archives in manuscript form.[87]

Centralization in the Later Nineteenth Century

Although Mormon imprints during the first decades were characterized by an informal and ad hoc quality, there was also a growing tendency toward centralization. As early as the fall of 1831, leaders made plans for a body of Mormon literature: books for children, a newspaper—*The Evening and the Morning Star*—the Emma Smith hymnal, and the first collection of Joseph Smith's revelations that eventually became A Book of Commandments or what later became known as the Doctrine and Covenants. These projects were to be financed by a newly formed Literary Firm.[88] In the late 1830s, the issue of where the Mormon scriptures should be published arose. In response, Joseph Smith requested that publication be completed near church headquarters, not in the eastern United States as some church members had advised.[89]

The tendency toward centralization gained momentum in the middle 1840s. Before Joseph Smith died, he gave the Quorum of the Twelve control of Nauvoo's *Times and Seasons.* "I believe you can do more good in the editorial department than preaching," Smith told the apostle John Taylor, whom he had chosen to edit a church newspaper. "You can write for thousands to read; while you can preach to but a few at a time."[90]

With rival aspirants claiming the departed prophet's mantle and using the press to advance their claims, the Quorum of the Twelve moved to defend its authority. Writing in behalf of the Quorum, Parley Pratt penned the directive "Regulations for the Publishing Department of the Latter-day Saints in the East," which was issued in New York City in January 1845.[91] This directive, the first attempt to establish LDS publishing guidelines under the authority of the new leadership, was favorably received by church leaders in Nauvoo. "There is nothing like order in the kingdom of God," they wrote.[92]

Pratt's document criticized the proliferation of Mormon authors, many of whom were producing a redundant and unsophisticated literature that competed with the apostles' own work—those church leaders "whose business it is to write and publish the truth." Singled out in Pratt's protest was the prolific early LDS pamphleteer Benjamin Winchester, who, Pratt believed, was writing for personal gain. Requesting an end to such personal writing, Pratt urged that the immediate future of Mormon publishing have only three "great emporiums of light, truth, and news": Nauvoo's *Times and Seasons,* Liverpool's *Millennial Star,* and Pratt's own *New York Prophet.* Six months later, Parley's brother Orson joined the call for missionary literature approved and sponsored by the church. "Open your purses, and stretch out the hand of assistance, and sustain us, and we will sustain you," Orson wrote church members.[93]

After the Pratt brothers issued these instructions, independent, free-lance writing became the exception to the rule. Although some unofficial publishing continued in the 1850s, this usually took place in areas geographically removed from church control, such as India, South Africa, or Australia. The era was, as George Ellsworth suggested, a time of transition for Mormon mission work. Likewise, it was a time of change for Mormon publishing.[94]

A NEW PUBLISHING HEADQUARTERS IN ENGLAND

During the middle decades of the nineteenth century, Liverpool assumed a greater responsibility for LDS printing. This trend partly reflected the Mormons' missionary success in Britain during the 1840s and early 1850s. It also reflected the Mormon migration to the Great Basin, which by the middle of the century meant the closing of the New York City and Nauvoo LDS printing centers. During the period of Liverpool's ascendancy, about 1850 to 1869, the mission headquarters located in the city published the *Millennial Star* and the *Journal of Discourses*. It also became the supply depot for LDS books and literature in Britain and for many other areas, including South Africa, India, Australia, the Pacific Islands, and even the United States.[95]

The growing centralization of the Liverpool mission headquarters permitted efficiencies of mass and scale; larger editions of Mormon mission literature could now be produced, advertised, and sold at lower costs. The system, in turn, encouraged the Mormons to expand greatly their pamphleteering. Orson Pratt's 1850 article "How to Warn the Whole British Nation in One Year" envisioned the placing of at least one LDS pamphlet in the hands of each British citizen.[96] Taking a first step in 1850, the London Conference ordered 57,000 additional tracts to be distributed during the Great Exhibition in London in 1851. During the 1850s, other LDS leaders continued to echo Pratt's call for flooding Queen Victoria's realm with LDS literature.[97]

The Mormons' mission literature had two ancillary developments. First, the growing variety of books, pamphlets, and other publications required the issuance of catalogues to list and identify the mission publications and to explain to the Mormon elders how they might be used. These catalogues were first printed as separate items but later appeared as a regular feature in the *Millennial Star*.[98] Second, the missionaries printed and distributed broadsides and handbills. These were used to advertise the location of their meetings and to explain the topics of their preaching. In the process, they often contained a brief statement of Mormon beliefs. Ephemeral in nature, these broadsides and handbills are now rare. However, like catalogues, they furnish overlooked information about midcentury proselytizing.[99]

Mission authorities in Liverpool, seeking the widest circulation for their literature, devised a complicated system of distribution. This system allowed each local unit or mission conference to establish a distribution agency that was eligible to secure literature on credit. The *Millennial Star* then published a quarterly statement of each local account and requested payment. The system had several advantages. It permitted mission officials to control the selection and printing of literature, while publishing these items in large runs at reduced costs. Independent vendors could publish approved materials and distribute them on credit through the Liverpool headquarters. Finally, missionaries could easily secure literature for their proselytizing and pay for it later. If enough items were sold, missionaries might even secure a limited income to defray their living expenses.

The system also had disadvantages, though. It discouraged private initiative and authorship; rank-and-file missionaries, even of exceptional talent, found it difficult to compete with "approved" mission writers, who were, almost without exception, either mission presidents or editors of the *Millennial Star*. The practice led to the perception that such leaders as Orson Hyde, Orson Spencer, Orson Pratt, Parley P. Pratt, and Franklin D. Richards used their church position to promote their own writing.

Second, the system created increasing levels of debt that became hard to manage. The Mormon lay missionaries did not always keep good records, and the frequent transfer or release of these men from their assignments did not promote accountability. The resulting debt levels and the practice of giving discounts to large orders too often introduced an economic factor into the spiritual endeavor of proselytizing: pamphlets and books could be peddled to reduce debts and secure profits.

Third, the centralization of Mormon publishing created currency exchange problems; the value of the British pound fluctuated even in British India, and internationally stationed missionaries did not always understand their exact financial obligation to the Liverpool office.

By the end of the 1850s, the system was breaking down. Difficulties with the "book business" became a frequent topic for discussion at the local conferences in the European mission's districts, and the *Millennial Star* ran editorials about the need to pay off debts and commended the missionaries who did so.[100] Despite such efforts, other missionaries continued to run up debts, which included the cost of printing of such incidental items as the engravings of church buildings, portraits of church leaders, and even pictures of the missionaries themselves. These practices apparently had a pecuniary motive. President Young warned the Mormon missionaries departing from Utah not to become "merchants" while serving in England, and he believed that some of the men who had earlier served in the country had taken advantage of the local Saints by their insistent selling of printed merchandise. Whatever the actual practices, by 1855 the cost of Liverpool publishing was £125,000, a sum that the church's general tithing funds were required to help retire.[101]

By the end of the 1850s, the formative years of Mormon publishing were coming to an end. The mounting abuses of the system were only a part of the situation. In the United States, the so-called Utah War (1857–58) had drained church finances and required stringency even in faraway Britain. At the same time, Mormon proselytizing in the European mission fell off sharply, and the demand for mission literature decreased. But some of the problem involved creative talent, too. By the end of the decade, such leading writers as Parley Pratt and Orson Spencer were dead, and partly because of their absence, no major new works—pamphlets or books—appeared during the rest of Brigham Young's presidency. Young probably was not disappointed. He seemed uncomfortable with Mormon pamphleteers' attempts to formalize Mormon doctrine, a practice that seemed to minimize his own teaching authority and the teaching authority of his possible successors. Besides, in Young's mind, the formalization of the church's doctrines appeared to be a "creedism" that threatened to undermine Mormonism's spirit and vibrancy.

GEORGE Q. CANNON AND NEW DIRECTIONS

Probably no first-generation figure personified the transition from independent free-lance writing to church-authorized writing so completely as George Q. Cannon. Cannon began his publishing career in Nauvoo under the tutelage of his father-in-law, John Taylor. Then, as a young missionary, Cannon translated the Book of Mormon into the Hawaiian language, and during the middle 1850s, with Parley Pratt initially directing his work, Cannon published the *Western Standard* in San Francisco. During that decade, he also was involved in the church's newspaper publishing in Utah and the eastern United States.[102]

In 1860, at the age of thirty-three, Cannon was called to be a member of the Quorum of the Twelve Apostles and placed in charge of the European mission. Arriving in Liverpool, he established a printing office that ended the mission's old practice of relying on outside job printers. In 1861, Cannon detailed to Young the state of church printing in Britain. He noted the waste of the system (it would "take half the Millennium to sell what are now on hand in this office"), provided an inventory of materials on hand that included each work's recent sales, and urged that the church assume control of the printing and distribution of its imprints. His letter, full of detail, provides a window to what LDS publishing in England had become:

> Were . . . [books and pamphlets] mine, with my present feelings, I would think it better to sell them to the Saints those disposed to buy our works at the price of waste paper, or even give them away, than to have them lie year after year rotting on shelves or in boxes doing no good to anybody. The publishing of such large editions has been unfortunate; it was doubtless [done] with the object of getting the works cheap. There are an immense number of Tracts, as you will see by the Miscellaneous Ac[coun]t which cannot be sold within any reasonable time, as the people have been sated with such works, and there is, therefore, but little demand for them; but they might be distributed and do good. Of books: there is the Harp of Zion, out of 3404 copies 21 have been sold in three years. Out of 2590 volumes of Sister E. R. Snow's Poems, 19 have been sold during the same period. There are 454 bound volumes of Joseph Smith the Prophet, and 5611 copies in sheets; of this work there have been 732 copies sold during the three years past. Of the Compendium there have been 201 copies sold, out of 1861 bound volumes and 1455 copies in sheets. And of the Journal of Discourses 481 Numbers have been sold, leaving now on hand 2884 unbound Volumes and 108,716 odd numbers out of which a good number of perfect volumes can be made. Were these works in the Valley, they might very likely be sold, if not for money at least for provisions &c.; but I think the prospect very dull here at present for their sale.[103]

Agreeing with the young apostle, Young advised Cannon to send the already bound volumes to Salt Lake City for sale, distribute the shorter tracts to church members gratis, and either destroy the remainder or sell them as waste paper.[104]

After Cannon returned to Utah, he played an even greater role in LDS publishing. Apparently inspired by the "home literature movement" in the United States, which sought to provide "good literature" as an alternative to the pulp novels of the period, in 1866 Cannon established the printing firm of "George Q. Cannon and Sons" and opened an affiliated bookstore.[105] The firm was a private enterprise only in name. Surviving catalogues (themselves important imprints) show that Cannon's press produced much of the literature issued by the church's auxiliary organizations, particularly the Sunday School organization that Cannon himself directed.[106] Seeking to "improve" the rising generation, Cannon published the *Juvenile Instructor,* a monthly magazine published from 1866 to 1929.[107] He also issued the multivolume "Faith-Promoting" series aimed at introducing Zion's young men and women to their pioneer heritage, and he prepared a series of biographies of Joseph Smith designed for various age groups. At the time of his death, Cannon had begun the first bookshelf version of the "History of Joseph Smith," a work that B. H. Roberts later completed. After his passing, the church acquired George Q. Cannon and Sons and in 1919 renamed the firm Deseret Book Company. By the end of the twentieth century, Deseret Book was a major publishing house, with retail outlets throughout the Intermountain West.[108]

Other periodicals emerged during the last decades of the nineteenth century. These included reading material for various age and gender groups: for women, *Woman's Exponent* (1872–1914); for young men, the *Contributor* (1879–1896); and for young women, the *Young Woman's Journal* (1889–1929).[109] The *Improvement Era* (1898–1970) served an evolving audience: first, young men; second, after 1929, young men and young women; and, third, during the 1930s and early 1940s, increasingly the adults of the church.[110]

Other church leaders played major roles in the development of these periodicals besides Cannon. The influence of Emmeline Wells and Susa Young Gates was especially strong in the development of women's literature.[111] The assistant church historian Andrew Jenson published a variety of historical and biographical volumes during this period.[112] These works, along with those published by Cannon and those that followed at the turn of the century, are especially helpful in revealing the evolving attitudes of Mormonism. They trace, among other controversial issues, the defense and abandonment of plural marriage, the rapprochement of Mormonism to the American mainstream, and the increasing codification of doctrine. For instance, the sixth edition of Parley P. Pratt's *Key to the Science of Theology* (1904) was reworked to correspond more closely to the church's new teachings about plural marriage as well as the nature and role of the Holy Ghost as expressed in James E. Talmage's *Articles of Faith*.[113] This body of literature also demonstrates the church's increasing insistence that its members abide by its Word of Wisdom health code—a teaching that many members had chosen to regard as only advisory.[114]

LDS Publishing in the Twentieth Century

PERIODICALS AND NEWSPAPERS

Until 1970, the church's auxiliary organizations continued to publish their own magazines and instruction manuals. Although this continued a pattern already established in the nineteenth century, a change had occurred. Increasingly, these magazines were no longer semiprivate periodicals but were owned by the church itself. The *Juvenile Instructor,* acquired earlier from Cannon, was retitled the *Instructor* in 1929.[115] The independently owned and managed *Woman's Exponent* was replaced in 1915 by the *Relief Society Bulletin* and was then retitled the *Relief Society Magazine* a year later.[116] The *Children's Friend,* the organ of the Primary organization, served the church's children, ages three through twelve. Even the Utah Genealogical Society published its own *Utah Genealogical and Historical Magazine* from 1910 to 1940.[117]

Some periodicals designed to serve the needs of the church's localized missions also continued. The *Millennial Star* remained the organ of the British mission, but as that mission declined, the *Star* found its status altered; once a premier LDS periodical, by the middle of the twentieth century the *Millennial Star* had become a local and derivative publication. In the United States, the earlier proselytizing periodicals that served the northern, eastern, and southern missions were combined into the *Liahona: The Elders' Journal,* published at Independence, Missouri, from 1907 to 1945.[118] The *Liahona*'s press also served Zion's Printing and Publishing Company. From the year of its establishment in 1907 to midcentury when its press was closed by a consolidation with the Deseret News Press, Zion's Printing and Publishing printed several English- and Spanish-language editions of the Book of Mormon as well as more than fifty titles written by LDS authors.[119]

With church membership growing and church publications proliferating, leaders felt the need for coordination. In 1912, a Correlation Committee was created under the direction of Apostle David O. McKay. A year later, the committee recommended that LDS headquarters take steps to correlate the activities of its priesthood and auxiliary organizations, which, if fully implemented, might have streamlined the church's publications. A more successful program was the creation in 1944 of the Committee on Publications, chaired by Apostle Joseph Fielding Smith. This committee supervised the preparation and publication of church literature.

In the 1960s, the correlation process was revived. Under the direction of Apostle Harold B. Lee, the General Priesthood Committee reviewed the church's teaching curriculum and recommended a closer correlation of published material. One result was the consolidation of the church's magazines under a central committee that urged further streamlining. Beginning in 1971, these recommendations were implemented when three new magazines replaced their earlier counterparts: the *Ensign* for adults, the *New Era* for teenagers, and the *Friend* for children.[120] At the same time, a monthly magazine for the international church was begun. This "international magazine," made up of articles drawn from the English-language magazines, replaced the several periodicals being published abroad, and by the end of the century it was issued in twenty-three languages.[121]

STATEMENTS OF DOCTRINE AND SCRIPTURAL GUIDES

Twentieth-century authors continued to explicate Mormon teaching. In some cases, their works carried the church's copyright and therefore represented officially approved teaching. James E. Talmage's two works, *The Articles of Faith* (1899) and *Jesus the Christ* (1915), were in this category.[122] In other cases, the authors were church leaders, and their works had the authority of their writers' position: B. H. Roberts's *Mormon Doctrine of Deity* and *The Seventy's Course in Theology* and John A. Widtsoe's *Rational Theology,* for example.[123] Especially important was the posthumously issued and church-copyrighted teachings of Joseph F. Smith: *Gospel Doctrine: Selections from the Sermons and Writings. . . .*[124] This book went through more than a dozen and a half printings and heavily influenced the writing of Smith's son, Joseph Fielding

Smith: *The Progress of Man; Answers to Gospel Questions; Man, His Origin and Destiny;* and *Doctrines of Salvation.*[125] It also influenced the popular codification of Mormon teaching written by Joseph F. Smith's grandson-in-law, Bruce R. McConkie.[126] Still another category was the books authored by such nonleaders as Lowell L. Bennion and Hugh W. Nibley, who, because of their popularity as teachers and writers, also helped shape twentieth-century Mormon thought.[127]

Two of these works stirred controversy at the time of their printing. Although Joseph Fielding Smith's *Man, His Origin and Destiny* was published by the Deseret Book Company and was promoted as a textbook for the church's educational system, President David O. McKay refused to approve the book as a statement of official doctrine, partly because of its fundamentalist, anti-Darwinian teaching.[128] The first edition (1958) of McConkie's *Mormon Doctrine,* intended as a handbook of LDS doctrine, was criticized as being "full of errors and misstatements" and was reissued in a second edition only after major revision.[129] Both books continued a strain of conservative literalism that had been present in Mormonism from its beginning.

The twentieth century saw the creation of several important scriptural guides, including George Reynolds's *Complete Concordance to the Book of Mormon;* Joseph B. Keeler's *Concordance to the Doctrine and Covenants;* John Bluth's *Concordance to the Doctrine and Covenants;* and Eldon Ricks's *Concordance of the LDS Standard Works.*[130] These guides prepared the way for the church's own scriptural index, *A Topical Guide to the Scriptures.*[131] This aid, along with a newly revised Bible dictionary, was included in the 1981 edition of the LDS scriptures.

THE MODERN MARKETING OF MAINSTREAM MORMONISM

During the last half of the century, church members produced a growing body of "uncorrelated," nonofficial literature that generally reflected the mainstream views of the twentieth-century church. The publishing firms Deseret Book Company and Bookcraft specialized in this kind of literature, and their merger at the end of the century recognized their longstanding similarity. Likewise, the Brigham Young University Press published conservative, institutional works, but with a greater academic orientation. During its stop-and-go existence, the BYU Press had several reincarnations, but among its distinctions was the publication of the academic journal *Brigham Young University Studies,* which began its modern run in 1959. Despite a degree of independence, these presses revealed a standardization of tone and content that reflected the public relations sensitivity of a growing, worldwide church. By the end of the century, the kind of public criticism of Mormon imprints that Brigham Young once exercised, or even David McKay in the 1960s, seemed out of the question.

The presentation of mainstream print–Mormonism, however, involved more than a homogenized approach and image. The Deseret Book Company's mass-marketed Book Club; Deseret Book's creation of special, market-driven imprint series (Bookcraft, Eagle Gate, and Shadow Mountain); the growing popularity of such electronic databases as Infobases and GospeLink; and the listing of many Mormon publications in the national *Books in Print* all suggested the growing sophistication of LDS publishing.

Another sign of maturity has been the growth of independent presses and jour-nals, many of which are discussed in chapter 3. The University of Illinois Press's Mormon series was especially distinguished, while Signature Books of Salt Lake City delivered works intended to appeal to readers seeking "non-correlated" and untraditional material on the liberal end of the interpretative spectrum. Similarly, LDS periodic literature became increasingly diverse, as such independent-minded journals as *Dialogue: A Journal of Mormon Thought* and *Sunstone* printed hundreds of specialized articles that showed the vitality of Mormon scholarship across a spec-trum of belief, viewpoint, and approach. While some church leaders censured these journals as an "alternate voice" to their own authoritative interpretation, the semiofficial *Encyclopedia of Mormonism* used this literature when creating, in 1992, Mormonism's most important modern synthesis of its scholarship. Notwithstand-ing the general authority's concerns, the line between approved and disapproved writing—or what can be used for church purposes and what might be ignored—was clearly becoming difficult to establish. It was a trend that the rapid increase of LDS material in electronic form will likely accelerate.[132]

ADMINISTRATIVE PUBLICATIONS

The church's dramatic growth in the twentieth century required it to become more bureaucratic in its procedures, spawning another kind of literature. This material detailed the church's administrative rules and procedures, and although its circula-tion was sometimes restricted to local and general church leaders, its importance to future historians is likely to grow. Joseph B. Keeler's priesthood handbooks were among the first of this genre.[133] More definitive were John A. Widtsoe's *Priesthood and Church Government* and, especially, the successive editions of the *Melchizedek Priesthood Handbook,* issued in the last part of the century.[134] Policy changes and directives between editions of the *Handbook* can be found in the *Priesthood Bulletin* (issued six times a year, 1965–74) or, more recently, in the *Bulletin* (1980–).

The church has encouraged a wider distribution of the sermons and proceedings of its annual and semiannual general conferences. Since the end of the nineteenth century, these have been published in the church's official *Conference Reports* (1880, 1897–present); more recently these proceedings can also be found the May and No-vember issues of the *Ensign* magazine. The reporting gaps between the publishing runs of *Journal of Discourses* and *Conference Reports* is partly filled by the five-vol-ume collection edited by Brian H. Stuy, *Collected Discourses, Delivered by Wilford Woodruff, His Two Counselors, the Twelve Apostles . . . ,* which is now included in the electronic collection of LDS sources, Infobases.[135]

Conclusion and Prospects

This review of Mormon publishing history, with its emphasis on early imprints, sug-gests the importance of the topic. From the beginning of LDS history, some of the church's most talented writers have devoted themselves to presenting and defend-ing Mormonism, while the church itself has committed a significant amount of its resources to the same task. Today, the topic is equally important to scholars, who have only begun to use this important source. By giving this resource greater attention, present-day researchers can more fully understand such Mormon-related topics as church administration, culture, economics, gender roles, image, leisure, polemics, rhetoric, and missiology—just to suggest a partial list of possibilities.

A study of Mormon imprints suggests the rich variety of Mormon thinking and the two approaches that often have been taken in presenting it. While Joseph Smith was the fountainhead of Mormon doctrine and enunciated its broad outlines, his disciples, then and now, have created two different strains or emphases. In general terms, just as Parley P. Pratt and Orson Pratt personified the romantic and the scientific traditions, their intellectual descendants seemed to be divided, on one hand, by an open-ended playfulness with ideas and, on the other, by a more serious-minded rationalism, if not legalism. While the first concerned itself with the moral dimension of religion, the second has given greater attention to the institutional demands of the faith. In the first category, we might place such writers as B. H. Roberts, John A. Widtsoe, Lowell Bennion, and Hugh Nibley; the second might include Joseph F. Smith, Joseph Fielding Smith, J. Reuben Clark, and Bruce R. McConkie. Doubtless, Mormon religion requires both approaches: one to conserve and formalize the traditions of the movement, the other to explore the core teachings of Joseph Smith and, in the process, provide the vitality of a living faith.

The study of Mormon imprints suggests the need to examine ancillary topics. By using print materials as cultural artifacts, researchers can study *authorship*—the who, what, and why of writing. Print material may be used to create the *history of texts*—compiling historical and analytical bibliography as well as studying how texts have changed. Mormon imprints can help illuminate the *history of reading*—such things as the nature of literature (the kinds of items people have read), audiences (the gender, age, class, occupation of the LDS reading public), the very nature of reading itself (whether in private or more obviously as a part of an interpretative community), or even the technology of reading (subjects range from eyeglasses to artificial lighting). Or Mormon imprints might be approached as a study of *distribution*—how men and women secured their reading matter and how libraries have gathered, preserved, and organized the printed word. Likewise, the study of imprints provides perspective on the question of *censorship*, with its subset topics of the relation between publication and authority, social and intellectual pluralism, or even religious dissent within the LDS community. Most broadly, the study of imprints is *intellectual history*, as each item of reading material may be seen as a vehicle for conveying information.

Nor have the various aspects of the economics of publishing, from authorship to marketing and distribution, been fully explored: *production and technology* (companies, bids, printing processes, insurance, contracts, copyright, paper, inks, presses, presswork, typefounding, and design); *editing*, from manuscript to typesetting in first as well as later editions; *advertising*, through advertisements, catalogues, trade publications, and personal promotion; *distribution*, including storage, sales, distributors, subscriptions, bookstores and book clubs, trade routes, and transportation (peddlers, mails, wagons, railroads, and trucks); *consumption,* including marketing to get products into the hands of readers through purchases, borrowing, gift-giving, and literary or tract societies; and finally, *piracy and counterfeiting,* or how printed works have been "poached"—stolen or plagiarized.[136]

Clearly, this is a fruitful field, awaiting further scholarly harvest.

Notes

1. The appendix does not consider several types of twentieth-century imprints because of their complexity and volume. For instance, a full discussion of the church's lesson manuals might require several essays. Nor does the appendix consider such electronic compilations as Infobases' *LDS Collectors' Library* and Deseret Book Company's *GospeLink,* each of which contains large and invaluable collections of LDS imprints. These electronic texts are briefly described in chapter 3.

2. The best guide to the first century of Mormon publication is Chad J. Flake, comp., *A Mormon Bibliography, 1830–1930: Books, Pamphlets, Periodicals, and Broadsides relating to the First Century of Mormonism* (Salt Lake City: University of Utah Press, 1978). A supplement to this volume appeared in 1989: Chad J. Flake and Larry W. Draper, comps., *A Mormon Bibliography, 1830–1930: Ten Year Supplement* (Salt Lake City: University of Utah Press, 1989). Both volumes are indexed in Chad J. Flake and Larry W. Draper, comps., *A Mormon Bibliography, 1830–1930: Indexes to a Mormon Bibliography and Ten Year Supplement* (Salt Lake City: University of Utah Press, 1992).

3. "Flooding the Earth with the Book of Mormon," *Ensign* 28 (March 1998): 75.

4. Literature discussing the print history of the Book of Mormon includes Jeffrey R. Holland, "An Analysis of Selected Changes in Major Editions of the Book of Mormon, 1830–1920" (Master's thesis, Brigham Young University, 1966); Stanley R. Larson, "A Study of Some Textual Variations in the Book of Mormon Comparing the Original and the Printer's Manuscripts and the 1830, the 1837, and the 1840 Editions" (Master's thesis, Brigham Young University, 1974); Hugh G. Stocks, "The Book of Mormon, 1830–1979: A Publishing History" (Master's thesis, University of California at Los Angeles, 1979); and Hugh Stocks, "The Book of Mormon in English, 1870–1920: A Publishing History and Analytical Bibliography" (Ph.D. diss., University of California at Los Angeles, 1986). For a short account of the first printing, see Gayle Goble Ord, "The Book of Mormon Goes to Press," *Ensign* 2 (December 1972): 66–70. See also Royal Skousen, "Towards a Critical Edition of the Book of Mormon," *BYU Studies* 30 (Winter 1990): 41–69. For a brief overview of the main studies of this volume of scripture, see John L. Sorenson, "Digging into the Book of Mormon: Our Changing Understanding of Ancient America and Its Scripture," *Ensign* 14 (September 1984): 26–37, and (October 1984): 12–23.

5. Donald W. Parry, Jeanette W. Miller, and Sandra A. Thorne, eds., *A Comprehensive Annotated Book of Mormon Bibliography* (Provo, Utah: Research Press, 1996).

6. Robert J. Woodford, "The Historical Development of the Doctrine and Covenants," 3 vols. (Ph.D. diss., Brigham Young University, 1974); Lyndon W. Cook, *The Revelations of the Prophet Joseph Smith* (1981; reprint, Salt Lake City: Deseret Book, 1985). See also Richard P. Howard, *Restoration Scriptures: A Study of Their Textual Development* (1969; 2d ed., Independence, Mo.: Herald Publishing House, 1995).

7. H. Michael Marquardt, *The Joseph Smith Revelations, Text and Commentary* (Salt Lake City: Signature Books, 1999).

8. James R. Clark, *The Story of the Pearl of Great Price* (Salt Lake City: Bookcraft, 1955); James R. Clark, "Our Pearl of Great Price: From Mission Pamphlet to Standard Work," *Ensign* 6 (August 1976): 12–17

9. Most of the controversy surrounding the Book of Abraham is surveyed and responded to in the work of Hugh W. Nibley. See especially "A New Look at the Pearl of Great Price," *Improvement Era* 71–73 (January 1968–May 1970); and *The Message of the Joseph Smith Papyri: An Egyptian Endowment* (Salt Lake City: Deseret Book, 1975). See also Jay M. Todd, *The Saga of the Book of Abraham* (Salt Lake City: Deseret Book, 1969); and H. Donl Peterson, *The Story of the Book of Abraham: Mummies, Manuscripts, and Mormonism* (Salt Lake City: Deseret Book, 1995).

10. The most comprehensive study of Smith's biblical revision is Robert J. Matthews, *"A Plainer Translation," Joseph Smith's Translation of the Bible: A History and Commentary* (Provo, Utah: Brigham Young University Press, 1975). See also Reed C. Durham Jr., "A History of Joseph Smith's Revision of the Bible" (Ph.D. diss., Brigham Young University, 1965); and Philip L. Barlow, *Mormons and the Bible: The Place of the Latter-day Saints in American Religion* (New York: Oxford University Press, 1991). For a useful bibliography of published material on the Joseph Smith "translation" of the Bible, see Thomas E. Sherry, *Joseph Smith's Translation of the Bible: A Bibliography of Publications, 1847–1987,* 3 vols. (Provo, Utah: By the author, 1988). In 1994 Sherry added a fourth volume that covered the literature published from 1988 to 1992.

11. These developments are discussed in Robert J. Matthews, "The New Publications of the Standard Works—1979, 1981," *BYU Studies* 22 (Fall 1982): 387–424.

12. Studies that help outsiders better understand the Mormon notion of an open canon include W. D. Davies, "Reflections on the Mormon Canon," *Harvard Theological Review* 79 (January/April/July 1986): 44–66; John W. Welch and David J. Whittaker, "Mormonism's Open Canon: Some Historical Perspectives on Its Religious Limits and Potentials" (paper responding to Davies and delivered at the annual meeting of the American Academy of Religion and the Society of Biblical Literature, Atlanta, Georgia, 24 November 1986), working paper distributed by FARMS; C. Wilfred Griggs, ed., *Apocryphal Writings and the Latter-day Saints* (Provo, Utah: Religious Studies Center, Brigham Young University, 1986); Edward J. Brandt, "The History, Content, and Latter-day Saint Use of the Book of Jasher" (Ph.D. diss., Brigham Young University, 1976); and Donald W. Parry and Dana M. Pike, eds, *LDS Perspectives on the Dead Sea Scrolls* (Provo, Utah: Foundation for Ancient Research and Mormon Studies, Brigham Young University, 1997).

13. Orson Hyde, *A Prophetic Warning to All the Churches* [Toronto, 1836]. Although no copy is extant, the text of the broadside was reprinted in the *Latter Day Saints' Messenger and Advocate* 2 (July 1836): 342–46; three years later it was reissued under the title *A Timely Warning.* Before running its course, the broadside was printed several more times. For bibliographic details of Hyde's pioneering effort, see Peter Crawley, *A Descriptive Bibliography of the Mormon Church,* vol. 1, *1830–47* (Provo, Utah: Religious Studies Center, Brigham Young University, 1997), 63–64 (items 30, 36, 54, 81, 332).

14. For discussion of this, see Durham, "A History of Joseph Smith's Revision of the Bible," 85–96.

15. Peter Crawley, "Parley P. Pratt: Father of Mormon Pamphleteering," *Dialogue: A Journal of Mormon Thought* 15 (Autumn 1982): 13–26.

16. The best available works on Pratt's life are Parley P. Pratt, *Autobiography of Parley Parker Pratt*, ed. Parley P. Pratt Jr. (New York: Russell Brothers, 1874); and Reva Stanley, *A Biography of Parley P. Pratt: The Archer of Paradise* (Caldwell, Idaho: Caxton, 1937). For details about his missionary activity and death, see David J. Whittaker, "Parley P. Pratt and the Pacific Mission: Mormon Publishing in 'That Very Questionable Part of the Civilized World,'" in *Mormons, Scripture, and the Ancient World: Studies in Honor of John L. Sorenson,* ed. Davis Bitton (Provo, Utah: Foundation for Ancient Research and Mormon Studies, Brigham Young University, 1998), 51–84; and Steve Pratt, "Eleanor McLean and the Murder of Parley P. Pratt," *BYU Studies* 15 (Winter 1975): 225–56. A modern, full-scale treatment of Pratt is much needed.

17. Parley P. Pratt, *Voice of Warning and Instruction to All People* (New York: W. Sandford, 1837).

18. Crawley, "Parley P. Pratt," 15. For further details about the book's first publishing, see Pratt's letter, dated New York City, 3 October 1837, *Elder's Journal* 1 (October 1837): 9. Bibliographical information is in Crawley, *A Descriptive Bibliography,* 69–70 (item 38).

19. For early missionary uses of Pratt's work, see Barbara McFarlane Higdon, "The Role of Preaching in the Early Latter Day Church, 1830–1846" (Ph.D. diss., University of Missouri, 1961), 87–88; and S. George Ellsworth, "A History of the Mormon Missions in the United States and Canada, 1830–1860" (Ph.D. diss., University of California at Berkeley, 1951), 46–47.

20. Pratt, *Voice of Warning and Instruction to All People,* esp. 97–104.

21. Parley P. Pratt, *Mormonism Unveiled: Zion's Watchman Unmasked, and Its Editor, Mr. L. R. Sunderland, Exposed: Truth Vindicated: The Devil Mad, and Priestcraft in Danger!* (Painesville, Ohio: Printed for William D. Pratt, 1838). The first edition of forty-seven pages appeared in April 1838; four years later, a subsequent edition appeared with some corrections. See Crawley, "Parley P. Pratt," 15, 19. For bibliographical information on the work's four 1838 printings, see Crawley, *A Descriptive Bibliography,* 76–79 (items 45–48).

22. Pratt, *Mormonism Unveiled,* 3. For information on Sunderland and the Spaulding theory on the origins of the Book of Mormon, see Edward D. Jervey, "LaRoy Sunderland: Zion's Watchman," *Methodist History* 6 (January 1968): 16–32; and Lester E. Bush Jr., "The Spaulding Theory Then and Now," *Dialogue: A Journal of Mormon Thought* 10 (Autumn 1977): 40–69.

23. His other replies include *Plain Facts, Showing the Falsehood and Folly of the Rev. C. S. Bush, (a Church Minister of the Parish of Peover,) Being a Reply to His Tract against the Latter-day Saints* (Manchester, England: W. R. Thomas, [1840]); *A Reply to Mr. Thomas Taylor's "Complete Failure," &c., and Mr. Richard Livesey's "Mormonism Exposed"* (Manchester, England: W. R. Thomas, 1840); *An Answer to Mr. William Hewitt's Tract against the Latter-day Saints* (Manchester, England: W. R. Thomas, 1840); and *Truth Defended; or, A Reply to the "Preston Chronicle," and to Mr. J. B. Rollo's "Mormonism Exposed": Extracted from the Millennial Star for July, 1841* (Manchester, England: P. P. Pratt, 1841). For further information on Pratt's works of disputation, see James B. Allen, Ronald K. Esplin, and David J. Whittaker, *Men with a Mission, 1837–1841: The Quorum of the Twelve Apostles in the British Isles* (Salt Lake City: Deseret Book, 1992), 255–59.

24. Parley P. Pratt, *The Millenium: A Poem, to Which Is Added Hymns and Songs* (Boston: n.p., 1835). For bibliographic details, see Crawley, *A Descriptive Bibliography*, 54 (item 21).

25. Parley P. Pratt, *The Millenium, and Other Poems to Which Is Annexed a Treatise on the Regeneration and Eternal Duration of Matter* (New York: W. Molineux, 1840).

26. Parley P. Pratt, *The World Turned Upside Down* (Liverpool: Millennial Star Office, Printed by James and Woodburn, 1841 and 1842); Parley P. Pratt, *An Appeal to the Inhabitants of the State of New York* (Nauvoo: John Taylor, 1844), 21–35, 36–40.

27. Crawley, "Parley P. Pratt," surveys Parley P. Pratt's influence on such writers as John Taylor, Benjamin Winchester, Orson Pratt, William Appleby, John E. Page, Moses Martin, and David Candland. Many of his ideas have survived into modern Mormon thought through Orson Pratt's writing and were still later used by B. H. Roberts, James E. Talmage, John A. Widtsoe, Joseph Fielding Smith, and Bruce R. McConkie.

28. Heber C. Kimball and Wilford Woodruff, *The Word of the Lord to the Citizens of London* (London: Doudney and Scrymgour, 1840); Erastus Snow and Benjamin Winchester, *An Address to the Citizens of Salem and Vicinity* (Salem, Mass.: Salem Observer, 1841); and Jesse Haven, *A Warning to All* (Capetown, South Africa: n.p., 1853). See also Parley P. Pratt, *Proclamation! To the People of the Coasts and Islands of the Pacific . . .* (Sydney, Australia: Hibernian, 1851); Parley P. Pratt, *Proclamation Extraordinary! To the Spanish Americans* (San Francisco: Monson, Haswell, 1852).

29. Orson Pratt to Parley P. Pratt, 12 September 1853, Parley P. Pratt Papers, LDS Library-Archives, Salt Lake City (hereafter LDS Archives). See also Orson's letter to his wife, Sarah, 6 January 1840, *Times and Seasons* 1 (February 1840): 61. For background on Orson Pratt's work as a writer and the wider context of his career, see David J. Whittaker, "Orson Pratt: Prolific Pamphleteer," *Dialogue: A Journal of Mormon Thought* 15 (Autumn 1982): 27–41; Breck England, *The Life and Thought of Orson Pratt* (Salt Lake City: University of Utah Press, 1985); and Craig James Hazen, *The Village Enlightenment in America: Popular Religion and Science in the Nineteenth Century* (Urbana: University of Illinois Press, 2000), 15–64.

30. Orson Pratt, *An Interesting Account of Several Remarkable Visions* (Edinburgh: Ballantyne and Hughes, 1840).

31. Orson Pratt, *The Absurdities of Immaterialism* (Liverpool: R. James, 1849). For other examples, see *Divine Authority; or, Was Joseph Smith Sent of God,* 16 pp. (30 September 1848); *The Kingdom of God,* Part 1, 8 pp. (31 October 1848), Part 2, 8 pp. (30 November 1848), Part 3, 8 pp. (14 January 1849), Part 4, 16 pp. (14 July 1849); *Reply to "Remarks on Mormonism,"* 16 pp. (30 April 1849); *New Jerusalem; or, The Fulfillment of Modern Prophecy,* 24 pp. (1 October 1849); *Divine Authenticity of the Book of Mormon,* 96 pp., No. 1 (15 October 1850), No. 2 (1 November 1850), No. 3 (1 December 1850), No. 4 (15 December 1850), No. 5 (7 January 1851), No. 6 (n.d. [probably 15 January 1851]); and *The Great First Cause; or, The Self Moving Forces of the Universe,* 16 pp. (1 January 1851). An early compilation of Orson Pratt's works appeared as *A Series of Pamphlets by Orson Pratt, One of the Twelve Apostles of the Church of Jesus Christ of Latter-day Saints* (Liverpool: Franklin D. Richards, 1851).

32. Orson Pratt, *The True Faith,* 16 pp. (25 August 1856); *True Repentance,* 16 pp. (8 September 1856); *Water Baptism,* 16 pp. (22 September 1856); *The Holy Spirit,* 16 pp. (15 No-

vember 1856); *Spiritual Gifts,* 16 pp. (15 December 1856); *Necessity for Miracles,* 16 pp. (15 January 1857); *Universal Apostasy; or, The Seventeen Centuries of Darkness,* 16 pp. (15 February 1857); and *Latter-day Kingdom; or, The Preparation for the Second Advent,* 16 pp. (15 March 1857). These pamphlets were published as a group in *[Tracts] by Orson Pratt . . .* (Liverpool and London: L. D. S. Book and Star Depot, 1856 and 1857).

33. For further discussion, see David J. Whittaker, "The Bone in the Throat: Orson Pratt and the Public Announcement of Plural Marriage," *Western Historical Quarterly* 18 (July 1987): 293–314.

34. Parley P. Pratt, *Key to the Science of Theology* (Liverpool: F. D. Richards, 1855); Orson Pratt, *The Key to the Universe* (Liverpool: William Budge, 1879).

35. Parley P. Pratt to Orson Pratt, 24 May 1853, Salt Lake City, Parley P. Pratt Papers, LDS Archives. For the historical circumstance that prompted this work, see Whittaker, "Parley P. Pratt and the Pacific Mission."

36. For efforts to record Joseph Smith's sermons, see Dean C. Jessee, "Priceless Words and Fallible Memories: Joseph Smith as Seen in the Effort to Preserve His Discourses," *BYU Studies* 31 (Spring 1991): 19–40.

37. Orson Pratt, *A[n] Interesting Account of Several Remarkable Visions, and the Late Discovery of Ancient American Records Giving an Account of the Commencement of the Work of the Lord in This Generation* (Edinburgh: Ballantyne and Hughes, 1840); Moses Martin, *A Treatise on the Fulness of the Everlasting Gospel . . .* (New York: J. W. Harrison, 1842); Benjamin Winchester, *History of the Priesthood . . .* (Philadelphia: Brown, Bicking, and Guilbert, 1843); David Candland, *A Fireside Visitor; or, Plain Reasoner* (Liverpool: R. James, 1846): Orson Spencer, *Letters Exhibiting the Most Prominent Doctrines . . .* (Liverpool: By the author, 1848).

38. Lorenzo D. Barnes, *References to Prove the Gospel in Its Fulness* (n.p.: n.p., 1841); *Gospel Reflector* 1 (15 June 1841): 315–16. Its publishing history is traced in Crawley, *A Descriptive Bibliography,* 164–65, 195–96 (items 115, 116, 152).

39. Charles Blancher Thompson, *Evidences in Proof of the Book of Mormon* (Batavia, N.Y.: D. D. Waite, 1841); Robert P. Crawford, *An Index; or, Reference to the Second and Third Editions of the Book of Mormon . . .* (Philadelphia: Brown, Bicking, and Guilbert, 1842); Benjamin Winchester, *Synopsis of the Holy Scriptures, and Concordance . . .* (Philadelphia: United States Book and Job Printing Office, 1842); John Routledge, *A Companion for the Bible or Important References . . .* (Liverpool: n.p., 1854).

40. John Jaques, *Catechism for Children* (Liverpool: F. D. Richards, 1854). For discussion of this point, see Davis Bitton, "Mormon Catechisms," in *Task Papers in LDS History,* no. 15 (Salt Lake City: Historical Department of the Church of Jesus Christ of Latter-day Saints, 1976).

41. Francis Gladden Bishop, *A Brief History of the Church* (Salem, Mass.: Blum and Son, 1839); John Corrill, *A Brief History of the Church of Christ . . .* (St. Louis: By the author, 1839); John Whitmer, "History," first printed in serial form, minus the last chapters, in the RLDS *Journal of History* 1 (1908) and more recently and completely in F. Mark McKiernan and Roger D. Launius, eds., *An Early Latter Day Saint History: The Book of John Whitmer* (Independence, Mo.: Herald House, 1980); and in Bruce N. Westergren, ed., *From Historian to Dissident: The Book of John Whitmer* (Salt Lake City: Signature Books,

1995). For the historical context of Whitmer's writing, see George H. Callcott, *History in the United States, 1800–1860* (Baltimore: Johns Hopkins University Press, 1970), 109–19. For a discussion of the broad trends of Mormon history, see chapter 1.

42. Heber C. Kimball, *Journal of Heber C. Kimball, an Elder of the Church . . . Giving an Account of His Mission to Great Britain and the Commencement of the Work of the Lord in That Land* (Nauvoo: Robinson and Smith, 1840); Orson Hyde, *A Voice from Jerusalem; or, A Sketch of the Travels and Ministry of Elder Orson Hyde, Missionary of the Church . . . to Germany, Constantinople, and Jerusalem . . .* (Liverpool: P. P. Pratt, 1842); Lorenzo Snow, *The Italian Mission* (London: W. Aubery, 1851); James B. Meynell, *A Few Incidents of Travel in England . . .* (Boston: John Gooch, 1845); Orson Spencer, *The Prussian Mission* (Liverpool: S. W. Richards, 1853); and Erastus Snow, *One Year in Scandinavia: Results of the Gospel in Denmark and Sweden* (Liverpool: F. D. Richards, 1851). For other mission histories, see George Q. Cannon, *My First Mission* (Salt Lake City: Juvenile Instructor Office, 1879); Andrew Jenson, *History of the Scandinavian Mission* (Salt Lake City: Deseret News, 1927); and Richard L. Evans, *A Century of Mormonism in Great Britain* (Salt Lake City: Deseret News, 1937). The study of Mormon missiology remains in its first stages, although a useful guide to the secondary literature is David J. Whittaker, "Mormon Missiology: An Introduction and Guide to the Sources," in *The Disciple as Witness: Essays on Latter-day Saint History and Doctrine in Honor of Richard Lloyd Anderson,* ed. Stephen D. Ricks, Donald W. Parry, and Andrew H. Hedges (Provo, Utah: Foundation for Ancient Research and Mormon Studies, Brigham Young University, 2000), 459–538.

43. For Smith's urging, see Doctrine and Covenants 123; and Paul C. Richards, "Missouri Persecutions: Petitions for Redress," *BYU Studies* 13 (Summer 1973): 520–43. For redress petitions that were prepared for government authorities, see Clark Johnson, ed., *Mormon Redress Petitions: Documents of the 1833–1838 Missouri Conflict* (Provo, Utah: Religious Studies Center, Brigham Young University, 1992). The best essay placing Joseph Smith at the center of the early Mormon effort to keep various kinds of written records is Dean C. Jessee, "Joseph Smith and the Beginning of Mormon Record Keeping," in *The Prophet Joseph: Essays on the Life and Mission of Joseph Smith,* ed. Larry C. Porter and Susan Easton Black (Salt Lake City: Deseret Book, 1988), 138–60.

44. For further examples of this literature, see B. H. Roberts, ed., *History of the Church of Jesus Christ of Latter-day Saints,* 7 vols. (Salt Lake City: Deseret Book, 1954), 3:347–48; and letter from Orson Hyde to Joseph Smith and George W. Robinson in *Times and Seasons* 1 (March 1840): 71–72. While a few pamphlets were the product of committees, individuals published accounts of their own mistreatment at the hands of their tormentors. See, for example, Parley P. Pratt, *A Short Account of a Shameful Outrage* [Kirtland, Ohio: n.p., 1835]; and Crawley, *A Descriptive Bibliography,* 53 (item 19). For a treatment of the emerging Mormon mood of distress and persecution, see the first chapters of Howard C. Searle, "Early Mormon Historiography: Writing the History of the Mormons, 1830–1858" (Ph.D. diss., University of California at Los Angeles, 1979).

45. Parley P. Pratt, *History of the Late Persecution Inflicted by the State of Missouri upon the Mormons . . .* (Detroit: Dawson and Bates, 1839); *Late Persecution of the Church of Jesus Christ of Latter Day Saints* (New York: J. W. Harrison, 1840).

46. Parley P. Pratt, *An Address by Judge Higbee and Parley P. Pratt . . . to the Citizens of Washington, and to the Public in General* (Washington: n.p., 1840); *An Address by a Min-*

ister of the Church of Jesus Christ of Latter-Day Saints, to the People of England (Manchester: W. R. Thomas, 1840). The publishing history of these two items is detailed in Crawley, *A Descriptive Bibliography,* 104–6 (item 67) and 113–14 (items 72, 73). For the development of the Mormons' faith testament, see David J. Whittaker, "The 'Articles of Faith' in Early Mormon Literature and Thought," in *New Views of Mormon History: A Collection of Essays in Honor of Leonard J. Arrington,* ed. Davis Bitton and Maureen Ursenbach Beecher (Salt Lake City: University of Utah Press, 1987), 63–92.

47. John P. Greene, *Facts Relative to the Expulsion of the Mormons from the State of Missouri* (Cincinnati: R. P. Brooks, 1839); John Taylor, *A Short Account of the Murders . . .* (Springfield, Ill.: n.p., 1839); Ephraim Owen Jr., *Mormons, Memorial of . . .* (Washington, D.C.: Thomas Allen, 1838); Sidney Rigdon, *An Appeal to the American People . . .* (Cincinnati: Glezen and Shepard, 1840); James Mulholland, *An Address to Americans . . .* (Nauvoo: E. Robinson, 1841). Later in the nineteenth century, Mormon imprints demonstrated this same defensive tendency, especially as the church came under assault for its belief in and practice of plural marriage. This topic is treated in David J. Whittaker, "Early Mormon Polygamy Defenses," *Journal of Mormon History* 11 (1984): 43–63; and Whittaker, "The Bone in the Throat," 293–314.

48. Thomas A. Lyne, *A True and Descriptive Account of the Assassination of Joseph and Hyrum Smith . . .* (New York: C. A. Calhoun, 1844); Freeman Nickerson [John Gooch], *Death of the Prophets Joseph and Hyrum Smith . . .* (Boston: J. Gooch, 1844); William M. Daniels, *A Correct Account of the Murder . . .* (Nauvoo, Ill.: J. Taylor, 1845); Lyman O. Littlefield, *A Correct Account of the Murder . . .* (Nauvoo, Ill.: Lyman O. Littlefield, 1845). For more bibliographical detail on the last two citations, see Crawley, *A Descriptive Bibliography,* 298–301 (item 261).

49. N. B. Lundwall, *The Fate of the Persecutors of the Prophet Joseph Smith* (Salt Lake City: Bookcraft, 1952).

50. Eber D. Howe, *Mormonism Unvailed; or, A Faithful Account of that Singular Imposition and Delusion* (Painesville, Ohio: By the author, 1834).

51. John C. Bennett, *History of the Saints; or, An Exposé of Joe Smith and the Mormons* (Cincinnati: E. S. Norris, 1842). For the literature spawned for Mormonism's various dissent movements, see the bibliographical guides compiled by Dale L. Morgan and published in *Western Humanities Review* (1950–53); and Steven L. Shields, *The Latter Day Saint Churches: An Annotated Bibliography* (New York: Garland, 1987).

52. John Hyde Jr., *Mormonism: Its Leaders and Designs* (New York: W. P. Fetridge, 1857); T. B. H. Stenhouse, *The Rocky Mountain Saints* (New York: D. Appleton, 1873); Fanny Stenhouse, *"Tell It All": The Story of a Life Experience in Mormonism* (Hartford, Conn.: A. D. Worthington, 1874); Frank J. Cannon and Harvey J. O'Higgins, *Under the Prophet in Utah: The National Menace of a Political Priestcraft* (Boston: C. M. Clark, 1911); Fawn M. Brodie, *No Man Knows My History* (New York: Alfred A. Knopf, 1945); Jerald Tanner and Sandra Tanner, *Mormonism—Shadow or Reality?* (Salt Lake City: Utah Lighthouse Ministry, 1964). For the beginning of scholarly attention to this literature, see Craig Foster, "Anti-Mormon Pamphleteering in Great Britain, 1837–1860" (Master's thesis, Brigham Young University, 1989); Lynne Watkins Jorgensen, "John Hyde, Jr., Mormon Renegade," *Journal of Mormon History* 17 (1991): 120–44; and Lawrence Foster, "Career Apostates: Reflections on the Works of Jerald and Sandra Tanner," *Dialogue: A Journal of Mormon*

Thought 17 (Summer 1984): 35–60. An extensive bibliography of the Tanners' published work is in Scott Faulring, "An Oral History of the Modern Microfilm Company, 1959–1982" (Senior Seminar Project, History Department, Brigham Young University, 1983). For further material on Mormon dissenters, see Leonard J. Arrington, "Mormonism: Views from Without and Within," *BYU Studies* 14 (Winter 1974): 140–53; and Ronald W. Walker, *Wayward Saints: The Godbeites and Brigham Young* (Urbana: University of Illinois Press, 1998).

53. Leonard J. Arrington, "Centrifugal Tendencies in Mormon History," in *To the Glory of God: Mormon Essays on Great Issues,* ed. Truman G. Madsen and Charles Tate Jr. (Salt Lake City: Deseret Book, 1972), 165–77.

54. See, for example, Benjamin Winchester, *An Examination of a Lecture Delivered by the Rev. H. Perkins . . .* (n.p.: n.p., [ca. 1840]); Samuel Bennett, *A Few Remarks by Way of Reply . . .* (Philadelphia: Brown, Bicking and Guilbert, 1840); John Taylor, *Truth Defended and Methodism Weighed in the Balance and Found Wanting: Being a Reply to . . .* (Liverpool: J. Tompkins, [1840]); George J. Adams, *A Few Plain Facts . . .* (Bedford, England: C. B. Merry, 1841); William Appleby, *Mormonism Consistent! . . .* (Wilmington, Del.: Porter and Neff, 1843); James F. Bell, *A Reply to Bare-Faced Falsehoods . . .* (Liverpool: F. D. Richards, [1851]); Charles W. Wandell, *Reply to Shall We Believe in Mormon?* (Sydney, Australia: n.p., 1852); and Richard Ballantyne, *A Reply to a Tract Written by the Rev. J. Richards* (Madras, India: S. Bowie, 1853). For another kind of "reply," see George Q. Cannon, *A Review of the Decision of the Supreme Court of the United States, in the Case of George Reynolds vs. the United States* (Salt Lake City: Deseret News, 1879).

55. See, for example, B. H. Roberts, *Defense of the Faith and the Saints,* 2 vols. (Salt Lake City: Deseret News, 1907–12); B. H. Roberts, *New Witnesses for God,* 3 vols. (Salt Lake City: Deseret News, 1909, 1911); Joseph Fielding Smith, *Blood Atonement and the Origin of Plural Marriage: A Discussion* (Salt Lake City: Deseret News, 1905); Ben[jamin] E. Rich, *Mr. Durant of Salt Lake City: "That Mormon"* (Salt Lake City: George Q. Cannon and Sons, 1893 and later printings); Hugh Nibley, *No Ma'am That's Not History: A Brief Review of Mrs. Brodie's Reluctant Vindication of a Prophet She Seeks to Expose* (Salt Lake City: Bookcraft, 1946); Hugh Nibley, *Tinkling Cymbals and Sounding Brass: The Art of Telling Tales about Joseph Smith and Brigham Young,* vol. 11 of *The Collected Works of Hugh Nibley,* ed. David J. Whittaker (Salt Lake City and Provo: Deseret Book and Foundation for Ancient Research and Mormon Studies, Brigham Young University, 1991); Gilbert W. Scharffs, *The Truth about "The Godmakers"* (Salt Lake City: Publishers Press, 1986); Paul Hedengren, *In Defense of Faith: Assessing Arguments against Latter-day Saint Belief* (Provo, Utah: Bradford and Wilson, 1985); Daniel C. Peterson and Stephen D. Ricks, *Offenders for a Word: How Anti-Mormons Play Word Games to Attack the Latter-day Saints* (Salt Lake City: Aspen Books, 1992); Stephen E. Robinson, *Are Mormons Christians?* (Salt Lake City: Bookcraft, 1991); Craig L. Blomberg and Stephen E. Robinson, *How Wide the Divide? A Mormon and an Evangelical in Conversation* (Downers Grove, Ill.: InterVarsity, 1997); many of the critical reviews contained in *FARMS Review of Books* (Brigham Young University).

56. For further discussion, see Warren A. Jennings, "Factors in the Destruction of the Mormon Press in Missouri, 1833," *Utah Historical Quarterly* 35 (Winter 1967): 57–76; and Ronald E. Romig and John H. Siebert, "First Impressions: The Independence, Missouri, Printing Operation, 1832–33," *John Whitmer Historical Association Journal* 10 (1990): 51–

66. The mob that destroyed the *The Evening and the Morning Star* press in July 1833 also destroyed the unbound printed sheets of A Book of Commandments. The Kirtland edition of 1835 was titled the Doctrine and Covenants, and the textual alterations in the *Evening and Morning Star* reflect those that appear in this "reprinting." See also Crawley, *A Descriptive Bibliography,* 32–34, 50–51 (items 3, 17); Melvin J. Petersen, "A Study of the Nature of the Significance of the Changes in the Revelations as Found in a Comparison of the *Book of Commandments* and Subsequent Editions of the Doctrine and Covenants" (Master's thesis, Brigham Young University, 1955); and Melvin J. Petersen, "Preparing Early Revelations for Publication," *Ensign* 15 (February 1985): 14–20.

57. See the correspondence between Oliver Cowdery and William W. Phelps in *Latter Day Saints' Messenger and Advocate* 1–2 (October 1834–October 1835). These letters were reprinted in other LDS periodicals and in 1844 as a pamphlet at Liverpool, England. Phelps's letters to his wife, Sally, during this period are in Bruce A. Van Orden, ed., "Writing to Zion: The William W. Phelps Kirtland Letters (1835–1836)," *BYU Studies* 33, no. 3 (1993): 542–93.

58. Max H. Parkin, "Mormon Political Involvement in Ohio," *BYU Studies* 9 (Summer 1969): 484–502; Crawley, *A Descriptive Bibliography,* 51–53 (item 18).

59. Parry D. Sorensen, "Nauvoo Times and Seasons," *Journal of the Illinois State Historical Society* 55 (Summer 1962): 117–35; Robert T. Bray, "*Times and Seasons:* An Archaeological Perspective on Early Latter Day Saints' Printing," *Historical Archaeology* 13 (1979): 53–119; Terence A. Tanner, "The Mormon Press in Nauvoo, 1839–1846," *Western Illinois Regional Studies* 11 (Fall 1988): 5–29.

60. Jerry C. Jolley, "The Sting of the WASP: Early Nauvoo Newspaper—April 1842 to April 1843," *BYU Studies* 22 (Fall 1982): 487–96; Lewis Clark Christian, "A Study of Mormon Knowledge of the American Far West prior to the Exodus (1830–February, 1846)" (Master's thesis, Brigham Young University, 1972). The *Hancock Eagle* was published by the Mormon press from April to October 1846, but it was not technically a Mormon imprint because its audience was non-Mormons. See Crawley, *A Descriptive Bibliography,* 21–22.

61. David J. Whittaker, "East of Nauvoo: Benjamin Winchester and the Early Mormon Church," *Journal of Mormon History* 21 (Fall 1995): 44–46. Winchester issued twelve numbers of twenty-four pages each between 1 January and 15 June 1841. See also Crawley, *A Descriptive Bibliography,* 222–23 (item 178).

62. The bibliographic details for this newspaper are in Ronald D. Dennis, *Welsh Mormon Writings from 1844 to 1862: A Historical Bibliography* (Provo, Utah: Religious Studies Center, Brigham Young University, 1988), 27–32. For the English edition, see Ronald D. Dennis, trans. and ed., *Prophet of the Jubilee* (Provo, Utah: Religious Studies Center, Brigham Young University, 1997).

63. Allen, Esplin, and Whittaker, *Men with a Mission,* 236–66; Crawley, *A Descriptive Bibliography,* 108–13 (item 71). For information on the history and operation of the *Millennial Star* printing office under the management of James Foggo, 1900 to 1930, see William D. Callister, "The Story of James Foggo," *Millennial Star* 92 (22 May 1930): 385–89; and the other articles in the same issue.

64. Crawley, *A Descriptive Bibliography,* 254–56, 306–7 (items 211, 267).

65. This period and the press can be approached in Richard E. Bennett, *Mormons at*

the Missouri, 1846–1852: "And Should We Die" (Norman: University of Oklahoma Press, 1987); Jean Marie Nederhiser, "The *Frontier Guardian:* A Study of Conflicting Loyalties, 1849–1852" (Master's thesis, Iowa State University, 1986); Jean Trumbo, "Orson Hyde's *Frontier Guardian,*" *Iowa Heritage Illustrated* 77 (Summer 1996): 74–85. See also Douglas C. McMurtrie, "The First Printing at Council Bluffs," *Annals of Iowa* 18 (July 1931): 2–11.

66. Paul T. Roberts, "A History of the Development and Objectives of the LDS Church News Section of the Deseret News" (Master's thesis, Brigham Young University, 1983).

67. Basic references for the study of Utah newspapers include Wendell J. Ashton, *Voice in the West: Biography of a Pioneer Newspaper* (New York: Duell, Sloan and Pearce, 1950); J. Cecil Alter, *Early Utah Journalism* (Salt Lake City: Utah State Historical Society, 1938); Luther L. Heller, "A Study of the Utah Newspaper War, 1870–1900" (Master's thesis, Brigham Young University, 1966); Robert P. Holley, ed., *Utah's Newspapers: Traces of Her Past* (Salt Lake City: Marriott Library, University of Utah, 1984) (papers presented at the Utah Newspaper Project Conference, University of Utah, 18 November 1983, includes Dennis McCargar's "Checklist of Utah Newspapers," 107–319); Joseph Sudweeks, *Discontinued LDS Periodicals* (Provo, Utah: Brigham Young University Press, 1955); Monte Burr McLaws, *Spokesman for the Kingdom: Early Mormon Journalism and the Deseret News, 1830–1898* (Provo, Utah: Brigham Young University Press, 1977), which contains an extensive bibliography; Monte Burr McLaws, "The Mormon *Deseret News:* Unique Frontier Newspaper," *Journal of the West* 19 (April 1980): 30–39; and A. R. Mortensen, "The *Deseret News* and Utah, 1850–1867" (Ph.D. diss., University of California at Los Angeles, 1949). See also an early survey by Edward W. Tullidge, "Journalism," an appendix in his *History of Salt Lake City and Its Founders* (Salt Lake City: Star, 1886).

68. David J. Whittaker, "Richard Ballantyne and the Defense of Mormonism in India in the 1850s," in *Supporting Saints: Life Stories of Nineteenth-Century Mormons,* ed. Donald Q. Cannon and David J. Whittaker (Provo, Utah: Religious Studies Center, Brigham Young University, 1985), 175–212.

69. For the Australian Mormon press, see Peter Crawley, "The First Australian Mormon Imprints," *Gradilis Review* [Brigham Young University Graduate Student Association of Library and Information Sciences] 2 (Fall 1973): 38–51.

70. After Pratt retired from the editorial office, Orson Hyde suggested the title, the *Western Standard.* See the introduction to George Q. Cannon, *Writings from the "Western Standard"* (Liverpool: George Q. Cannon, 1864); Jerreld L. Newquist, "The Western Standard," *Improvement Era* 62 (April 1959): 238–39, 274–82; Whittaker, "Parley P. Pratt and the Pacific Mission," 64–71; Lawrence R. Flake, *George Q. Cannon: His Missionary Years* (Salt Lake City: Bookcraft, 1998), 91–124; and Davis Bitton, *George Q. Cannon: A Biography* (Salt Lake City: Deseret Book, 1999), 75–87.

71. For the Mormon publishing campaign, see Whittaker, "The Bone in the Throat," 293–314. For the role of Snow, see Andrew Karl Larson, *Erastus Snow: The Life of a Missionary and Pioneer for the Early Mormon Church* (Salt Lake City: University of Utah Press, 1971), 257–75. Taylor's eastern publishing is detailed in B. H. Roberts, *The Life of John Taylor, Third President of the Church of Jesus Christ of Latter-day Saints* (Salt Lake City: George Q. Cannon and Sons, 1892), 246–71; and Samuel W. Taylor, *The Kingdom or Nothing: The Life of John Taylor, Militant Mormon* (New York: Macmillan, 1976), 177–90. Taylor had

edited a Mormon newspaper in Paris, *Etoile du Deseret [Star of Deseret]*, from May 1851 to April 1852.

72. Ronald W. Walker, "The Stenhouses and the Making of a Mormon Image," *Journal of Mormon History* 1 (1974): 51–72.

73. John Lyon, *The Harp of Zion* (Liverpool and London: S. W. Richards and T. C. Armstrong, 1853); Eliza R. Snow, *Poems: Religious, Political, and Historical* (Liverpool: F. D. Richards, 1856); Orson F. Whitney, *The Poetical Writings of Orson F. Whitney* (Salt Lake City: Juvenile Instructor Office, 1889).

74. Carol Lynn Pearson, *Beginnings* (Garden City, N.Y.: Doubleday, 1975); Clinton F. Larson, *Counterpoint: A Book of Poems* (Provo, Utah: Brigham Young University Press, 1973). For more information about contemporary LDS poetry, see Richard H. Cracroft and Neal E. Lambert, eds., *A Believing People: Literature of the Latter-day Saints* (Provo, Utah: Brigham Young University Press, 1974); the various issues of the *Annual Association of Mormon Letters;* and Eugene England, preface to *Harvest: Contemporary Mormon Poems*, ed. Eugene England and Dennis Clark (Salt Lake City: Signature Books, 1989). For the nineteenth century, see especially J. N. Washburn, "A Critical Study of Latter-day Saint Poetry from 1847–1877" (Master's thesis, Brigham Young University, 1936); T. Edgar Lyon Jr., "Publishing a Book of Mormon Poetry: *The Harp of Zion,*" *BYU Studies* 27 (Winter 1987): 84–95; T. Edgar Lyon Jr., *John Lyon: The Life of a Pioneer Poet* (Provo, Utah: Religious Studies Center, Brigham Young University, 1989); and Maureen Ursenbach Beecher, ed., *The Personal Writings of Eliza Roxcy Snow* (Salt Lake City: University of Utah Press, 1995).

75. Crawley, *A Descriptive Bibliography,* 57–59 (item 23). For a detailed study of early LDS hymnals, see Helen Hanks Macaré, "The Singing Saints: A Study of the Mormon Hymnal, 1835–1950" (Ph.D. diss., University of California at Los Angeles, 1961). For a more recent examination, see Karen Lynn Davidson, *Our Latter-day Hymns: The Stories and the Messages* (Salt Lake City: Deseret Book, 1988); and Michael Hicks, *Mormonism and Music: A History* (Urbana: University of Illinois Press, 1989).

76. These last two hymnals are treated in Crawley, *A Descriptive Bibliography,* 82–83 (item 50) and 96–97 (item 61).

77. J[esse] C. Little and G[eorge] B. Gardner, *A Collection of Sacred Hymns for the Use of the Latter Day Saints* (Bellow Falls, Vt.: Blake and Bailey, 1844). The most recent church hymnal is *Hymns of the Church of Jesus Christ of Latter-day Saints* (Salt Lake City: Deseret Book, 1985).

78. For an overview of the American rural almanac tradition, see Marion Barber Stowell, *Early American Almanacs* (New York: Artemis Books of Burt Franklin, 1977). On the Mormon almanac tradition, see David J. Whittaker, "Almanacs in the New England Heritage of Mormonism," *BYU Studies* 29 (Fall 1989): 89–113; for their larger context, see D. Michael Quinn, *Early Mormonism and the Magic World View,* rev. ed. (Salt Lake City: Signature Books, 1998), 21–24, 277–91.

79. For biographical information on Phelps, see Walter D. Bowen, "The Versatile W. W. Phelps—Mormon Writer, Educator, and Pioneer" (Master's thesis, Brigham Young University, 1958). Valuable in revealing the LDS almanac tradition and Phelps's role in early Utah affairs are the letters Phelps wrote to Brigham Young: 17 September 1855, 9 Septem-

ber 1856, 11 September 1859, 20 September 1860, 4 December 1864, 19 October 1865, 12 December 1865, 29 March 1866, 22 October 1866, Brigham Young Papers, LDS Archives.

80. Sidney Rigdon, *Oration Delivered by Mr. Rigdon on the 4th of July, 1838, at Far West, Caldwell Co., Missouri* (Far West, Mo.: Journal Office, 1838). The oration was reprinted in James H. Hunt, *Mormonism: Embracing the Origin, Rise and Progress of the Sect* (St. Louis, Mo.: Ustick and Davies, 1844), 167–80. A more recent publication is Peter Crawley, "Two Rare Missouri Documents," *BYU Studies* 14 (Summer 1974): 502–27.

81. Joseph Smith, *General Joseph Smith's Views of the Power and Policy of the Government of the United States* (Nauvoo: John Taylor, 1844). Phelps's role in the preparation of this document is revealed in W. W. Phelps to Brigham Young, 6 August 1863, Brigham Young Papers, LDS Archives.

82. Parley P. Pratt, "Proclamation of Twelve Apostles of the Church of Jesus Christ of Latter-day Saints [on death of Joseph and Hyrum Smith]," New York City, 6 April 1845, in *Messages of the First Presidency of the Church of Jesus Christ of Latter-day Saints*, 6 vols, comp. James R. Clark (Salt Lake City: Bookcraft, 1965–1975), 1:252–66. For an examination of the issues that led to Smith's death, which included the suppression of the anti-Smith newspaper, see Dallin H. Oaks, "The Suppression of the *Nauvoo Expositor*," *Utah Law Review* 9 (Winter 1965): 862–903.

83. The text of four of these documents are in "Proclamations of the First Presidency and the Quorum of the Twelve Apostles," *Encyclopedia of Mormonism*, 5 vols., ed. Daniel H. Ludlow (New York: Macmillan, 1992), 3:1151–57.

84. These documents are now most easily accessed in *Messages of the First Presidency*, comp. Clark, vols. 1 and 2.

85. Brigham Young, "Circular of the First Presidency to Stake Presidents, Bishops, and Members," in *Messages of the First Presidency*, comp. Clark, 2:283–95. Its larger significance is discussed in William G. Hartley, "The Priesthood Reorganization of 1877: Brigham Young's Last Achievement," *BYU Studies* 20 (Fall 1979): 3–36. The *Messages of the First Presidency* remains the best printed source for these statements, although the Church Record files, organized by the issuing organization in the LDS Archives, has the most extensive collection of these pronouncements.

86. While a comprehensive guide to these Utah territorial imprints is yet to be issued, a preliminary work is in Douglas C. McMurtrie, *The Beginnings of Printing in Utah, with a Bibliography of the Issues of the Utah Press, 1849–1860* (Chicago: John Calhoun Club, 1931); Douglas C. McMurtrie, "Early Printing in Utah Outside of Salt Lake City," *Utah Historical Quarterly* 5 (July 1932): 83–87; Helen West Conner, "A Check List of Utah Imprints for the Years 1862–1882" (Master's thesis, Catholic University of America, 1962); Brigham Young University Library, comp., "Index to Theater Bills, Salt Lake Theater, 1862–1874," 1971, Brigham Young University Library, Provo, Utah; and Flake, *A Mormon Bibliography*, which lists items issued to the year 1930. During the twentieth century, the church continued to send information to its members by issuing newsletters, study guides, manuals of instruction, and even periodicals. This important literature is beyond the scope of this essay.

87. Many of Young's unpublished sermons are in Elden J. Watson, comp. and ed., *Brigham Young Addresses*, 6 vols. (Salt Lake City: By the compiler, 1979–84). The published sermons are referenced in Watson's work but are not reprinted. For George D. Watt's key

role in beginning this series, see Ronald G. Watt, "Sailing 'The Old Ship Zion': The Life of George D. Watt," *BYU Studies* 18 (Fall 1977): 48–65.

88. Doctrine and Covenants 55:4; 57:11; Lyndon W. Cook, *Joseph Smith and the Law of Consecration* (Provo, Utah: Grandin Book, 1985), 45–55.

89. Parley P. Pratt to Joseph Smith, 22 November 1839, and the reply written by Hyrum Smith, 22 December 1839, Joseph Smith Collection, LDS Archives. For a further discussion of this issue, see Allen, Esplin, and Whittaker, *Men with a Mission*, 244–46.

90. *History of the Church*, 5:367, 19 April 1843. This decision is traced in Robert Bruce Flanders, *Nauvoo: Kingdom on the Mississippi* (Urbana: University of Illinois Press, 1965), 250–51. Wilford Woodruff's Journal, 3–4 February 1842, LDS Archives, contained Smith's revelation on the topic on 4 January 1842, as well as information about the church's purchase of the newspaper. Ebenezer Robinson, an important editor and publisher in Nauvoo until 1842, recalls these events in his "Personal Items of History of the Editor," *Return* (Davis City, Iowa) 2 (May 1880): 258–62.

91. Parley Pratt, "Regulations for the Publishing Department of the Latter-day Saints in the East," *Times and Seasons* 6 (15 January 1845): 778.

92. Ibid. For the context of these events, see Whittaker, "East of Nauvoo," 30–83. Clearly, church authorities recognized the power of the press in the "succession crisis" that followed Smith's death, and events bore them out. Those claimants to Smith's mantle that had the most extensive publishing usually had the greatest number of followers. For the publications of one claimant, James J. Strang, see *Northern Islander*, 24 January 1856; Henry E[dward] Legler, "King Strang's Press," *Literary Collector* 8 (June 1904): 33–40; and Jean Hughes Raber, "Beaver Island King, Prophet and Editor: James Jesse Strang and the Northern Islander," *Michigan History* 75 (September/October 1991): 24–30.

93. Orson Pratt to "The Saints in the Eastern and Middle States," 25 August 1845, *New York Messenger* 2 (30 August 1845): 70–71, reprinted in *Times and Seasons* 6 (15 August 1845) [*sic*]: 997; compare the editorial a month later in *New York Messenger* 2 (20 September 1845): 93. The move to centralize LDS literature was not simply a question of ecclesiastical control; the Mormon leaders understood that the press was crucial to their proselytizing. See the *Prophet* 1 (6 July 1844): 2; and *Times and Seasons* 1 (August 1840): 155; *Times and Seasons* 6 (15 February 1845): 810. By July 1844, women were being urged to organize societies for the distribution of tracts to nonmembers.

94. For Mormon printing in India, see Whittaker, "Richard Ballantyne and the Defense of Mormonism in India in the 1850s," 175–212; for South Africa, see David J. Whittaker, "Early Mormon Imprints in South Africa," *BYU Studies* 20 (Summer 1980): 404–16; George S. Ellsworth, "A History of Mormon Missions in the United States and Canada, 1830–1960" (Ph.D. diss., University of California, 1950), 295.

95. The importance of Liverpool is traced in Philip A. M. Taylor, *Expectations Westward: The Mormons and the Emigration of Their British Converts in the Nineteenth Century* (Edinburgh: Oliver and Boyd, 1965), 160–75; and W. H. G. Armytage, "Liverpool, Gateway to Zion," *Pacific Northwest Quarterly* 48 (April 1957): 39–44. Even during Liverpool's dominance, local and regional printing, especially non-English printing, continued elsewhere. Helpful guides to this non-Liverpool publishing include David J. Whittaker, "Early Mormon Pamphleteering" (Ph.D. diss., Brigham Young University, 1982), appendices E, H, and J; Lyn R. Jacobs, *Mormon Non-English Scriptures, Hymns, and Periodicals, 1830–*

1986: A Descriptive Bibliography (Ithaca, N.Y.: By the author, 1986); Ronald D. Dennis, *Welsh Mormon Writings from 1844 to 1862: A Historical Bibliography* (Provo, Utah: Religious Studies Center, Brigham Young University, 1988); Andrew Jenson, "Scandinavian Latter-Day Saint Literature," *Utah Genealogical and Historical Magazine* 13 (October 1922): 181–91; and William Mulder, "Denmark and the Mormons: The Jørgen W. Schmidt Collection," *Princeton University Library Chronicle* 52 (Spring 1991): 331–57. The important "European Mission Publication Account Books and Ledgers" in the Historical Department of the LDS Church have yet to be studied in detail.

96. Cited in Whittaker, "Early Mormon Pamphleteering," 67, 87–88.

97. *Millennial Star* 12 (1 February 1850): 40–41, 17 (19 May 1855): 315, and 12 (15 May 1851): 153–56; E. L. Sloan, "Publications of the Church," ibid., 20 (23 October 1858): 683–85. For advice given on tract distribution, see Eli B. Kelsey to F. D. Richards, 7 January 1850, ibid., 13 (1 February 1851): 33–37; "Tract Distributing," ibid., 15 (29 October 1853): 713–14, 18 (12 January 1856): 27–29, and 18 (27 September 1856): 617; and *Seer* 1 (November 1853): 166–68.

98. See *Millennial Star* 17 (21 July 1855): 464, 18 (18 October 1856): 665, and 18 (1 November 1856): 697, where the reader is told that with every order an equal number of catalogues will be sent, bound with the pamphlets ordered. Samples of these catalogues are helpful for historians of Mormon Americana.

99. Flake, comp, *A Mormon Bibliography,* lists many of these handbills, and examples can be found both at the LDS Archives and at Special Collections, Harold B. Lee Library, Brigham Young University, Provo, Utah.

100. For instance, see the cautions expressed by Franklin D. Richards and S. W. Richards, *Millennial Star* 13 (15 December 1851): 372, and 14 (3 July 1852): 297. For other references dealing with the Mormon publishing practices, see ibid., 12 (1 February 1850): 40–41, 14 (18 September 1852): 474–75, 17 (12 May 1855): 298–300, 17 (23 June 1855): 399, 18 (5 January 1856): 12, 18 (16 August 1856): 526, 18 (6 September 1856): 564, and 18 (15 November 1856): 734.

101. Quoted in Wilford Woodruff Diary, 9 September 1860, LDS Archives. For examples of the regularly published advertisements for portraits and pictures, see *Millennial Star* 15 (8 January 1853): 27, and 18 (21 June 1856): 394. Brigham Young voiced concerns about LDS publishing in England throughout the 1850s; see, for example, Brigham Young to Orson Pratt, 30 August 1856, Brigham Young Papers, LDS Archives.

102. For Cannon's career, see Andrew Jenson, *LDS Biographical Encyclopedia,* 4 vols. (Salt Lake City: Andrew Jenson History Co., 1901–36), 1:42–51; Flake, *George Q. Cannon;* and Bitton, *George Q. Cannon.*

103. Cannon to Young, 30 March 1861, Brigham Young Papers, LDS Archives. This letter reminds the book historian that the total of items printed did not equal the total of items bound. Because of binding costs, it is clear specific titles were bound only as needed after a few hundred were bound when first printed.

104. Brigham Young to George Q. Cannon, 15 May and 12 November 1861, Brigham Young Papers, LDS Archives. See also "Office Journal of Brigham Young," 11 and 14 May and 12 November 1861, LDS Archives. Young's decision reflected more than an impatience with inventory; he felt some of the material was filled with error, probably including several tracts written by Orson Pratt, *The Great First Cause* and *The Holy Spirit,* and Lucy

Mack Smith's *Biographical Sketches of Joseph Smith the Prophet and His Progenitors for Many Generations* (Liverpool: S. W. Richards, 1853). This last volume had the added disadvantage, in Young's mind, of providing an unduly positive picture of some members of the Smith family, who by 1860 had begun to organize an opposition church. For Orson Pratt's tracts, see Whittaker, "Orson Pratt," 27–41. For information about the Lucy Mack Smith history, see Jan Shipps, *Mormonism: The Story of a New Religious Tradition* (Urbana: University of Illinois Press, 1985), 87–107.

105. For a sampling of sources dealing with Cannon's attitudes, the home literature movement, and Mormon historical attitudes toward fiction, see Stephen Kent Ehat, "How to Condemn Noxious Novels," *Century II* (1 December 1976): 36–48; Orson F. Whitney, "Home Literature," *Contributor* 9 (June 1888): 297–302; Richard H. Cracroft, "Seeking 'The Good, the Pure, the Elevating': A Short History of Mormon Fiction, (Pt. I)," *Ensign* 11 (June 1981): 56–62; Richard H. Cracroft, "Nephi, Seer of Modern Times: The Home Literature Novels of Nephi Anderson," *BYU Studies* 25 (Spring 1985): 3–15; and Matthew Durrant and Neal E. Lambert, "From Foe to Friend: The Mormon Embrace of Fiction," *Utah Historical Quarterly* 50 (Fall 1982): 325–39.

106. For examples of these book catalogues, see Flake and Draper, comps., *A Mormon Bibliography, 1830–1930, Indexes*, 22–23.

107. Lawrence R. Flake, "The Development of the *Juvenile Instructor* under George Q. Cannon and Its Functions in Latter-day Saint Religious Education" (Master's thesis, Brigham Young University, 1969); Edwin F. Parry, "Early Writers for the *Juvenile Instructor*," *Juvenile Instructor* 50 (October 1915): 684–86.

108. An overview of Deseret Book's history is provided in Eleanor Knowles, *Deseret Book Company: 125 Years of Inspiration, Information and Ideas* (Salt Lake City: Deseret Book, 1991). See also Deseret Book Company, *Deseret Book Company, 1866–1976* (Salt Lake City: Deseret Book, 1976). More recent developments are surveyed in Leonard J. Arrington and Davis Bitton, *The Mormon Experience: A History of the Latter-day Saints* (New York: Alfred A. Knopf, 1979), 270; and in an 11 June 1999 press release by Deseret Book announcing Deseret Book's purchasing of Bookcraft and the restructuring of the new company, copy in possession of the authors.

109. The literature dealing with these periodicals is large and growing. For *Woman's Exponent,* see Carol Cornwall Madsen, "'Remember the Women of Zion': A Study of the Editorial Content of the *Woman's Exponent,* a Mormon Woman's Journal, 1872–1914" (Master's thesis, University of Utah, 1977); Alfene Page, "*Woman's Exponent:* Cradle of Literary Culture among Early Mormon Women" (Master's thesis, Utah State University, 1988); and Tarla Rai Peterson, "The *Woman's Exponent,* 1872–1914: Champion for 'The Rights of the Women of Zion and the Rights of Women of All Nations,'" in *A Voice of Their Own: The Woman Suffrage Press, 1840–1910,* ed. Martha M. Solomon (Tuscaloosa: University of Alabama Press, 1991), 165–82.

For *Young Woman's Journal,* see R. Paul Cracroft, "Susa Young Gates: Her Life and Literary Work" (Master's thesis, University of Utah, 1951); and Sherry Baker, "Creating a Shared History: Serial Narratives in the *Young Woman's Journal,* 1889–1894" (Master's thesis, University of Utah, 1988).

For the *Contributor,* see Junius F. Wells, "The Contributor," *Improvement Era* 33 (November 1929): 55–57.

110. B. H. Roberts, "The Beginning of the *Improvement Era*, 1897," *Improvement Era* 28 (July 1925): 869–72.

111. The essays of Carol Cornwall Madsen, written in preparation of a biography, present the best view of Wells. See especially Madsen's "A Bluestocking in Zion: The Literary Life of Emmeline B. Wells," *Dialogue: A Journal of Mormon Thought* 16 (Spring 1983): 126–40; "Emmeline B. Wells, a Voice for Mormon Women," *John Whitmer Historical Association Journal* 2 (1982): 11–21; and "Emmeline B. Wells: Romantic Rebel," in *Supporting Saints,* ed. Cannon and Whittaker, 305–41. On Gates, see James B. Allen and Jessie L. Embry, "'Provoking the Brethren to Good Works': Susa Young Gates, the Relief Society, and Genealogy," *BYU Studies* 31 (Spring 1991): 115–38; and Rebecca Foster Cornwall, "Susa Young Gates: The Thirteenth Apostle," in *Sister Saints,* ed. Vicky Burgess-Olsen (Provo, Utah: Brigham Young University Press, 1978), 61–93; and Cracroft, "Susa Young Gates."

112. For more on Jenson, see Keith W. Perkins, "A Study of the Contributions of Andrew Jenson to the Writing and Preservation of LDS Church History" (Master's thesis, Brigham Young University, 1971); Louis G. Reinwand, "Andrew Jenson, Latter-day Saint Historian," *BYU Studies* 14 (Autumn 1973): 29–46; and Allan Kent Powell, "Andrew Jenson," in *Utah History Encyclopedia,* ed. Allan Kent Powell (Salt Lake City: University of Utah Press, 1994), 284.

113. James E. Talmage, *Articles of Faith* (Salt Lake City: Deseret News, 1899).

114. For more detail about the maturing of Mormon doctrine, see Thomas G. Alexander, *Mormonism in Transition: A History of the Latter-day Saints, 1890–1930* (Urbana: University of Illinois Press, 1986), esp. 272–306. There were other thorny issues as well. The first edition of the documentary *History of the Church* failed to contain Smith's celebrated King Follett Discourse, which presented the untraditional views of Smith on the Godhead. The speech had been typeset but the signature containing it (around pages 302–17 of volume 6) had been deleted when the work went to the binders, without the permission of B. H. Roberts, the editor of the work. Returning to Utah, Roberts ordered 10,000 copies of the discourse printed and circulated to local church leaders, and the material was replaced in later editions of the *History of the Church.* See Edgar Lyon, "Church Historians I Have Known," *Dialogue: A Journal of Mormon Thought* 11 (Winter 1978): 14–22. This is traced in more detail in Lyon's oral history, copy in the LDS Archives.

115. Lorin F. Wheelwright, "'The Instructor': A Voice of Truth for 105 Years, 1866–1970," *Improvement Era* 73 (October 1970): 16–19; David Lawrence McKay, "Goodbye, the Instructor," *Instructor* 105 (December 1970): 444–48; Vern Maeser Young, "A Readership Study of the *Instructor* Magazine" (Master's thesis, Brigham Young University, 1970).

116. Patricia Ann Mann, "A History of the *Relief Society Magazine,* 1914–1970" (Master's thesis, Brigham Young University, 1971).

117. For general studies of Mormon periodicals, see A. Richard Robertson, "A Comparative History of Periodicals of the Church of Jesus Christ of Latter-day Saints" (Master's thesis, University of Utah, 1951); Richard G. Moore, "A History of Mormon Periodicals from 1830–1838" (Master's thesis, Brigham Young University, 1983); Harrison R. Merrill, "The Latter-day Saint Press, 1830–1930" (Master's thesis, Columbia University, 1930); Virgil V. Peterson, "Early Mormon Journalism," *Mississippi Valley Historical Review* 35 (March 1949): 627–38; and "Church Periodicals," appendix 3, in *Encyclopedia of Mormonism,* ed.

Ludlow, 4:1659–64. In this appendix, we have ignored the important foreign-language publications and periodicals.

118. For more on the *Liahona*, see Arnold K. Garr, "A History of *Liahona: The Elders' Journal:* A Magazine for the Mormon Missions of America, 1903–1945" (Ph.D. diss., Brigham Young University, 1986).

119. The best overview is the unpublished essay of Glen and Barbara Wahlquist, "Zion's Printing and Publishing Company: A Page from the Past" (paper presented at the annual meeting of the Mormon History Association, Omaha, Nebraska, May 1983).

120. Jay M. Todd, "A Status Report on Church Magazines: A Look at How They Came to Be as They Are," *Ensign* 6 (February 1976): 70–74; Jay M. Todd, "Power in Their Pages," *Ensign* 26 (January 1996): 65–67.

121. For a listing of church periodicals, see "Church Periodicals," appendix 3, in *Encyclopedia of Mormonism*, ed. Ludlow, 4:1659–60. For a brief summary of the magazines, see *Ensign* 27 (July 1997): 80.

122. James E. Talmage, *Jesus the Christ* (Salt Lake City: Deseret News, 1915).

123. B. H. Roberts, *The Mormon Doctrine of Deity* (Salt Lake City: Deseret News, 1903); B. H. Roberts, *The Seventy's Course in Theology*, 5 vols. (Salt Lake City: Deseret News, 1907–12); John A. Widtsoe, *A Rational Theology* (Salt Lake City: General Priesthood Committee, 1915). For a useful guide to the published works of LDS general authorities through the late 1970s, see Gary Gillum, "Out of the Books Which Shall Be Written," *Dialogue: A Journal of Mormon Thought* 12 (Summer 1979): 99–123.

124. Joseph F. Smith, *Gospel Doctrine: Selections from the Sermons and Writings . . .* (Salt Lake City: Deseret News, 1919).

125. Joseph Fielding Smith, *The Progress of Man* (Salt Lake City: Genealogical Society of Utah, 1936); *Answers to Gospel Questions*, 5 vols. (Salt Lake City: Deseret Book, 1957–66); *Man, His Origin and Destiny* (Salt Lake City: Deseret Book, 1954); *Doctrines of Salvation*, 3 vols. (Salt Lake City: Bookcraft, 1954).

126. Bruce R. McConkie, *Mormon Doctrine*, 2d ed. (Salt Lake City: Bookcraft, 1966).

127. Lowell L. Bennion, *Religion and the Pursuit of Truth* (Salt Lake City: Deseret Book, 1959); Lowell L. Bennion, *The Best of Lowell L. Bennion: Selected Writings, 1928–1988*, ed. Eugene England (Salt Lake City: Deseret Book, 1988); Hugh W. Nibley, *The Collected Works of Hugh W. Nibley*, 14 vols. to date (Salt Lake City and Provo, Utah: Deseret Book and Foundation for Ancient Research and Mormon Studies, Brigham Young University, 1986–).

128. J. Reuben Clark, McKay's counselor, also indirectly repudiated the book as official doctrine in a speech reported in the *Deseret News*, Church News Section, 87 (10 July 1954): 2, 9–11. The talk was given on 7 July 1954. For one of McKay's statements, see William Lee Stokes, "An Official Position," *Dialogue: A Journal of Mormon Thought* 12 (Winter 1979): 90–92.

129. One reviewer claimed to have found 1,200 "errors" of fact and interpretation. See David O. McKay Diary, 7, 8 and 27, 28 January 1960, David O. McKay Papers, LDS Archives, which contains copies of the evaluations. See also David John Buerger, "Speaking with Authority: The Theological Influence of Elder Bruce R. McConkie," *Sunstone* 10 (March 1985): 8–13. The second edition of *Mormon Doctrine* was published in 1966. The textual changes can be seen in the useful parallel column comparison by Dennis C. Davis (1971),

copy in Harold B. Lee Library, Brigham Young University. See also Erich Robert Paul, *Science, Religion, and Mormon Cosmology* (Urbana: University of Illinois Press, 1992), esp. chapter 8.

130. George Reynolds, *A Complete Concordance to the Book of Mormon* (Salt Lake City: n.p., 1900); Joseph B. Keeler, *Concordance to the Doctrine and Covenants* (printed with the 1918 edition); John Bluth, *Concordance to the Doctrine and Covenants* (Salt Lake City: Deseret Book, 1945); Eldon Ricks, *Concordance of the LDS Standard Works* (Provo, Utah: Foundation for Ancient Research and Mormon Studies, Brigham Young University, 1995 edition).

131. *A Topical Guide to the Scriptures of the Church of Jesus Christ of Latter-day Saints* (Salt Lake City: Deseret Book, 1977).

132. For a useful overview of these publications, see Bryan Waterman, "A Guide to the Mormon Universe: Mormon Organizations and Periodicals," *Sunstone* 17 (December 1994): 44–64. Mormon publishing in cyberspace is treated in Lauramaery Gold, *Mormons on the Internet, 2000–2001* (Roseville, Calif.: Prima, 2000).

133. For Keeler's work, see Clinton D. Christensen, "Joseph Brigham Keeler: The Master's Builder" (Master's thesis, Brigham Young University, 1997), 153–69.

134. John A. Widtsoe, *Priesthood and Church Government* (Salt Lake City: Deseret Book, 1939); *General Handbook of Instructions* (Salt Lake City: Church of Jesus Christ of Latter-day Saints, 1976–89); *Melchizedek Priesthood Handbook* (Salt Lake City: Church of Jesus Christ of Latter-day Saints, 1948, 1956, 1959, 1962, 1964, 1975, 1984).

135. Brian H. Stuy, *Collected Discourses, Delivered by Wilford Woodruff, His Two Counselors, the Twelve Apostles . . .* (Burbank, Calif.: B. H. S. Publishing, 1987–). Studies of the church's general conferences include Jay R. Lowe, "A Study of the General Conferences of the Church of Jesus Christ of Latter-day Saints, 1830–1901" (Ph.D. diss., Brigham Young University, 1972); Gordon Shepherd and Gary Shepherd, *A Kingdom Transformed: Themes in the Development of Mormonism* (Salt Lake City: University of Utah Press, 1984), which examines themes in the context of doctrinal change; and Noel B. Reynolds, "The Coming Forth of the Book of Mormon in the Twentieth Century," *BYU Studies* 38, no. 2 (1999): 6–47, which examines the frequency of Book of Mormon citations at general conference and notes an increasing emphasis.

136. Suggestions for further research in Mormon imprint literature are explored by David J. Whittaker, "The Web of Print: Toward a History of the Book in Early Mormon Culture," *Journal of Mormon History* 23 (Spring 1997): 1–41.

Mormon Americana:
A Guide to Reference Works and Bibliographies

TOO LITTLE ATTENTION is paid to those hardy souls who track the sources, organize specialized bibliographies, or compile other reference works that historians find so valuable. Like maps to an unknown terrain, these "helps" start the researcher in the right direction and remain essential tools to those who continue to navigate the difficult geography of scholarly research.

There are numerous such reference works that can assist the student of Mormon history. This appendix describes some of the more valuable ones. Most of these are also listed in James B. Allen, Ronald W. Walker, and David J. Whittaker's *Studies in Mormon History, 1830–1997: An Indexed Bibliography* (Urbana: University of Illinois Press, in cooperation with the Smith Institute for LDS History, Brigham Young University, 2000). However, for those who do not have access to this work or who may be overwhelmed by its number of references, we provide here a guide to basic historical research in Mormon sources.

Reference Works and Encyclopedias

Perhaps the first thing a beginner to Mormon history should do is consult a general survey. We recommend three works: (1) B. H. Roberts, *A Comprehensive History of the Church,* 6 vols. (Salt Lake City: Deseret News, 1930), a dated but still valuable multivolume series written by one of Mormonism's leading intellectuals of the time; (2) James B. Allen and Glen M. Leonard, *The Story of the Latter-day Saints* (Salt Lake City: Deseret Book, 1976; 2d ed., rev., 1992), a more concise and recent volume that examines the entire compass of Mormon history, including the often neglected twentieth-century church; and (3) Leonard J. Arrington and Davis Bitton, *The Mormon Experience: A History of the Latter-day Saints* (New York: Alfred A. Knopf, 1979), which approaches Mormonism through a series of themes and is designed for the more advanced or scholarly reader.

Beyond these general works, the student of Mormon history will want to consult reference works and bibliographies, even older ones because these can provide a window to the attitudes and scholarship of former times. The earliest such publications were printed as interviews or statements meant for use in larger works. Examples include Joseph Young's essay in John Hayward, *The Religious Creeds and Statistics of Every Christian Denomination in the United States and British Provinces* (Boston: John Hayward, 1836), 139–40, or Joseph Smith's response to an inquiry made by the Chicago newspaperman John Wentworth, who wanted information about the church. Smith's "Wentworth letter," now considered a seminal statement about church history and belief, was published in the *Times and Seasons* 3 (1 March 1842): 706–10.

When the church was later established in Utah, more lengthy reference works began to appear. Most continued the pattern of combining doctrine and history. These included Franklin D. Richards, *A Compendium of the Faith and Doctrines of the Church of Jesus Christ of Latter-day Saints* (London: LDS Book Depot, 1857); and George A. Smith, *The Rise, Progress, and Travels of the Church of Jesus Christ of Latter-day Saints* (Salt Lake City: Deseret News, 1869). See also John Jaques, *The Church of Jesus Christ of Latter-day Saints: Its Priesthood, Organization, Doctrines, Ordinances and History* (Salt Lake City: Deseret News, 1882); Abraham H. Cannon, *A Hand-book of Reference to the History, Chronology, Religion, and Country of the Latter-day Saints* (Salt Lake City: Juvenile Instructor Office, 1884); Andrew Jenson, *The Historical Record: A Monthly Periodical Devoted Exclusively to Historical, Biographical, Chronological, and Statistical Matters,* 9 vols. (Salt Lake City: By the author, 1882–90); and Andrew Jenson, *Encyclopedic History of the Church of Jesus Christ of Latter-day Saints* (Salt Lake City: Deseret News, 1941). Two twentieth-century general reference guides are Melvin R. Brooks, *LDS Reference Encyclopedia,* 2 vols. (Salt Lake City: Bookcraft, 1960–65); and Rulon T. Burton, *We Believe: Doctrine and Principles of the Church of Jesus Christ of Latter-day Saints* (Salt Lake City: Tabernacle Books, 1994).

The most well-known summary of Mormon beliefs is the "Articles of Faith," a set of thirteen brief doctrinal statements. For a history of the "Articles of Faith" in LDS print literature, see David J. Whittaker, "The 'Articles of Faith' in Early Mormon Literature and Thought," in *New Views of Mormon History: A Collection of Essays in Honor of Leonard J. Arrington,* ed. Davis Bitton and Maureen Ursenbach Beecher (Salt Lake City: University of Utah Press, 1987), 63–92. A popular, twentieth-century summary of doctrine is Bruce R. McConkie, *Mormon Doctrine,* 2d ed. (Salt Lake City: Bookcraft, 1966). Although this work was not meant as an official church publication, because of McConkie's prominence as a general church authority and his authoritative writing style, many Mormons have considered it such. Some of McConkie's sweeping and controversial statements were modified in the second edition.

In recent years, Mormon scholars have produced a number of general reference works, including Davis Bitton, *Historical Dictionary of Mormonism* (Metuchen, N.J.: Scarecrow, 1994), which contains a bibliography of basic works, 275–321; Allan Kent Powell, ed., *Utah History Encyclopedia* (Salt Lake City: University of Utah Press, 1994);

and David J. Whittaker, ed., *Mormon Americana: A Guide to Sources and Collections in the United States* (Provo, Utah: BYU Studies, 1995). This last work is frequently cited in the pages that follow because (1) its essays describe the libraries that hold Mormon material as well as offering some information about their collections; and (2) it contains essays that focus on specific topics in Mormon history.

The most comprehensive guide to the Mormon experience is Daniel H. Ludlow, ed., *Encyclopedia of Mormonism,* 5 vols. (New York: Macmillan, 1992). Edited from Brigham Young University but using the scholarly talents of many people throughout the United States and even beyond, including some non-Mormons, this reference work is rich in photographs, charts, and statistical information. It also has short bibliographies following most entries. Volume 5 is an appendix volume containing the texts of the unique Mormon scriptures: the Book of Mormon, the Doctrine of Covenants, and the Pearl of Great Price.

The *Deseret News Church Almanac* (1974–) offers brief information on history, biography, chronology, statistical data, and other items of popular interest. Since many of these annual volumes have focused on a special topic, succeeding issues have a comprehensive but selective index.

Place Guides and Atlases

When moving to the Intermountain West, the Mormons depended on the works of such government-sponsored explorers and cartographers as John C. Frémont and Howard Stansbury. However, the settlers also made maps and trail guides of their own. No comprehensive study of these efforts has been published (some remain in manuscript), but a number of useful, specifically focused works have appeared in recent years. The best studies of the Mormon awareness of the West prior to their emigration are written by Lewis Clark Christian: "A Study of Mormon Knowledge of the American Far West prior to the Exodus (1830–February, 1846)" (Master's thesis, Brigham Young University, 1972); and "A Study of the Mormon Western Migration between February 1846 and July 1847 with Emphasis on and Evaluation of the Factors That Led to the Mormons' Choice of Salt Lake Valley as the Site of Their Initial Colony" (Ph.D. diss., Brigham Young University, 1976). Additional trail information is provided in *West from Fort Bridger: The Pioneering of Immigrant Trails across Utah, 1846–1850,* edited with an introduction by J. Roderic Korns and Dale L. Morgan, revised and updated by Will Bagley and Harold Schindler (Logan: Utah State University Press, 1994); and Alexander L. Baugh, "John C. Frémont's Expeditions into Utah: An Historical Analysis of the Explorer's Contributions and Significance to the Region" (Master's thesis, Brigham Young University, 1986). Works that emphasize the exploration and trails of Utah include William B. Smart and Donna T. Smart, eds., *Over the Run: The Parley P. Pratt Exploring Expedition to Southern Utah, 1849–50* (Logan: Utah State University Press, 1999); and Peter H. DeLaFosse, ed., *Trailing the Pioneers: A Guide to Utah's Emigrant Trails, 1829–1869* (Salt Lake City: University of Utah Press and Utah Crossroads, Oregon-California Trails Association, 1994). An excellent guide to nineteenth-century cartography is Riley M. Moffat, *Maps of Utah to 1900: An Annotated Cartobibliography* (Santa Cruz, Calif.: Western Association of Map Libraries, 1980), which is the published version of Moffat's master's thesis.

For sources dealing with the Mormon trail and the organizations that sponsor or encourage research on western trails, see Stanley B. Kimball, "Mormon Emigration Trails," in *Mormon Americana: A Guide to Sources and Collections in the United States,* ed. David J. Whittaker (Provo, Utah: BYU Studies, 1995), 406–36. (References to this volume will hereafter be cited as *Mormon Americana.*) A useful guide is William E. Hill, *The Mormon Trail, Yesterday and Today* (Logan: Utah State University Press, 1996). For this topic and for most of the topics listed below, readers should also consult the appropriate subject headings in *Studies in Mormon History.*

A specialized reference work that deals with Mormon oceanic migration is Conway B. Sonne, *Ships, Saints, and Mariners: A Maritime Encyclopedia of Mormon Migration, 1830–1890* (Salt Lake City: University of Utah Press, 1987).

Two recent and professionally prepared atlases are Wayne L. Wahlquist, ed. *Atlas of Utah* (Provo, Utah: Brigham Young University Press, 1981); and S. Kent Brown, Donald Q. Cannon, and Richard H. Jackson, eds., *Historical Atlas of Mormonism* (New York: Simon and Schuster, 1994). In addition, LaMar C. Berrett is working with others on a six-volume guide to Mormon history sites that will include maps and local information. The first of these is A. Gary Anderson, Donald Q. Cannon, Larry E. Dahl, and Larry C. Porter, *Sacred Places: New England and Eastern Canada, a Comprehensive Guide to Early LDS Historical Sites,* general ed. LaMar C. Berrett (Salt Lake City: Bookcraft, 1999).

Guides to specific areas and eras of Mormon history have also appeared. Three volumes by Richard Neitzel Holzapfel and T. Jeffery Cottle are useful for their combination of historic photographs, historical description, and locally focused maps for the Joseph Smith era: *Old Mormon Palmyra and New England: Historic Photographs and Guide* (Santa Ana, Calif.: Fieldbook Productions, 1991); *Old Mormon Kirtland and Missouri: Historic Photographs and Guide* (Santa Ana, Calif.: Fieldbook Productions, 1991); and *Old Mormon Nauvoo, 1839–1846: Historic Photographs and Guide* (Provo, Utah: Grandin Book, 1990). Each contains bibliographies.

For other place guides, see R. Don Oscarson and Stanley B. Kimball, *The Travelers' Guide to Historic Mormon America* (Salt Lake City: Bookcraft, 1965); William C. and Eloise Anderson, *Guide to Mormon History Travel,* 5th ed. (Spanish Fork, Utah: Banta ISG, 1997); and Stanley B. Kimball, *Historic Sites and Markers along the Mormon and Other Great Western Trails* (Urbana: University of Illinois Press, 1988). Karl R. Anderson and Keith W. Perkins's *Walk through the Sacred Land of "The Ohio": A Personal Guidebook through the Land* (n.p.: By the authors, 1995) introduces readers to Mormon sites in Ohio. For the LDS sites in the United Kingdom, see James Moss and Lavelle Moss, *Historic Sites of the Church of Jesus Christ of Latter-day Saints in the British Isles* (Salt Lake City: Publishers Press for the Church of Jesus Christ of Latter-day Saints, 1987).

In the twentieth century, private foundations, such as the Utah Heritage Foundation, and the LDS Church itself have sought to preserve and restore important Mormon historical places. These range in size and location from the large community of Nauvoo, Illinois, to such smaller locations as central Utah's Cove Fort. A useful descriptive and bibliographical guide to these locations is Steven L. Olsen, "Museums and Historic Sites of Mormonism," in *Mormon Americana*, 522–37. A number of guides have been published for Utah sites and, more particularly, for Salt Lake City's architectural history. For an extended list of such guides, see the keyword "Guidebooks" in *Studies in Mormon History*.

Identifying and describing Mormon historic sites is one thing, but the student of Mormon history should also be aware of the interpretive works dealing with Mormon historical and cultural geography. No fully adequate guide to this kind of work exists, but many helpful sources are indexed in *Studies in Mormon History* under the keywords "Cultural geography," "Historical geography," "Mormon cultural region," "Mormon landscape," and "Mormon village."

Mormons in Manuscripts: The Records of LDS History

The published "secondary" works mentioned above are recommended as starting points for research. But the most difficult and most exciting work comes when the student deals with primary sources. These sources include personal and institutional records, most of which exist in manuscript form, although the number of published primary sources is growing.

From the day the church was organized, Latter-day Saints were commanded to keep records (see Doctrine and Covenants 21:1, April 6, 1830), and various individuals were assigned to collect historical material relating to the institutional history of the church. This process is described in Dean C. Jessee, "Joseph Smith and the Beginning of Mormon Record Keeping," in *The Prophet Joseph: Essays on the Life and Mission of Joseph Smith,* ed. Larry C. Porter and Susan Easton Black (Salt Lake City: Deseret Book, 1988), 138–60.

These manuscripts as well as other sources were taken to Utah during the church's exodus to the Great Basin to become the first holdings of the Church Historian's Office in Salt Lake City. Now known as the LDS Historical Department, this archive has become the single most important repository of Mormon records, with material spanning the entire history of the church. Historical Department collections range from individual journals and papers, including those of most presidents of the church, to local church records and manuscript histories of the church's "missions" or proselytizing areas. Not all of these collections are available for research because the church, like other private archives, controls access to its institutional records. Registers describing the Historical Department's larger collections are available for research.

A useful introduction to the resources of the Historical Department is Glenn N. Rowe, "The Historical Department and Library of the LDS Church," in *Mormon Americana*, 154–71. Other helpful guides include Charles P. Adams and Gustive O. Larson, "A Study of the LDS Church Historian's Office, 1830–1900," *Utah Historical Quarterly* 40 (Fall 1972): 370–89; Davis Bitton and Leonard J. Arrington, *Mormons and Their Historians* (Salt Lake City: University of Utah Press, 1988); and the index listing of *Studies in Mormon History* under the keyword "Historical Department."

The L. Tom Perry Special Collections of the Harold B. Lee Library at Brigham Young University in Provo, Utah, has the second largest Mormon manuscript collection. Managed as an open research facility (with the exception of BYU's own institutional archives), this institution has a broader focus than the LDS Historical Department; it holds and collects material that places Mormonism in its wider cultural matrix, especially the American West. A brief overview of the Harold B. Lee Library's Special Collections is provided by David J. Whittaker, "The Archives of the Mormon Experience at Brigham Young University," in *Mormon Americana*, 100–110.

Still another important Mormon-run archive is the LDS Family History Library. Its main facility is located in Salt Lake City, but branch libraries exist throughout the United States and at Mormon population centers throughout the world. Several of the main research tools of the Family History Library are available on the Internet at the address "familysearch.org," including the library's main index of material. Those researchers who are interested in examining the library's microfilmed materials may secure them either in Salt Lake City or at one of the Family History Library's satellite locations. While the library's primary function is to gather records helpful to members who are completing their family histories and genealogies, its worldwide microfilmers have gathered records useful to historians with many other interests, including family history, community history, and demographic research. For an introduction to this repository, see James B. Allen, "The LDS Family History Library, Salt Lake City," in *Mormon Americana*, 135–53; and Johni Cerny and Wendy Elliott, eds., *The Library: A Guide to the LDS Family History Library* (Salt Lake City: Ancestry, 1988).

Mormon material is also found in libraries outside Utah. The Library of Congress's "National Union Catalogue of Manuscript Collections" contains a number of Mormon entries, while other U.S. libraries have issued guides to their Mormon-related materials. *Mormon Americana* provides information on many of these repositories, including the major libraries in Utah; the Hubert Howe Bancroft Library at the University of California, Berkeley; the Henry E. Huntington Library, San Marino, California; the Houghton Library, Harvard University; the New York Public Library; the State Historical Society of Wisconsin; the Beinecke Library, Yale University; and the Archives of the Reorganized Church of Jesus Christ of Latter Day Saints, Independence, Missouri. The concluding essay in *Mormon Americana* surveys other libraries holding Mormon or Mormon-related material.

No union catalogue exists for these widely scattered materials, although students will find Davis Bitton's *Guide to Mormon Diaries and Autobiographies* (Provo, Utah: Brigham Young University Press, 1977) helpful. This reference work provides detailed annotations to more than 2,800 diaries, memoirs, and autobiographies, including information about where these documents can be found and the publishing data if they have been printed. Since Bitton's work was issued more than twenty-five years ago and since libraries continue to access material at a rapid rate, the *Guide to Mormon Diaries and Autobiographies* lists no more than half of this genre's now available literature.

The task of research has been helped by the growing number of published sources that have been issued in recent years. When completing their editing projects, Mormon scholars have used a variety of approaches. On one end of the editing spectrum is the exemplary work of Dean C. Jessee, whose publications include materials drawn from the papers of Joseph Smith and Brigham Young and are cited below. Jessee has refused to publish any document until he has examined it several times, double-checked its spelling and punctuation, and provided background notes. In contrast, less careful editors have produced works without consulting original documents or even seeking to understand them.[1]

The documentary approach to Mormon history began with the first generation of Mormon record keepers, who, following the fashion of the time, concentrated on publishing collections of primary documents. One example of this compiling method to history was "Joseph Smith's History" (sometimes known as the *Documentary History of the Church* or simply the *History of the Church*), which was first published in the *Times and Seasons,* the *Deseret News,* and the *Latter-day Saints' Millennial Star.* Other examples include the published missionary diaries of the early Mormon leaders Wilford Woodruff and Heber C. Kimball. Although these early collections and several like them were not edited according to modern scholarly standards, they retain value and should be consulted by researchers.

The following items are representative of some of the significant documentary collections to appear in the last half-century: William E. Berrett and Alma P. Burton, *Readings in L.D.S. Church History,* 3 vols. (Salt Lake City: Deseret Book, 1953–58); William Mulder and A. Russell Mortensen, eds., *Among the Mormons: Historic Accounts by Contemporary Observers* (New York: Alfred A. Knopf, 1958); LeRoy R. Hafen and Ann W. Hafen, eds., *The Utah Expedition, 1857–1858: A Documentary Account of the United States Military Movement under Colonel Albert Sidney Johnston and the Resistance by Brigham Young and the Mormon Nauvoo Legion* (1958; reprint, Glendale, Calif.: Arthur H. Clark, 1982); James R. Clark, ed., *Messages of the First Presidency,* 6 vols. (Salt Lake City: Bookcraft, 1965–75); Dan Vogel, ed., *Early Mormon Documents,* 3 vols. (Salt Lake City: Signature Books, 1996, 1998, 2000); and Carol Cornwall Madsen, comp. and ed., *Journey to Zion: Voices from the Mormon Trail* (Salt Lake City: Deseret Book, 1997).

Editions of minute books include Donald Q. Cannon and Lyndon W. Cook, eds., *Far West Record: Minutes of the Church of Jesus Christ of Latter-day Saints, 1830–1844* (Salt Lake City: Deseret Book, 1983); and Fred C. Collier and William S. Harwell, eds., *Kirtland Council Minute Book* (October 1832–November 1837) (Salt Lake City: Collier's, 1996).

Yet another kind of documentary work is diaries, a staple of Mormon historiography. Some of the best editions of the diaries of Mormon males include Dean C.

Jessee, comp. and ed., *The Papers of Joseph Smith*, 2 vols. (Salt Lake City: Deseret Book, 1989, 1992); Scott G. Kenney, ed., *Wilford Woodruff's Journal*, 9 vols., including an index by Susan Staker and Brent D. Corcoran (Midvale, Utah, and Salt Lake City: Signature Books, 1983–85, 1991); Jan Shipps and John W. Welch, eds., *The Journals of William E. McLellin, 1831–1836* (Provo, Utah: BYU Studies, Brigham Young University; Urbana: University of Illinois Press, 1994); James B. Allen and Thomas G. Alexander, eds., *Manchester Mormons: The Journal of William Clayton, 1840 to 1842* (Santa Barbara, Calif.: Peregrine Smith, 1974); Robert Glass Cleland and Juanita Brooks, eds., *A Mormon Chronicle: The Diaries of John D. Lee, 1848–1876*, 2 vols. (1955; reprint, Salt Lake City: University of Utah Press, 1983); Stanley B. Kimball, ed., *On the Potter's Wheel: The Diaries of Heber C. Kimball* (Salt Lake City: Signature Books, in association with Smith Research Associates, 1987); Juanita Brooks, ed., *On the Mormon Frontier: The Diary of Hosea Stout, 1844–1861*, 2 vols. (Salt Lake City: University of Utah Press and Utah State Historical Society, 1964); Dean C. Jessee, ed., *Letters of Brigham Young to His Sons* (Salt Lake City: Deseret Book, 1974); A. Karl Larson and Katharine Miles Larson, eds., *Diary of Charles Lowell Walker*, 2 vols. (Logan: Utah State University Press, 1980); and Will Bagley, ed., *The Pioneer Camp of the Saints: The 1846 and 1847 Mormon Trail Journals of Thomas Bullock* (Spokane, Wash.: Arthur H. Clark, 1997).

Readers may also want to consult three volumes edited and compiled by Elden J. Watson: *The Orson Pratt Journals* (Salt Lake City: Elden J. Watson, 1975); *Manuscript History of Brigham Young, 1801–1844* (Salt Lake City: Elden J. Watson, 1968); and *Manuscript History of Brigham Young, 1846–1847* (Salt Lake City: Elden J. Watson, 1971).

Significant editions of Mormon women's diaries or diary excerpts include Kenneth W. Godfrey, Audrey M. Godfrey, and Jill Mulvay Derr, eds., *Women's Voices: An Untold History of the Latter-day Saints, 1830–1900* (Salt Lake City: Deseret Book, 1982); Carol Cornwall Madsen, comp. and ed., *In Their Own Words: Women and the Story of Nauvoo* (Salt Lake City: Deseret Book, 1994); Maureen Ursenbach Beecher, ed., *The Personal Writings of Eliza Roxcy Snow* (Salt Lake City: University of Utah Press, 1995); Maurine Carr Ward, ed., *Winter Quarters: The 1846–1848 Life Writings of Mary Haskin Parker Richards* (Logan: Utah State University Press, 1996); Donna Toland Smart, ed., *Mormon Midwife: The 1846–1888 Diaries of Patty Bartlett Sessions* (Logan: Utah State University Press, 1997); Noel A. Carmack and Karen Lynn Davidson, eds., *Out of the Black Patch: The Autobiography of Effie Marquess Carmack, Folk Musician, Artist, and Writer* (Logan: Utah State University Press, 1999); Maria S. Ellsworth, ed., *Mormon Odyssey: The Story of Ida Hunt Udall, Plural Wife* (Urbana: University of Illinois Press, 1992); and Jeni Broberg Holzapfel and Richard Neitzel Holzapfel, eds., *A Woman's View: Helen Mar Whitney's Reminiscences of Early Church History* (Provo, Utah: Religious Studies Center, Brigham Young University, 1997).

These listings of documentary material are only representative. Comprehensive bibliographies can be found in the index to *Studies in Mormon History* under the keywords "Diaries and journals" and "Sources."

Oral History Projects and Programs

Oral histories constitute another rich source for research. The James M. Moyle Oral History Program at the Historical Department of the LDS Church, begun in 1972, has collected material on about 1,300 men and women throughout the world, dealing with many aspects of LDS life. Most interviews have been transcribed, except for the approximately 10 percent done in non-English languages. However, the use of some of these materials is restricted. The Moyle oral histories of living general authorities can be used only by their permission; interviews less than ten years old also require the permission of the people who were interviewed or the permission of their families.

The Charles Redd Center for Western Studies at Brigham Young University began its oral history program in 1973. Most of these interviews focus on such specialized topics as ethnic groups, polygamy, and women missionaries and have been transcribed and placed in the L. Tom Perry Special Collections of the Harold B. Lee Library, Brigham Young University. For information on this program, see Jessie L. Embry, "Charles Redd Center for Western Studies: The Oral History Program," in *Mormon Americana*, 111–19.

Brigham Young University has completed other oral histories. Along with the Redd Center's interviews, these are listed in five collection guides compiled by John F. Bluth, LeGrand Baker, Kristen Goehring, and Albert Winkler. Published by the L. Tom Perry Special Collections, Harold B. Lee Library, BYU, these reference works contain information on more than one thousand interviews. Still another oral history collection is the five hundred hours of interviews conducted by E. Dale LeBaron, 1988–93, featuring Mormon converts in Africa. Transcriptions of the LeBaron interviews are in BYU's Special Collections.

Indexes

Another valuable aid to the researcher is the indexes that have been prepared of major Mormon publications. Newburn I. Butt, a BYU librarian and index specialist from 1922 to 1968, directed a number of such projects. These included indexing the *Contributor* (vols. 1–17, 1880–96); *Times and Seasons* (vols. 1–6, 1839–46); and the *Millennial Star* (vol. 1–15, 1840–53) and creating a three-volume compilation entitled *Indexes to First Periodicals of the Church of Jesus Christ of Latter-day Saints.* This last project indexed the *Evening and Morning Star* (vols. 1–2, 1832–34), the *Latter Day Saints' Messenger and Advocate* (vols. 1–3, 1834–36), the *Elders' Journal* (vol. 1, 1837–38), and the *Relief Society Magazine* (vols. 1–19, 1913–32). Butt and his assistants also provided indexes for several important books and other collections, including the *History of the Church*, ed. B. H. Roberts; *Utah since Statehood,* by Noble Warrum; *Conference Reports of the Church of Jesus Christ of Latter-day Saints* (50th [1880] and 68th–129th [1897–1959]); the *Journal of Discourses* (26 vols., 1854–86); and an index to newspaper clippings about Brigham Young University, 1875–1966. Copies of most of these indexes are available in the major Utah libraries, but they must be used with caution. Because students of varying talent were assigned to Burt's projects, index-ing was neither comprehensive nor definitive.

Other important indexing projects have been completed. Gary Gillum compiled and Daniel Maryon edited *Dialogue: A Journal of Mormon Thought: Index to Volumes 1–20, 1966–1987,* published in 1989; Gary Gillum and the *Sunstone* staff prepared the *Sunstone and Sunstone Review Index* (1975–1980) in 1981. Gary Gillum also prepared the *LDS Periodicals Index* for 1991–92 (issued in May 1993) and 1993–96 (issued in October 1997). A cumulative index for *Brigham Young University Studies* (vols. 1–31, 1959–91) was published as *BYU Studies* 31 (Fall 1991). Jane Carpenter, a student work-ing in BYU Special Collections, prepared an index for *Exponent II* in 1984. In 1970, the LDS Church published the two-volume *Cumulative Index to Periodicals for the Church of Jesus Christ of Latter-day Saints, 1961–1970* and continued to publish indexes thereafter (1971–75; 1976–80; 1986–90; 1991–95). Also valuable is the index to the *Deseret News, Church News Section;* first covering 1952–65, this index was updated annually from 1958 to 1965 and thereafter merged with the larger *Cumulative Index* mentioned above.

Early Bibliographic Efforts

The earliest efforts to describe or catalogue Mormon books came from at least four directions. The first was internal and appeared in unpublished inventories of the earliest LDS libraries. Examples of this type of bibliography include the 1844 listing "Nauvoo Library and Literary Institute," which can be examined at the LDS Historical Department, and the *Catalogue of the Utah Territorial Library,* prepared by William C. Staines and published by Brigham H. Young in Great Salt Lake City in 1852. Staines's bibliography no doubt included volumes that church members had gath-ered in Nauvoo; these were supplemented and greatly enlarged when Utah was granted territorial status in 1850 and the U.S. government established a territorial library.

The second impetus for listing Mormon books came from nineteenth-century authors who wanted readers to know about their sources. For example, Richard F. Burton provided references to the books that he consulted when writing *The City of the Saints, and across the Rocky Mountains to California* (London: Longman, Green, Longman and Roberts, 1861). Burton's chapter 4 contains a valuable listing of the literature then available about Mormonism, in both the United States and England. Likewise, T. B. H. Stenhouse, whose *Rocky Mountain Saints* (New York: D. Appleton, 1873), perhaps the most widely read history between 1873 and 1905, provided an im-portant listing of early sources in a section of his book called "Writers on Mormon-ism" (741–46).

A third and closely related effort came from collectors of western Americana. One of the most avid collectors was Hubert Howe Bancroft, who scoured the West in search of manuscript and printed items for his multivolume History of the Pacific States of North America series.[2] Bancroft's *History of Utah, 1540–1886* (San Francisco: History Company, 1889), a part of this larger series, had twenty-seven pages of "Authorities Consulted." Because Bancroft secured copies of this material and because these manuscripts were later placed in the Hubert Howe Bancroft Library at the University of California at Berkeley, this listing is a partial indication of the present-day Mormon holding of this important archive. For further information about the Bancroft's Mormon collection, see S. George Ellsworth, "A Guide to the Manuscripts in the Bancroft Library Relating to the *History of Utah*," *Utah Historical Quarterly* 22 (July 1954): 196–247; and Bonnie Hardwick, "Mormon Manuscripts in the Bancroft Library," in *Mormon Americana,* 93–99.

Other collectors prepared descriptive catalogues of their materials when offering them for sale. In the process, these sale catalogues became pioneering bibliographies. The earliest may have been Charles L. Woodward, *Bibliothica-Scallawagiana: Catalogue of a Matchless Collection of Books, Pamphlets, Autographs, Pictures, etc. relating to Mormonism and the Mormons* (New York: n.p., 1880). More famous was the William Berrian Collection that in 1899 became a part of the New York Public Library. Described in William Berrian, *Catalogue of Books, Early Newspapers and Pamphlets on Mormonism* (New York: V. H. Everson, 1898), the collection became the basis for a "List of Works in the New York Public Library Relating to Mormons," *Bulletin of the New York Public Library* 13 (March 1909): 183–239. The personal collection of Salt Lake City businessman Herbert S. Auerbach was the basis of two catalogues: *The Distinguished Collection of Western Americana: Books, Newspapers and Pamphlets, Many relating to the Mormon Church,* 2 parts (New York: Parke-Bernet Galleries, 1947–48); and *"The Auerbach Collection": Manuscripts and Other Selections from the Herbert S. Auerbach Collection of Western Americana* (Northampton, Mass.: L and T Research Books, 1992). Still another collection was Edward Eberstadt, *Utah and the Mormons . . . Rare Books, Manuscripts, Paintings, etc., Offered for Sale by Edward Eberstadt and Sons* (New York: n.p., ca. 1956).

A fourth source of early Mormon materials was the Mormon listings in larger bibliographies, even though these efforts did not focus on the LDS Church. Such was the classic listing by Joseph Sabin, Wilberforce Eames, and R. W. G. Vail, *Bibliotheca Americana: A Dictionary of Books relating to America, from Its Discovery to the Present Time,* 29 vols. (New York: n.p., 1868–1936), which also included titles placing Mormonism in its larger cultural environment. Two supplements to Sabin's work are especially helpful to students of Mormonism: John Edgar Molnar, *Author-Title Index to Joseph Sabin's Dictionary of Books relating to America,* 3 vols. (Metuchen, N.J.: Scarecrow, 1974); and S. George Ellsworth, "A List of References to Mormonism, the Mormons and Utah in Joseph Sabin," typescript, Berkeley, Calif., July 1950, copy in L. Tom Perry Special Collections, Harold B. Lee Library, Brigham Young University.

A more recent work in this same tradition is Nelson R. Burr, *A Critical Bibliography of Religion in America,* 2 parts, vol. 4 of *Religion in American Life,* ed. James Ward Smith and A. Leland Jameson (Princeton, N.J.: Princeton University Press, 1961); see especially 329–34. Because the Mormon experience was so much a part of the American westward movement, the major bibliographies on the West also provide guides to Mormon and Mormon-related materials. See especially Henry R. Wagner and

Charles L. Camp, *The Plains and the Rockies: A Critical Bibliography of Exploration, Adventure and Travel in the American West, 1800–1865*, 4th ed., rev. and enl., ed. Robert H. Becker (San Francisco: John Howell Books, 1982); Merrill J. Mattes, *Platte River Road Narratives: A Descriptive Bibliography of Travel over the Great Central Overland Route to Oregon, California, Utah, Colorado, Montana, and Other Western States and Territories, 1812–1866* (Urbana: University of Illinois Press, 1988), which includes over two hundred Mormon narratives; Lannon W. Mintz, *The Trail: A Bibliography of the Travelers on the Overland Trail to California, Oregon, Salt Lake City and Montana during the Years 1841–1864* (Albuquerque: University of New Mexico Press, 1987); and John M. Townley, *The Trail West: A Bibliography—Index to Western American Trails, 1841–1869* (Reno, Nev.: Jamison Station, 1988).

Scholarly Approaches to General Bibliographies

Bernard De Voto's 1936 comment that a complete bibliography of articles on Mormonism by qualified scholars would hardly fill one page was provocative but misleading.[3] At the time of De Voto's statement, over 2,000 items dealing with Mormon history had already been produced. While many of these were "faith-promoting" or polemical in nature, serious scholarship was on its way: such authors as Nels Anderson, Hubert Howe Bancroft, Juanita Brooks, Richard T. Ely, John Henry Evans, LeRoy R. Hafen, Gustive O. Larson, Lowry Nelson, Milo Quaife, B. H. Roberts, Orson F. Whitney, and John A. Widtsoe had begun their publishing careers. As a further sign, more than 120 theses and dissertations had been produced. Even as De Voto deprecated Mormon historical writing, the time was ripe for serious bibliographic study.

A Brigham Young University professor of psychology, M. Wilford Poulson, led off. Poulson's interest in Mormonism's early historical setting was reflected in his short note, "Library Resources for the Scientific Study of Mormonism," which was printed in the *Proceedings of the Utah Academy of Sciences* 7 (15 July 1930): 37–38. More substantial was the work of Dale L. Morgan. Working with the Works Progress Administration's Historical Records Survey and later with the Utah's Writers' Project, which he supervised after July 1940, Morgan helped produce three bibliographies under the title "Inventory of the Church Archives of Utah" (vol. 1, "History and Bibliography of Religions," June 1940; vol. 2, "Baptist Church," August 1940; and vol. 3, "Smaller Denominations," February 1941, copies in Utah libraries). Morgan was also involved in the production of *Utah: A Guide to the State* (New York: Hastings House for WPA, 1941), which contained an extensive bibliography. While his plans to produce a history of the Mormon church never materialized in his own lifetime (his early drafts were issued posthumously),[4] the project led him to continue his bibliographic study. One result was the publication of a series of listings on Mormon dissent groups, the core of which he published in the *Western Humanities Review* from 1949 to 1953. These are cited below. Morgan also sold copies of his larger bibliographies to a number of libraries, including the Beinecke Library at Yale University; the Henry E. Huntington Library in San Marino, California; and the Harold B. Lee Library at Brigham Young University. Morgan was involved in informal bibliographic projects, too. He helped supply reference material for Fawn M. Brodie's biography of Joseph Smith and assisted other midcentury scholars with sources for their work.

As early as 1951, Morgan proposed the creation of the "Union Catalogue of Works on Mormonism." Originally conceived as a comprehensive guide to all sources on Mormonism, to be housed at the Utah State Historical Society in Salt Lake City, the project involved many scholars: John James, a librarian at the Utah State Historical Society; S. Lyman Tyler, the director of the Brigham Young University Library; Everett L. Cooley and Ray Canning at the University of Utah Library; Earl E. Olson, assistant LDS Church historian; S. George Ellsworth, a history professor at Utah State University; and Morgan himself. Eventually Tyler brought the project to BYU in the hope of providing a tool for developing the university's Mormon holdings. It was there that BYU specialist Chad J. Flake became the project's key bibliographer, and the resulting work was published under his name: Chad J. Flake, comp., *A Mormon Bibliography, 1830–1930: Books, Pamphlets, Periodicals, and Broadsides relating to the First Century of Mormonism* (Salt Lake City: University of Utah Press, 1978). Morgan reviewed the volume's early drafts, wrote its introduction, and received Flake's dedication. A ten-year supplement appeared in 1989: Chad J. Flake and Larry W. Draper, comps., *A Mormon Bibliography, 1830–1930: Ten Year Supplement* (Salt Lake City: University of Utah Press, 1989). A title index to both volumes was added in 1992: Chad J. Flake and Larry W. Draper, comps., *A Mormon Bibliography, 1830–1930: Indexes to a Mormon Bibliography and Ten Year Supplement* (Salt Lake City: University of Utah Press). While these works did not have the breadth of coverage originally intended—government documents, periodical literature, newspapers, and manuscripts were only partly addressed—these volumes remain the closest thing that Mormon studies has to a "union catalogue" of published source documents. They are enhanced by Susan L. Fales and Chad J. Flake, comps., *Mormons and Mormonism in U.S. Government Documents: A Bibliography* (Salt Lake City: University of Utah Press, 1989).

Other bibliographies have also appeared. S. Lyman Tyler produced a short note, "The Availability of Information Concerning the Mormons," in the inaugural issue of *Dialogue: A Journal of Mormon Thought* 1 (Autumn 1966): 172–75. He also produced several guides that were published after he left Brigham Young University, including *The Historiography of Utah, the Mormons, and the West: A Personal Approach* (Salt Lake City: American West Center, University of Utah, 1978); and *Greater Utah, the Mormons, et al.: The Region and the Record* (Salt Lake City: American West Center, University of Utah, 1981). Ralph W. Hansen, a BYU Special Collections staff member and book review editor of *Dialogue*, prepared several short guides on materials that had been recently published on the Mormons: "Among the Mormons: A Survey of Current Literature," *Dialogue: A Journal of Mormon Thought* 5 (Autumn 1970): 107–12; and "Among the Mormons: A Survey of Current Literature," *Dialogue: A Journal of Mormon Thought* 6 (Autumn/Winter 1971): 133–38. Stephen W. Stathis expanded Hansen's original approach and made bibliographies of newly published material a regular *Dialogue* feature.[5] When *Brigham Young University Studies* was reestablished in 1959, it, too, began an annual Mormon bibliography of newly issued works. First supervised by Flake and later by Scott H. Duvall and other members of the Special Collections staff, the *Brigham Young University Studies* bibliographies included a wide range of Mormon studies and were not limited to history. Yet another attempt to provide a listing of recent literature was the mimeographed catalogues that Flake circulated from 1960 to 1986 under the title of "Mormon Americana," a complete set of which is in BYU Special Collections. After 1986, it was issued as an in-house accessions list, and the circulation of this listing became more limited.

Several important bibliographies appeared as scholarly writing greatly expanded at midcentury. In 1954, Wayne Stout completed but never published a pioneering, 1,042-page "A Bibliography on Mormonism," available in BYU Special Collections. Another indefatigable scholar, S. George Ellsworth, compiled a massive card listing of Mormon and western American sources that remains housed with his private papers at the Utah State University Library. Following the growing convention of the time, Leonard J. Arrington's monograph *Great Basin Kingdom: An Economic History of the Latter-day Saints, 1830–1900* (Cambridge, Mass.: Harvard University Press, 1958) had an exemplary listing of the sources used in the preparation of this work. Another useful measure of Mormon bibliography as the new professionalism was emerging was William V. Nash, "Library Resources for the Study of Mormons and Mormonism" (Urbana: Graduate School of Library Science, University of Illinois, 1960, typescript, copy in BYU Library).

Early Scholarly Approaches to Specialized Bibliographies

Some scholars approached the bibliographical task by focusing on specific topics, regions, or print media. In 1944, the Division of Religion at BYU published the topically organized *A Practical Bibliography of Works on Mormonism.* Three years later L. H. Kirkpatrick and Ruth Jones prepared "A Current Regional Bibliography," *Utah Humanities Review* 1 (January 1947): 97–103. Leonard H. Kirkpatrick's *Holdings of the University of Utah on Utah and the Church of Jesus Christ of Latter-day Saints* was published by the University of Utah libraries in 1954. A year later, Joseph Sudweeks's *Discontinued L.D.S. Periodicals,* the first major attempt to survey the history of LDS newspapers and periodical literature, was published by Brigham Young University.

J. Cecil Alter offered readers of the *Utah Historical Quarterly* the "Bibliographers' Choice of Books on Utah and the Mormons" in the July 1956 issue (215–31). From 1955 to 1959, the *UHQ* continued to provide its readers with guides to graduate studies on Mormon and Utah history: see Ruth M. Jones and Robert N. McMillan, "Utah, the Mormons and the West: A Bibliography and a Check List of Theses at the University of Utah," *Utah Historical Quarterly* 23 (January 1955): 79–85;[6] and Ida-Marie Clark Logan, "A Bibliography of Theses and Dissertations concerning Utah or the Mormons Written outside the State of Utah." Logan's work, written as a master's thesis at Utah State University in 1956, was published as a series: *Utah Historical Quarterly* 27 (January 1959): 85–100, and 27 (April 1959): 169–90. A more comprehensive listing of graduate studies on Mormonism was published in 1971 by the College of Religious Instruction at Brigham Young University: *A Catalogue of Theses and Dissertations concerning the Church of Jesus Christ of Latter-day Saints, Mormonism and Utah.* Three years later, the College of Religious Instruction followed with a small, mimeographed update of its earlier publication, which was titled "Additions."

In 1972 and 1973, Velton Peabody of Williamsville, New York, compiled and published the *Mormonia: A Quarterly Bibliography of Works on Mormonism,* available in the BYU Library and elsewhere. It was suspended after seven issues.

In May 1973, Roger Wright Harris compiled "Copyright Entries: Works by and about the Mormons, 1829–1870," a collection of typescripts of copyright entries in the Rare Book Room of the Library of Congress. A copy of this valuable work is available in BYU's Special Collections.

Much effort remains to acquire bibliographic control of newspapers. In addition to the work of Joseph Sudweeks, other early works included Cecil A. Snider, "A Syllabus on Mormonism in Illinois from the Angle of the Press: Newspaper Source Materials, 1838–1848" (Master's thesis, State University of Iowa, 1933); Cecil A. Snider and Helen Fulton Snider, comps., "Mormons in Ohio, Illinois, Missouri, etc., Newspaper Clippings, 1831–1849," 8 vols. and index (n.p., 1953) (copy available at BYU Special Collections); Douglas C. McMurtrie, *The Beginnings of Printing in Utah: With a Bibliography of the Issues of the Utah Press, 1849–1860* (Chicago: John Calhoun Club, 1931); Douglas C. McMurtrie, "Early Printing in Utah outside of Salt Lake City," *Utah Historical Quarterly* 5 (July 1932): 83–87; and J. Cecil Alter, *Early Utah Journalism: A Half Century of Forensic Warfare, Waged by the West's Most Militant Press* (Salt Lake City: Utah State Historical Society, 1938); Winifred Gregory, ed., *American Newspapers, 1821–1936: A Union List of Files Available in the United States and Canada* (New York: H. W. Wilson, 1937). More recently, see *United States Newspaper Program National Union List,* 3d ed. (Dublin, Ohio: OCLC Online Computer Library Center, 1989). Finally, Chad J. Flake's *Mormon Bibliography* lists many newspapers, arranged under the title of the periodical, not the founding editor.

Scholarly Bibliographies in the Modern Era

After years of study and experimentation, the church consolidated its bureaucracy in the early 1970s and began to issue curricula under its newly established Correlation Program. This "correlation movement" had implications for church scholarship and the preparation of scholarly guides. New curriculum committees needed a more professionalized library and archives for their work. They also needed indexes and bibliographies of past research. The result of these twin needs was the expansion of staff at the LDS Historical Department, which in turn produced a growing number of research guides.

Most of these guides were for internal or institutional use, but some had a wider impact. Two important "guides to guides" were produced: Kip Sperry, *A Guide to Indexes to Mormon Works, Mormon Collections, and Utah Collections* (Salt Lake City: Historical Department of the Church of Jesus Christ of Latter-day Saints, 1974); and Gordon Irving, "Utah since 1847: A Guide to Bibliographies, Finding Aids, and Major Source Repositories" (Salt Lake City: Historical Department of the Church of Jesus Christ of Latter-day Saints, 1981). Both of these works are available at the LDS Historical Department and BYU's Special Collections. The bibliographic work of Melvin L. Bashore was especially important. Bashore, a longtime employee at church headquarters, prepared guides to the LDS Historical Department's collections on Mormon immigration, which appeared under the titles *Mormon Pioneer Companies Crossing the Plains (1847–1869) Narratives: Guide to Sources in Utah Libraries and Archives,* 3d rev. ed. (Salt Lake City: Historical Department of the Church of Jesus Christ of Latter-day Saints, 1989); and, with Linda L. Haslam, *Mormons on the High Seas: Ocean Voyage Narratives to America (1840–1890): Guide to Sources in the Historical Department of the Church of Jesus Christ of Latter-day Saints and Other Utah Repositories,* 3d rev. ed. (Salt Lake City: Historical Department of the Church of Jesus Christ of Latter-day Saints, 1990). Bashore has also been responsible for an ongoing index that traces the most recent work published about Mormonism. Bashore's index, which includes nonscholarly items, is available at the LDS Library in the Historical Department.

A second event that helped shaped the creation of modern scholarly reference material was the rise of the new approach to the writing of Mormon history. Sometimes described as the "new Mormon history," this new historical school is described in chapter 3 and in an essay in *Studies in Mormon History* and had as one of its manifestations the organization, in 1965, of the Mormon History Association (MHA). The MHA's *Newsletter* featured bibliographies on a wide range of topics, many of which were prepared by David J. Whittaker. The MHA's *Journal of Mormon History* published a series of path-breaking bibliographic essays, some of which are cited below. Two other journals that printed "new Mormon history"—*Dialogue: A Journal of Mormon Thought* and *Brigham Young University Studies*—also published bibliographic material. For instance, the inaugural issue of *Dialogue* (1 [Spring 1966]: 15–32) issued Leonard J. Arrington's "Scholarly Studies of Mormonism in the Twentieth Century." This path-breaking article included an appendix that listed Ph.D. dissertations on Mormon topics.

By the mid-1960s, bibliographic studies were increasingly common. For an introduction to this material, see Susan L. Fales and Lanell M. Reeder, "Mormonism: Bibliography of Bibliographies," MHA *Newsletter,* no. 72 (April 1989): 5–8, and no. 74 (October 1989): 4–7. A more recent guide is David J. Whittaker, "The Study of Mormon History: A Guide to the Published Sources," in *Mormon Americana,* 45–90. The researcher should also consult the keyword "Bibliographies" or the "bibliographies" subdivision of specific topics in *Studies in Mormon History.*

James B. Allen and Glen M. Leonard, *The Story of the Latter-day Saints,* 2d ed. (Salt Lake City: Deseret Book, 1992), contains the most extensive and useful bibliography available in any general history of the church. This annotated listing is organized by topics and subtopics. It is particularly helpful to students seeking a selective and quick guide to Mormon historical literature.

Other bibliographic studies emerged in the last half of the twentieth century. They often retain utility because of their annotation, commentary, and classification—or they reveal the state of Mormon history and bibliography at the time they were compiled. Listed chronologically, some of the most important of the general bibliographies are Philip A. M. Taylor, "Recent Writing on Utah and the Mormons," *Arizona and the West* 4 (Autumn 1962): 249–60; Thomas G. Alexander and James B. Allen, "The Mormons in the Mountain West: A Selected Bibliography," *Arizona and the West* 9 (Winter 1967): 365–84; James B. Allen, "Since 1950: Creators and Creations of Mormon History," in *New Views of Mormon History: A Collection of Essays in Honor of Leonard J. Arrington,* ed. Davis Bitton and Maureen Ursenbach Beecher (Salt Lake City: University of Utah Press, 1987), 407–38; William C. Miller, "Recent Scholarship on Mormonism," *American Theological Library Association Proceedings* 44 (1990): 202–15; David L. Laughlin, "A Selective, Evaluative, and Annotated Bibliography on Mormonism," *Bulletin of Bibliography* 48 (June 1991): 75–101; and David L. Laughlin, "It Began with a Book: A Didactically Annotated Bibliography on Mormonism," *Journal of Religious and Theological Information* 2, no. 1 (1994): 45–94.

Many bibliographies detail the literature chronologically. For the cultural matrix that gave rise to Mormonism, see David J. Whittaker, "The Religious Context of Mormon History: A Bibliography for the American Setting," MHA *Newsletter,* no. 45 (November 1980): 8–17. For sources dealing with the first stages of Mormonism, see Peter L. Crawley, *A Descriptive Bibliography of the Mormon Church,* vol. 1, *1830–1847* (Provo: Religious Studies Center, Brigham Young University, 1998); David J. Whittaker, "Joseph Smith's First Vision: A Source Essay," MHA *Newsletter,* no. 42 (November 1979): 7–9; and David J. Whittaker, "Sources on Mormon Origins in New York and Pennsylvania," MHA *Newsletter,* no. 43 (March 1980): 8–13. The Ohio period of Mormonism (1831–38) is detailed in Stanley B. Kimball, "Sources on the History of the Mormons in Ohio, 1830–1838," *BYU Studies* 11 (Summer 1971): 524–40; and Roger D. Launius, "The Latter Day Saints in Ohio: Writing the History of Mormonism's Middle Period," *John Whitmer Historical Association Journal* 16 (1996): 31–57. Some of the best listings on the Illinois era of Mormonism (1839–46) have been prepared by Glen M. Leonard: "Recent Writing on Mormon Nauvoo," *Western Illinois Regional Studies* 11 (Fall 1988): 69–93; "Selected Nauvoo Bibliography: Work since 1978," MHA *Newsletter,* no. 71 (January 1989): 4–8; and "Remembering Nauvoo: Historiographical Considerations," *Journal of Mormon History* 16 (1990): 25–39.

For the Iowa period and the trek west (1846–47), two histories by Richard E. Bennett provide extensive references: *Mormons at the Missouri, 1846–1852: "And Should We Die . . ."* (Norman: University of Oklahoma Press, 1987); and *We'll Find the Place: The Mormon Exodus, 1846–1848* (Salt Lake City: Deseret Book, 1997). For early Utah (1847–69), see S. George Ellsworth, "Utah History: Retrospect and Prospect," *Utah Historical Quarterly* 40 (Fall 1972): 342–67; Wayne L. Wahlquist, "A Review of Mormon Settlement Literature," *Utah Historical Quarterly* 45 (Winter 1977): 4–21; and Thomas G. Alexander, "Toward the New Mormon History: An Examination of the Literature on the Latter-day Saints in the Far West," in *Historians and the American West,* ed. Michael P. Malone (Lincoln: University of Nebraska Press, 1983), 344–68.

Among the best bibliographic guides to the later Utah territorial experience (1869–1900) are the listings accompanying the chapters in Richard D. Poll, Thomas G. Alexander, Eugene E. Campbell, and David E. Miller, *Utah's History* (Provo, Utah: Brigham Young University Press, 1978); and Douglas D. Alder's more specialized listing: "Writing Southern Utah History: An Appraisal and a Bibliography," *Journal of Mormon History* 20 (Fall 1994): 156–78. Bibliographies dealing with Mormonism in the twentieth century (like the historical literature itself) are more difficult to find. The relevant chapter bibliographies in Allen and Leonard's *Story of the Latter-day Saints* are an important pioneering effort.

Women and Plural Marriage

An early attempt to survey the sources on women in LDS history was Carol Cornwall Madsen and David J. Whittaker, "History's Sequel: A Source Essay on Women in Mormon History," *Journal of Mormon History* 6 (1979): 123–45. More recent efforts include Patricia Lyn Scott and Maureen Ursenbach Beecher, "Mormon Women: A Bibliography in Process, 1977–1985," *Journal of Mormon History* 12 (1985): 113–27; and Karen Purser Frazier, *Bibliography of Social Scientific, Historical, and Popular Writings about Mormon Women* (Provo, Utah: Women's Research Institute, Brigham Young University, 1990). Still another listing, Patricia Lyn Scott, "Writing Women's Lives: A Bibliography on Writing Biographies on Women," *Genealogical Journal* 27, no. 1 (1999): 3–23, focuses on national and regional women's biography, although some Mormon titles are included as well.

Mormon plural marriage continues to receive attention. Two guides to this literature are Davis Bitton's "Mormon Polygamy: A Review Article," *Journal of Mormon History* 4 (1977): 101–18; and Patricia Lyn Scott's "Mormon Polygamy: A Bibliography, 1977–92," *Journal of Mormon History* 19 (Spring 1993): 133–55.

Scripture and the Printed Word

Mormonism began with claims of modern revelation. While accepting the Old Testament and New Testament as authoritative (although Smith produced a nonbinding interpretation of these texts in an "inspired translation"), Mormons accept three additional books of "new" scripture: the Book of Mormon, the Doctrine and Covenants, and the Pearl of Great Price. These scriptures have produced a body of secondary literature that, while often devotional and theological, has had a historical dimension. Especially numerous have been works dealing with the Book of Mormon—and the bibliographies that attempt to organize and categorize these works. The most ambitious of these Book of Mormon listings have been issued by the Foundation for Ancient Research and Mormon Studies (FARMS) at Brigham Young University: Donald W. Parry, Jeanette W. Miller, and Sandra A. Thorne, eds., *A Comprehensive Annotated Book of Mormon Bibliography* (Provo, Utah: Research Press, 1996). Earlier Book of Mormon bibliographies include Hugh G. Stocks, "The Book of Mormon, 1830–1879: A Publishing History" (Master's thesis, University of California at Los Angeles, 1979) and "The Book of Mormon in English, 1870–1920: A Publishing History and Analytical Bibliography" (Ph.D. diss., University of California at Los Angeles, 1986). All of these listings contain material of historical interest.

For works about Joseph Smith's "inspired translation" of the Bible, see David J. Whittaker, "The Mormon Scriptures: History and Textual Development (Pt. 2: The Joseph Smith Translation)," MHA *Newsletter*, no. 52 (February 1983): 7–10; and Thomas E. Sherry, *Joseph Smith's Translation of the Bible: A Bibliography of Publications, 1847–1987*, 3 vols. (Provo, Utah: By the author, 1988). In 1994, Sherry produced a supplement to his earlier work covering titles published from 1988 to 1992.

An extended introduction to the subject of Mormon publishing history is David J. Whittaker, "The Web of Print: Toward a History of the Book in Early Mormon Culture," *Journal of Mormon History* 23 (Spring 1997): 1–41, which has an appendix that lists sources dealing with early Mormon publishing. For a detailed bibliographical guide to the first seventeen years of Mormon imprints, see Peter L. Crawley, *A Descriptive Bibliography of the Mormon Church*, vol. 1, *1830–1847* (Provo, Utah: Religious Studies Center, Brigham Young University, 1998). A useful guide to official Mormon publications in languages other than English is L[ynn] R. Jacobs, *Mormon Non-English Scriptures, Hymnals, and Periodicals, 1830–1986: A Descriptive Bibliography* (Ithaca, N.Y.: By the author, 1986). Bryan Waterman has brought together sources on a related topic: "A Guide to the Mormon Universe: Mormon Organizations and Periodicals," *Sunstone* 17 (December 1994): 44–65, which discusses the organizations and publications that issue information about the church.

Mormons in Periodical Literature

While no comprehensive guide has been published on the topic of Mormons in the periodical literature (Chad J. Flake and Larry W. Draper have such a project underway), two dissertations provide extensive references: Richard O. Cowan, "Mormonism in National Periodicals" (Ph.D. diss., Stanford University, 1961); and Dennis L. Lythgoe, "The Changing Image of Mormonism in Periodical Literature" (Ph.D. diss., University of Utah, 1969). The topic can also be approached by three articles by Linda Thatcher published in *Dialogue: A Journal of Mormon Thought:* "Selected Newspaper Articles on Mormons and Mormonism Published during 1977," 11 (Winter 1978): 105–11; "Selected Newspaper Articles on Mormons and Mormonism Published during 1978," 12 (Winter 1979): 114–26; and "Selected Newspaper Articles on Mormons and Mormonism Published during 1982," 17 (Spring 1984): 135–49.

Schismatic Movements

Since the listings of *Studies in Mormon History* is restricted to mainline Mormonism and therefore contains bibliographies of schismatic movements only as they relate to the larger institutional church, the researcher will want to consult a variety of supplemental listings, especially Steven L. Shields, *The Latter Day Saint Churches: An Annotated Bibliography* (New York: Garland, 1987). A supplemental work is Shields's

Divergent Paths of the Restoration: A History of the Latter-day Saints Movement, 4th ed., rev. and enl. (Los Angeles: Restoration Research, 1990), which provides brief historical and doctrinal commentaries for most schismatic groups as well as information about their publications. Russell Rich, a longtime professor of church history and doctrine at Brigham Young University, had an interest in schismatic groups. His papers in the BYU Special Collections contain student papers as well as Rich's own research and correspondence on the topic.

The largest and most studied nonmainline group is the Reorganized Church of Jesus Christ of Latter Day Saints, founded in 1860 and first led by Joseph Smith III. Roger D. Launius has prepared several bibliographical guides to this movement: "The Reorganized Church in the Nineteenth Century: A Bibliographical Review," *Restoration Studies* 4 (1988): 171–87; "A New Historiographical Frontier: The Reorganized Church in the Twentieth Century," *John Whitmer Historical Association Journal* 6 (1986): 53–63; and "Whither Reorganization Historiography?" *John Whitmer Historical Association Journal* 10 (1990): 24–37. For a guide to manuscript collections relating to Joseph Smith III, see Daniel T. Muir, "Sources for Studies in the Life of Joseph Smith III," *Courage: A Journal of History, Thought and Action* 1 (December 1970): 93–99. See also Sara Hallier Nyman and L. Madelon Brunsom, "The Archives of the Reorganized Church of Jesus Christ of Latter Day Saints," in *Mormon Americana,* 27–80.

As earlier mentioned, Dale L. Morgan published bibliographies on Mormonism's schisms. Students should be aware of such Morgan publications as "A Bibliography of the Church of Jesus Christ, Organized at Green Oak, Pennsylvania, July, 1862," *Western Humanities Review* 4 (Winter 1949–50): 44–70; "A Bibliography of the Church of Jesus Christ of Latter Day Saints [Strangite]," *Western Humanities Review* 5 (Winter 1950–51): 42–114; and "A Bibliography of the Churches of the Dispersion," *Western Humanities Review* 7 (Summer 1953): 255–66. In 1991, BYU's Special Collections prepared an index to these articles.

Ethnic Groups and Mormonism outside the United States

As Mormonism expanded to become a worldwide, multicultural church during the last half of the twentieth century, scholars began to study the role of ethnic groups in the church's history. Bibliographic studies have followed. Native American bibliography is the subject of David J. Whittaker's "Mormons and Native Americans: A Historical and Bibliographical Introduction," *Dialogue: A Journal of Mormon Thought* 18 (Winter 1985): 33–64. Studies of African Americans are compiled in Chester L. Hawkins, "Selective Bibliography on African-Americans and Mormons, 1830–1990," *Dialogue: A Journal of Mormon Thought* 25 (Winter 1992): 113–31; and in Lester E. Bush Jr. and Armand L. Mauss, eds., *Neither White nor Black: Mormon Scholars Confront the Race Issue in a Universal Church* (Midvale, Utah: Signature Books, 1984).

Bibliographical aids on other ethnic groups and nationalities include Robert D. Bingham, "Swedish-Americans in Utah: A Bibliography," *Swedish Pioneer History Quarterly* 30 (July 1979): 205–10; Mark L. Grover, "The Mexican-American in Utah:

A Bibliography," *Utah Libraries* 18 (Spring 1975): 34–38; Mark L. Grover, *The Mormon Church in Latin America: A Periodical Index (1830–1976)* (Provo, Utah: Harold B. Lee Library, Brigham Young University, 1977); D. L. Ashliman, "Mormonism and the Germans: An Annotated Bibliography, 1848–1966," *BYU Studies* 8 (Autumn 1967): 73–94; Russell T. Clement, comp., *Mormons in the Pacific: A Bibliography* (Laie, Hawaii: Institute for Polynesian Studies, Brigham Young University–Hawaii Campus, 1981); Michael W. Homer, "The Church's Image in Italy from the 1840s to 1946: A Bibliographic Essay," *BYU Studies* 31 (Spring 1991): 83–114; David J. Whittaker, "Mormonism in Victorian Britain: A Bibliographical Essay," in *Mormons in Early Victorian Britain,* ed. Richard L. Jensen and Malcolm R. Thorp (Salt Lake City: University of Utah Press, 1989), 258–71; Robert L. Lively Jr., "Bodleian Sources for the Study of Two Nineteenth-Century Millenarian Movements in Britain," *Bodleian Library Record* 13 (April 1991): 491–500; Ronald D. Dennis, *Welsh Mormon Writings from 1844–1862: A Historical Bibliography* (Provo, Utah: Religious Studies Center, Brigham Young University, 1988); and David J. Whittaker, *Mormon Americana: A Bibliographical Guide to Printed Material in the British Library relating to the Church of Jesus Christ of Latter-day Saints* (London: David and Mary Eccles Centre for American Studies, British Library, 1994). For a discussion of an extensive Mormon-Danish imprint collection, see William Mulder, "Denmark and the Mormons: The Jørgen W. Schmidt Collection," *Princeton University Library Chronicle* 52 (Spring 1991): 331–57.

Miscellaneous Bibliographies

Bibliographers have also produced "niche" works on specific topics. Mormon political history has been on the agenda of historians for decades, but few substantive bibliographies have followed. Frank H. Jonas, "Bibliography on Utah Politics," *Western Political Quarterly* 11, supplement (December 1958): 132–51, was an early beginning but is now outdated. Eugene England produced several bibliographies on Mormon literature; the most complete is "Mormon Literature: Progress and Prospects," in *Mormon Americana,* 455–505. Richard F. Haglund Jr. and Erich Robert Paul have surveyed the literature on science and technology in Mormon culture in their essay in *Mormon Americana,* 559–606; they observe that the most comprehensive guide to this literature, Robert Miller's "Science/Mormonism Bibliography, 1932–1986," remains unpublished, although copies of Miller's work are in the libraries at Brigham Young University and the University of Utah. Drawing on his rich background in Mormon folklore, William A. Wilson prepared several guides on the topic: "A Bibliography of Studies in Mormon Folklore," *Utah Historical Quarterly* 44 (Fall 1976): 389–94; and, most fully, "Mormon Folklore," in *Mormon Americana,* 437–54.

Mormonism's experience with the performing arts is surveyed in Michael Hicks, "The Performing Arts and Mormonism: An Introductory Guide," in *Mormon Americana,* 538–58. Richard G. Oman undertakes a similar task for Mormon art and artists in "Sources for Mormon Visual Arts," in *Mormon Americana,* 607–66. Both essays provide extensive bibliographical references. An introduction to the records and literature relating to Mormon architects and architecture, covering both vernacular and public structures, is Brad Westwood, "Mormon Architectural Records," in *Mormon Americana,* 336–405. In the same volume, Carol A. Edison guides the researcher through the sources on such topics as furniture, domestic artifacts, gravestone iconography, and Mormon quilting in "Material Culture: An Introduction and Guide to Mormon Vernacular," 306–35. The only comprehensive guide to the literature on Mormon temples is Richard O. Cowan and Frank Alan Bruno, *Bibliography on Temples and Temple Work* (Provo, Utah: Brigham Young University, 1985). Mormon proselytizing is the subject of David J. Whittaker's bibliographic essay, "Mormon Missiology: An Introduction and Guide to the Sources," in *The Disciple as Witness: Essays on Latter-day Saint History and Doctrine in Honor of Richard Lloyd Anderson,* ed. Stephen D. Ricks, Donald W. Parry, and Andrew H. Hedges (Provo, Utah: Foundation for Ancient Research and Mormon Studies, Brigham Young University, 2000), 459–538. Still another kind of bibliography is presented by Gregory A. Prince, "A Bibliography on Mormon Reprints," *Dialogue: A Journal of Mormon Thought* 11 (Autumn 1978): 120–23, which suggests the growing market for out-of-print items.

Biographical Aids

The most comprehensive aid to students seeking Mormon biographical information about the men and women who have populated LDS history is Marvin E. Wiggins, *Mormons and Their Neighbors: An Index to over 75,000 Biographical Sketches from 1820 to the Present,* 2 vols. (Provo, Utah: Harold B. Lee Library, Brigham Young University, 1984). Wiggins provides an index to a large number of Mormon and Mormon-related publications, including the standard early biographical reference work by Andrew Jenson, *LDS Biographical Encyclopedia,* 4 vols. (Salt Lake City: Jenson History Co., 1901–36). Also useful is the work by Susan Easton Black, under whose supervision three data bases have been prepared: *Membership of the Church of Jesus Christ of Latter-day Saints, 1830–1848,* 50 vols. (Provo, Utah: Religious Studies Center, Brigham Young University, 1989); *Early Members of the Reorganized Church of Jesus Christ of Latter Day Saints,* 6 vols. (Provo, Utah: Religious Studies Center, Brigham Young University, 1993); and *Pioneers of 1847: A Sesquicentennial Remembrance* (Provo, Utah[?]: Brigham Young University[?], 1980[?]). Black has made much of her research available for electronic computer searching in the *LDS Family History Suite,* a CD-ROM issued by Infobases. For information about Mormon biography as a genre and the approach that scholars have taken in writing biography, the researcher should examine the biography section in David J. Whittaker, "The Study of Mormon History: A Guide to the Published Sources," *Mormon Americana,* 70–74, pertinent indexing in *Studies in Mormon History,* and, most important, the chapter in this volume that deals with the topic of biography.

Some bibliographic guides and essays focus on LDS leaders. The best place to begin a study of Joseph Smith is Dean C. Jessee, "Sources for the Study of Joseph Smith," in *Mormon Americana,* 7–28. See also David J. Whittaker, "Joseph Smith in Recent Research: A Selected Bibliography," in *Mormon Americana,* 29–44; and Davis Bitton, "Select Bibliography," in his *Images of the Prophet Joseph Smith* (Salt Lake City: Aspen Books, 1996), 171–96. There are no comparable guides to sources relating to other LDS leaders, although a few review essays have utility. The literature dealing with Brigham Young is introduced in Donald R. Moorman, "Shadows of Brigham Young as Seen by His Biographers," *Utah Historical Quarterly* 45 (Summer 1977): 251–64; Dean C. Jessee, "The Writings of Brigham Young," *Western Historical Quarterly* 4 (June 1973): 273–94; and Ronald K. Esplin, "From Rumors to the Records: Historians and the Sources for Brigham Young," *BYU Studies* 18 (Spring 1978): 453–65. Gary P. Gillum's "Out of the Books Which Shall be Written . . . ," *Dialogue: A Journal of Mormon Thought* 12 (Summer 1979): 99–123, offers a bibliography of published works written by church leaders.

Polemical Literature

Mormon polemical literature has been profuse. According to one survey, by 1989 almost two thousand anti-Mormon books, novels, pamphlets, tracts, and flyers had been issued in English alone.[7] Despite these numbers, Mormon polemics has attracted only a few reference guides—largely because of the limited scholarly value of polemics. While such works may provide clues to the social and religious milieu and occasionally tell something about the Mormon past, this literature is generally filled with distorting emotion and "facts" that are either faulty or lacking context. The purpose of polemics, of course, is to convince, often by slight-of-hand.

For those interested in this literature, one place to begin is William P. Connors, "Mormon Opposition Literature: A Historiographical Critique and Case Study, 1844–57" (Master's thesis, Brigham Young University, 1994), which includes a listing of early anti-Mormon works. For Britain, see Craig L. Foster, "Anti-Mormon Pamphleteering in Great Britain, 1837–1860" (Master's thesis, Brigham Young University, 1989). For information about Jerald Tanner and Sandra Tanner, leading polemicists of the last part of the twentieth century, see Scott H. Faulring's oral history of Sandra Tanner: "An Oral History of the Modern Microfilm Company, 1959–1982" (Senior Seminar Oral History Project, Brigham Young University, 1983); and Lawrence Foster, "Career Apostates: Reflections on the Works of Jerald and Sandra Tanner," *Dialogue: A Journal of Mormon Thought* 17 (Summer 1984): 35–60. H. Michael Marquardt lists some of the polemical literature and historical reproductions generated by the Tanners in his work, *A Tanner Bibliography, 1959–1983* (Bountiful, Utah: Restoration Research, 1984).

Of course, not all polemical literature has been authored by non-Mormons or anti-Mormons. Mormons, too, have been active writers of this type of literature, although few substantial guides to Mormon polemics have been authored.

Conclusion

Mormon reference material has greatly expanded during the past half-century as Mormon historical scholarship itself accelerated. Present-day scholars have available to them reference works and encyclopedias, place guides and atlases, guides to manuscript and oral history programs, indexes, and a considerable array of bibliographies, which in the last case should be used with the more current and universal listings found in *Studies of Mormon History.* These works serve simultaneously as guides and artifacts. They help steer researchers to primary and secondary sources while providing a record of past accomplishment. For scholars interested in the development of Mormon historical scholarship, they are useful signposts to the past journey of Mormon scholarship, telling of its quantity and quality when a particular reference work was produced.

In this vein, Mormon reference materials tell about the current state of scholarship. They suggest the professionalism and the growing resources committed by libraries and universities to its work. But they also measure what needs to be done. The profession still awaits the development of better-crafted lists of primary and secondary literature. We also await specialized bibliographies of such things as Mormon-related newspapers and how the Mormons have been treated in the periodic literature. Reference materials to the large volume of polemical literature have hardly begun to be produced. The clever compiler of reference material will no doubt craft many other new projects as well. As always, the hourglass is both half filled and half empty. That condition makes us appreciate past effort while encouraging new ventures by a future generation of scholars.

Notes

1. For an example of questionable editing practice, see Leland R. Nelson, comp., *The Journal of Joseph: The Personal Diary of a Modern Prophet by Joseph Smith, Jr.* (Mapleton, Utah: Council, 1979). Because Nelson used the *History of the Church* as his source, he mixed Smith's writings with those of Smith's contemporaries. The *History of the Church* itself did not distinguish in its narrative Smith's holograph material from that of his followers. For scholarly debate about such practices, see Howard C. Searle, "Authorship of the History of Joseph Smith: A Review Essay," *BYU Studies* 21 (Winter 1981): 101–22; and the discussion between James B. Allen and George D. Smith in *Dialogue: A Journal of Mormon Thought* 30 (Summer 1997): 129–56. The latter interchange focused on *An Intimate Chronicle: The Diaries of William Clayton,* ed. George Smith (Salt Lake City: Smith Research Associates and Signature Books, 1991), which Smith had issued without seeing the Clayton diaries in manuscript.

2. For Bancroft's procedures, which heavily relied on the work of Bancroft's associates, see John Walton Caughey, *Hubert Howe Bancroft: Historian of the West* (Berkeley: University of California Press, 1946).

3. Bernard De Voto, *Forays and Rebuttals* (Boston: Little, Brown, 1936), 82–83.

4. For information on this project, along with previously unpublished chapters he did manage to write, see Dale L. Morgan, *Dale Morgan on Early Mormonism: Correspondence and a New History,* ed. John Phillip Walker (Salt Lake City: Signature Books, 1986).

5. For example, see Stephen W. Stathis, "A Survey of Current Literature: Dissertations and Theses relating to Mormons and Mormonism," *Dialogue: A Journal of Mormon Thought* 11 (Summer 1978): 96–100; Stephen W. Stathis, "A Survey of Current Literature: A Selected Bibliography of Recent Works on Mormons and Mormonism," *Dialogue: A*

Journal of Mormon Thought 11 (Autumn 1978): 107–19; and Stephen W. Stathis, "Periodical Articles on Mormons and Mormonism," *Dialogue: A Journal of Mormon Thought* 13 (Spring 1980): 108–16. A more complete list can be found in the published index to volumes 1–20 of *Dialogue,* 15–16.

6. Also in this series were bibliographies on graduate work at Brigham Young University ([July 1955]: 279–84) and at Utah State Agricultural College, later to become Utah State University, ([April 1957]: 163–70).

7. William O. Nelson, "Anti-Mormon Publications," in *Encyclopedia of Mormonism,* 5 vols., ed. Daniel H. Ludlow (New York: Macmillan, 1992), 1:45.

Index

RONALD W. WALKER is a professor of history and the director of research at the Joseph Fielding Smith Institute, Brigham Young University. He is the author, editor, and compiler of three books, including the award-winning *Wayward Saints: The Godbeites and Brigham Young* (1998). He has also published more than four dozen articles on western and Mormon history.

DAVID J. WHITTAKER is the curator of Western and Mormon Manuscripts, L. Tom Perry Special Collections at the Harold B. Lee Library, Brigham Young University, where he is also an associate professor of history. His publications include *Men with a Mission, 1837-1841: The Quorum of the Twelve Apostles in the British Isles* (1992) and *Mormon Americana: A Guide to Sources and Collections in the United States* (1995).

JAMES B. ALLEN is a professor emeritus of history and a senior research fellow at the Joseph Fielding Smith Institute, Brigham Young University. He has served as chair of the BYU history department and as assistant church historian. His numerous publications include *The Story of the Latter-day Saints* (1976) and *Trials of Discipleship: The Story of William Clayton, a Mormon* (1987).

ARMAND L. MAUSS, a professor emeritus of sociology and religious studies at Washington State University, has published widely on religious movements, including *The Angel and the Beehive: The Mormon Struggle with Assimilation* (1994). He is past editor of the *Journal for the Scientific Study of Religion*.

Typeset in 10.5/13 Minion
Composed by Barbara Evans
at the University of Illinois Press
Manufactured by Thomson-Shore, Inc.

University of Illinois Press
1325 South Oak Street
Champaign, IL 61820-6903
www.press.uillinois.edu

CARMEL CLAY PUBLIC LIBRARY
55 4th Avenue SE
Carmel, IN 46032
(317) 844-3361
Renewal Line: (317) 814-3936
www.carmel.lib.in.us